Amazing
FOREST

1
Tank
Art by
Julien Dufour

2
Wolf Mother
Art by
Matt Rota

3
Ronnie The Robot
Art by
Melody Often

4
The Bird Watcher
Art by
Yumi Sakugawa

5
Detective Dunk
Art by
Caitlin Rose Boyle

Written by
Ulises Farinas & Erick Freitas

6
Van Dark
Art by
Angelica Blevins

8
Agroman
Art by
Buster Moody

7
Stardust
Art by
Sean Pryor

9
Ben Franklin, Dragon Hunter
Art by
Job Yamen
Colors & Lettering by
Austin Breed

Cover Art by **Ulises Farinas**
Collection Edits by **Justin Eisinger** and **Alonzo Simon**
Collection Design by **Clyde Grapa**
Publisher: **Ted Adams**

For international rights, contact **licensing@idwpublishing.com**

Special thanks to Hannah Nance Partlow for the Amazing Forest logo!

ISBN: 978-1-63140-677-5

19 18 17 16 1 2 3 4

IDW®
www.IDWPUBLISHING.com

Ted Adams, CEO & Publisher
Greg Goldstein, President & COO
Robbie Robbins, EVP/Sr. Graphic Artist
Chris Ryall, Chief Creative Officer/Editor-in-Chief
Matthew Ruzicka, CPA, Chief Financial Officer
Dirk Wood, VP of Marketing
Lorelei Bunjes, VP of Digital Services
Jeff Webber, VP of Licensing, Digital and Subsidiary Rights
Jerry Bennington, VP of New Product Development

Facebook: **facebook.com/idwpublishing**
Twitter: **@idwpublishing**
YouTube: **youtube.com/idwpublishing**
Tumblr: **tumblr.idwpublishing.com**
Instagram: **instagram.com/idwpublishing**

Originally published as AMAZING FOREST issues #1-6.

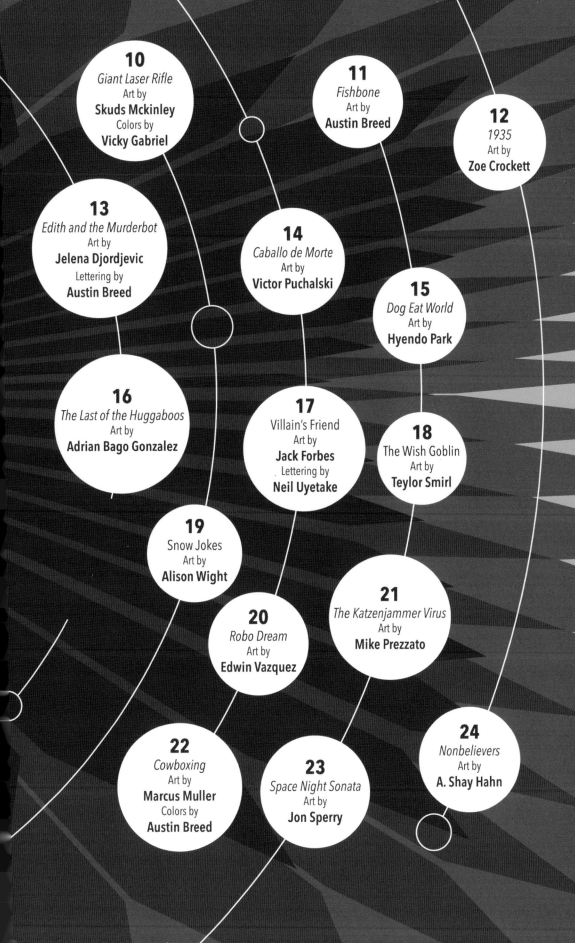

10
Giant Laser Rifle
Art by
Skuds Mckinley
Colors by
Vicky Gabriel

11
Fishbone
Art by
Austin Breed

12
1935
Art by
Zoe Crockett

13
Edith and the Murderbot
Art by
Jelena Djordjevic
Lettering by
Austin Breed

14
Caballo de Morte
Art by
Victor Puchalski

15
Dog Eat World
Art by
Hyendo Park

16
The Last of the Huggaboos
Art by
Adrian Bago Gonzalez

17
Villain's Friend
Art by
Jack Forbes
Lettering by
Neil Uyetake

18
The Wish Goblin
Art by
Teylor Smirl

19
Snow Jokes
Art by
Alison Wight

20
Robo Dream
Art by
Edwin Vazquez

21
The Katzenjammer Virus
Art by
Mike Prezzato

22
Cowboxing
Art by
Marcus Muller
Colors by
Austin Breed

23
Space Night Sonata
Art by
Jon Sperry

24
Nonbelievers
Art by
A. Shay Hahn

INTRODUCTION

I'm a cartoonist. In comics, everyone has a role, a position. It's a fantastic collaboration that happens constantly, consistently, and makes amazing stories happen all year round, for decades. Eventually, it will be centuries. Artists, writers, editors, colorists, letterers, flatters, designers, all working together to tell stories. Planting seeds into other's minds that grow into the next generation of cartoonists. That's what Erick Freitas and I set out to do. That's why we called this project, *Amazing Forest*. After almost four years since we conceived of this anthology, a barrage of ballistic ideas contained in eight pages, we are finally seeing that the seeds have grown into mighty trees.

I couldn't imagine the texture and colors and how vibrant each individual story would become. Each issue brought a new personal favorite, a new challenge for the both of us to find a new approach. When you write fantasy and science fiction and you enjoy a good plot twist, you set the bar higher each time to out-twist yourself. We got to work with fantastic artists: Paul Chadwick, Yumi Sakugawa, Steven Russell Black, Job Yamen, Hannah Nance Partlow, and they all made each story their own.

The *Amazing Forest* reflects the world of comics today. Inclusive, diverse, struggling, unexpected, growing. Men, women, people of color, lgbtq. Cartoonists telling stories. Thank you for reading and thanks to Monkeybrain Comics and IDW for helping bring this to readers all year round. Perennial.

Ulises Farinas

TANK

STORY: ERICK FREITAS + ULISES FARINAS

ART: JULIEN DUFOUR

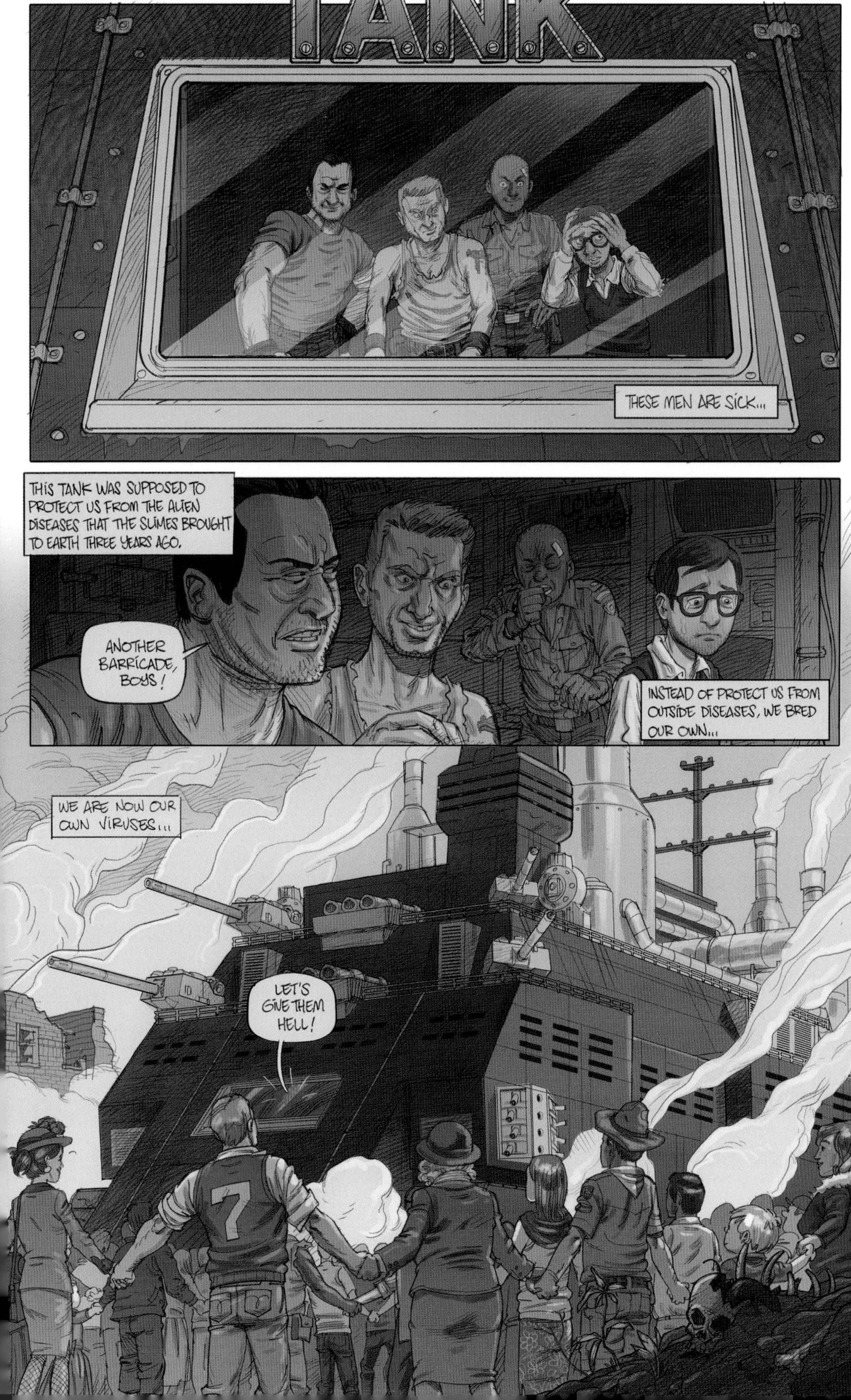
THESE MEN ARE SICK...
THIS TANK WAS SUPPOSED TO PROTECT US FROM THE ALIEN DISEASES THAT THE SLIMES BROUGHT TO EARTH THREE YEARS AGO.
ANOTHER BARRICADE, BOYS!
COUGH COUGH
INSTEAD OF PROTECT US FROM OUTSIDE DISEASES, WE BRED OUR OWN...
WE ARE NOW OUR OWN VIRUSES...
LET'S GIVE THEM HELL!

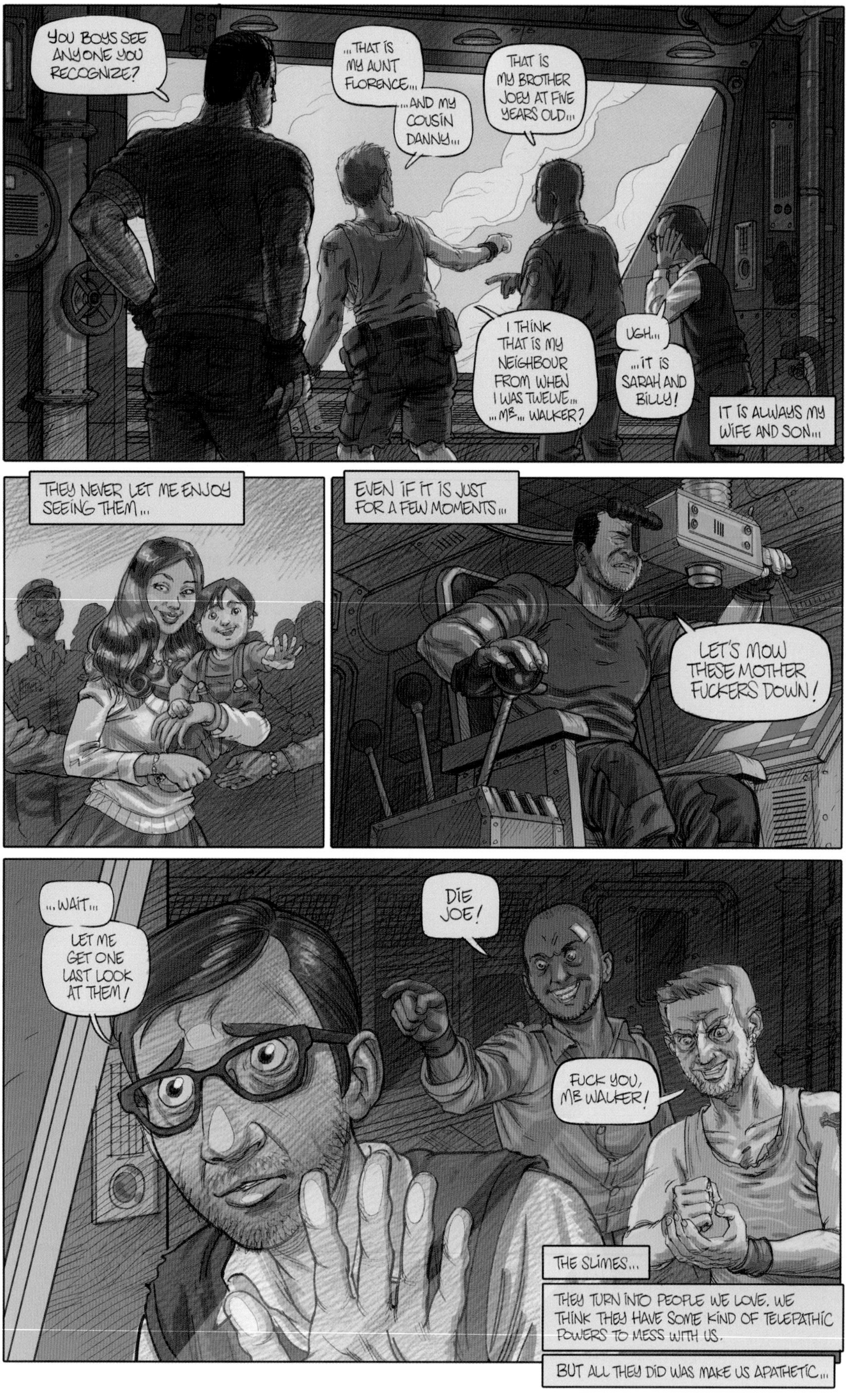

YOU BOYS SEE ANYONE YOU RECOGNIZE?
...THAT IS MY AUNT FLORENCE...
...AND MY COUSIN DANNY...
THAT IS MY BROTHER JOEY AT FIVE YEARS OLD...
I THINK THAT IS MY NEIGHBOUR FROM WHEN I WAS TWELVE... ...MR... WALKER?
UGH...
...IT IS SARAH AND BILLY!
IT IS ALWAYS MY WIFE AND SON...
THEY NEVER LET ME ENJOY SEEING THEM...
EVEN IF IT IS JUST FOR A FEW MOMENTS...
LET'S MOW THESE MOTHER FUCKERS DOWN!
...WAIT...
LET ME GET ONE LAST LOOK AT THEM!
DIE JOE!
FUCK YOU, MR WALKER!
THE SLIMES...
THEY TURN INTO PEOPLE WE LOVE. WE THINK THEY HAVE SOME KIND OF TELEPATHIC POWERS TO MESS WITH US.
BUT ALL THEY DID WAS MAKE US APATHETIC...

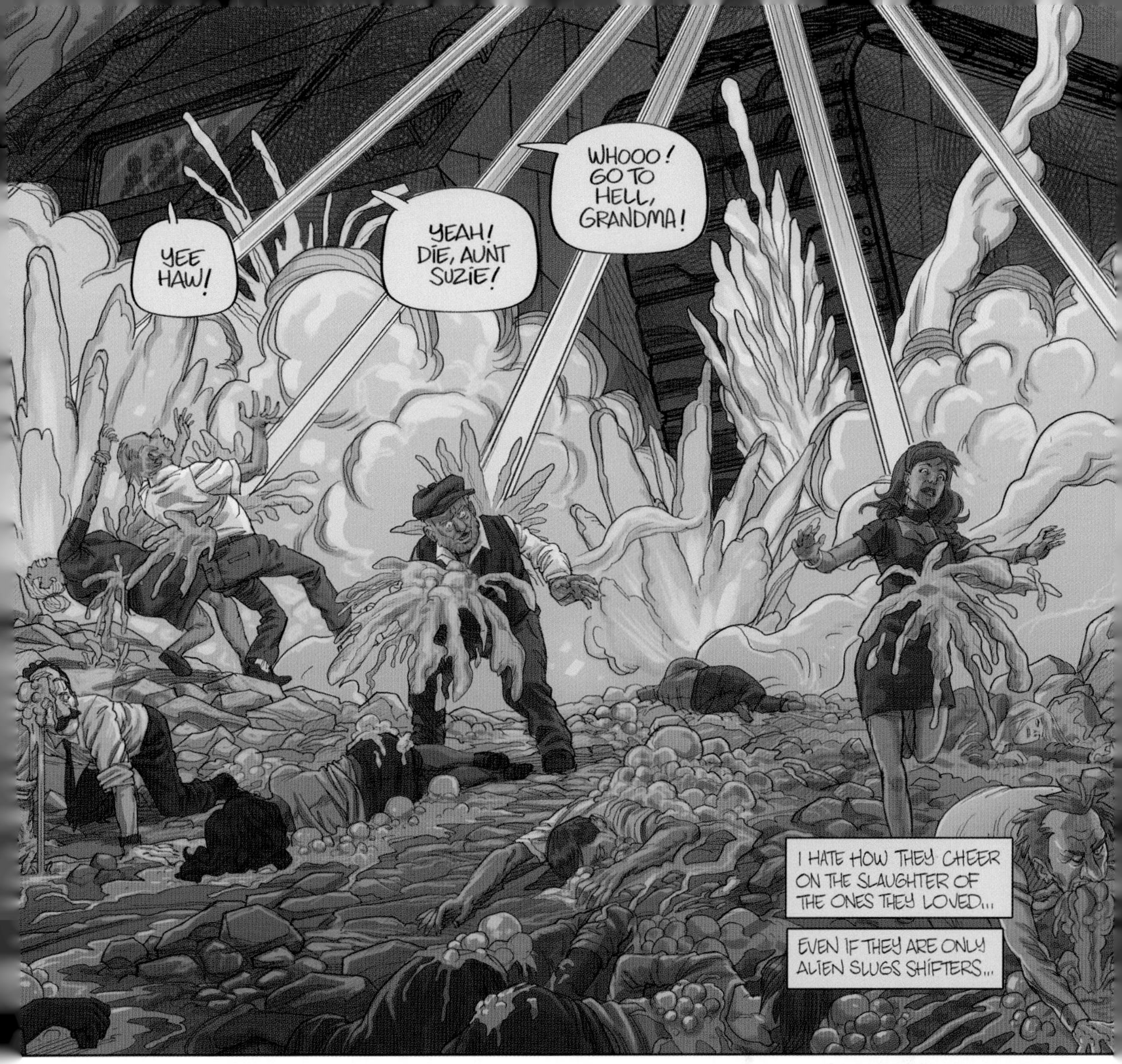
YEE HAW!
YEAH! DIE, AUNT SUZIE!
WHOOO! GO TO HELL, GRANDMA!
I HATE HOW THEY CHEER ON THE SLAUGHTER OF THE ONES THEY LOVED...
EVEN IF THEY ARE ONLY ALIEN SLUGS SHIFTERS...

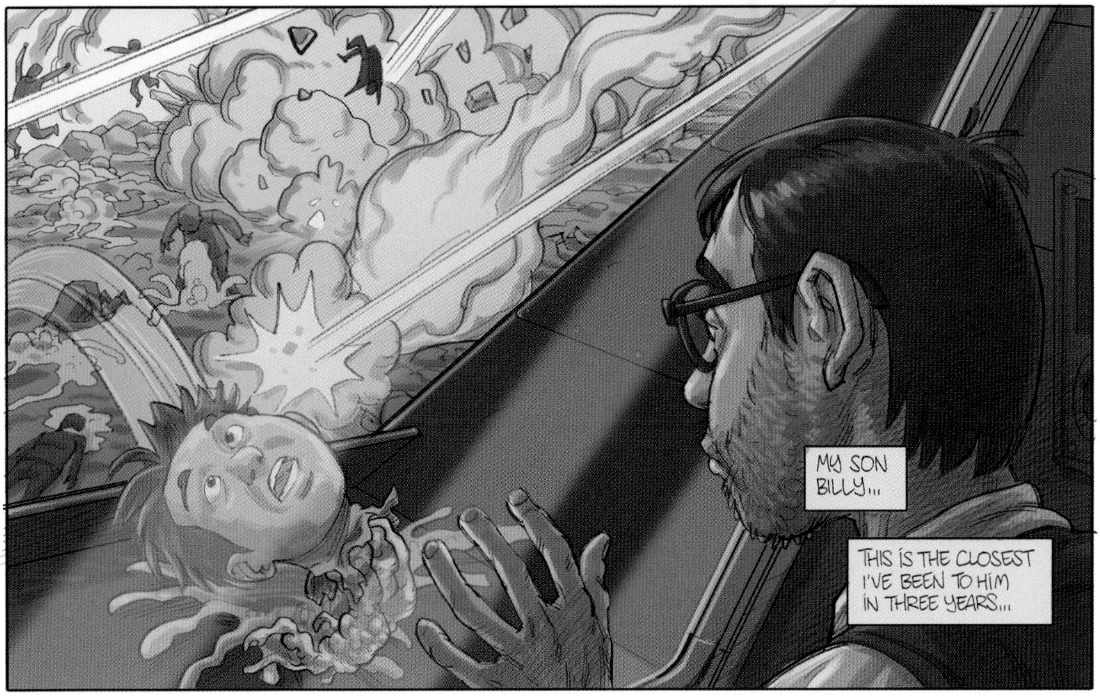
MY SON BILLY...
THIS IS THE CLOSEST I'VE BEEN TO HIM IN THREE YEARS...

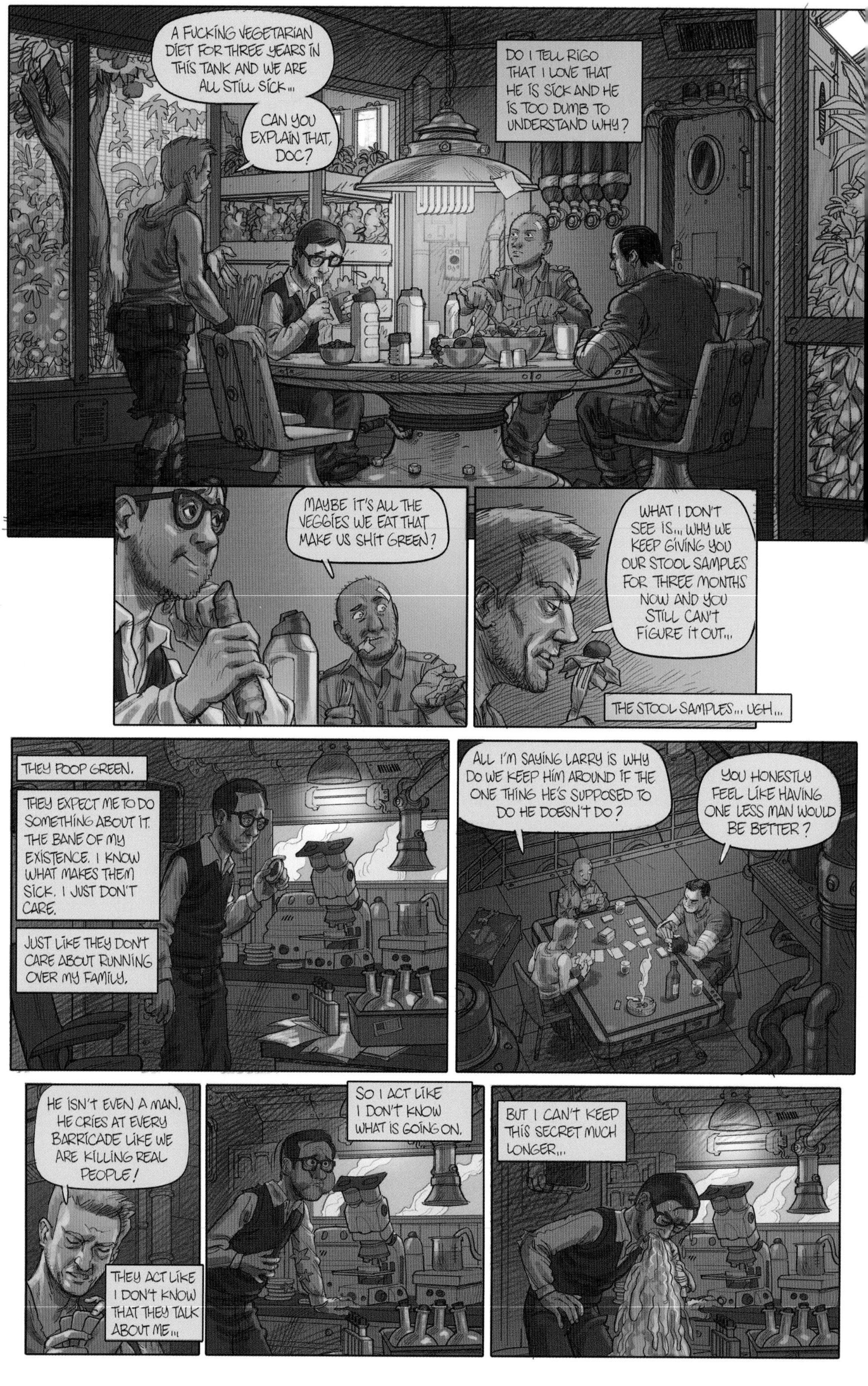
A FUCKING VEGETARIAN DIET FOR THREE YEARS IN THIS TANK AND WE ARE ALL STILL SICK...
CAN YOU EXPLAIN THAT, DOC?
DO I TELL RIGO THAT I LOVE THAT HE IS SICK AND HE IS TOO DUMB TO UNDERSTAND WHY?
MAYBE IT'S ALL THE VEGGIES WE EAT THAT MAKE US SHIT GREEN?
WHAT I DON'T SEE IS... WHY WE KEEP GIVING YOU OUR STOOL SAMPLES FOR THREE MONTHS NOW AND YOU STILL CAN'T FIGURE IT OUT...
THE STOOL SAMPLES... UGH...
THEY POOP GREEN.
THEY EXPECT ME TO DO SOMETHING ABOUT IT. THE BANE OF MY EXISTENCE. I KNOW WHAT MAKES THEM SICK. I JUST DON'T CARE.
JUST LIKE THEY DON'T CARE ABOUT RUNNING OVER MY FAMILY.
ALL I'M SAYING LARRY IS WHY DO WE KEEP HIM AROUND IF THE ONE THING HE'S SUPPOSED TO DO HE DOESN'T DO?
YOU HONESTLY FEEL LIKE HAVING ONE LESS MAN WOULD BE BETTER?
HE ISN'T EVEN A MAN. HE CRIES AT EVERY BARRICADE LIKE WE ARE KILLING REAL PEOPLE!
THEY ACT LIKE I DON'T KNOW THAT THEY TALK ABOUT ME...
SO I ACT LIKE I DON'T KNOW WHAT IS GOING ON.
BUT I CAN'T KEEP THIS SECRET MUCH LONGER...

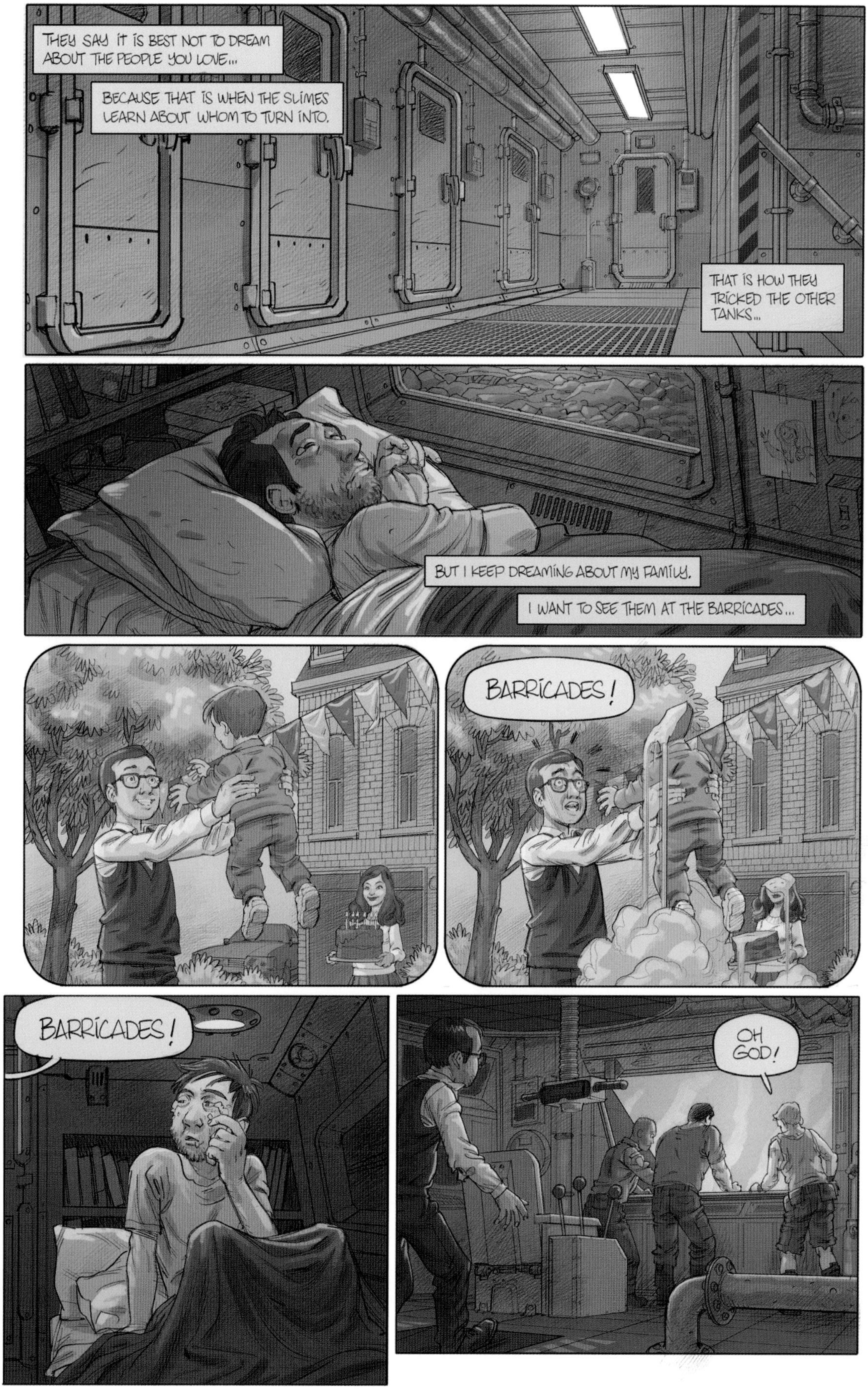
THEY SAY IT IS BEST NOT TO DREAM ABOUT THE PEOPLE YOU LOVE...
BECAUSE THAT IS WHEN THE SLIMES LEARN ABOUT WHOM TO TURN INTO.
THAT IS HOW THEY TRICKED THE OTHER TANKS...
BUT I KEEP DREAMING ABOUT MY FAMILY.
I WANT TO SEE THEM AT THE BARRICADES...
BARRICADES!
BARRICADES!
OH GOD!

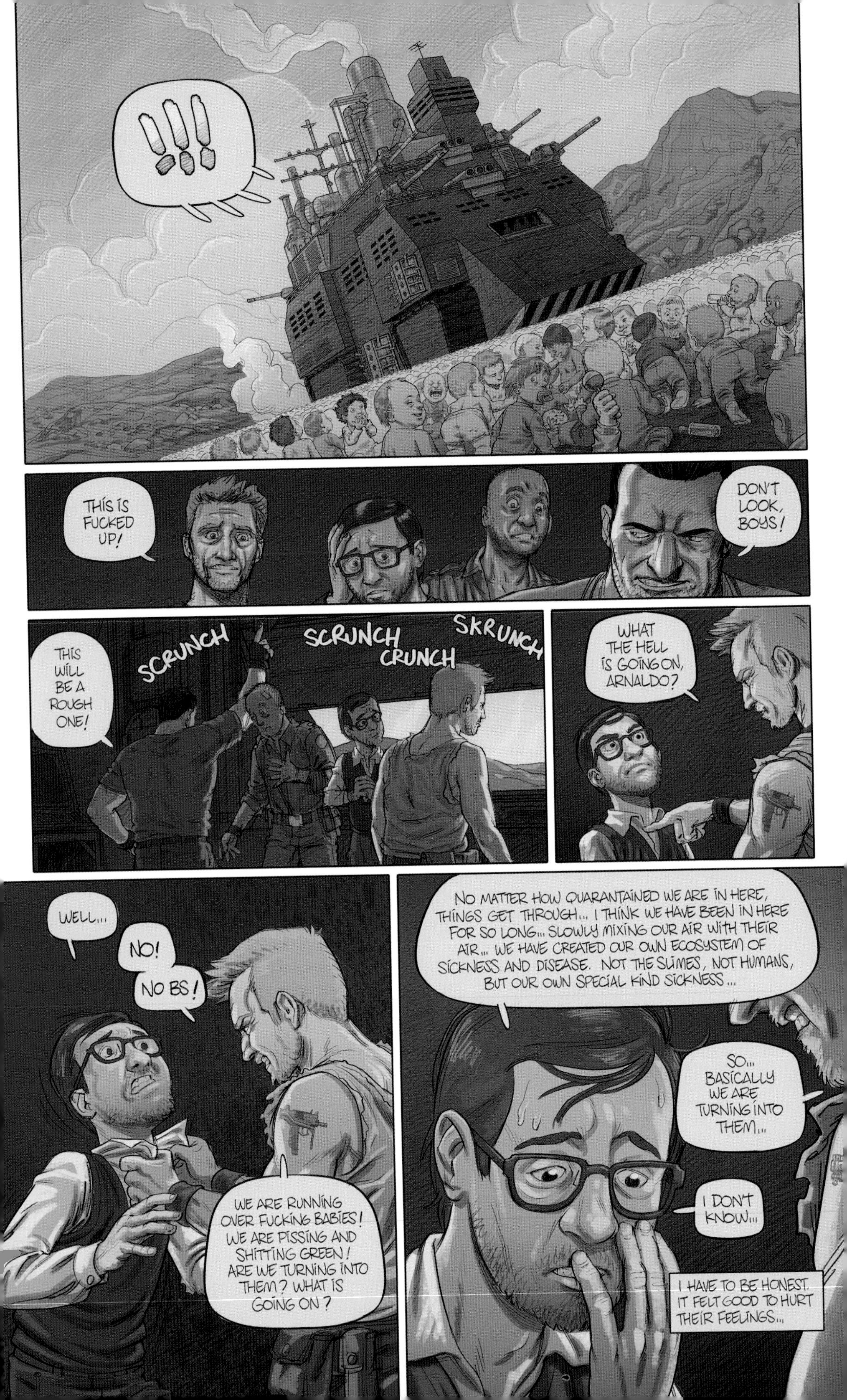
!!!
THIS IS FUCKED UP!
DON'T LOOK, BOYS!
THIS WILL BE A ROUGH ONE!
SCRUNCH
SCRUNCH
CRUNCH
SKRUNCH
WHAT THE HELL IS GOING ON, ARNALDO?
WELL...
NO!
NO BS!
WE ARE RUNNING OVER FUCKING BABIES! WE ARE PISSING AND SHITTING GREEN! ARE WE TURNING INTO THEM? WHAT IS GOING ON?
NO MATTER HOW QUARANTAINED WE ARE IN HERE, THINGS GET THROUGH... I THINK WE HAVE BEEN IN HERE FOR SO LONG... SLOWLY MIXING OUR AIR WITH THEIR AIR... WE HAVE CREATED OUR OWN ECOSYSTEM OF SICKNESS AND DISEASE. NOT THE SLIMES, NOT HUMANS, BUT OUR OWN SPECIAL KIND SICKNESS...
SO... BASICALLY WE ARE TURNING INTO THEM...
I DON'T KNOW...
I HAVE TO BE HONEST. IT FELT GOOD TO HURT THEIR FEELINGS...

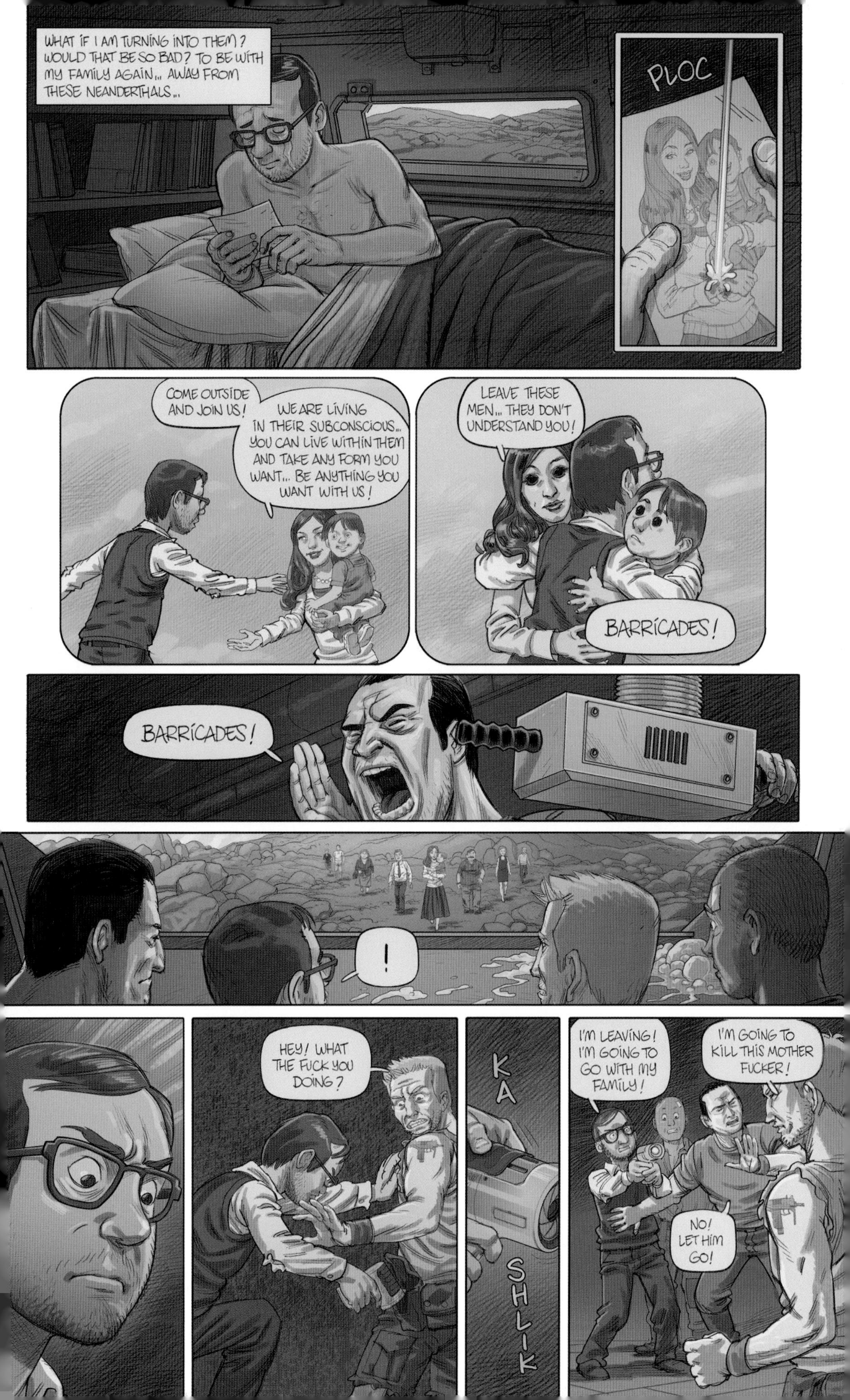
WHAT IF I AM TURNING INTO THEM? WOULD THAT BE SO BAD? TO BE WITH MY FAMILY AGAIN... AWAY FROM THESE NEANDERTHALS...
PLOC
COME OUTSIDE AND JOIN US!
WE ARE LIVING IN THEIR SUBCONSCIOUS... YOU CAN LIVE WITHIN THEM AND TAKE ANY FORM YOU WANT... BE ANYTHING YOU WANT WITH US!
LEAVE THESE MEN... THEY DON'T UNDERSTAND YOU!
BARRICADES!
BARRICADES!
!
HEY! WHAT THE FUCK YOU DOING?
KA
SHLIK
I'M LEAVING! I'M GOING TO GO WITH MY FAMILY!
I'M GOING TO KILL THIS MOTHER FUCKER!
NO! LET HIM GO!

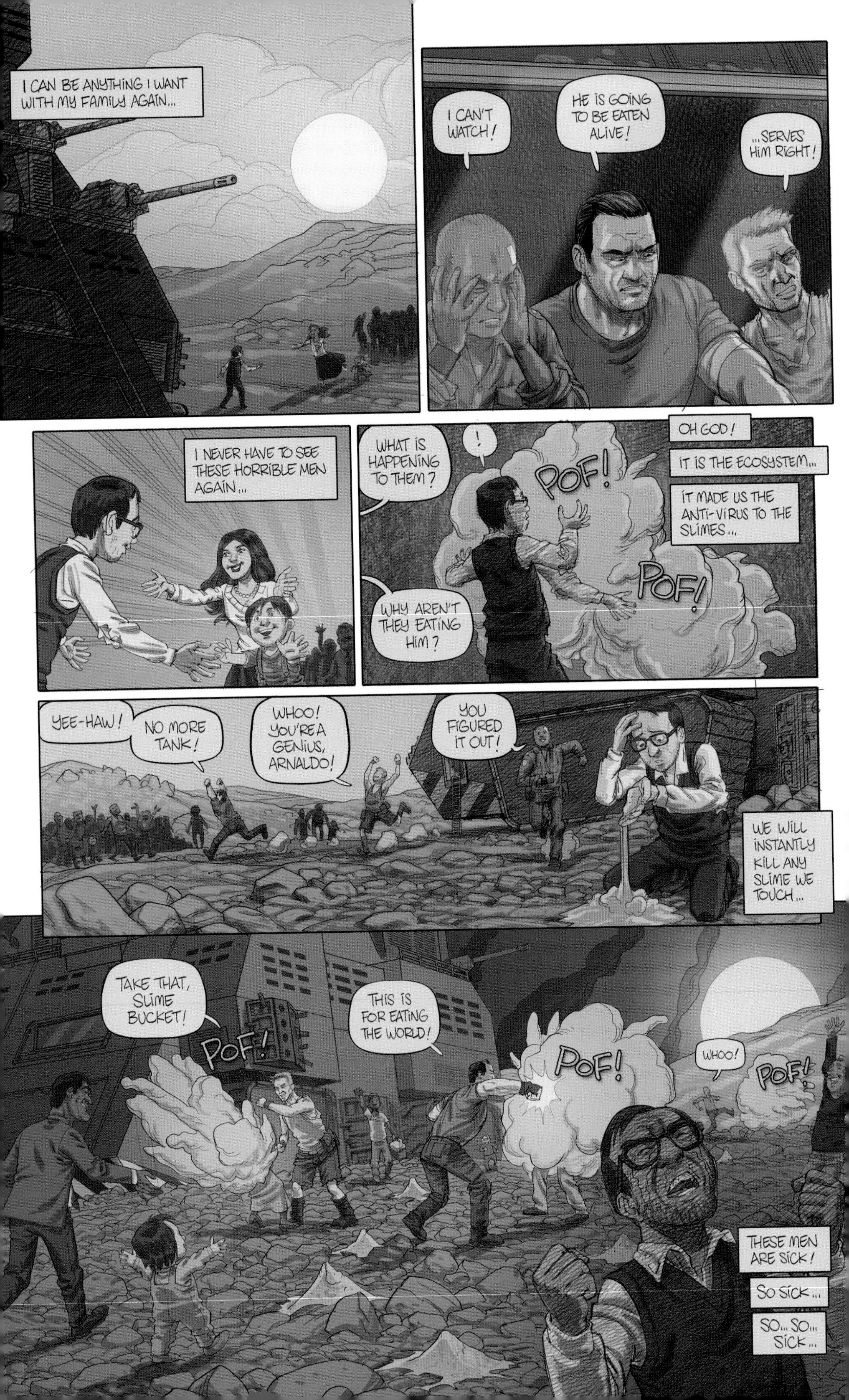
I CAN BE ANYTHING I WANT WITH MY FAMILY AGAIN...
I CAN'T WATCH!
HE IS GOING TO BE EATEN ALIVE!
...SERVES HIM RIGHT!
I NEVER HAVE TO SEE THESE HORRIBLE MEN AGAIN...
WHAT IS HAPPENING TO THEM?
!
POF!
OH GOD!
IT IS THE ECOSYSTEM...
IT MADE US THE ANTI-VIRUS TO THE SLIMES...
POF!
WHY AREN'T THEY EATING HIM?
YEE-HAW!
NO MORE TANK!
WHOO! YOU'RE A GENIUS, ARNALDO!
YOU FIGURED IT OUT!
WE WILL INSTANTLY KILL ANY SLIME WE TOUCH...
TAKE THAT, SLIME BUCKET!
POF!
THIS IS FOR EATING THE WORLD!
POF!
WHOO!
POF!
THESE MEN ARE SICK!
SO SICK...
SO... SO... SICK...

Wolf Mother

Art by **Matt Rota**

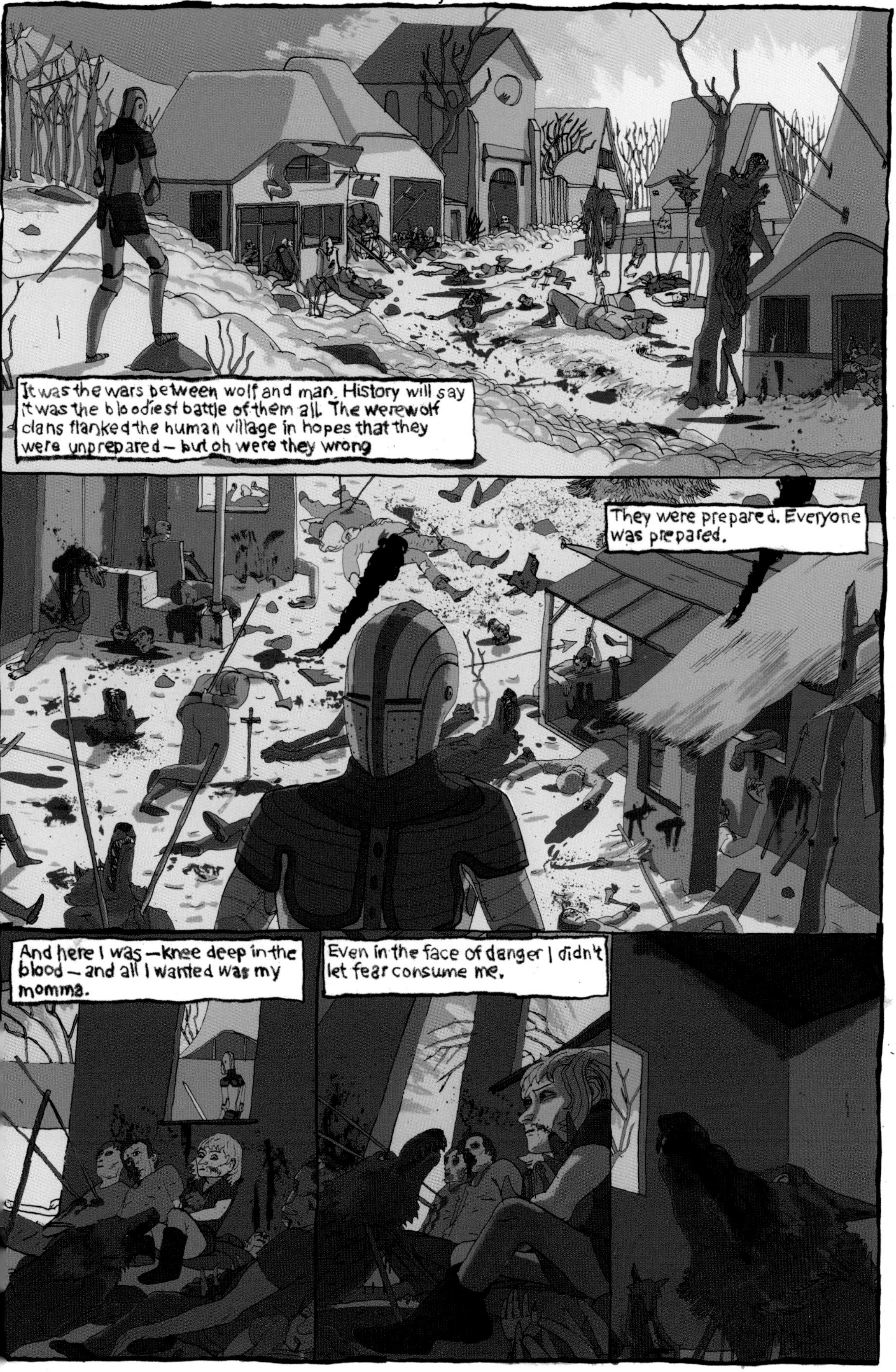
It was the wars between wolf and man. History will say it was the bloodiest battle of them all. The werewolf clans flanked the human village in hopes that they were unprepared — but oh were they wrong
They were prepared. Everyone was prepared.
And here I was — knee deep in the blood — and all I wanted was my momma.
Even in the face of danger I didn't let fear consume me.

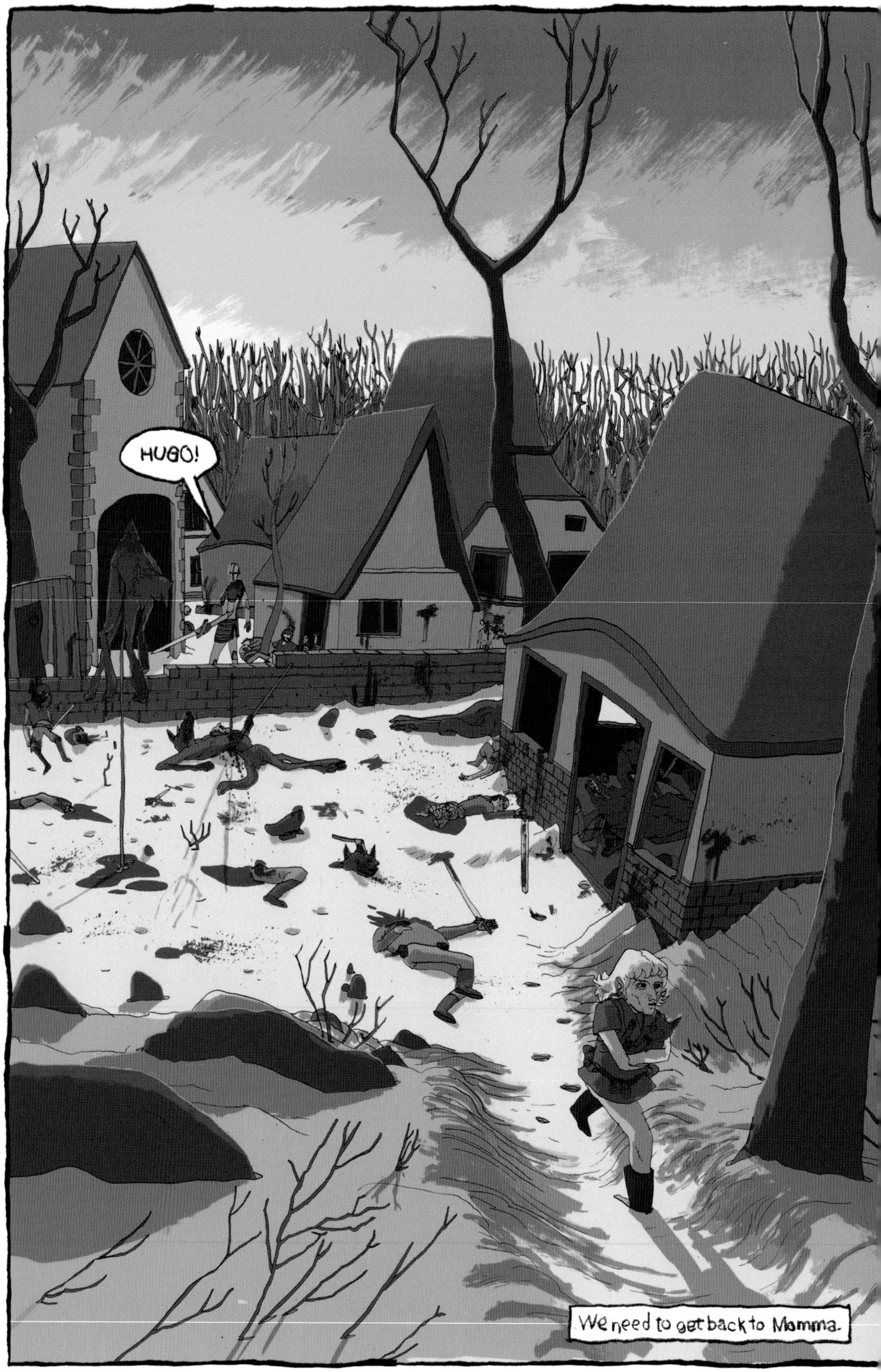
HUGO!
We need to get back to Momma.

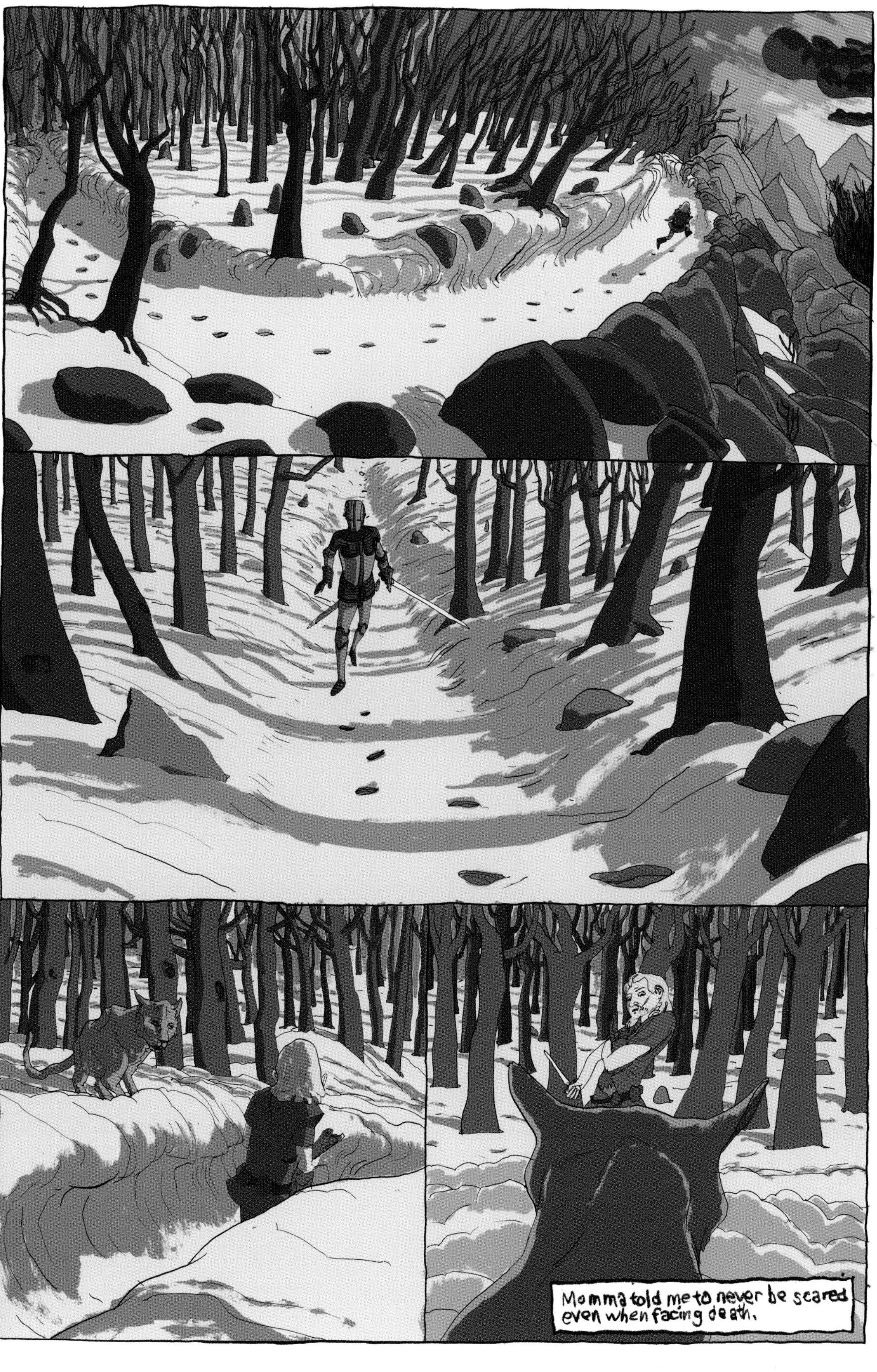
Momma told me to never be scared even when facing death.

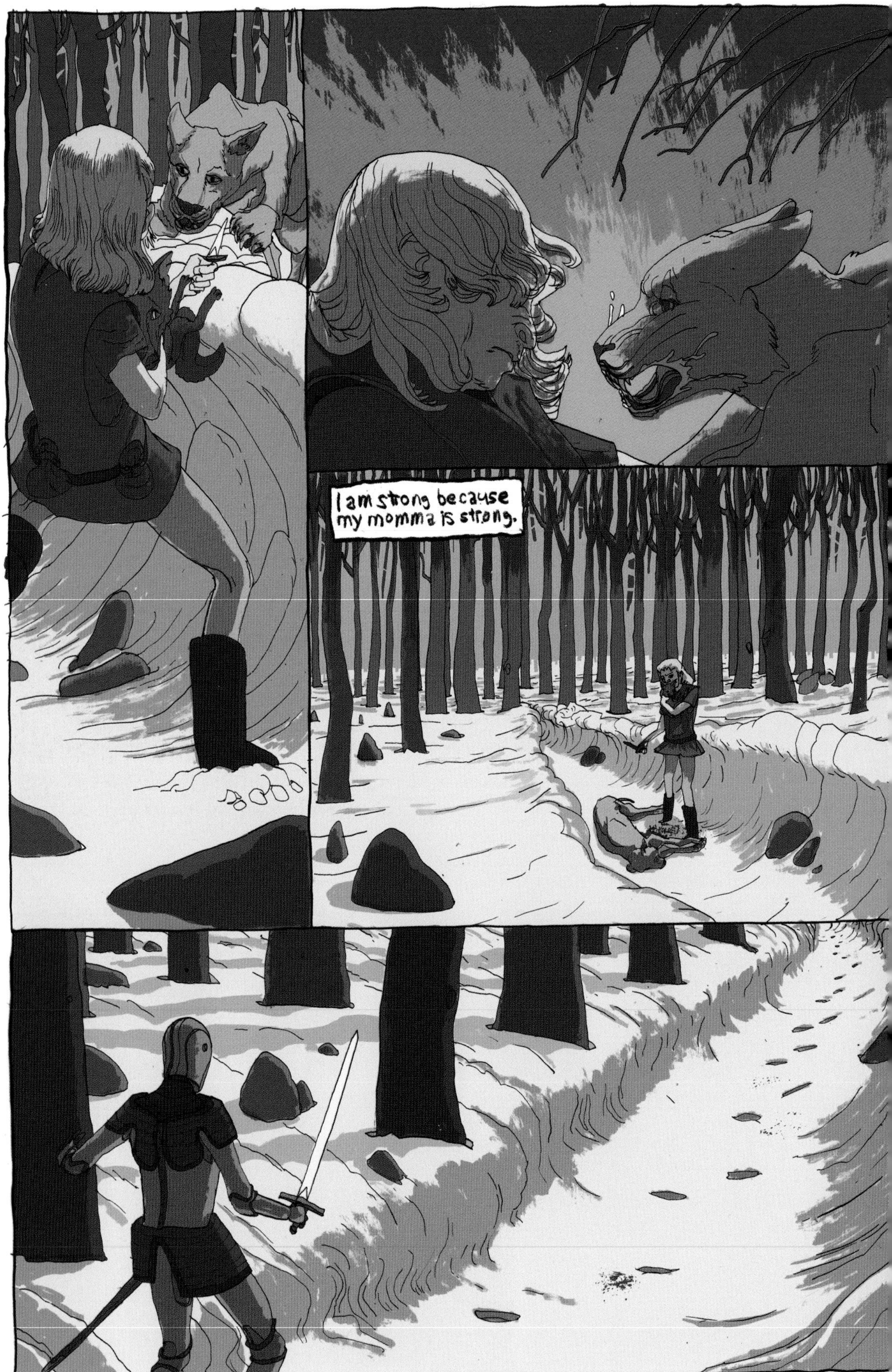
I am strong because my momma is strong.

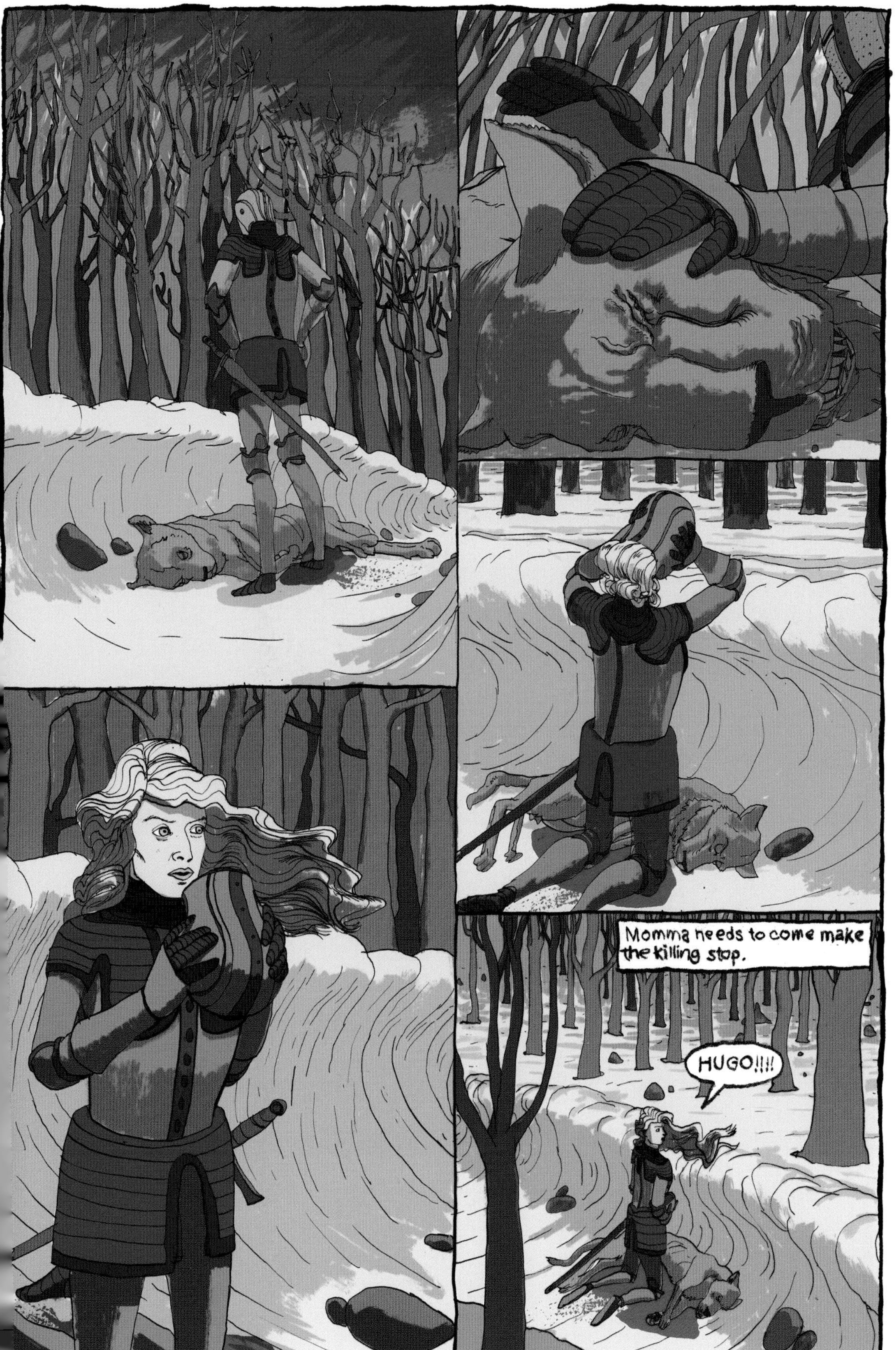
Momma needs to come make the killing stop.
HUGO!!!!

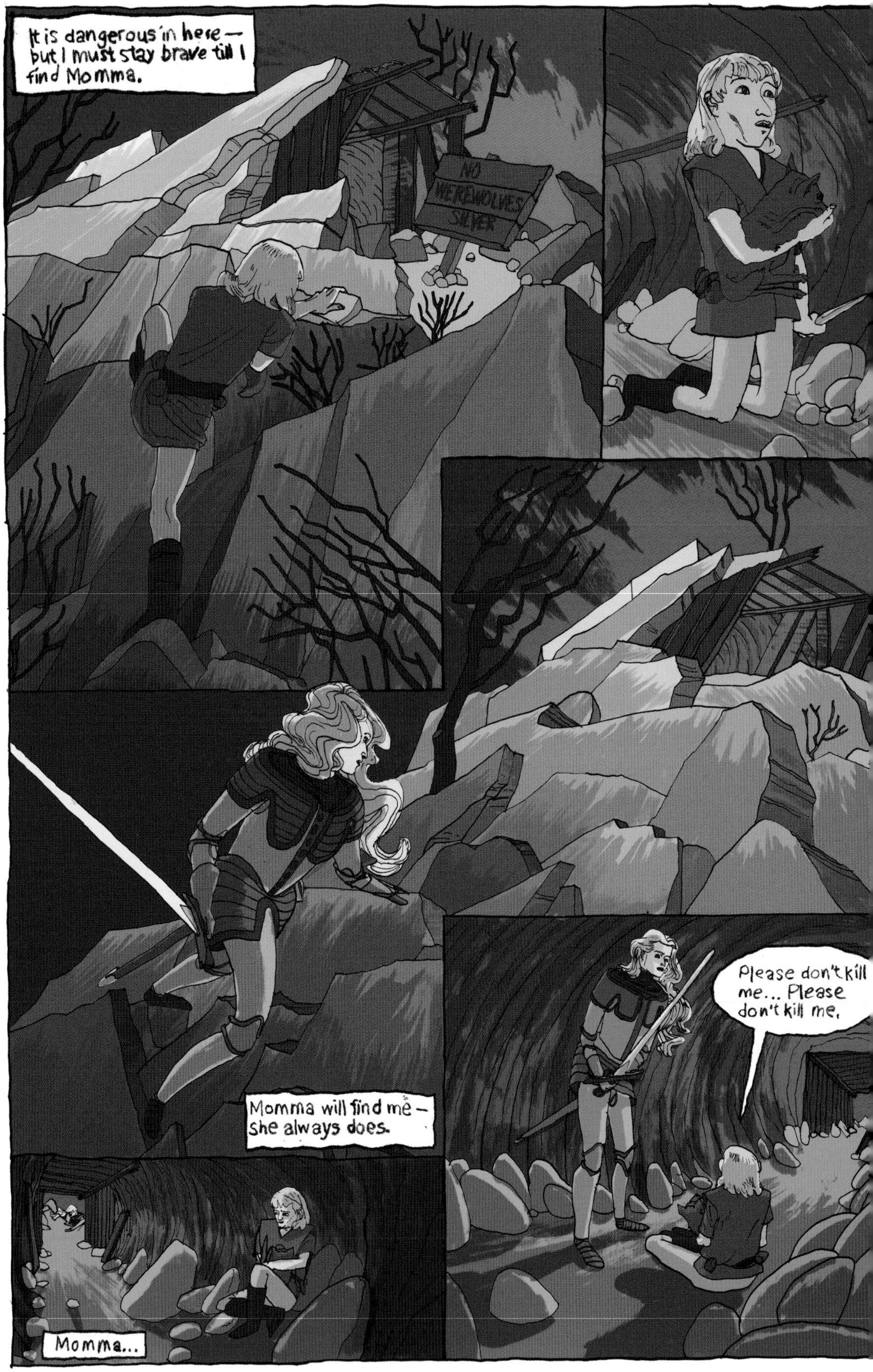
It is dangerous in here — but I must stay brave till I find Momma.
NO WEREWOLVES SILVER
Momma will find me — she always does.
Please don't kill me... Please don't kill me.
Momma...

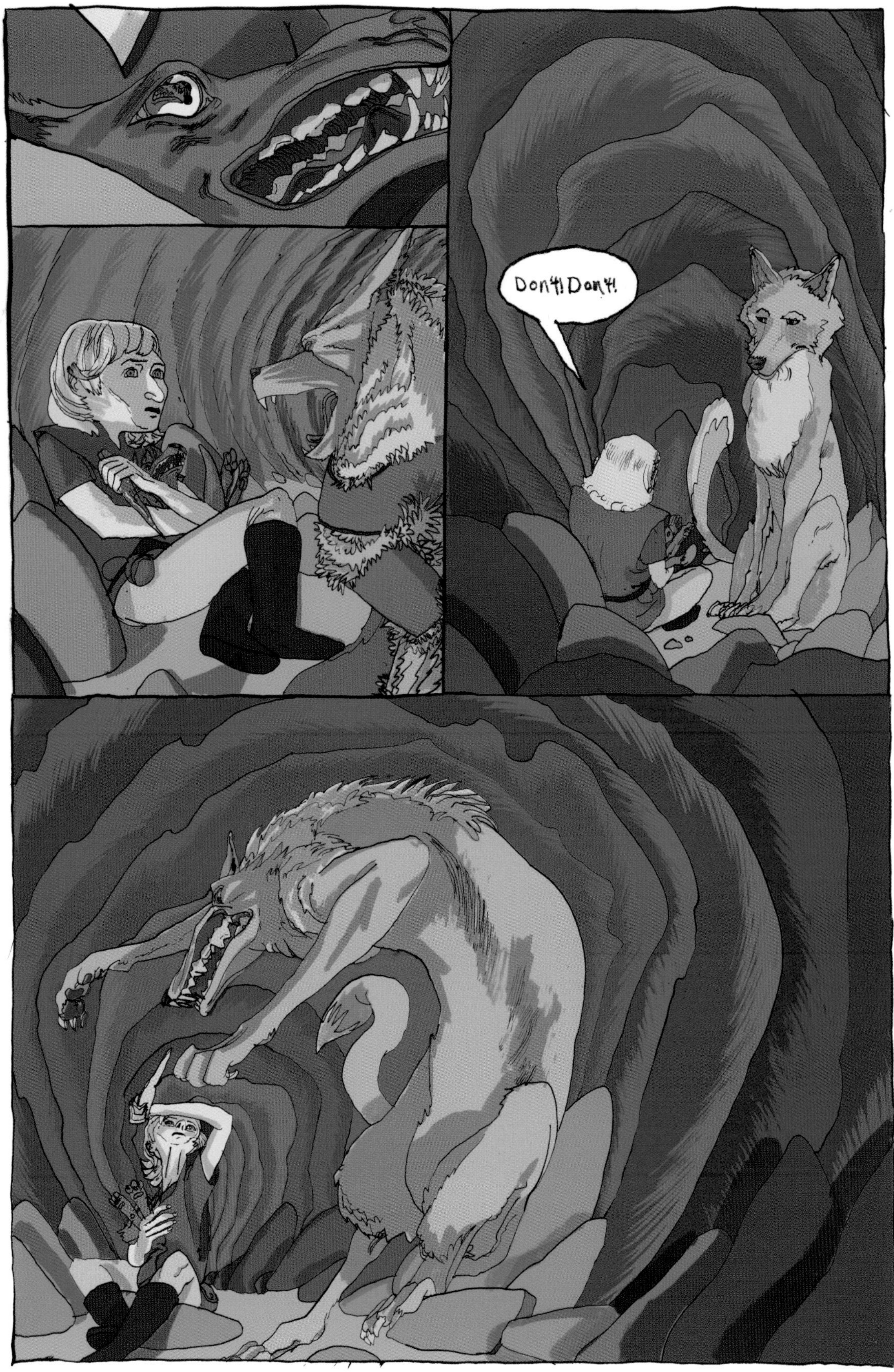
Don't! Don't!

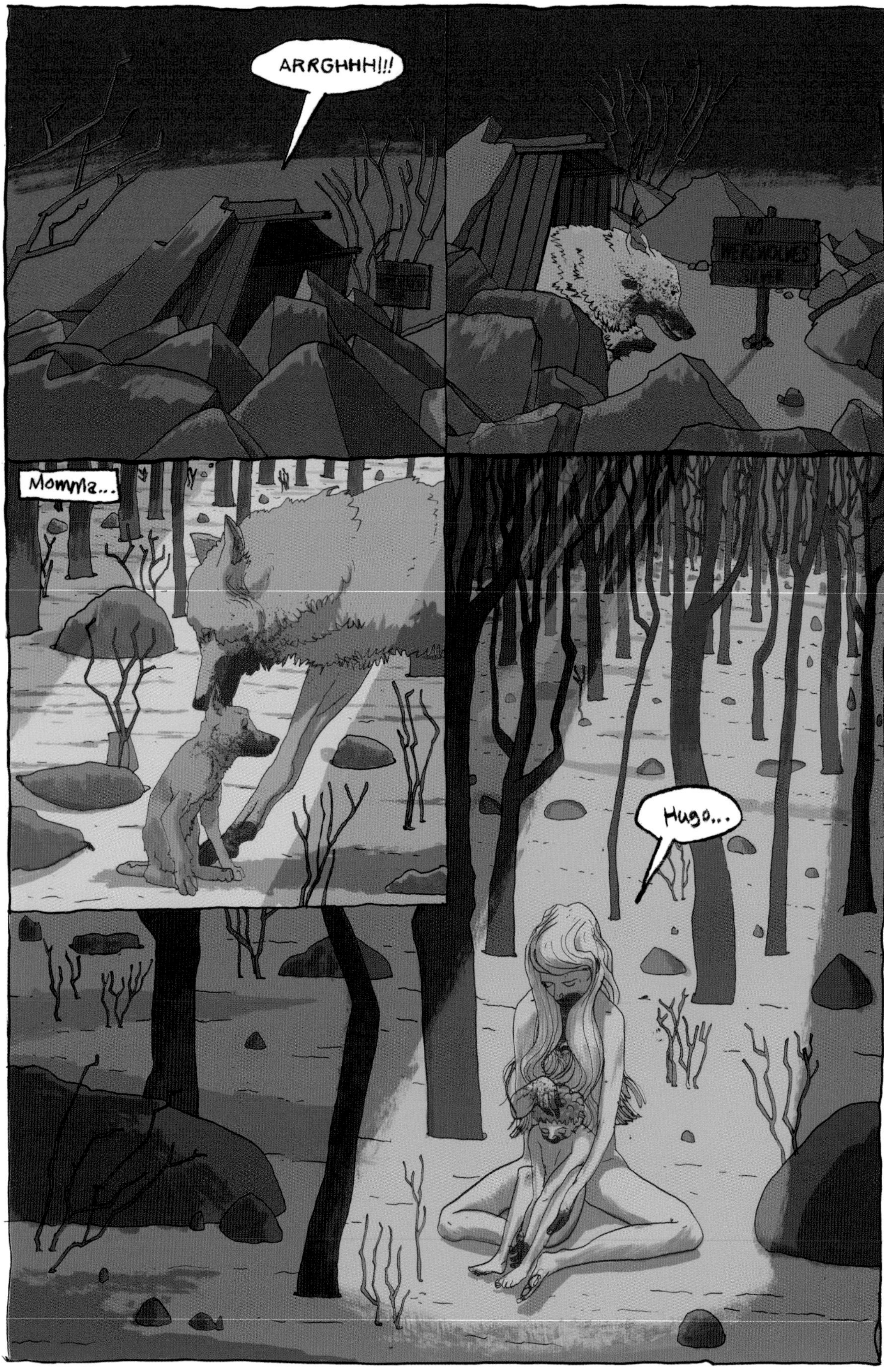
ARRGHHH!!!
Momma...
Hugo...

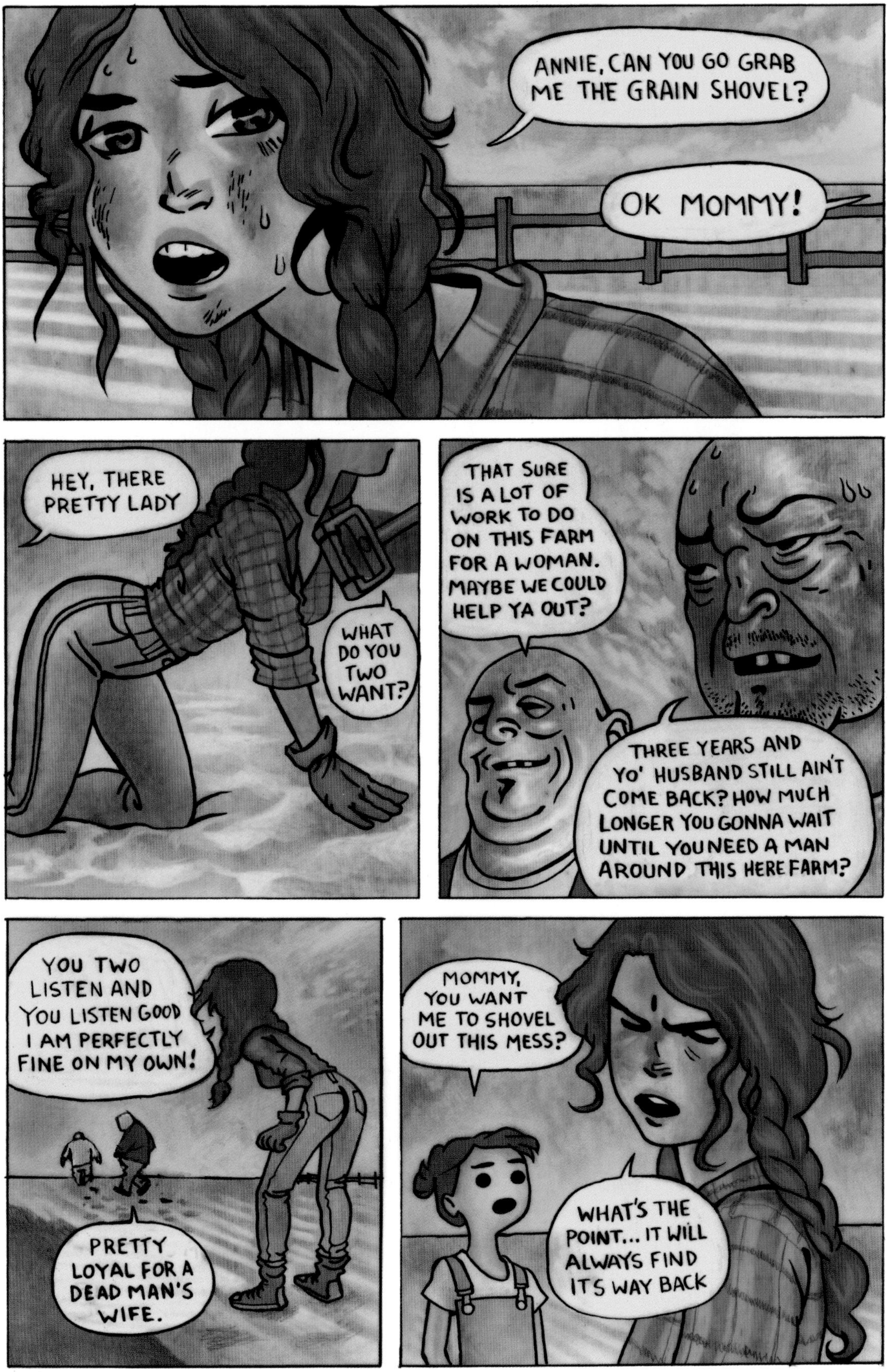
ANNIE, CAN YOU GO GRAB ME THE GRAIN SHOVEL?
OK MOMMY!
HEY, THERE PRETTY LADY
WHAT DO YOU TWO WANT?
THAT SURE IS A LOT OF WORK TO DO ON THIS FARM FOR A WOMAN. MAYBE WE COULD HELP YA OUT?
THREE YEARS AND YO' HUSBAND STILL AIN'T COME BACK? HOW MUCH LONGER YOU GONNA WAIT UNTIL YOU NEED A MAN AROUND THIS HERE FARM?
YOU TWO LISTEN AND YOU LISTEN GOOD I AM PERFECTLY FINE ON MY OWN!
PRETTY LOYAL FOR A DEAD MAN'S WIFE.
MOMMY, YOU WANT ME TO SHOVEL OUT THIS MESS?
WHAT'S THE POINT... IT WILL ALWAYS FIND ITS WAY BACK

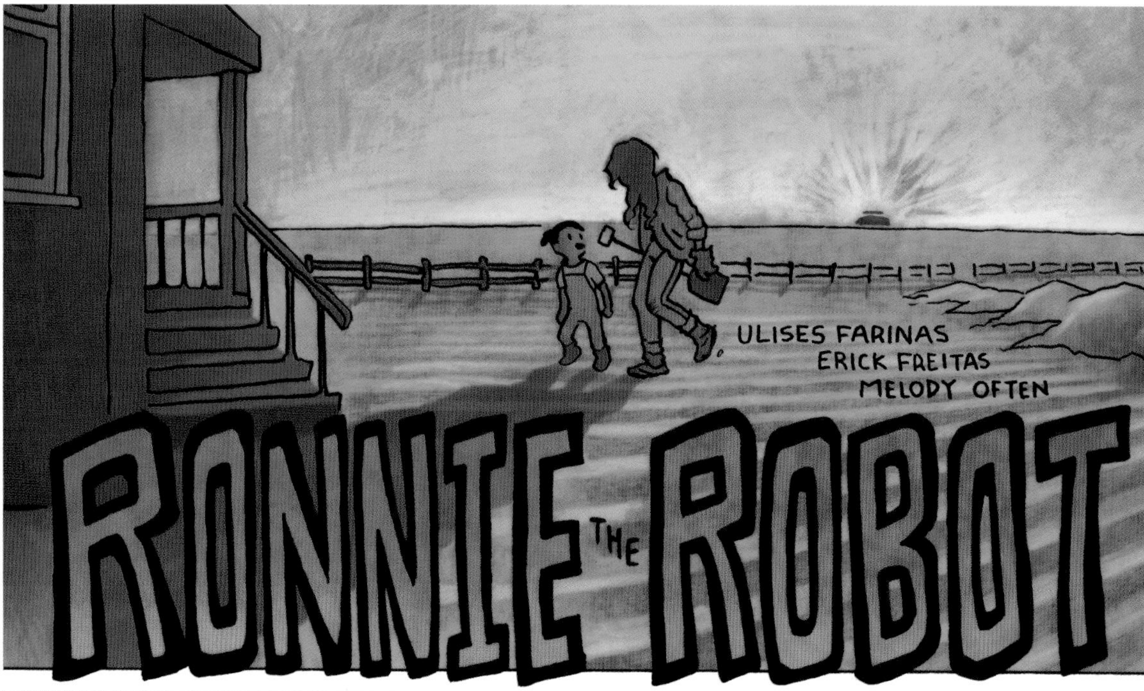

ULISES FARINAS
ERICK FREITAS
MELODY OFTEN
RONNIE THE ROBOT

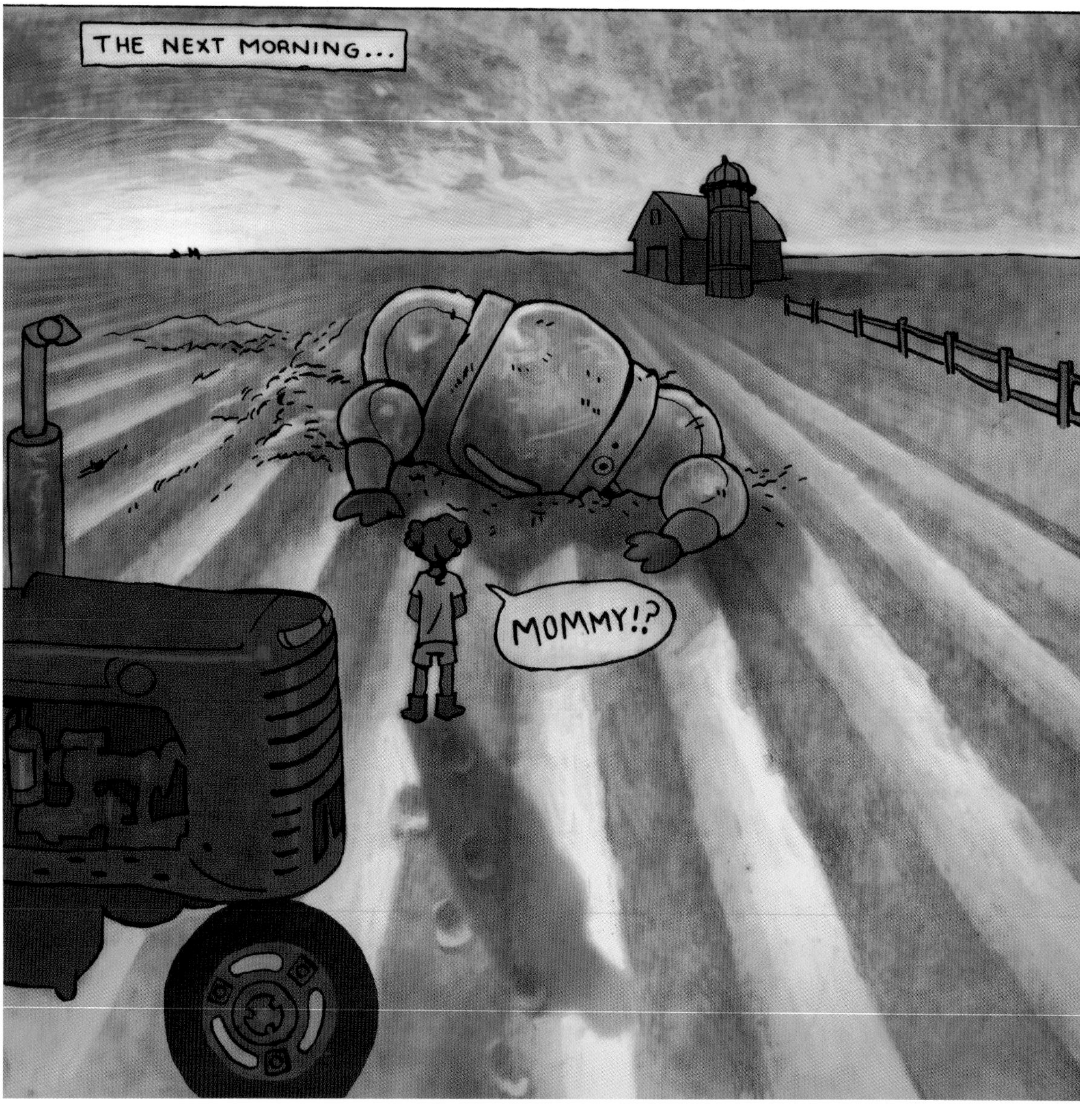

THE NEXT MORNING...
MOMMY!?

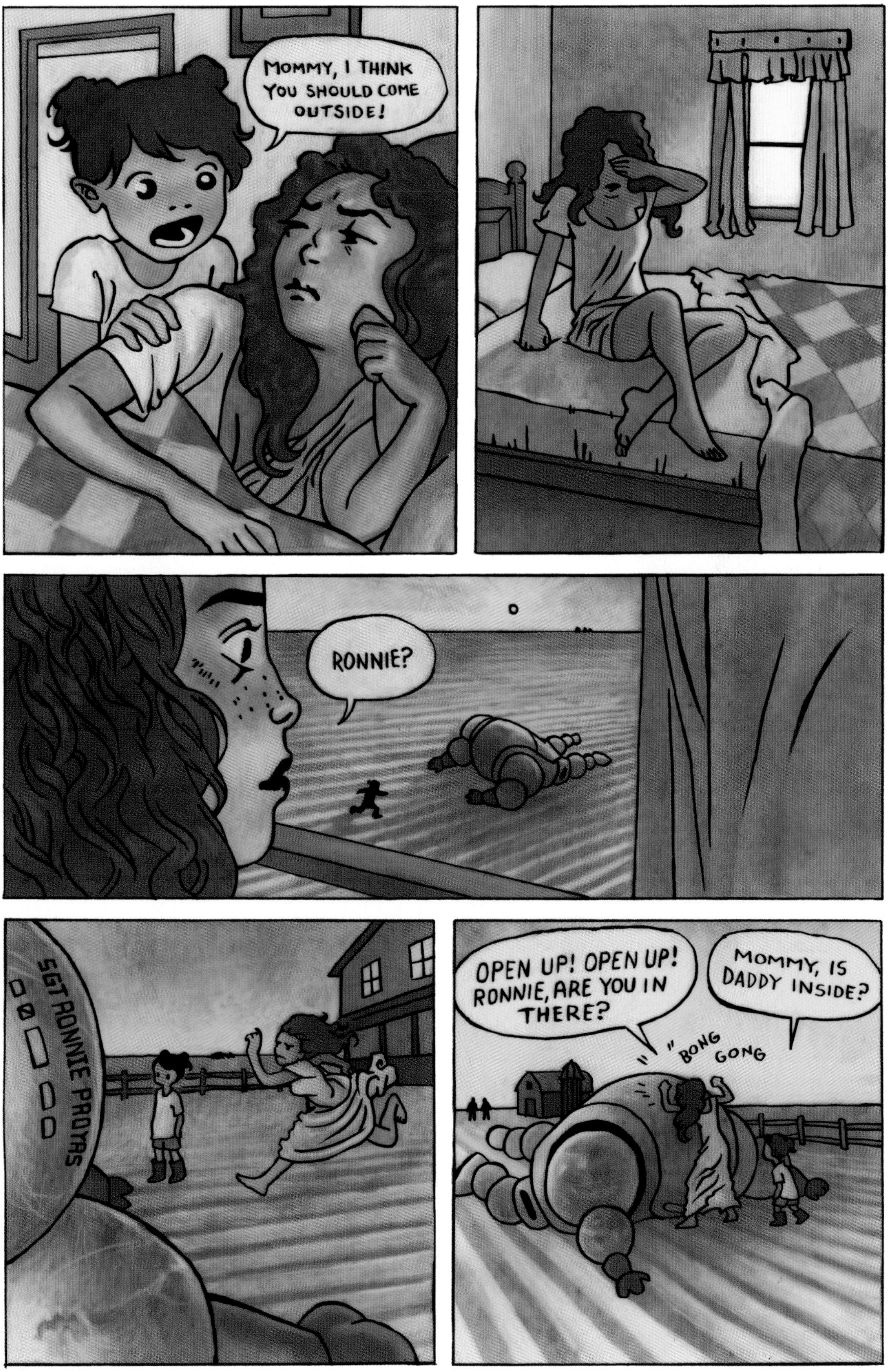
MOMMY, I THINK YOU SHOULD COME OUTSIDE!
RONNIE?
SGT RONNIE PROYAS
OPEN UP! OPEN UP! RONNIE, ARE YOU IN THERE?
MOMMY, IS DADDY INSIDE?
BONG
GONG

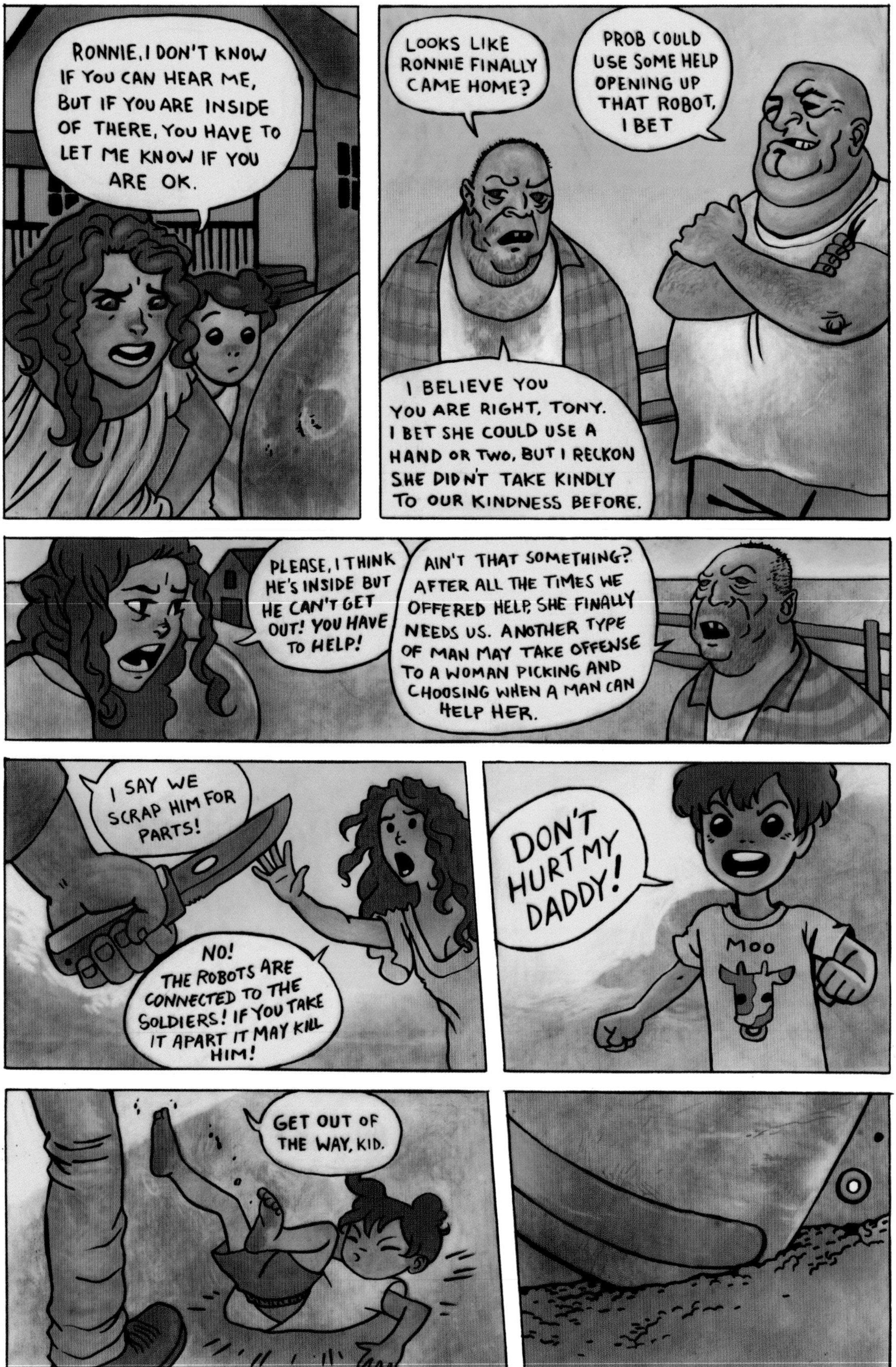
RONNIE, I DON'T KNOW IF YOU CAN HEAR ME, BUT IF YOU ARE INSIDE OF THERE, YOU HAVE TO LET ME KNOW IF YOU ARE OK.
LOOKS LIKE RONNIE FINALLY CAME HOME?
PROB COULD USE SOME HELP OPENING UP THAT ROBOT, I BET
I BELIEVE YOU YOU ARE RIGHT, TONY. I BET SHE COULD USE A HAND OR TWO, BUT I RECKON SHE DIDN'T TAKE KINDLY TO OUR KINDNESS BEFORE.
PLEASE, I THINK HE'S INSIDE BUT HE CAN'T GET OUT! YOU HAVE TO HELP!
AIN'T THAT SOMETHING? AFTER ALL THE TIMES WE OFFERED HELP, SHE FINALLY NEEDS US. ANOTHER TYPE OF MAN MAY TAKE OFFENSE TO A WOMAN PICKING AND CHOOSING WHEN A MAN CAN HELP HER.
I SAY WE SCRAP HIM FOR PARTS!
NO! THE ROBOTS ARE CONNECTED TO THE SOLDIERS! IF YOU TAKE IT APART IT MAY KILL HIM!
DON'T HURT MY DADDY!
MOO
GET OUT OF THE WAY, KID.

WHOK

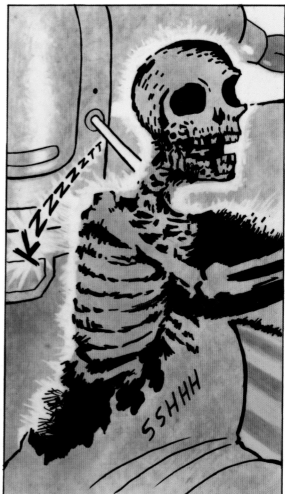

ZZZZZZTT

SSHHH

RONNIE, IS THAT YOU?

OH GOD... WHAT DID I DO?

RONNIE! COME BACK!

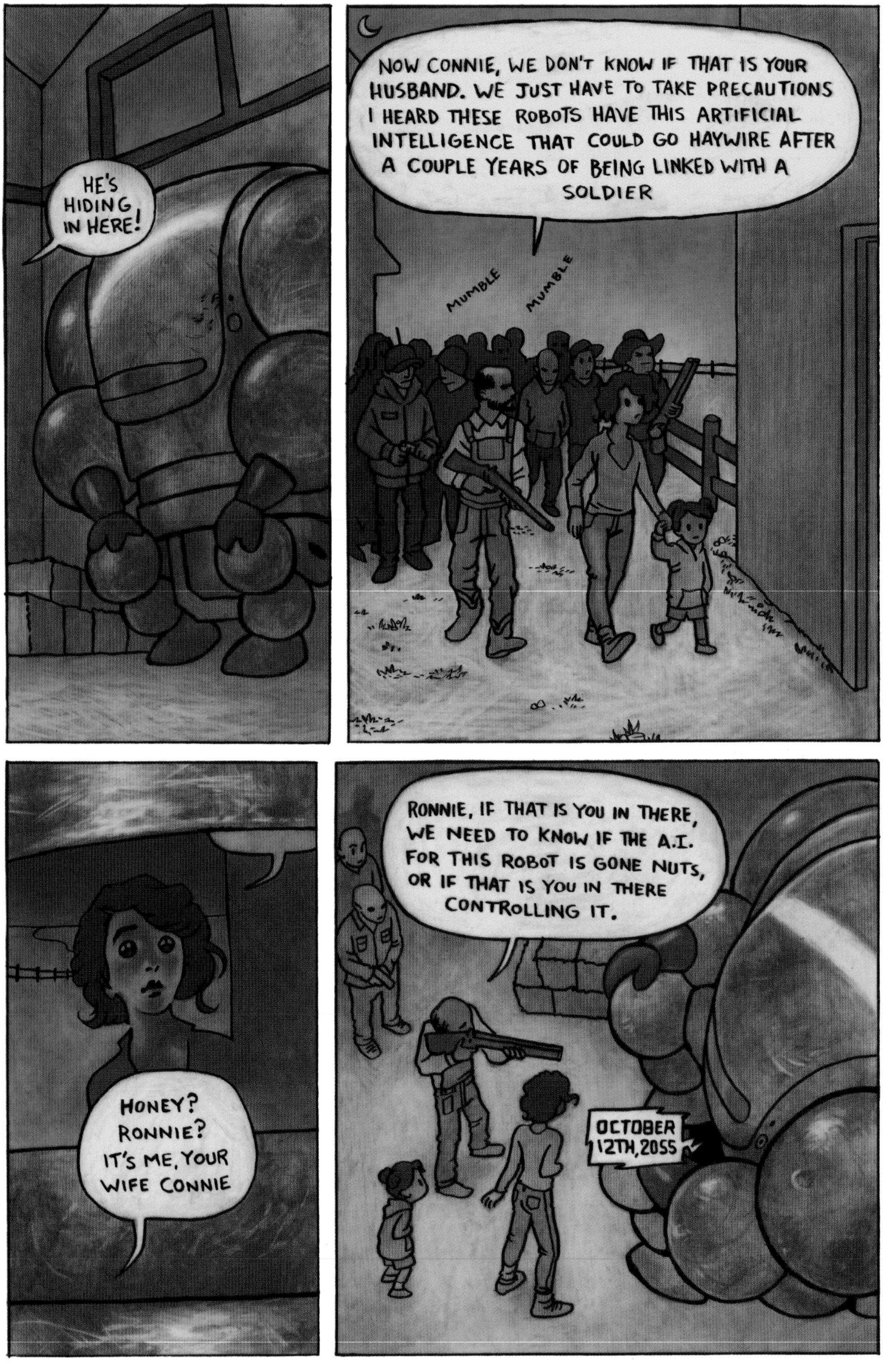
HE'S HIDING IN HERE!
NOW CONNIE, WE DON'T KNOW IF THAT IS YOUR HUSBAND. WE JUST HAVE TO TAKE PRECAUTIONS I HEARD THESE ROBOTS HAVE THIS ARTIFICIAL INTELLIGENCE THAT COULD GO HAYWIRE AFTER A COUPLE YEARS OF BEING LINKED WITH A SOLDIER
MUMBLE
MUMBLE
HONEY? RONNIE? IT'S ME, YOUR WIFE CONNIE
RONNIE, IF THAT IS YOU IN THERE, WE NEED TO KNOW IF THE A.I. FOR THIS ROBOT IS GONE NUTS, OR IF THAT IS YOU IN THERE CONTROLLING IT.
OCTOBER 12TH, 2055

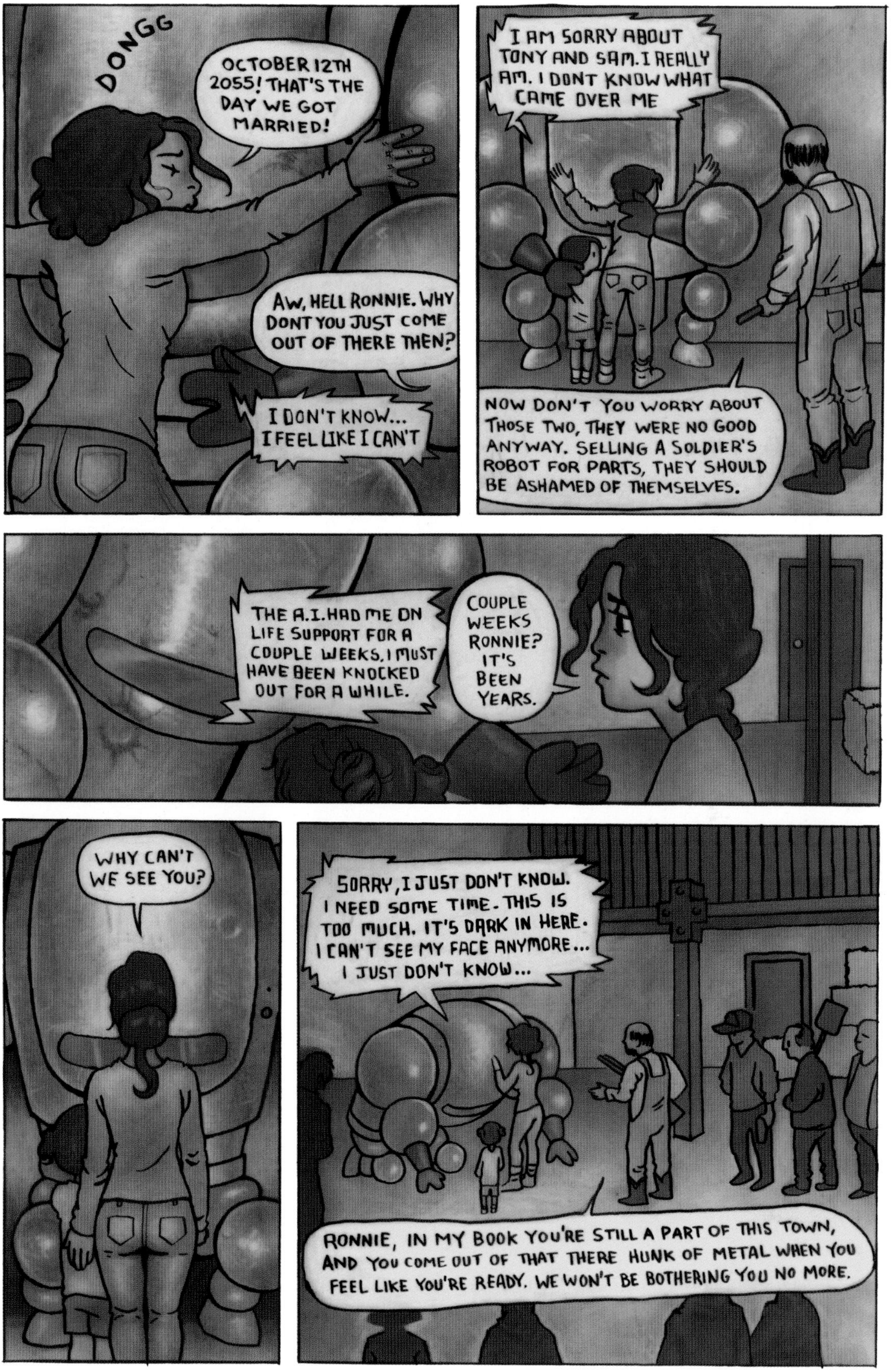
DONGG
OCTOBER 12TH 2055! THAT'S THE DAY WE GOT MARRIED!
AW, HELL RONNIE. WHY DONT YOU JUST COME OUT OF THERE THEN?
I DON'T KNOW... I FEEL LIKE I CAN'T
I AM SORRY ABOUT TONY AND SAM. I REALLY AM. I DONT KNOW WHAT CAME OVER ME
NOW DON'T YOU WORRY ABOUT THOSE TWO, THEY WERE NO GOOD ANYWAY. SELLING A SOLDIER'S ROBOT FOR PARTS, THEY SHOULD BE ASHAMED OF THEMSELVES.
THE A.I. HAD ME ON LIFE SUPPORT FOR A COUPLE WEEKS. I MUST HAVE BEEN KNOCKED OUT FOR A WHILE.
COUPLE WEEKS RONNIE? IT'S BEEN YEARS.
WHY CAN'T WE SEE YOU?
SORRY, I JUST DON'T KNOW. I NEED SOME TIME. THIS IS TOO MUCH. IT'S DARK IN HERE. I CAN'T SEE MY FACE ANYMORE... I JUST DON'T KNOW...
RONNIE, IN MY BOOK YOU'RE STILL A PART OF THIS TOWN, AND YOU COME OUT OF THAT THERE HUNK OF METAL WHEN YOU FEEL LIKE YOU'RE READY. WE WON'T BE BOTHERING YOU NO MORE.

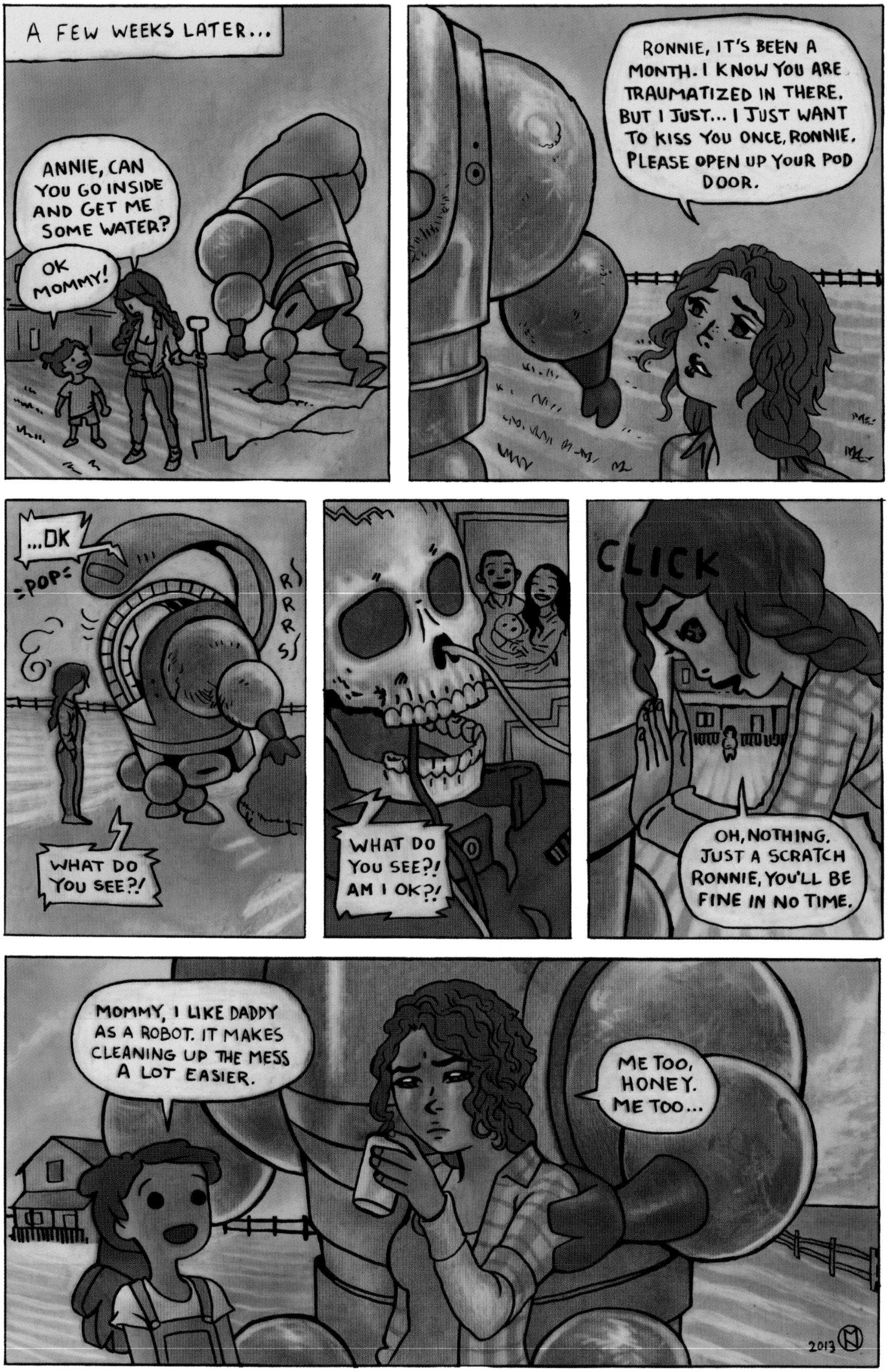
A FEW WEEKS LATER...
ANNIE, CAN YOU GO INSIDE AND GET ME SOME WATER?
OK MOMMY!
RONNIE, IT'S BEEN A MONTH. I KNOW YOU ARE TRAUMATIZED IN THERE. BUT I JUST... I JUST WANT TO KISS YOU ONCE, RONNIE. PLEASE OPEN UP YOUR POD DOOR.
...OK
POP
RRRS
WHAT DO YOU SEE?!
WHAT DO YOU SEE?! AM I OK?!
CLICK
OH, NOTHING. JUST A SCRATCH RONNIE, YOU'LL BE FINE IN NO TIME.
MOMMY, I LIKE DADDY AS A ROBOT. IT MAKES CLEANING UP THE MESS A LOT EASIER.
ME TOO, HONEY. ME TOO...
2013

THE BIRD WATCHER

ART BY YUMI SAKUGAWA

THE IVORY-BILLED WOODPECKER IS ONE OF THE LARGEST WOODPECKERS IN THE WORLD. IT WAS NAMED A CLASS 6 SPECIES A FEW YEARS AGO.

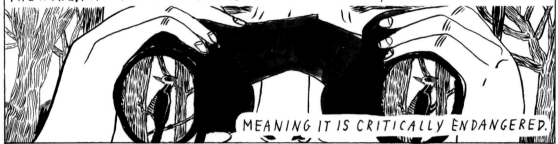

MEANING IT IS CRITICALLY ENDANGERED.

THE BIRDWATCHER. HE IS OF AVERAGE SIZE AND HAS AVERAGE THOUGHTS.

THERE ARE MANY LIKE HIM.

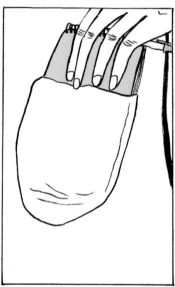

ONCE A BIRD IS SUCCESSFULLY VIEWED HE WILL CHECK IT FROM HIS LIST.

THIS IS THE WAY OF THE BIRDWATCHER.

TO BE CONTENT AND UNCOMPLICATED.

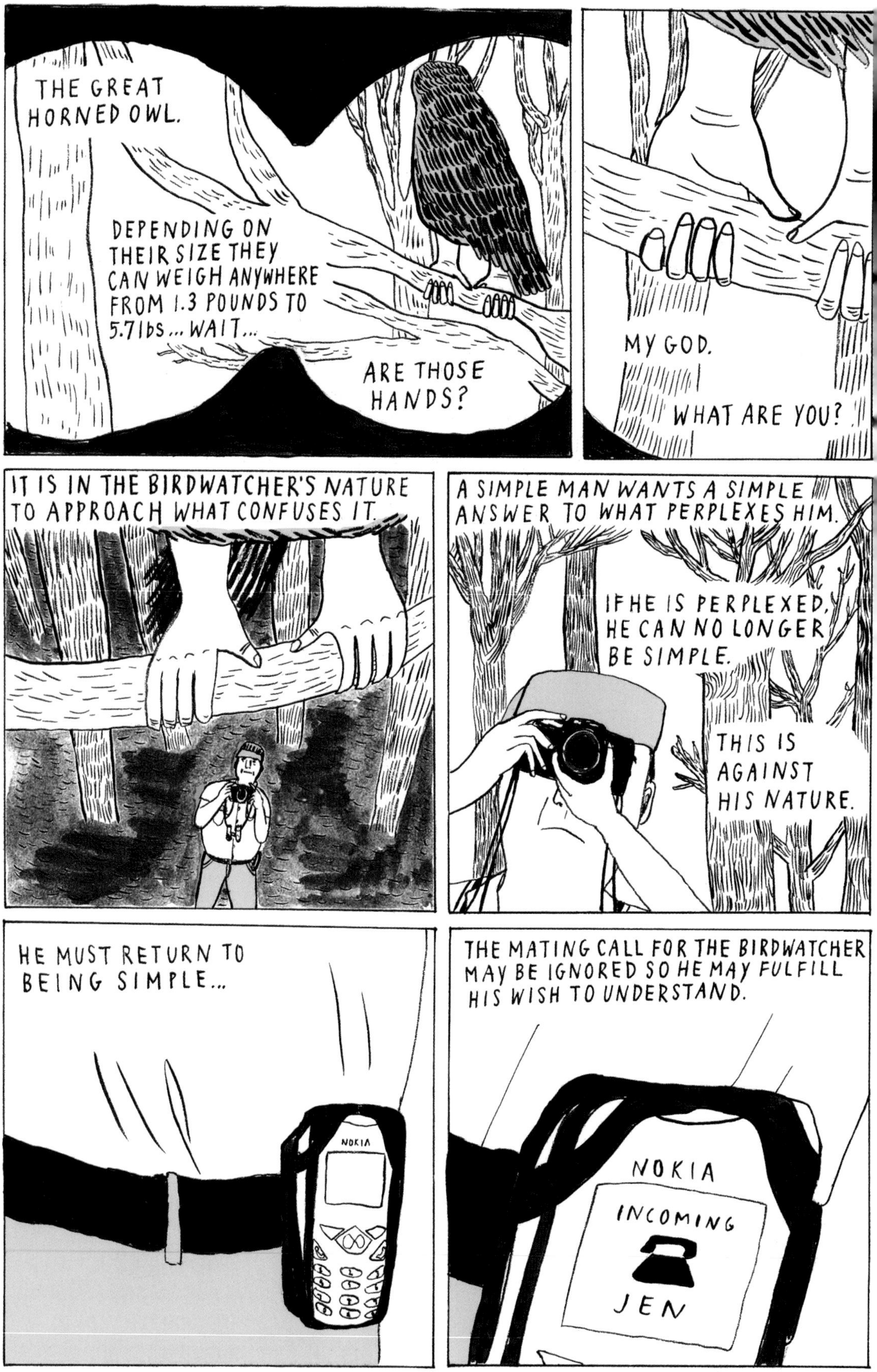
THE GREAT HORNED OWL.
DEPENDING ON THEIR SIZE THEY CAN WEIGH ANYWHERE FROM 1.3 POUNDS TO 5.71bs... WAIT...
ARE THOSE HANDS?
MY GOD.
WHAT ARE YOU?
IT IS IN THE BIRDWATCHER'S NATURE TO APPROACH WHAT CONFUSES IT.
A SIMPLE MAN WANTS A SIMPLE ANSWER TO WHAT PERPLEXES HIM.
IF HE IS PERPLEXED, HE CAN NO LONGER BE SIMPLE.
THIS IS AGAINST HIS NATURE.
HE MUST RETURN TO BEING SIMPLE...
NOKIA
THE MATING CALL FOR THE BIRDWATCHER MAY BE IGNORED SO HE MAY FULFILL HIS WISH TO UNDERSTAND.
NOKIA
INCOMING
JEN

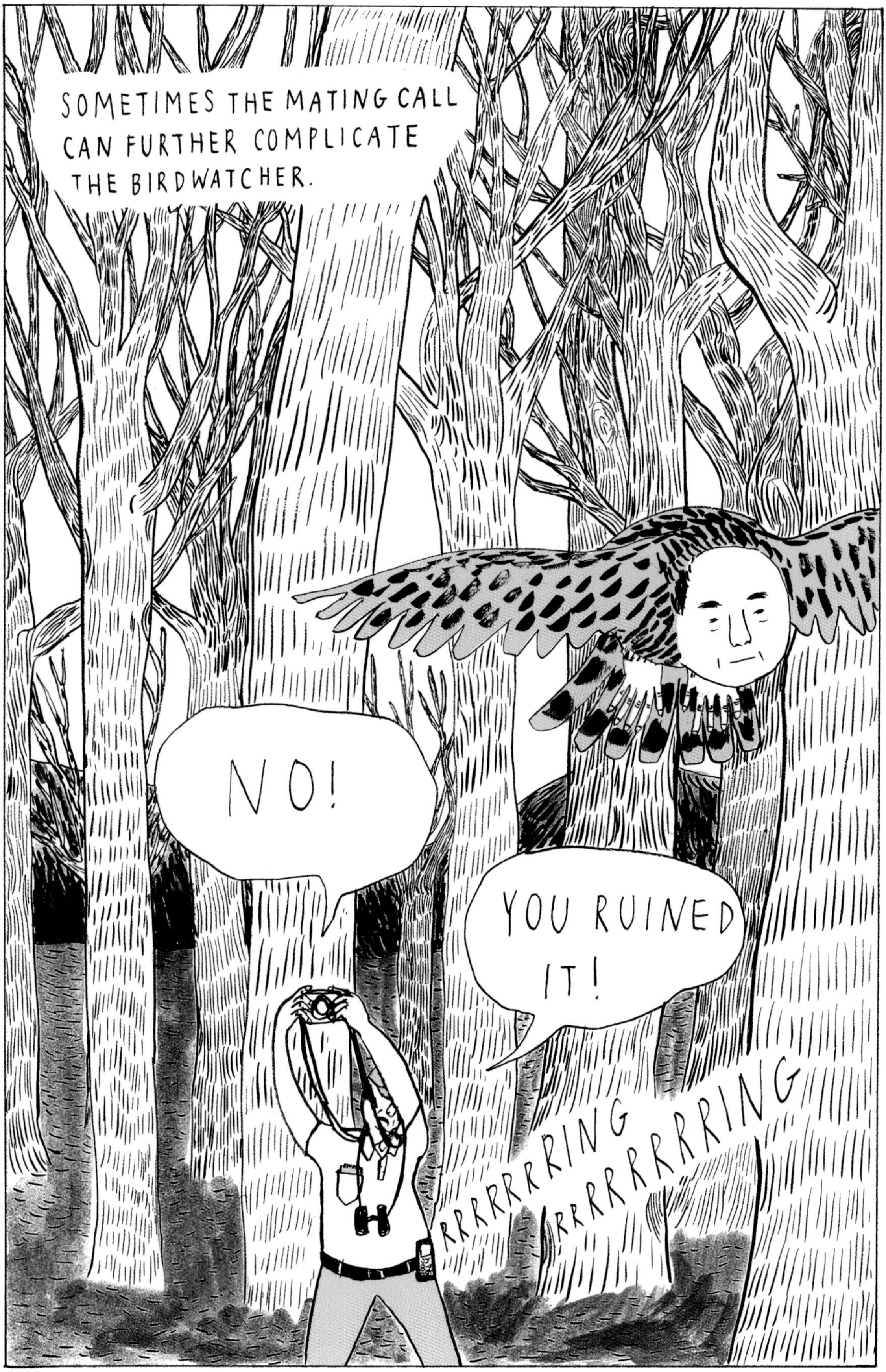
SOMETIMES THE MATING CALL CAN FURTHER COMPLICATE THE BIRDWATCHER.
NO!
YOU RUINED IT!
RRRRRRRING
RRRRRRRRRING

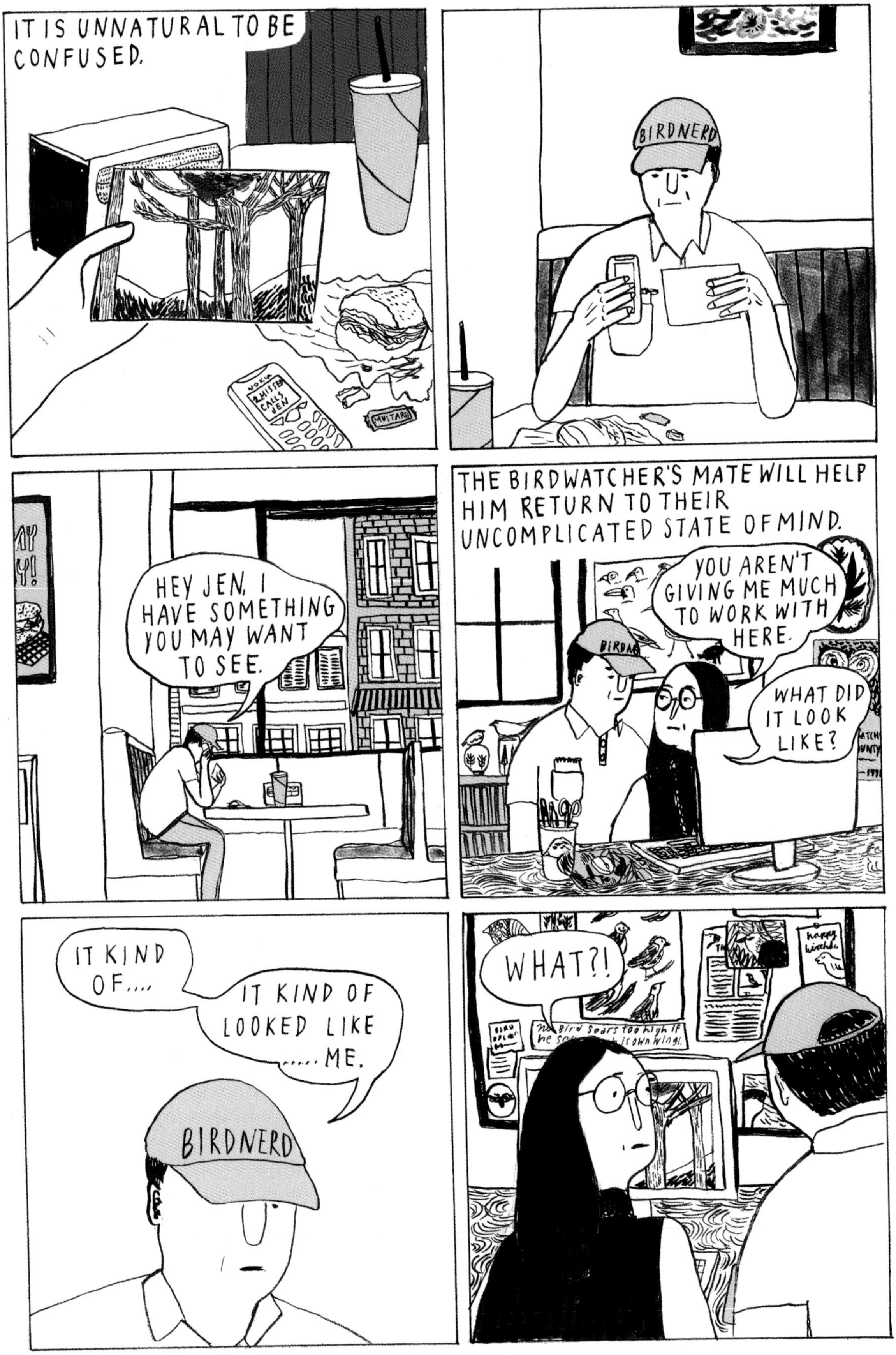
IT IS UNNATURAL TO BE CONFUSED.
MUSTARD
BIRDNERD
HEY JEN, I HAVE SOMETHING YOU MAY WANT TO SEE.
THE BIRDWATCHER'S MATE WILL HELP HIM RETURN TO THEIR UNCOMPLICATED STATE OF MIND.
YOU AREN'T GIVING ME MUCH TO WORK WITH HERE.
WHAT DID IT LOOK LIKE?
IT KIND OF....
IT KIND OF LOOKED LIKE .....ME.
BIRDNERD
WHAT?!

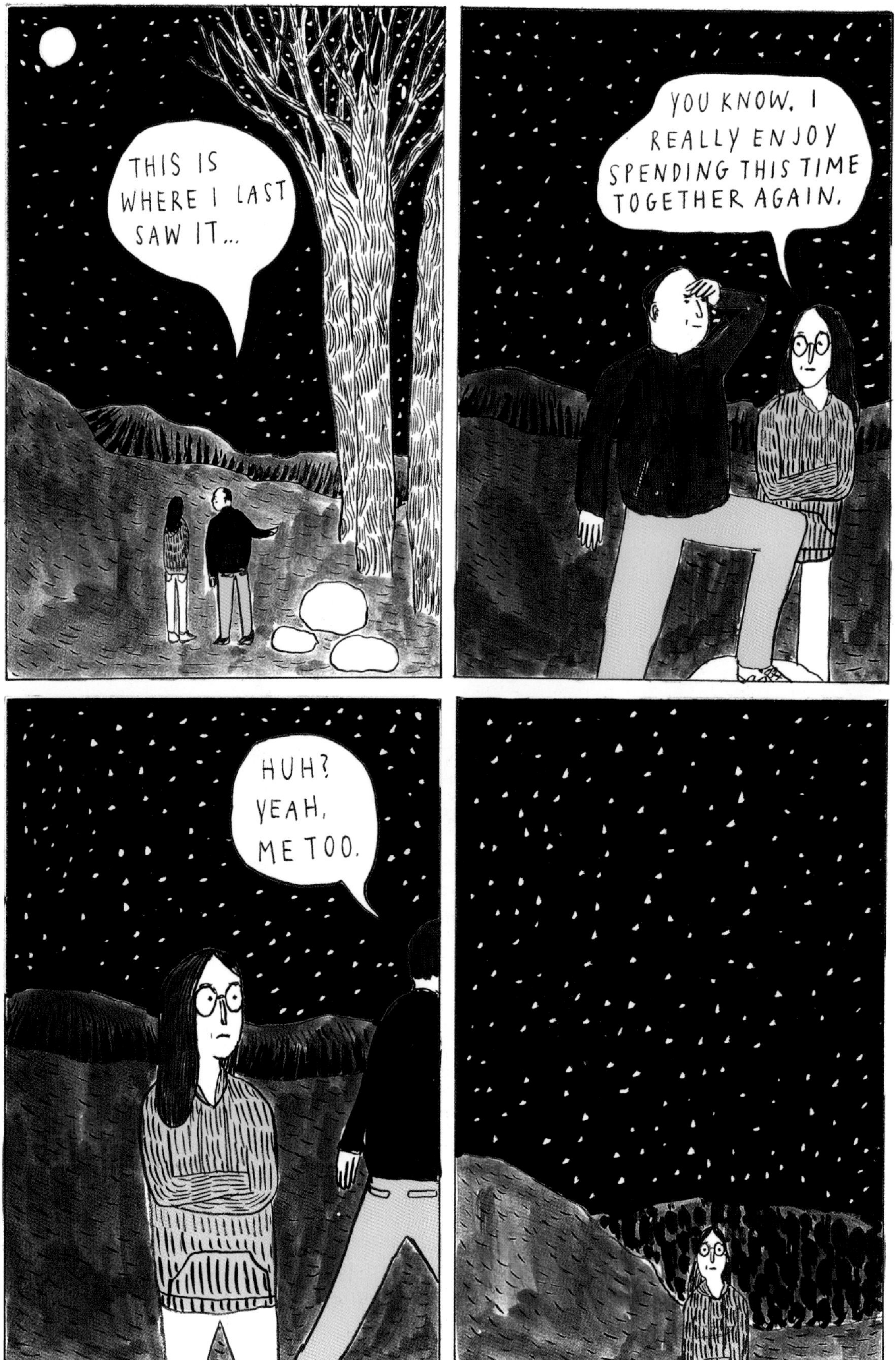
THIS IS WHERE I LAST SAW IT...
YOU KNOW, I REALLY ENJOY SPENDING THIS TIME TOGETHER AGAIN.
HUH? YEAH, ME TOO.

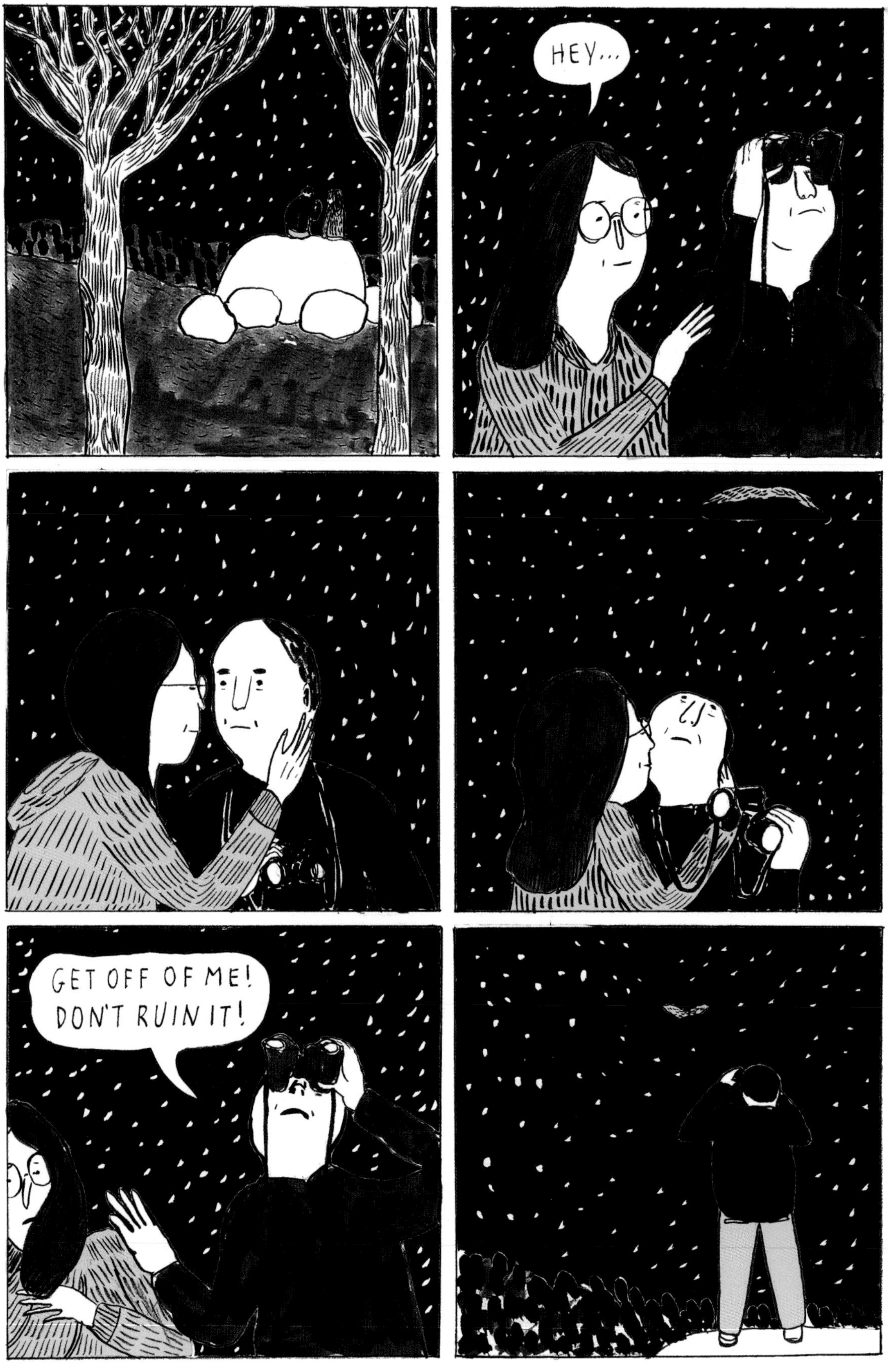
HEY...
GET OFF OF ME! DON'T RUIN IT!

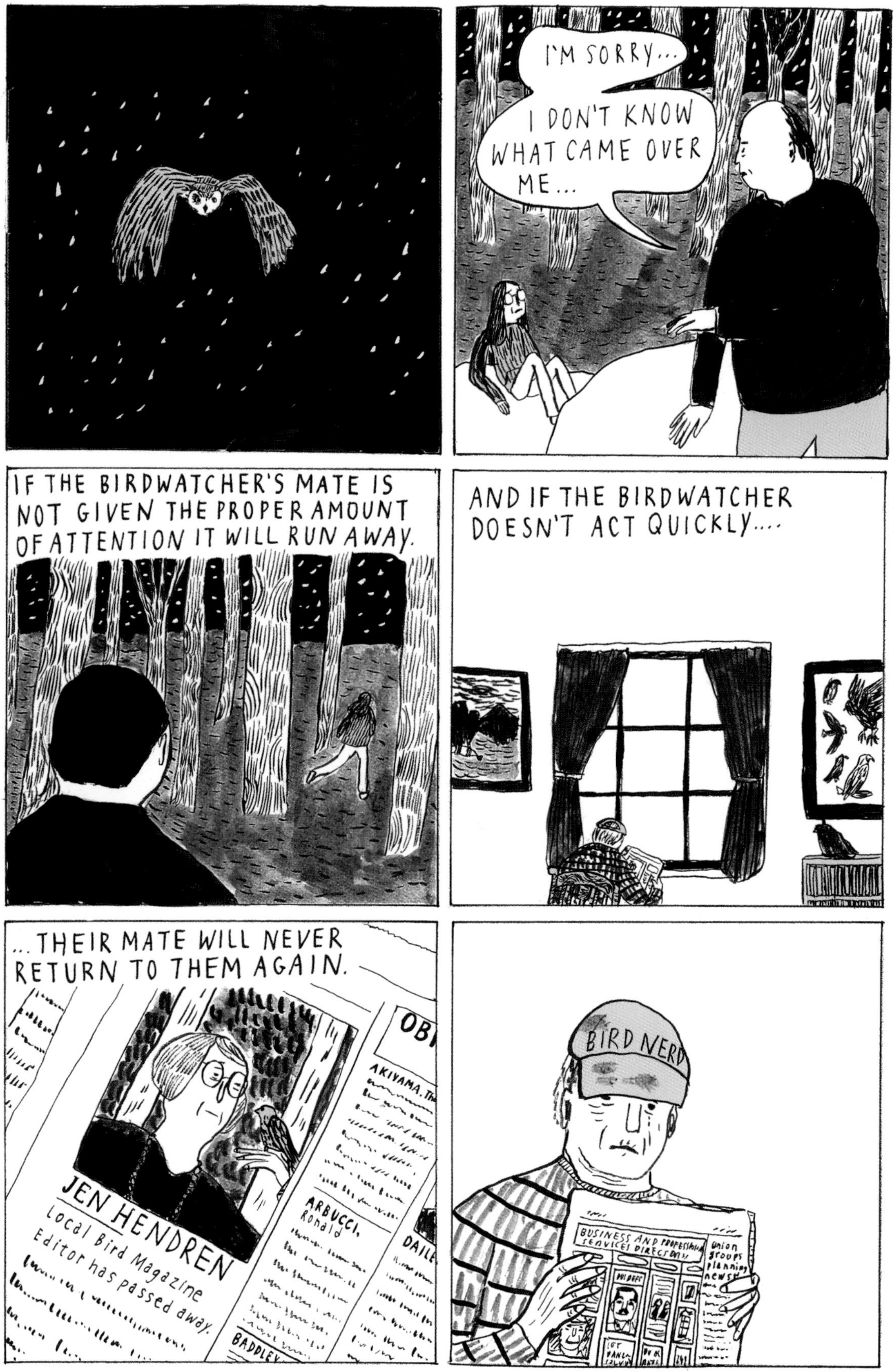
I'M SORRY...
I DON'T KNOW WHAT CAME OVER ME...
IF THE BIRDWATCHER'S MATE IS NOT GIVEN THE PROPER AMOUNT OF ATTENTION IT WILL RUN AWAY.
AND IF THE BIRDWATCHER DOESN'T ACT QUICKLY....
...THEIR MATE WILL NEVER RETURN TO THEM AGAIN.
JEN HENDREN
Local Bird Magazine Editor has passed away.
AKIYAMA
ARBUCCI, Ronald
BADDLEY
BIRD NERD
BUSINESS AND PROFESSIONAL SERVICES DIRECTORY
Union groups planning news

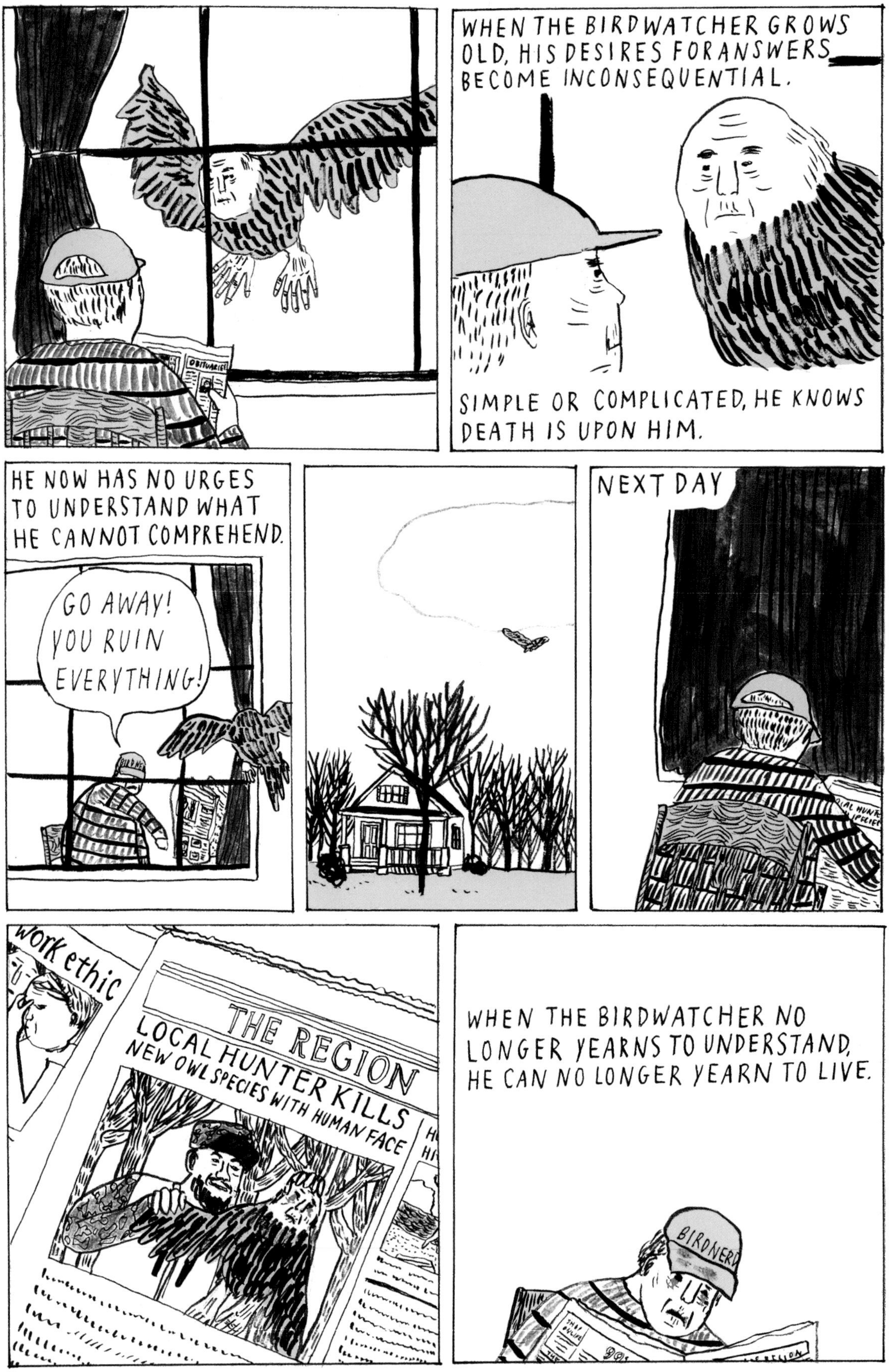

WHEN THE BIRDWATCHER GROWS OLD, HIS DESIRES FOR ANSWERS BECOME INCONSEQUENTIAL.
SIMPLE OR COMPLICATED, HE KNOWS DEATH IS UPON HIM.
HE NOW HAS NO URGES TO UNDERSTAND WHAT HE CANNOT COMPREHEND.
GO AWAY! YOU RUIN EVERYTHING!
NEXT DAY
work ethic
THE REGION
LOCAL HUNTER KILLS NEW OWL SPECIES WITH HUMAN FACE
WHEN THE BIRDWATCHER NO LONGER YEARNS TO UNDERSTAND, HE CAN NO LONGER YEARN TO LIVE.
BIRDNERD

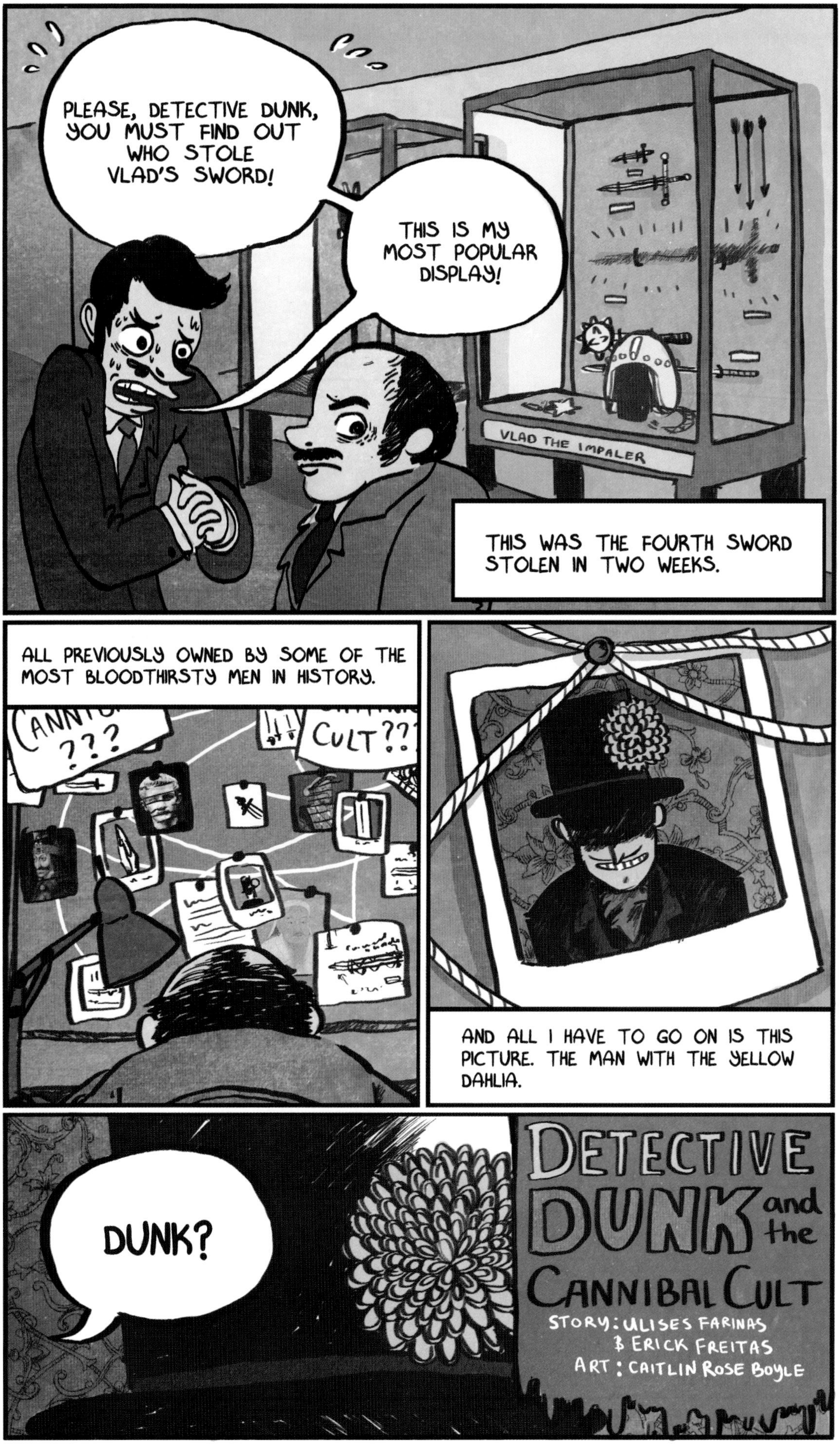
PLEASE, DETECTIVE DUNK, YOU MUST FIND OUT WHO STOLE VLAD'S SWORD!
THIS IS MY MOST POPULAR DISPLAY!
VLAD THE IMPALER
THIS WAS THE FOURTH SWORD STOLEN IN TWO WEEKS.
ALL PREVIOUSLY OWNED BY SOME OF THE MOST BLOODTHIRSTY MEN IN HISTORY.
???
CULT???
AND ALL I HAVE TO GO ON IS THIS PICTURE. THE MAN WITH THE YELLOW DAHLIA.
DUNK?
DETECTIVE DUNK and the CANNIBAL CULT
STORY: ULISES FARINAS $ ERICK FREITAS
ART: CAITLIN ROSE BOYLE

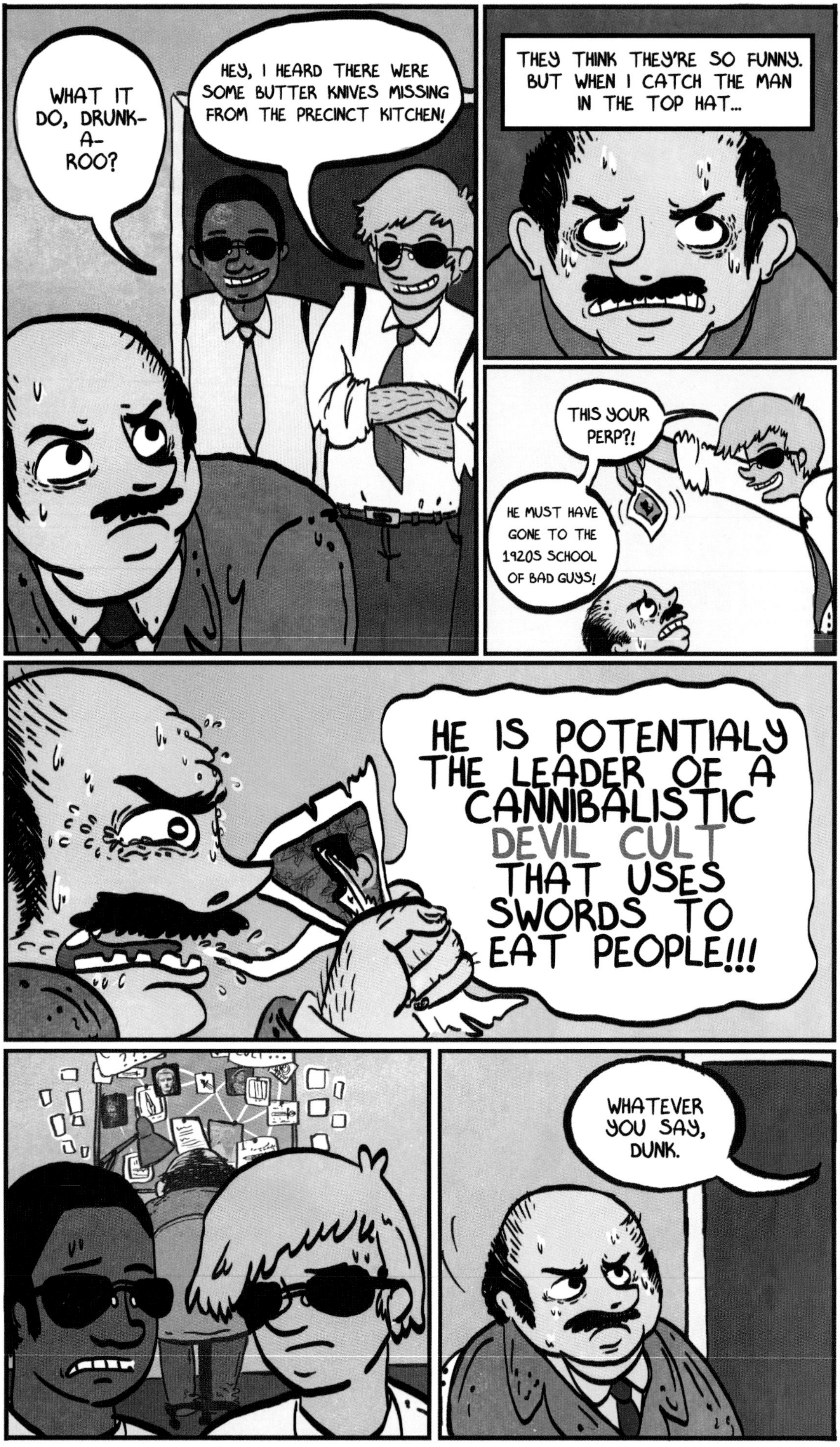
WHAT IT DO, DRUNK-A-ROO?
HEY, I HEARD THERE WERE SOME BUTTER KNIVES MISSING FROM THE PRECINCT KITCHEN!
THEY THINK THEY'RE SO FUNNY. BUT WHEN I CATCH THE MAN IN THE TOP HAT...
THIS YOUR PERP?!
HE MUST HAVE GONE TO THE 1920S SCHOOL OF BAD GUYS!
HE IS POTENTIALY THE LEADER OF A CANNIBALISTIC DEVIL CULT THAT USES SWORDS TO EAT PEOPLE!!!
WHATEVER YOU SAY, DUNK.

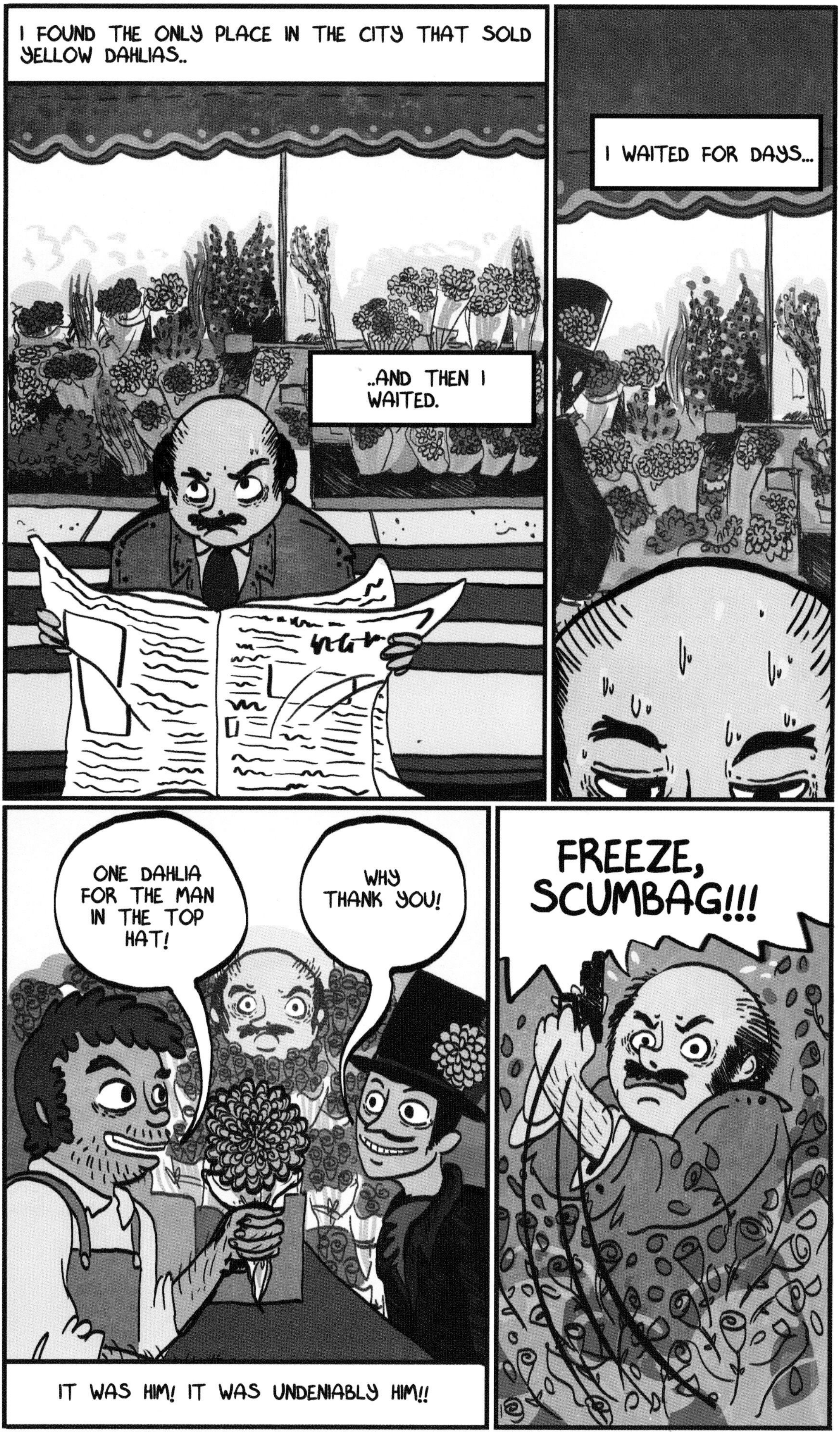
I FOUND THE ONLY PLACE IN THE CITY THAT SOLD YELLOW DAHLIAS..
..AND THEN I WAITED.
I WAITED FOR DAYS...
ONE DAHLIA FOR THE MAN IN THE TOP HAT!
WHY THANK YOU!
IT WAS HIM! IT WAS UNDENIABLY HIM!!
FREEZE, SCUMBAG!!!

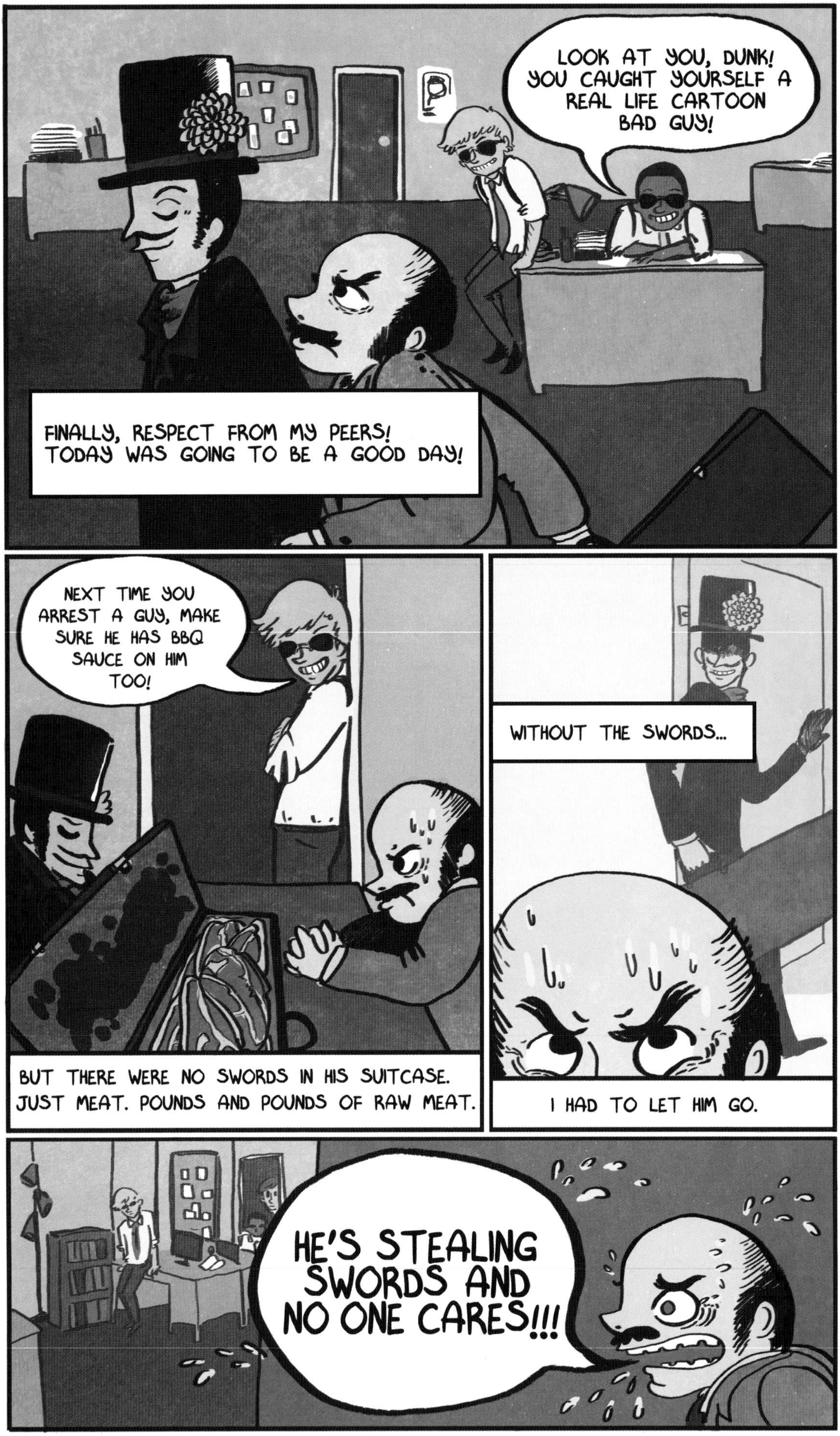
LOOK AT YOU, DUNK! YOU CAUGHT YOURSELF A REAL LIFE CARTOON BAD GUY!
FINALLY, RESPECT FROM MY PEERS! TODAY WAS GOING TO BE A GOOD DAY!
NEXT TIME YOU ARREST A GUY, MAKE SURE HE HAS BBQ SAUCE ON HIM TOO!
BUT THERE WERE NO SWORDS IN HIS SUITCASE. JUST MEAT. POUNDS AND POUNDS OF RAW MEAT.
WITHOUT THE SWORDS...
I HAD TO LET HIM GO.
HE'S STEALING SWORDS AND NO ONE CARES!!!

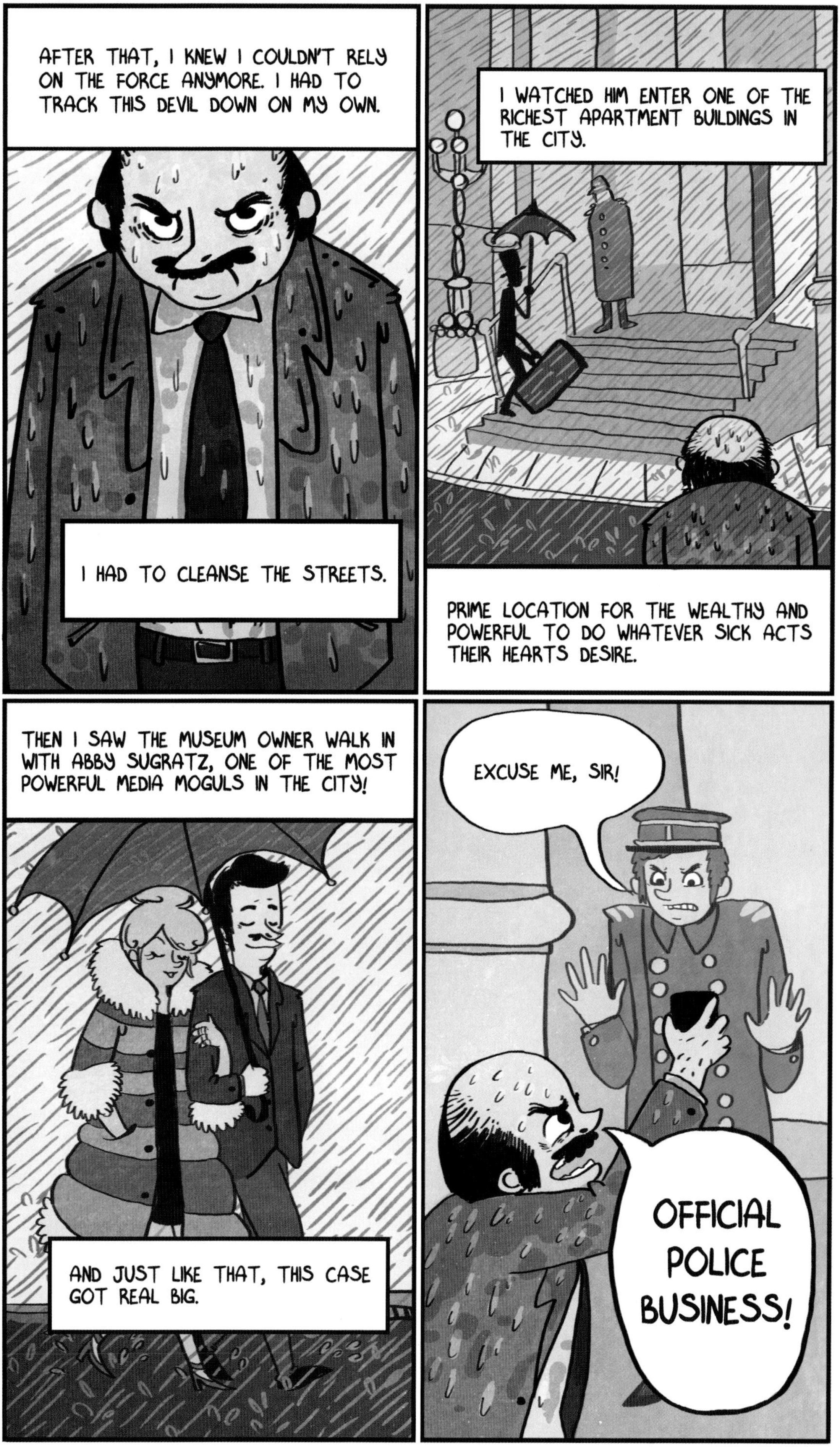
AFTER THAT, I KNEW I COULDN'T RELY ON THE FORCE ANYMORE. I HAD TO TRACK THIS DEVIL DOWN ON MY OWN.
I HAD TO CLEANSE THE STREETS.
I WATCHED HIM ENTER ONE OF THE RICHEST APARTMENT BUILDINGS IN THE CITY.
PRIME LOCATION FOR THE WEALTHY AND POWERFUL TO DO WHATEVER SICK ACTS THEIR HEARTS DESIRE.
THEN I SAW THE MUSEUM OWNER WALK IN WITH ABBY SUGRATZ, ONE OF THE MOST POWERFUL MEDIA MOGULS IN THE CITY!
AND JUST LIKE THAT, THIS CASE GOT REAL BIG.
EXCUSE ME, SIR!
OFFICIAL POLICE BUSINESS!

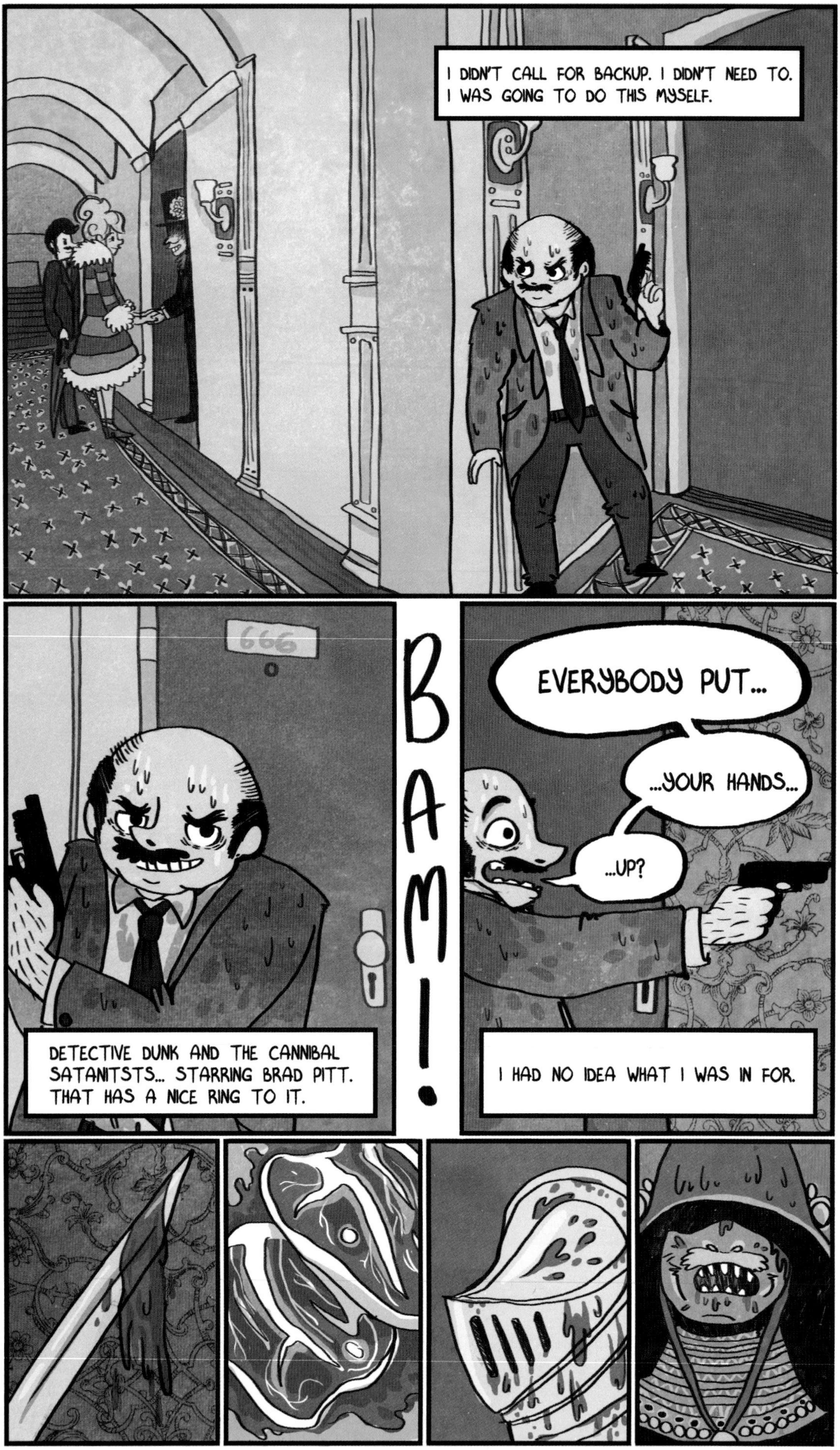
I DIDN'T CALL FOR BACKUP. I DIDN'T NEED TO. I WAS GOING TO DO THIS MYSELF.
666
DETECTIVE DUNK AND THE CANNIBAL SATANITSTS... STARRING BRAD PITT. THAT HAS A NICE RING TO IT.
BAM!
EVERYBODY PUT...
...YOUR HANDS...
...UP?
I HAD NO IDEA WHAT I WAS IN FOR.

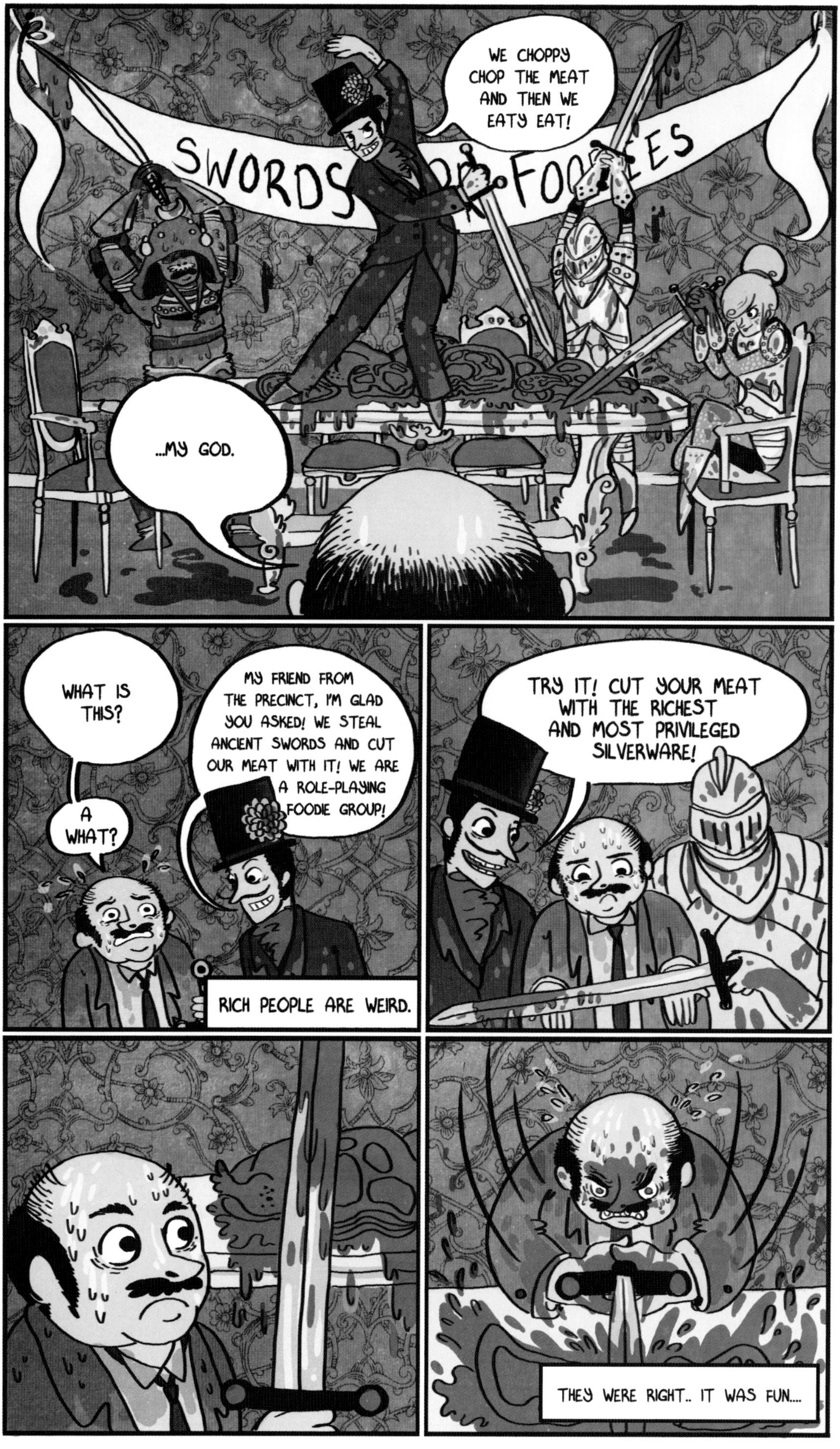
SWORDS
WE CHOPPY CHOP THE MEAT AND THEN WE EATY EAT!
...MY GOD.
WHAT IS THIS?
MY FRIEND FROM THE PRECINCT, I'M GLAD YOU ASKED! WE STEAL ANCIENT SWORDS AND CUT OUR MEAT WITH IT! WE ARE A ROLE-PLAYING FOODIE GROUP!
A WHAT?
RICH PEOPLE ARE WEIRD.
TRY IT! CUT YOUR MEAT WITH THE RICHEST AND MOST PRIVILEGED SILVERWARE!
THEY WERE RIGHT.. IT WAS FUN....

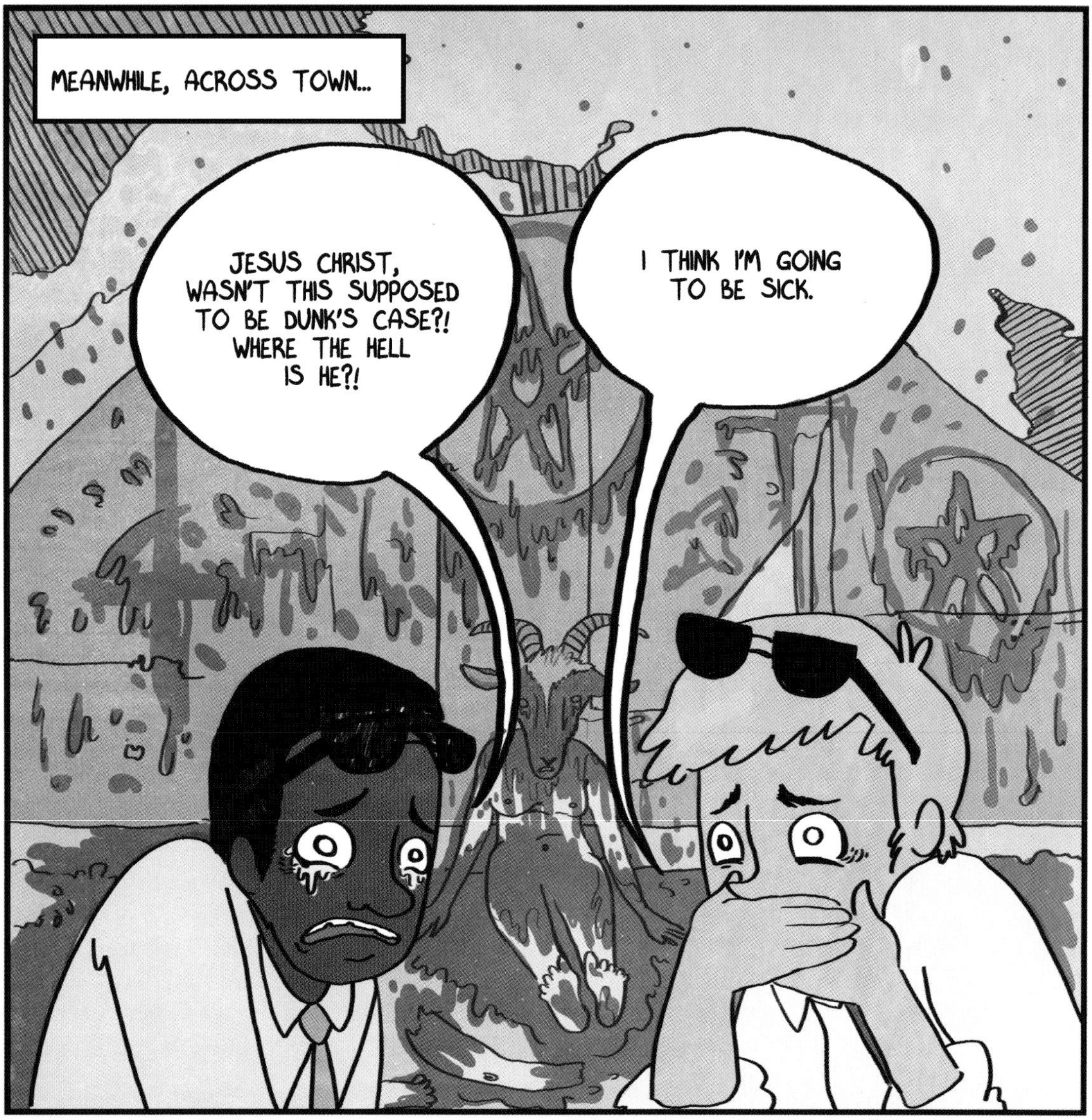
MEANWHILE, ACROSS TOWN...
JESUS CHRIST, WASN'T THIS SUPPOSED TO BE DUNK'S CASE?! WHERE THE HELL IS HE?!
I THINK I'M GOING TO BE SICK.

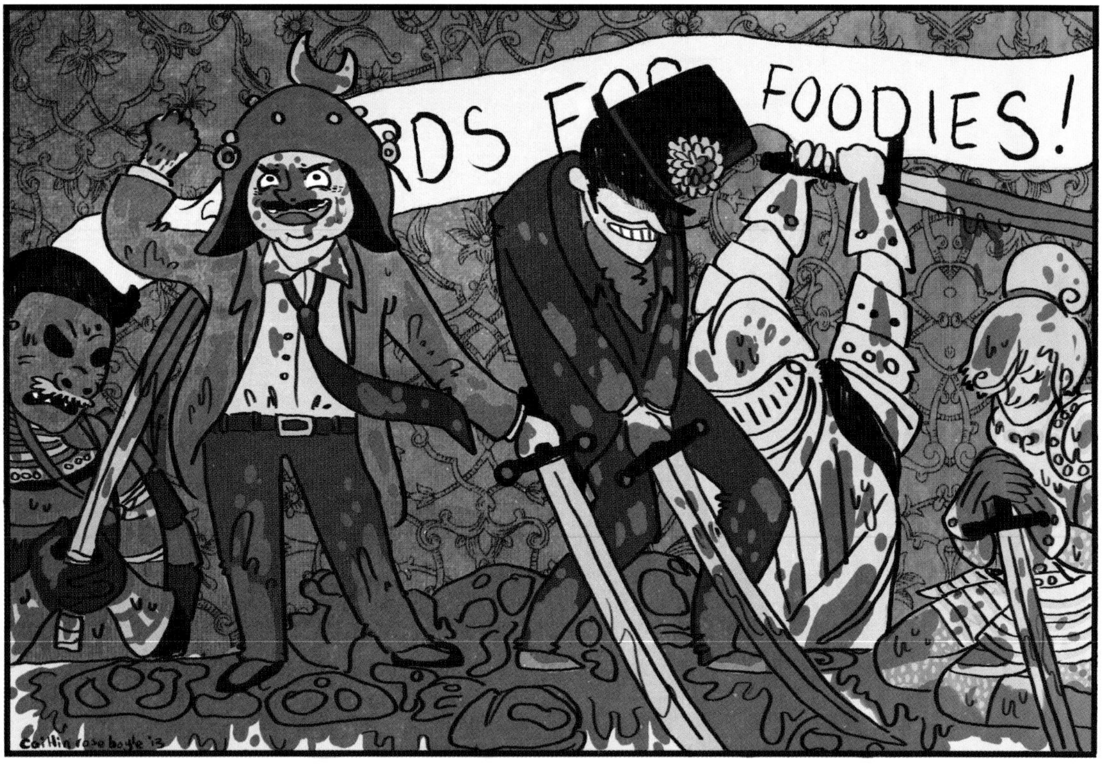
FOODIES!
caitlin rose boyle '13

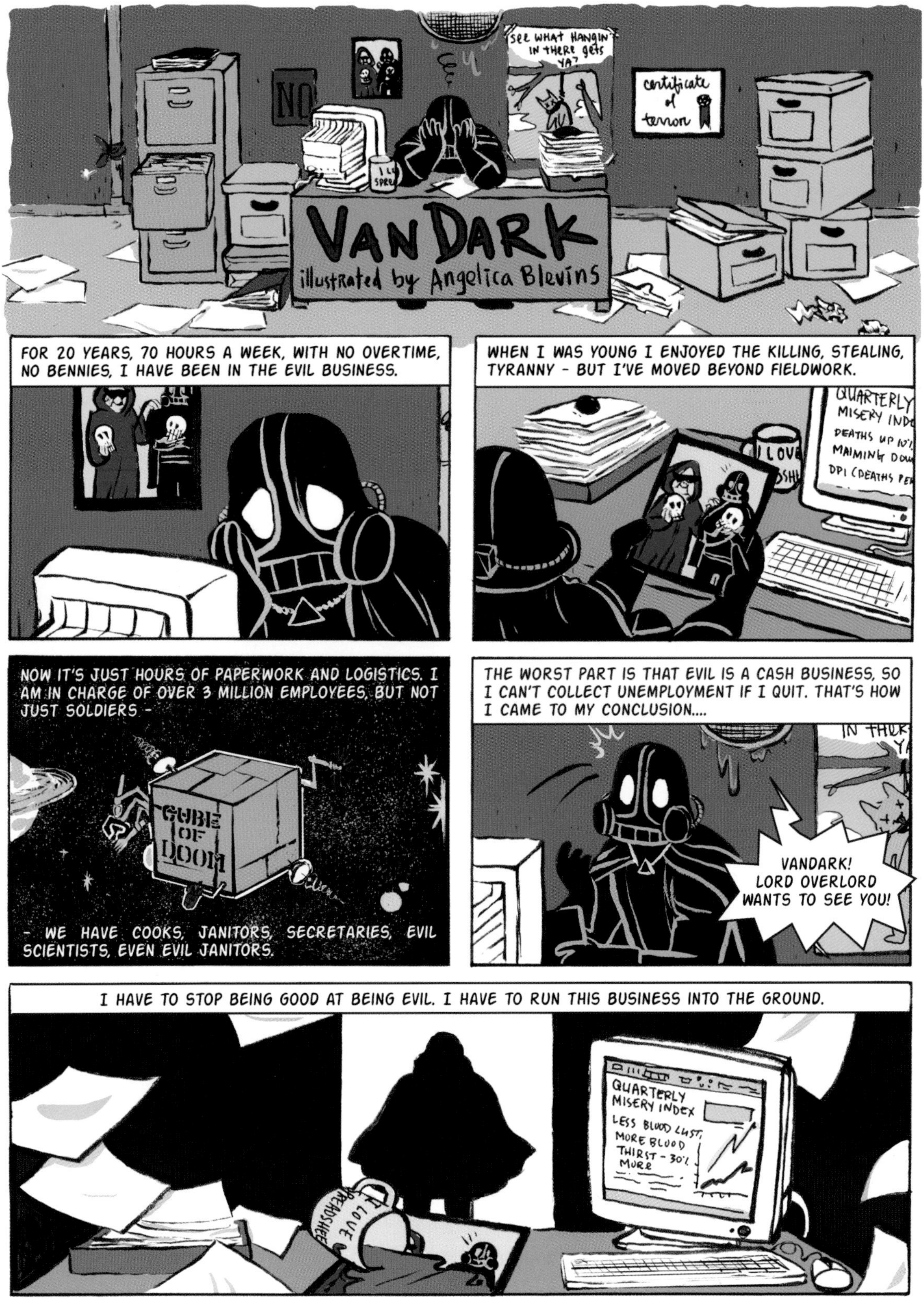
see what hangin in there gets ya?
certificate of terror
NO
VAN DARK
illustrated by Angelica Blevins
FOR 20 YEARS, 70 HOURS A WEEK, WITH NO OVERTIME, NO BENNIES, I HAVE BEEN IN THE EVIL BUSINESS.
WHEN I WAS YOUNG I ENJOYED THE KILLING, STEALING, TYRANNY - BUT I'VE MOVED BEYOND FIELDWORK.
QUARTERLY MISERY IND
DEATHS UP 10%
MAIMING DOW
DPI (DEATHS PER
NOW IT'S JUST HOURS OF PAPERWORK AND LOGISTICS. I AM IN CHARGE OF OVER 3 MILLION EMPLOYEES, BUT NOT JUST SOLDIERS -
CUBE OF DOOM
- WE HAVE COOKS, JANITORS, SECRETARIES, EVIL SCIENTISTS, EVEN EVIL JANITORS.
THE WORST PART IS THAT EVIL IS A CASH BUSINESS, SO I CAN'T COLLECT UNEMPLOYMENT IF I QUIT. THAT'S HOW I CAME TO MY CONCLUSION....
VANDARK! LORD OVERLORD WANTS TO SEE YOU!
I HAVE TO STOP BEING GOOD AT BEING EVIL. I HAVE TO RUN THIS BUSINESS INTO THE GROUND.
QUARTERLY MISERY INDEX
LESS BLOOD LUST, MORE BLOOD THIRST - 30% MORE
I LOVE SPREADSHEE

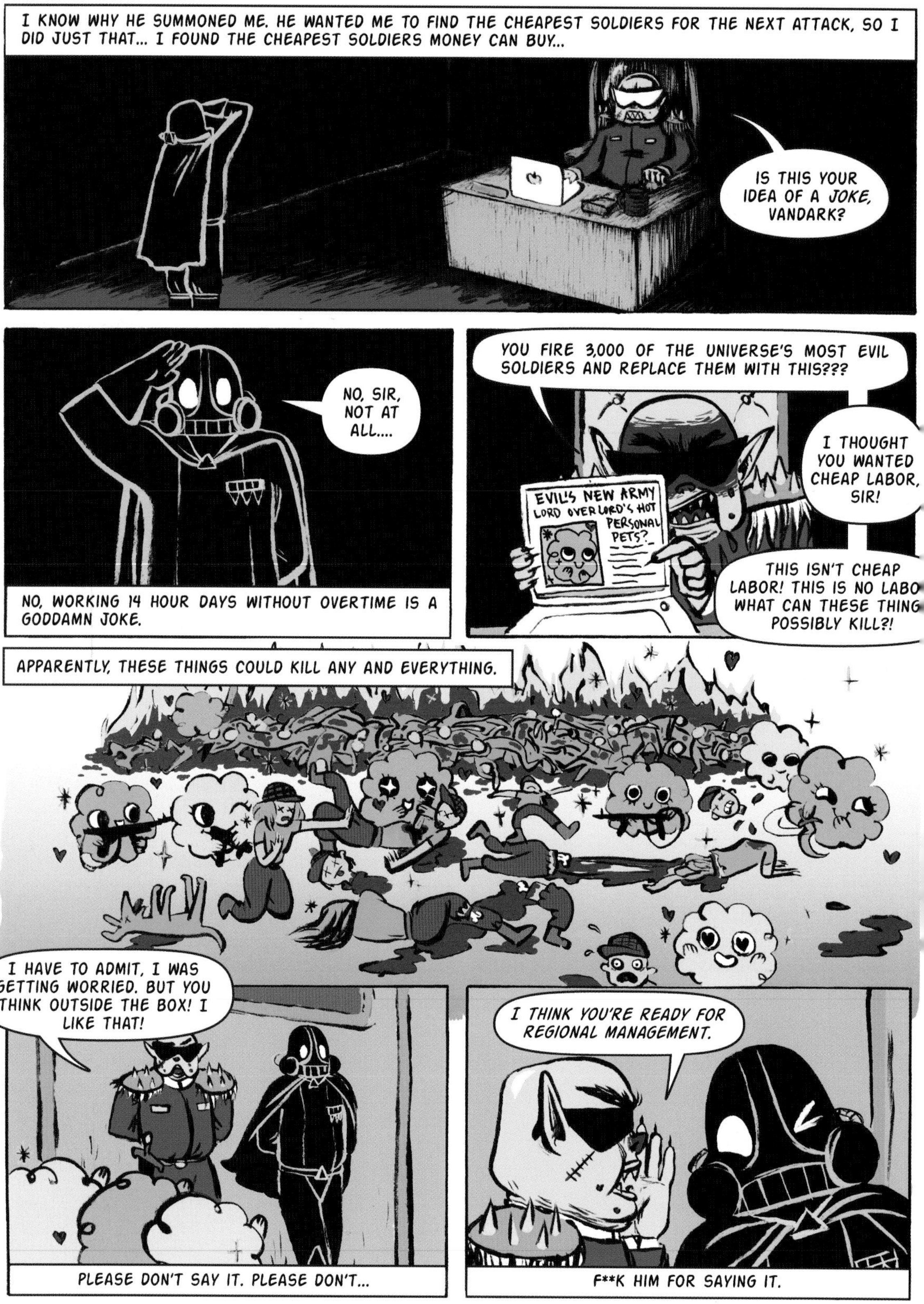
I KNOW WHY HE SUMMONED ME. HE WANTED ME TO FIND THE CHEAPEST SOLDIERS FOR THE NEXT ATTACK, SO I DID JUST THAT... I FOUND THE CHEAPEST SOLDIERS MONEY CAN BUY...
IS THIS YOUR IDEA OF A *JOKE*, VANDARK?
NO, SIR, NOT AT ALL....
NO, WORKING 14 HOUR DAYS WITHOUT OVERTIME IS A GODDAMN JOKE.
YOU FIRE 3,000 OF THE UNIVERSE'S MOST EVIL SOLDIERS AND REPLACE THEM WITH THIS???
EVIL'S NEW ARMY
LORD OVERLORD'S HOT PERSONAL PETS?
I THOUGHT YOU WANTED CHEAP LABOR, SIR!
THIS ISN'T CHEAP LABOR! THIS IS NO LABO
WHAT CAN THESE THING POSSIBLY KILL?!
APPARENTLY, THESE THINGS COULD KILL ANY AND EVERYTHING.
I HAVE TO ADMIT, I WAS GETTING WORRIED. BUT YOU THINK OUTSIDE THE BOX! I LIKE THAT!
PLEASE DON'T SAY IT. PLEASE DON'T...
I THINK YOU'RE READY FOR REGIONAL MANAGEMENT.
F**K HIM FOR SAYING IT.

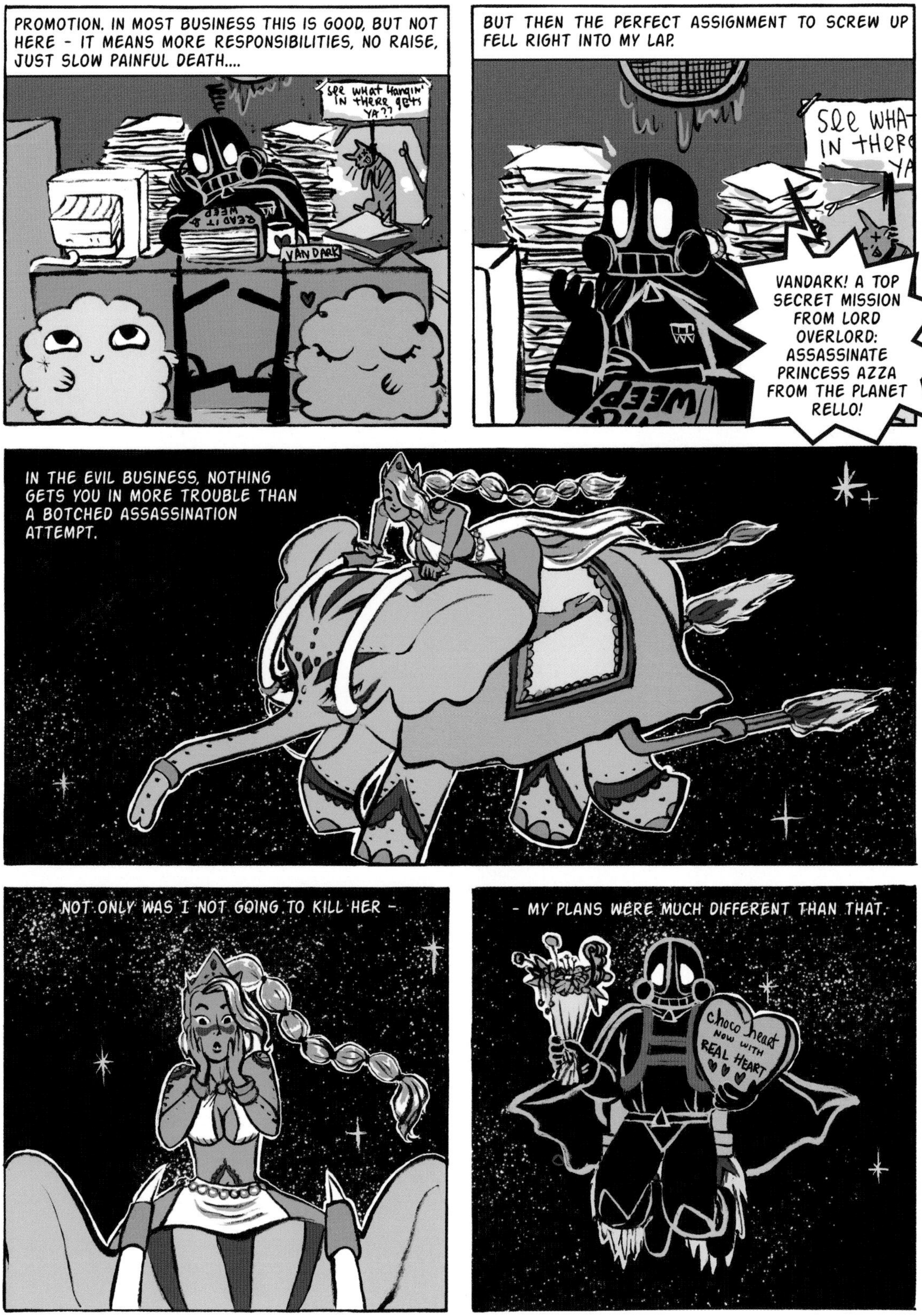
PROMOTION. IN MOST BUSINESS THIS IS GOOD, BUT NOT HERE - IT MEANS MORE RESPONSIBILITIES, NO RAISE, JUST SLOW PAINFUL DEATH....
See what Hangin' in there gets ya??
READ IT & WEEP
VANDARK
BUT THEN THE PERFECT ASSIGNMENT TO SCREW UP FELL RIGHT INTO MY LAP.
VANDARK! A TOP SECRET MISSION FROM LORD OVERLORD: ASSASSINATE PRINCESS AZZA FROM THE PLANET RELLO!
IN THE EVIL BUSINESS, NOTHING GETS YOU IN MORE TROUBLE THAN A BOTCHED ASSASSINATION ATTEMPT.
NOT ONLY WAS I NOT GOING TO KILL HER -
- MY PLANS WERE MUCH DIFFERENT THAN THAT.
choco heart now with REAL HEART

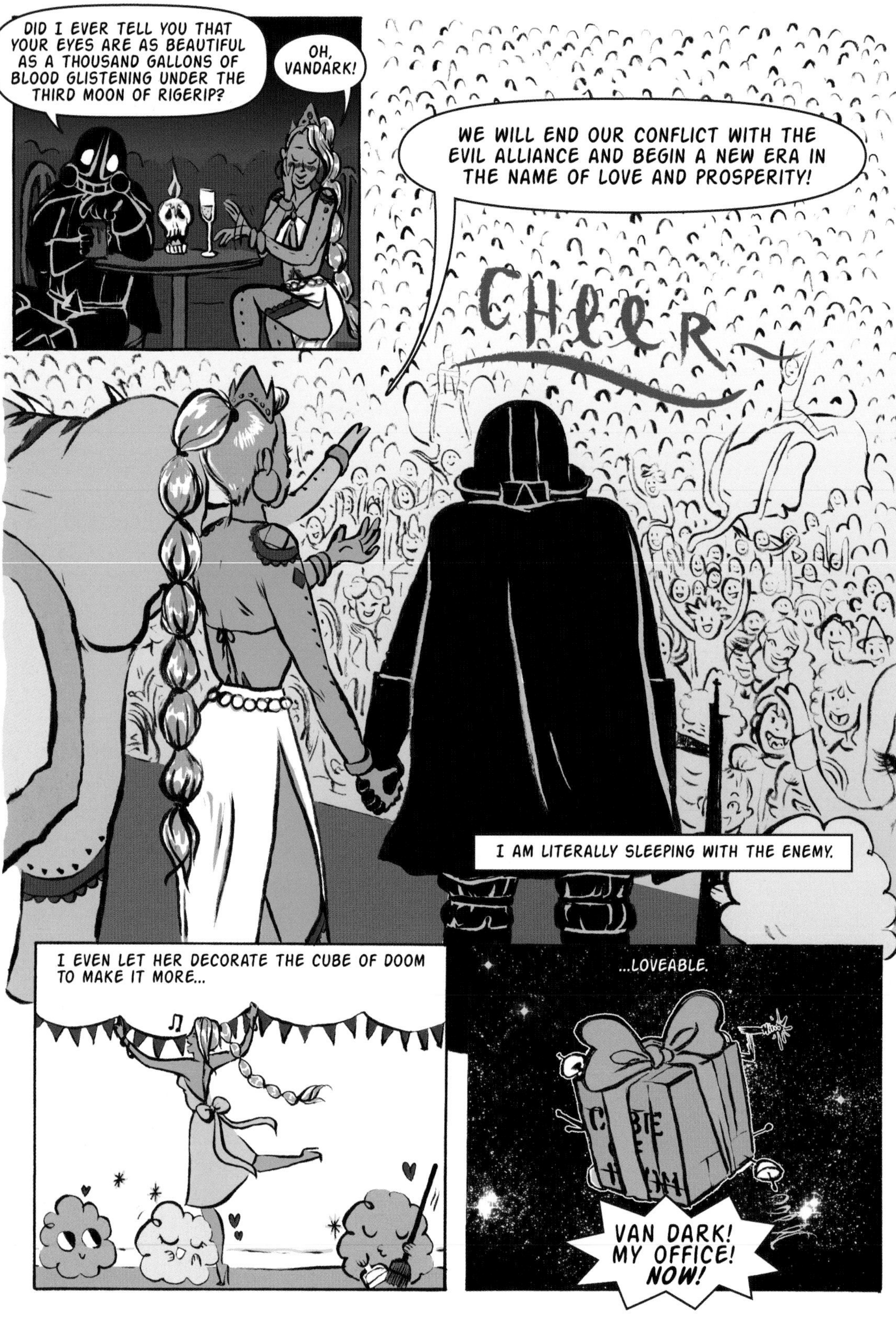
DID I EVER TELL YOU THAT YOUR EYES ARE AS BEAUTIFUL AS A THOUSAND GALLONS OF BLOOD GLISTENING UNDER THE THIRD MOON OF RIGERIP?
OH, VANDARK!
WE WILL END OUR CONFLICT WITH THE EVIL ALLIANCE AND BEGIN A NEW ERA IN THE NAME OF LOVE AND PROSPERITY!
CHEER
I AM LITERALLY SLEEPING WITH THE ENEMY.
I EVEN LET HER DECORATE THE CUBE OF DOOM TO MAKE IT MORE...
...LOVEABLE.
VAN DARK! MY OFFICE! NOW!

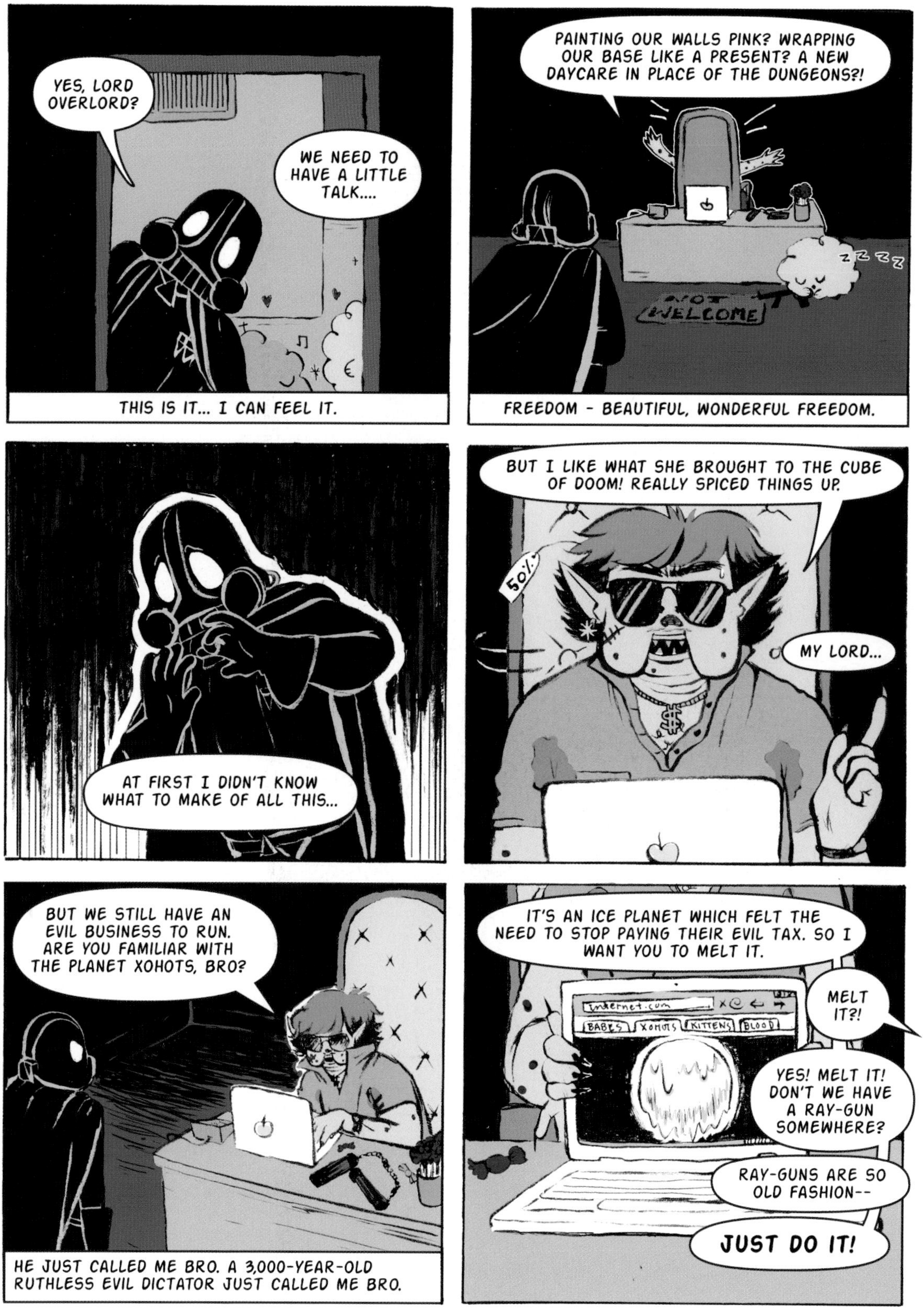
YES, LORD OVERLORD?
WE NEED TO HAVE A LITTLE TALK....
THIS IS IT... I CAN FEEL IT.
PAINTING OUR WALLS PINK? WRAPPING OUR BASE LIKE A PRESENT? A NEW DAYCARE IN PLACE OF THE DUNGEONS?!
Z Z Z Z
NOT WELCOME
FREEDOM - BEAUTIFUL, WONDERFUL FREEDOM.
AT FIRST I DIDN'T KNOW WHAT TO MAKE OF ALL THIS...
BUT I LIKE WHAT SHE BROUGHT TO THE CUBE OF DOOM! REALLY SPICED THINGS UP.
50%
MY LORD...
BUT WE STILL HAVE AN EVIL BUSINESS TO RUN. ARE YOU FAMILIAR WITH THE PLANET XOHOTS, BRO?
HE JUST CALLED ME BRO. A 3,000-YEAR-OLD RUTHLESS EVIL DICTATOR JUST CALLED ME BRO.
IT'S AN ICE PLANET WHICH FELT THE NEED TO STOP PAYING THEIR EVIL TAX. SO I WANT YOU TO MELT IT.
internet.com
BABES
XOHOTS
KITTENS
BLOOD
MELT IT?!
YES! MELT IT! DON'T WE HAVE A RAY-GUN SOMEWHERE?
RAY-GUNS ARE SO OLD FASHION--
JUST DO IT!

I WAS SUPPOSED TO BURN THE PEOPLE OF XOHOTS.

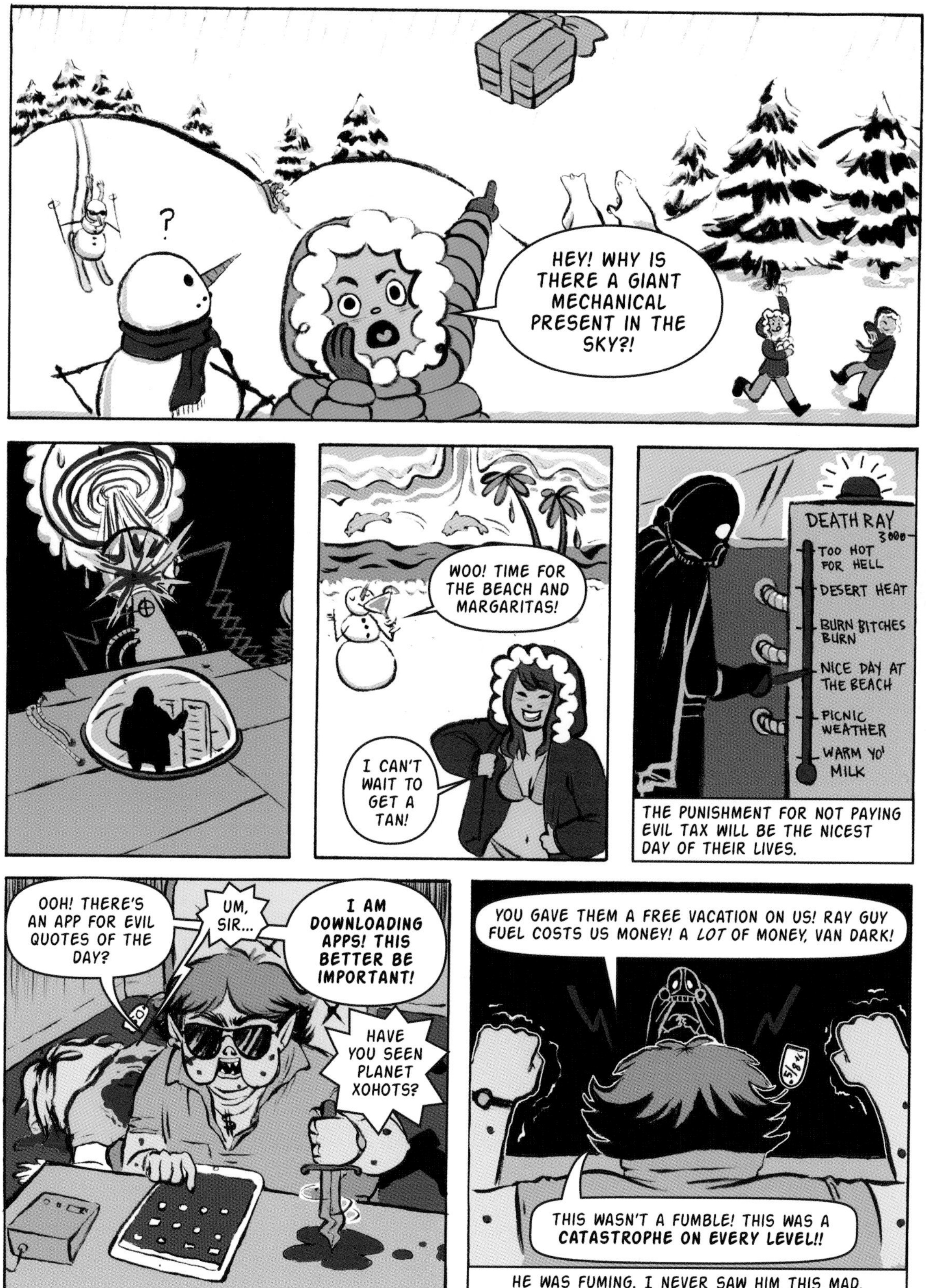
?
HEY! WHY IS THERE A GIANT MECHANICAL PRESENT IN THE SKY?!
WOO! TIME FOR THE BEACH AND MARGARITAS!
I CAN'T WAIT TO GET A TAN!
DEATH RAY 3000
TOO HOT FOR HELL
DESERT HEAT
BURN BITCHES BURN
NICE DAY AT THE BEACH
PICNIC WEATHER
WARM YO' MILK
THE PUNISHMENT FOR NOT PAYING EVIL TAX WILL BE THE NICEST DAY OF THEIR LIVES.
OOH! THERE'S AN APP FOR EVIL QUOTES OF THE DAY?
UM, SIR...
I AM DOWNLOADING APPS! THIS BETTER BE IMPORTANT!
HAVE YOU SEEN PLANET XOHOTS?
YOU GAVE THEM A FREE VACATION ON US! RAY GUY FUEL COSTS US MONEY! A LOT OF MONEY, VAN DARK!
THIS WASN'T A FUMBLE! THIS WAS A CATASTROPHE ON EVERY LEVEL!!
HE WAS FUMING. I NEVER SAW HIM THIS MAD.

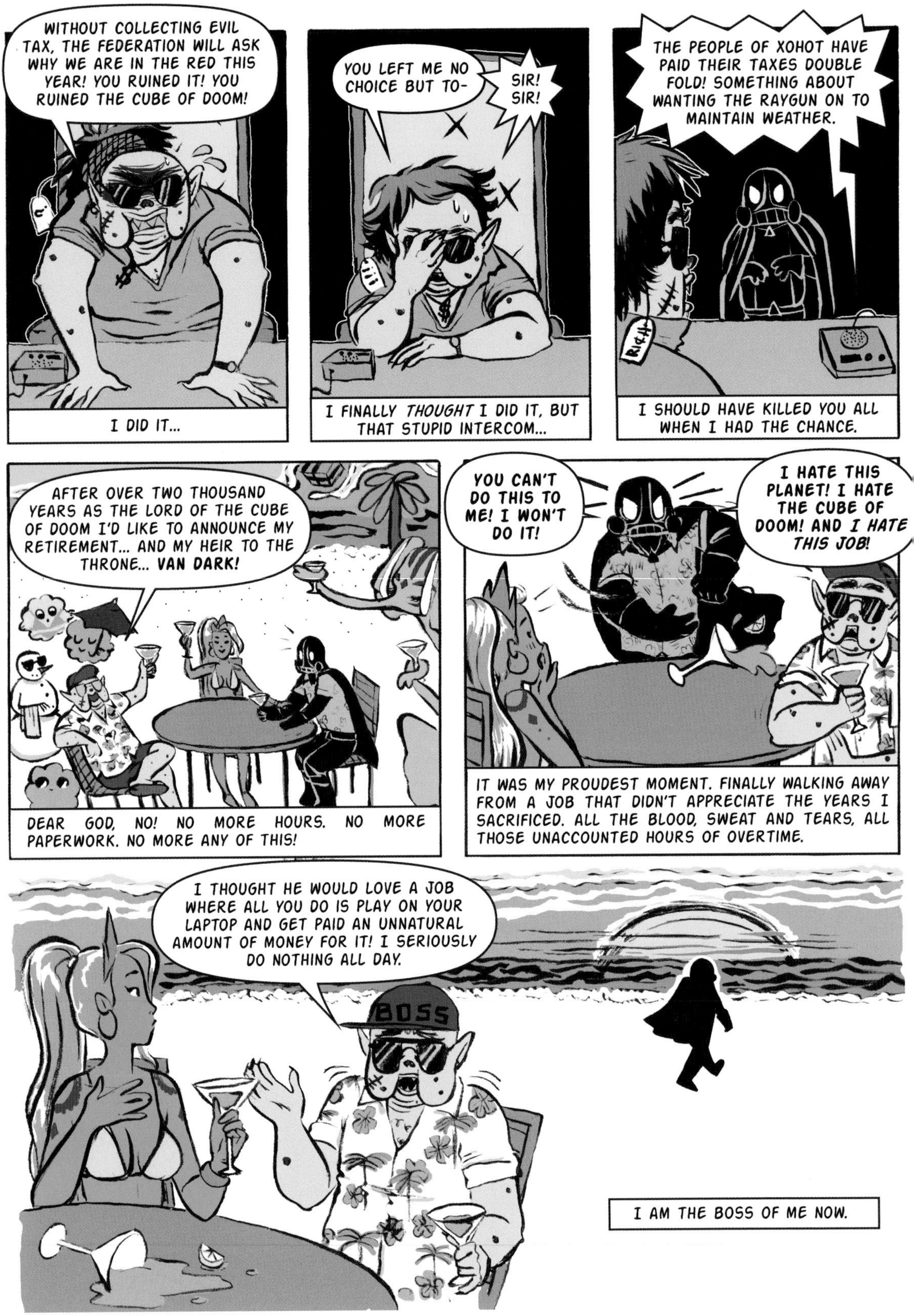
WITHOUT COLLECTING EVIL TAX, THE FEDERATION WILL ASK WHY WE ARE IN THE RED THIS YEAR! YOU RUINED IT! YOU RUINED THE CUBE OF DOOM!
I DID IT...
YOU LEFT ME NO CHOICE BUT TO-
SIR! SIR!
I FINALLY *THOUGHT* I DID IT, BUT THAT STUPID INTERCOM...
THE PEOPLE OF XOHOT HAVE PAID THEIR TAXES DOUBLE FOLD! SOMETHING ABOUT WANTING THE RAYGUN ON TO MAINTAIN WEATHER.
I SHOULD HAVE KILLED YOU ALL WHEN I HAD THE CHANCE.
AFTER OVER TWO THOUSAND YEARS AS THE LORD OF THE CUBE OF DOOM I'D LIKE TO ANNOUNCE MY RETIREMENT... AND MY HEIR TO THE THRONE... **VAN DARK!**
DEAR GOD, NO! NO MORE HOURS. NO MORE PAPERWORK. NO MORE ANY OF THIS!
YOU CAN'T DO THIS TO ME! I WON'T DO IT!
I HATE THIS PLANET! I HATE THE CUBE OF DOOM! AND *I HATE THIS JOB!*
IT WAS MY PROUDEST MOMENT. FINALLY WALKING AWAY FROM A JOB THAT DIDN'T APPRECIATE THE YEARS I SACRIFICED. ALL THE BLOOD, SWEAT AND TEARS, ALL THOSE UNACCOUNTED HOURS OF OVERTIME.
I THOUGHT HE WOULD LOVE A JOB WHERE ALL YOU DO IS PLAY ON YOUR LAPTOP AND GET PAID AN UNNATURAL AMOUNT OF MONEY FOR IT! I SERIOUSLY DO NOTHING ALL DAY.
BOSS
I AM THE BOSS OF ME NOW.

Stardust Art by Sean Pryor

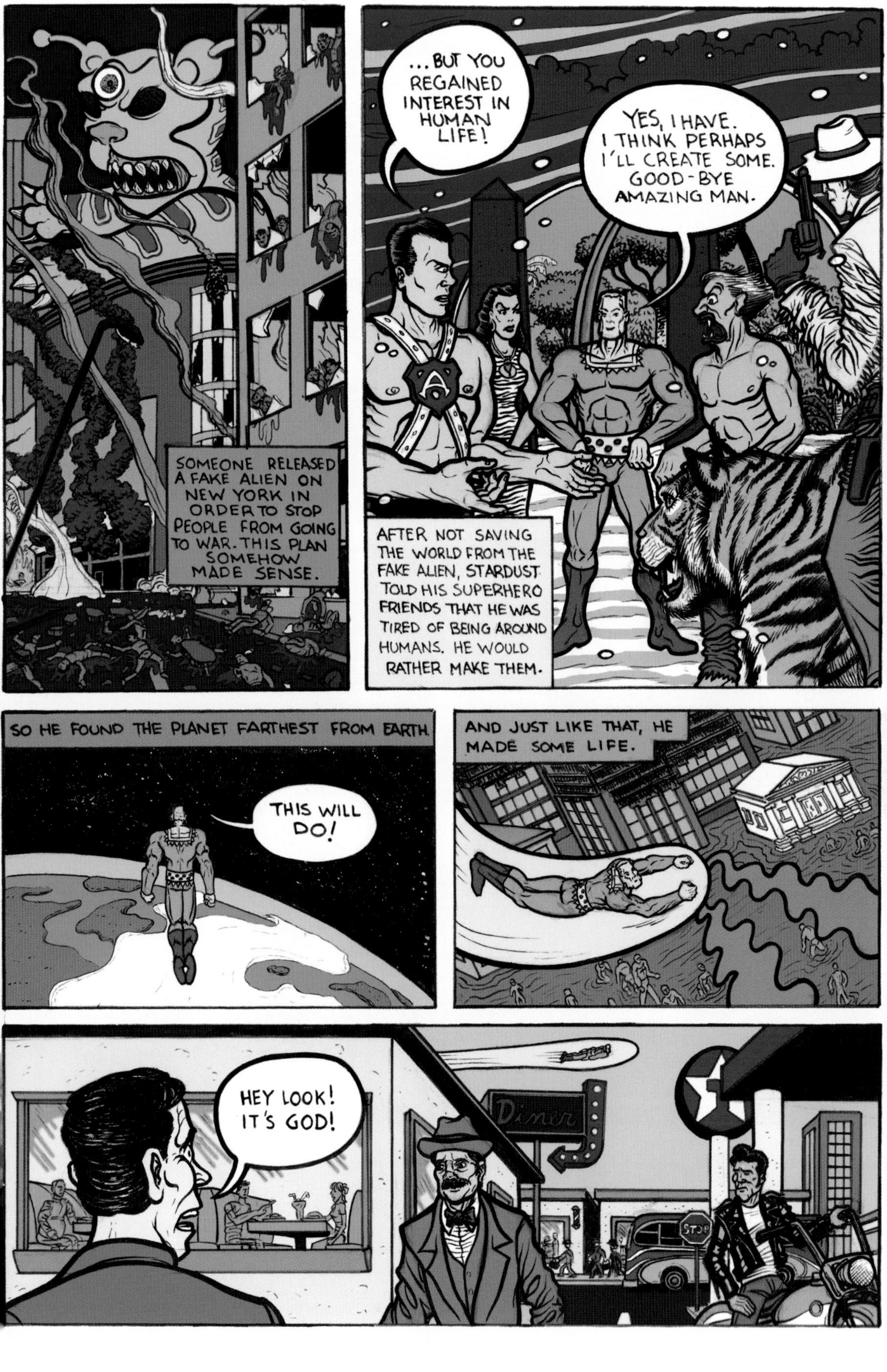
SOMEONE RELEASED A FAKE ALIEN ON NEW YORK IN ORDER TO STOP PEOPLE FROM GOING TO WAR. THIS PLAN SOMEHOW MADE SENSE.
...BUT YOU REGAINED INTEREST IN HUMAN LIFE!
YES, I HAVE. I THINK PERHAPS I'LL CREATE SOME. GOOD-BYE AMAZING MAN.
AFTER NOT SAVING THE WORLD FROM THE FAKE ALIEN, STARDUST TOLD HIS SUPERHERO FRIENDS THAT HE WAS TIRED OF BEING AROUND HUMANS. HE WOULD RATHER MAKE THEM.
SO HE FOUND THE PLANET FARTHEST FROM EARTH.
THIS WILL DO!
AND JUST LIKE THAT, HE MADE SOME LIFE.
HEY LOOK! IT'S GOD!
Diner
STOP

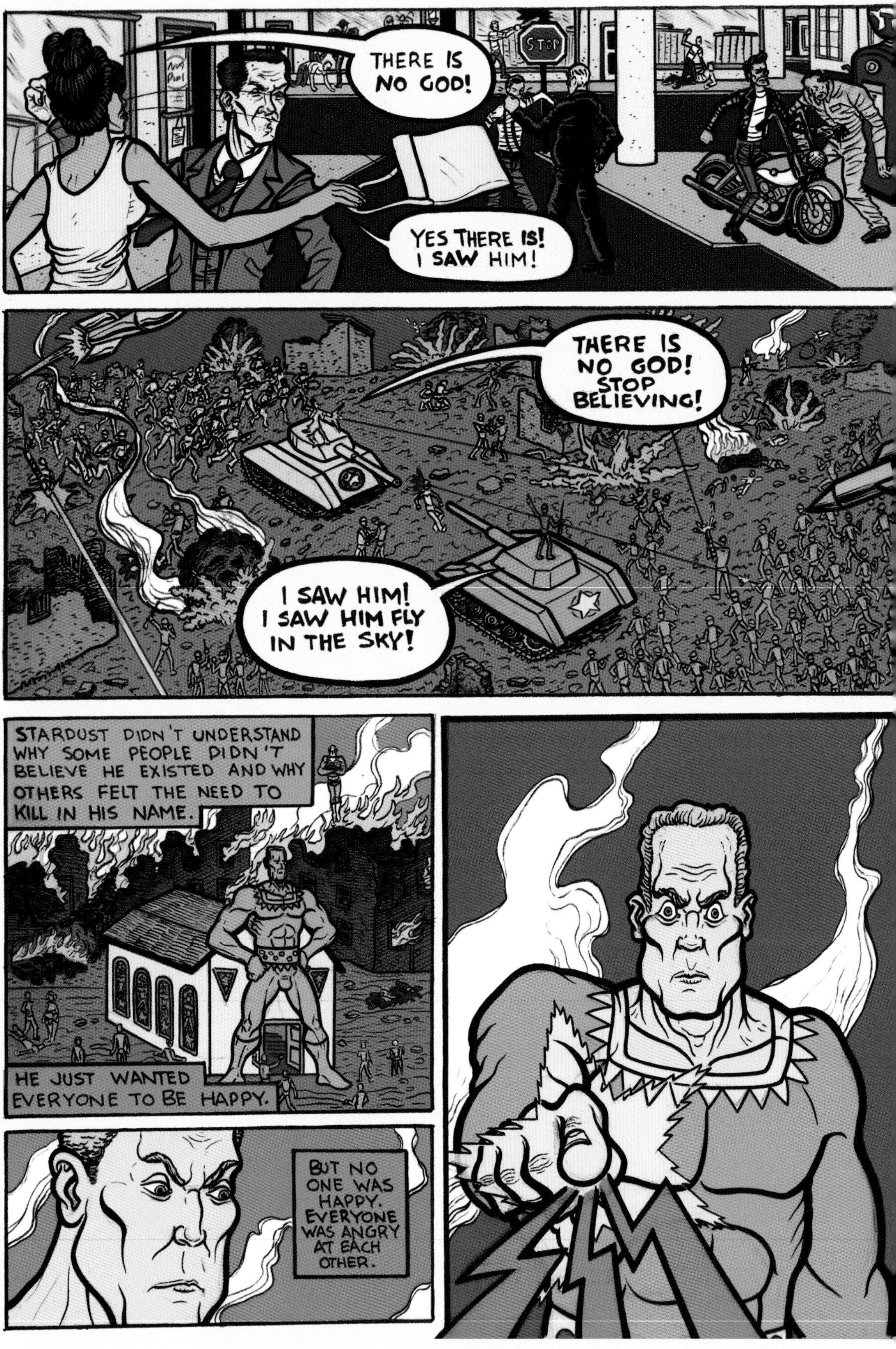

THERE IS NO GOD!
YES THERE IS! I SAW HIM!
THERE IS NO GOD! STOP BELIEVING!
I SAW HIM! I SAW HIM FLY IN THE SKY!
STARDUST DIDN'T UNDERSTAND WHY SOME PEOPLE DIDN'T BELIEVE HE EXISTED AND WHY OTHERS FELT THE NEED TO KILL IN HIS NAME.
HE JUST WANTED EVERYONE TO BE HAPPY.
BUT NO ONE WAS HAPPY. EVERYONE WAS ANGRY AT EACH OTHER.

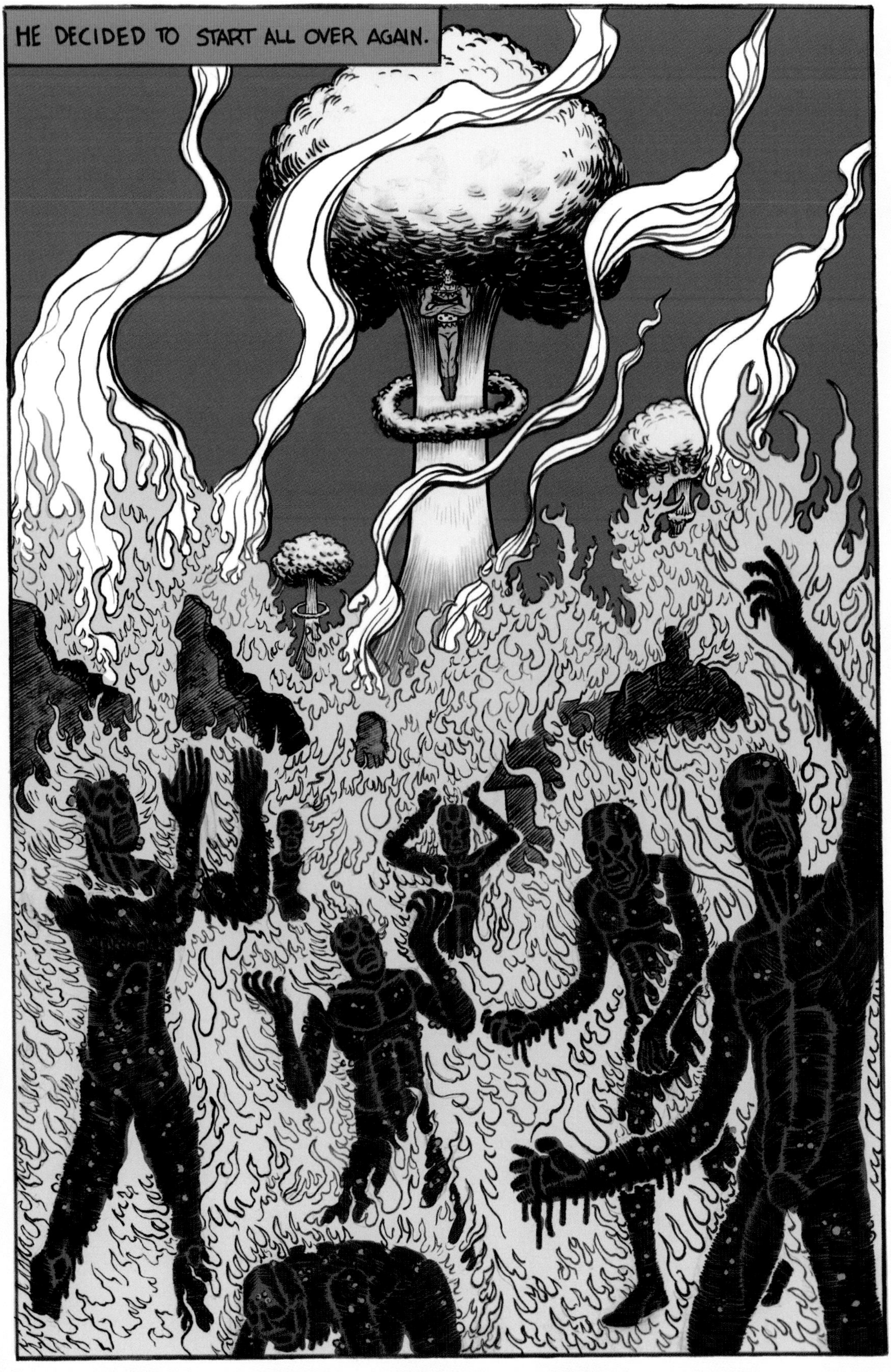
HE DECIDED TO START ALL OVER AGAIN.

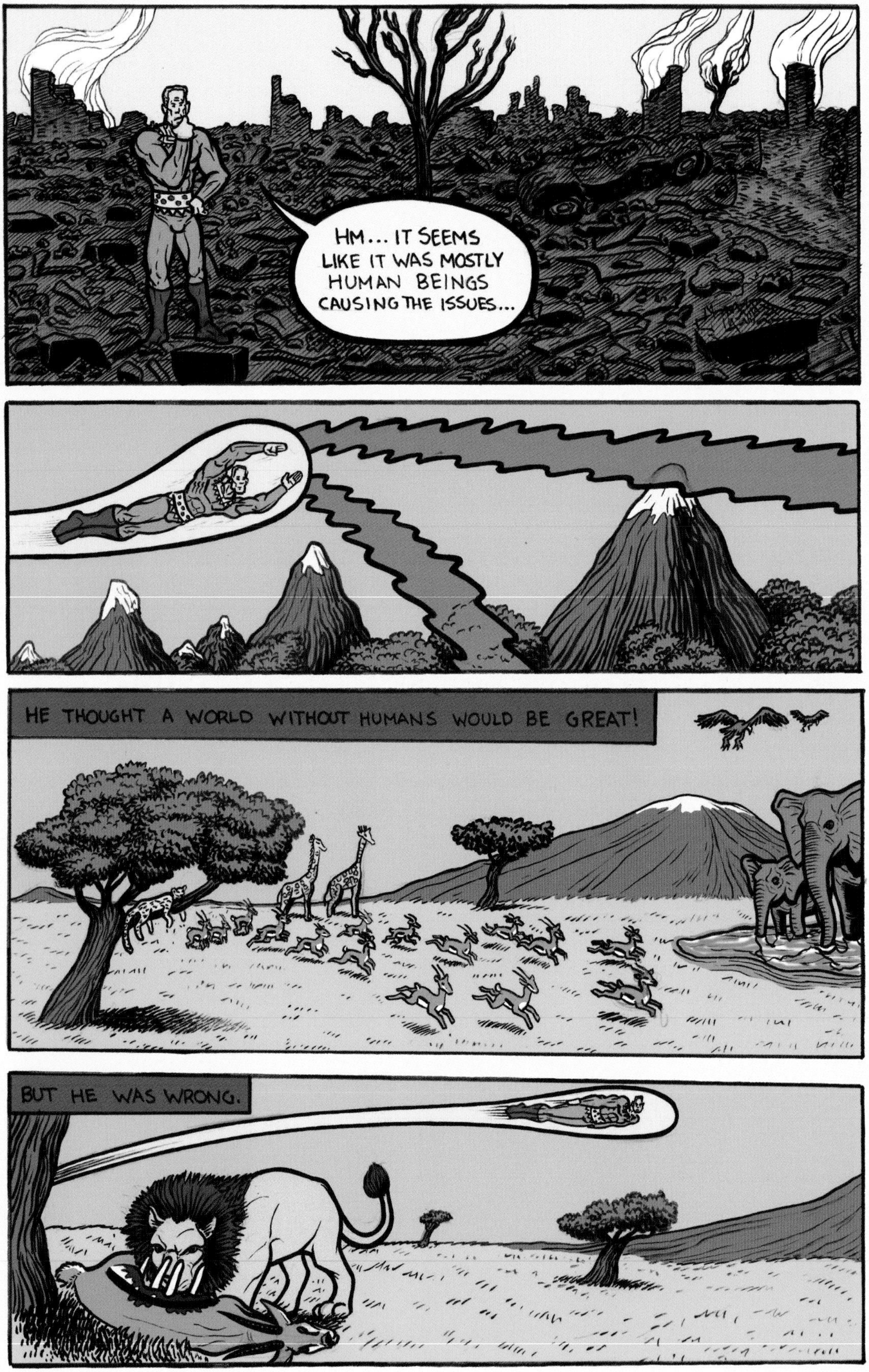
HM... IT SEEMS LIKE IT WAS MOSTLY HUMAN BEINGS CAUSING THE ISSUES...
HE THOUGHT A WORLD WITHOUT HUMANS WOULD BE GREAT!
BUT HE WAS WRONG.

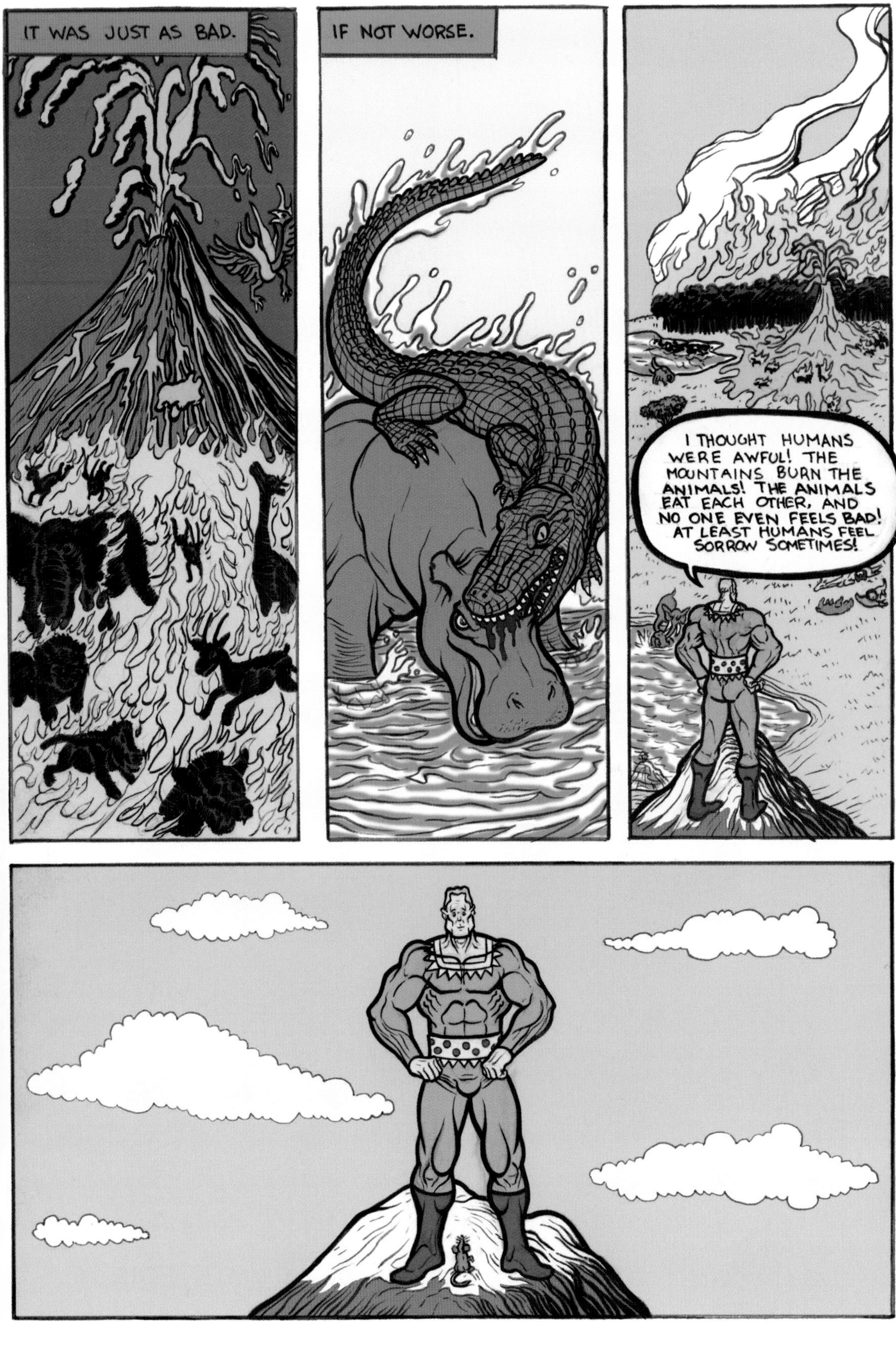
IT WAS JUST AS BAD.
IF NOT WORSE.
I THOUGHT HUMANS WERE AWFUL! THE MOUNTAINS BURN THE ANIMALS! THE ANIMALS EAT EACH OTHER, AND NO ONE EVEN FEELS BAD! AT LEAST HUMANS FEEL SORROW SOMETIMES!

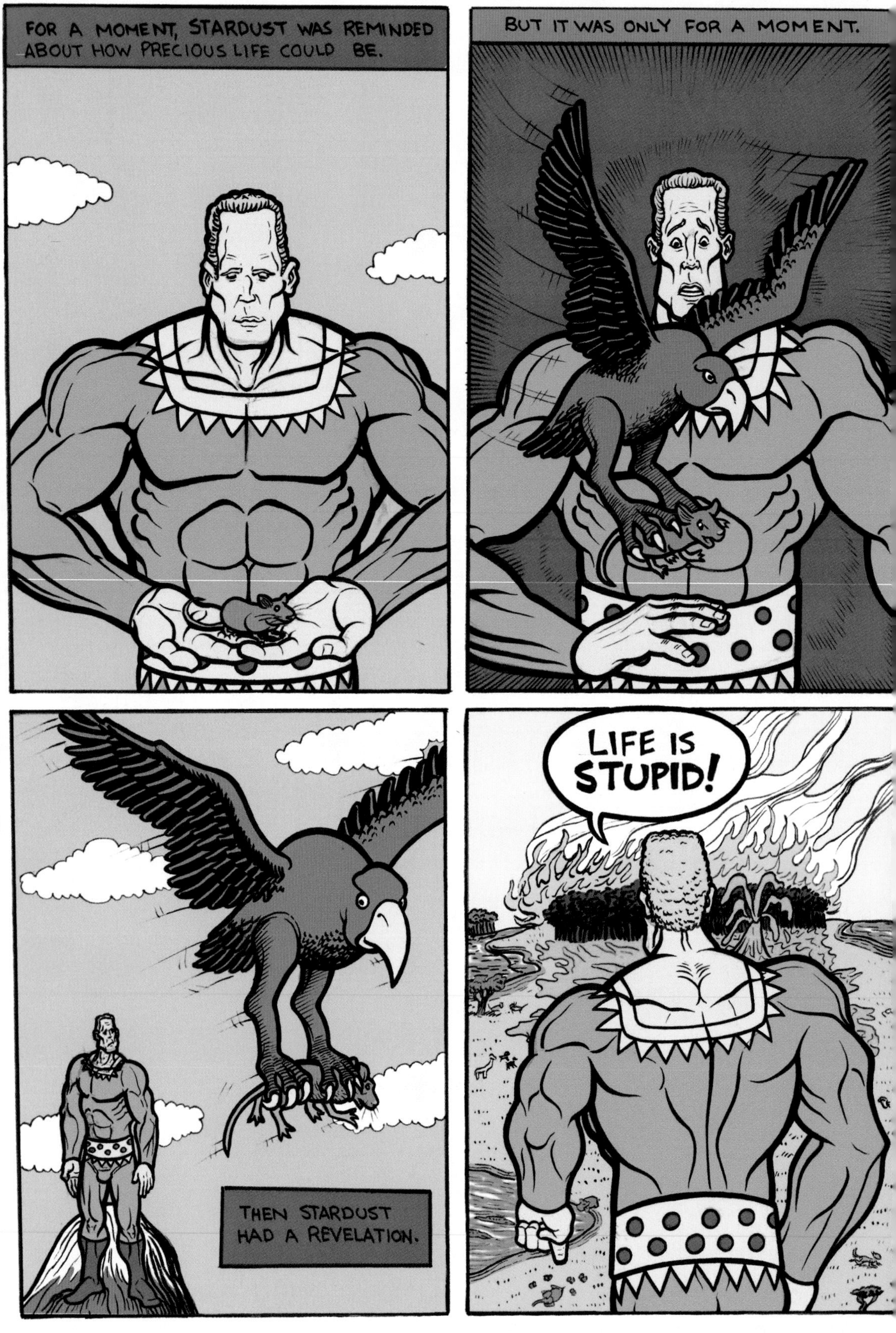
FOR A MOMENT, STARDUST WAS REMINDED ABOUT HOW PRECIOUS LIFE COULD BE.
BUT IT WAS ONLY FOR A MOMENT.
THEN STARDUST HAD A REVELATION.
LIFE IS STUPID!

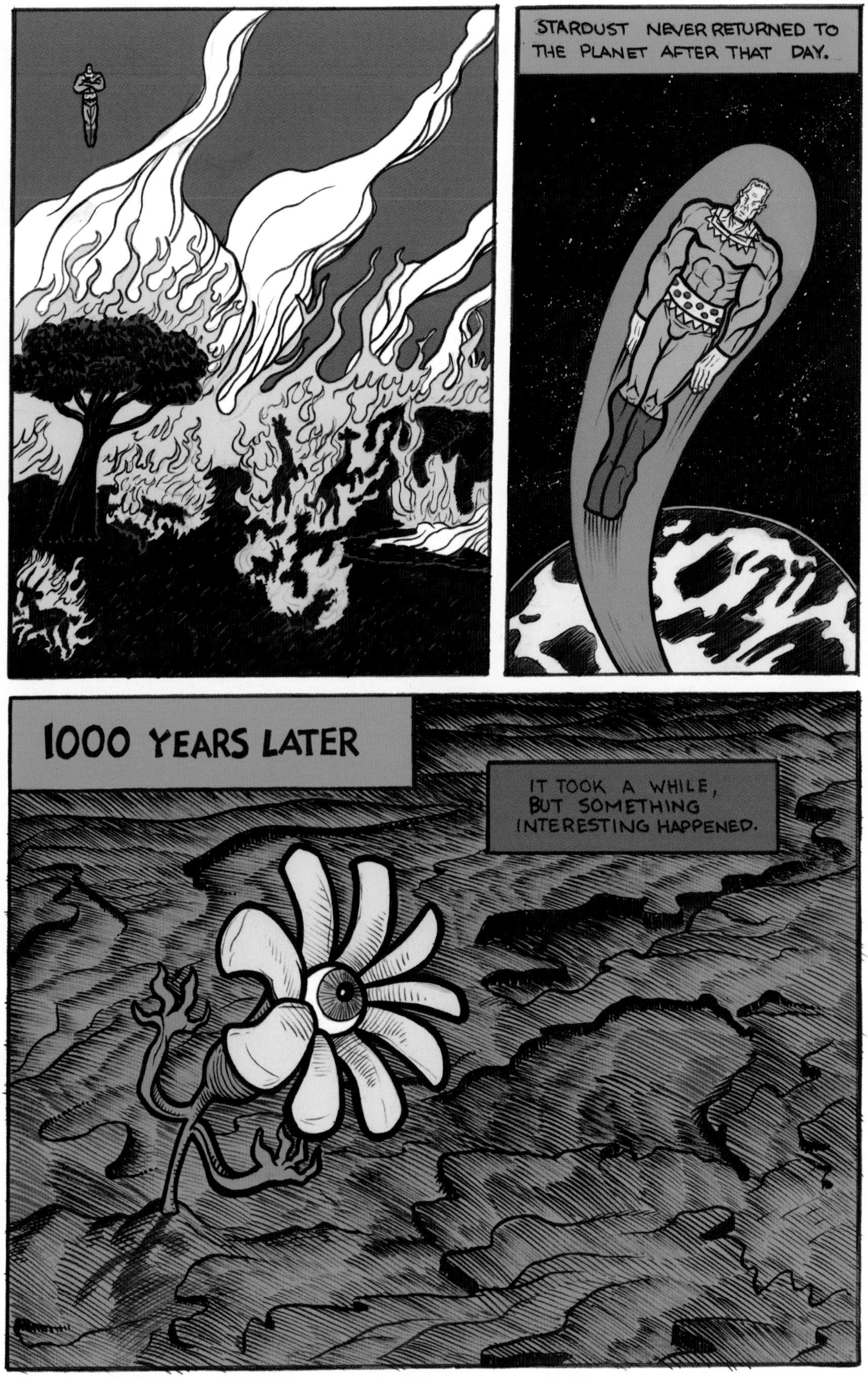
STARDUST NEVER RETURNED TO THE PLANET AFTER THAT DAY.
1000 YEARS LATER
IT TOOK A WHILE, BUT SOMETHING INTERESTING HAPPENED.

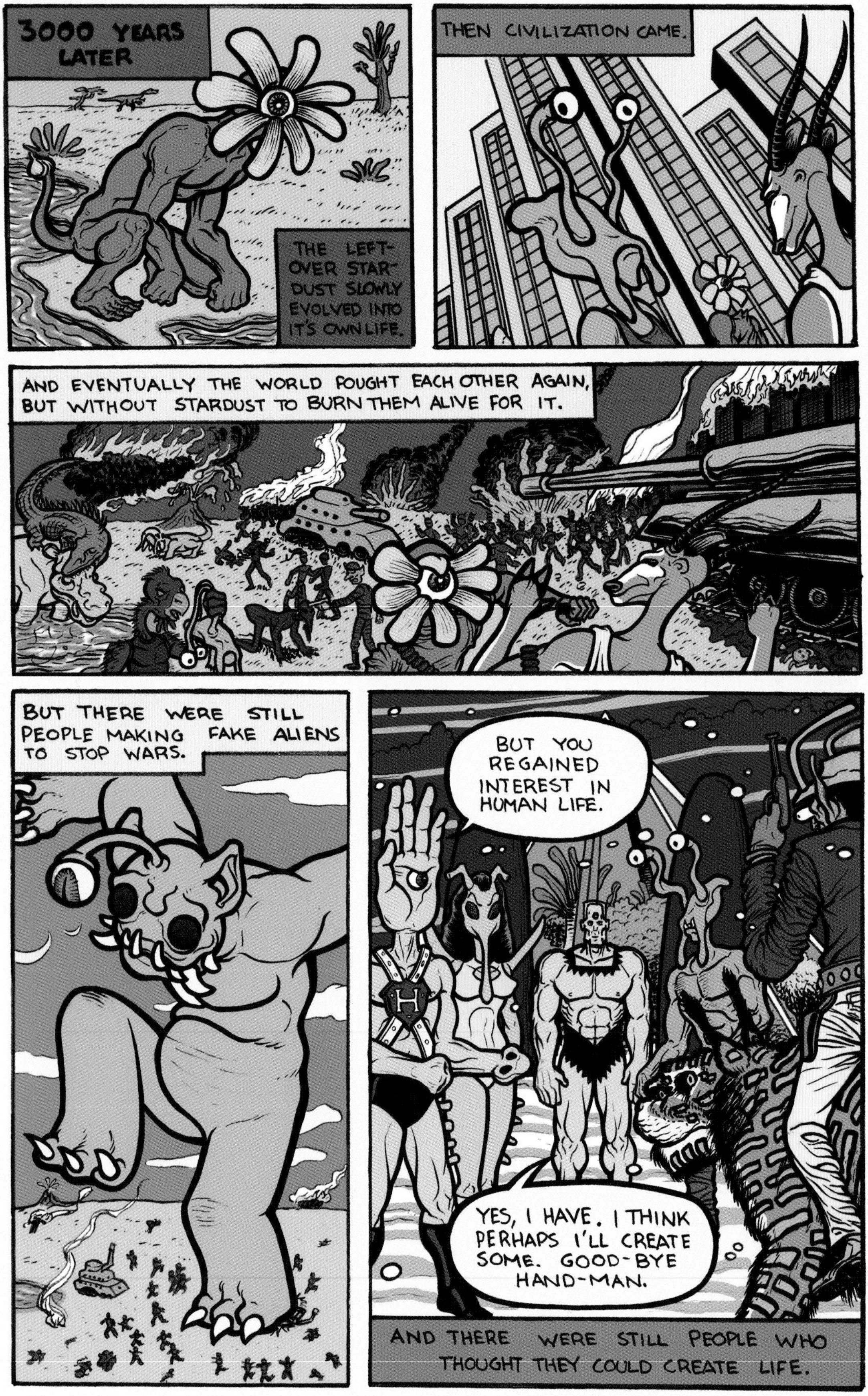
3000 YEARS LATER
THE LEFT-OVER STAR-DUST SLOWLY EVOLVED INTO IT'S OWN LIFE.
THEN CIVILIZATION CAME.
AND EVENTUALLY THE WORLD FOUGHT EACH OTHER AGAIN, BUT WITHOUT STARDUST TO BURN THEM ALIVE FOR IT.
BUT THERE WERE STILL PEOPLE MAKING FAKE ALIENS TO STOP WARS.
BUT YOU REGAINED INTEREST IN HUMAN LIFE.
YES, I HAVE. I THINK PERHAPS I'LL CREATE SOME. GOOD-BYE HAND-MAN.
AND THERE WERE STILL PEOPLE WHO THOUGHT THEY COULD CREATE LIFE.

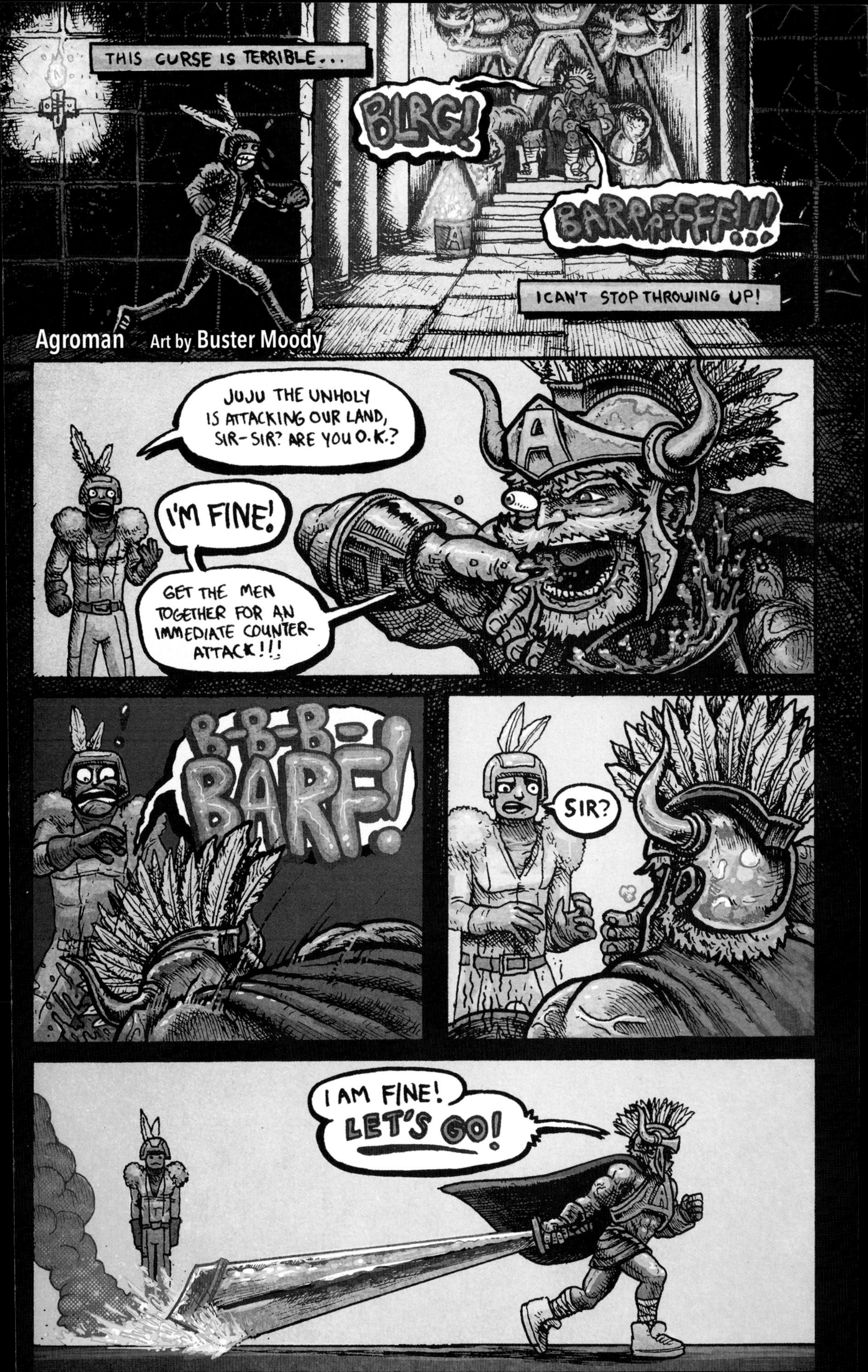
THIS CURSE IS TERRIBLE...
BLRG!
BARRFFFF!!!
I CAN'T STOP THROWING UP!
Agroman Art by Buster Moody
JUJU THE UNHOLY IS ATTACKING OUR LAND, SIR- SIR? ARE YOU O.K.?
I'M FINE!
GET THE MEN TOGETHER FOR AN IMMEDIATE COUNTER-ATTACK!!!
B-B-B-BARF!
SIR?
I AM FINE! LET'S GO!

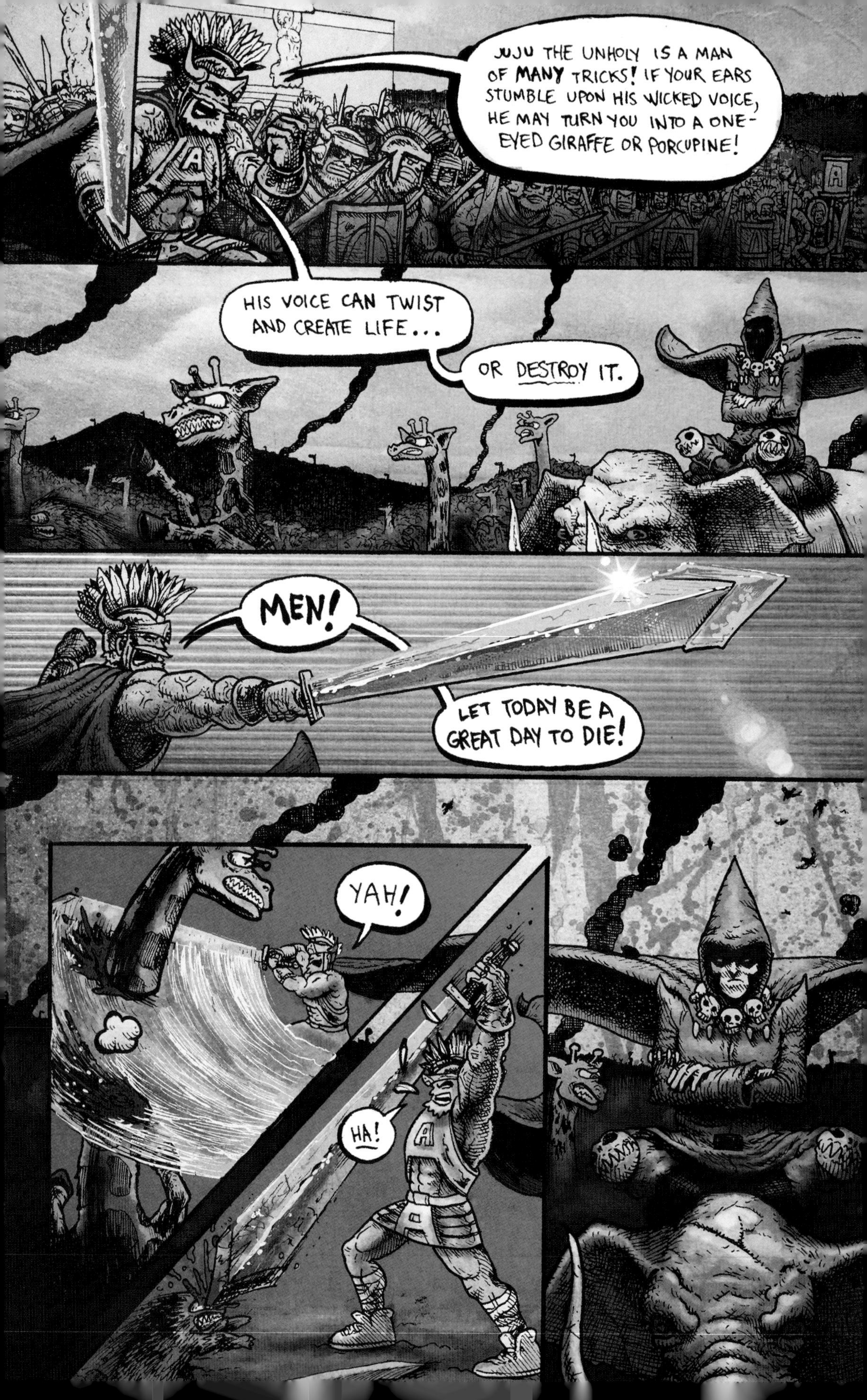
JUJU THE UNHOLY IS A MAN OF MANY TRICKS! IF YOUR EARS STUMBLE UPON HIS WICKED VOICE, HE MAY TURN YOU INTO A ONE-EYED GIRAFFE OR PORCUPINE!
HIS VOICE CAN TWIST AND CREATE LIFE...
OR DESTROY IT.
MEN!
LET TODAY BE A GREAT DAY TO DIE!
YAH!
HA!

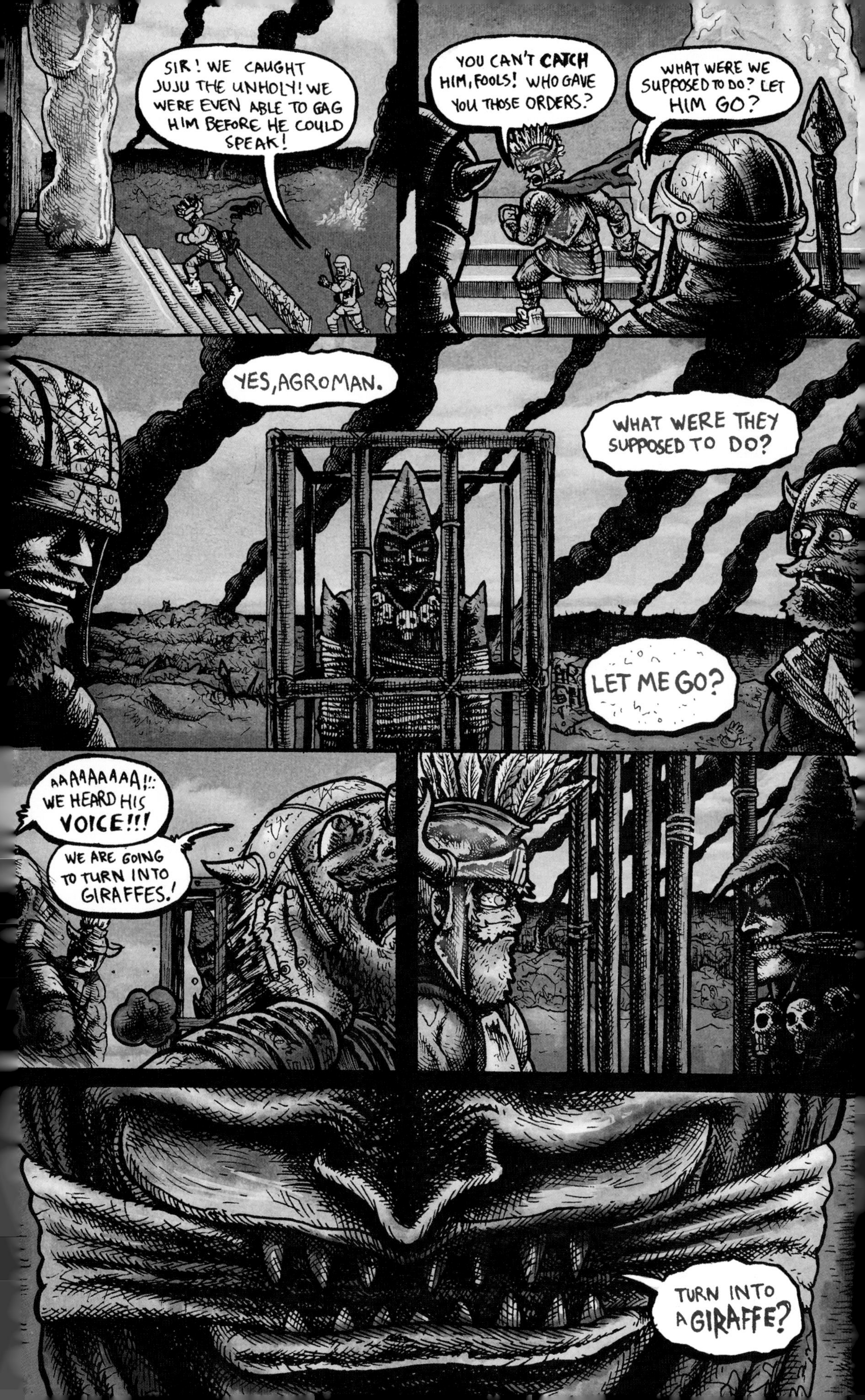
SIR! WE CAUGHT JUJU THE UNHOLY! WE WERE EVEN ABLE TO GAG HIM BEFORE HE COULD SPEAK!
YOU CAN'T **CATCH** HIM, FOOLS! WHO GAVE YOU THOSE ORDERS?
WHAT WERE WE SUPPOSED TO DO? LET HIM GO?
YES, AGROMAN.
WHAT WERE THEY SUPPOSED TO DO?
LET ME GO?
AAAAAAAAA!!! WE HEARD HIS **VOICE!!!**
WE ARE GOING TO TURN INTO GIRAFFES!
TURN INTO A GIRAFFE?

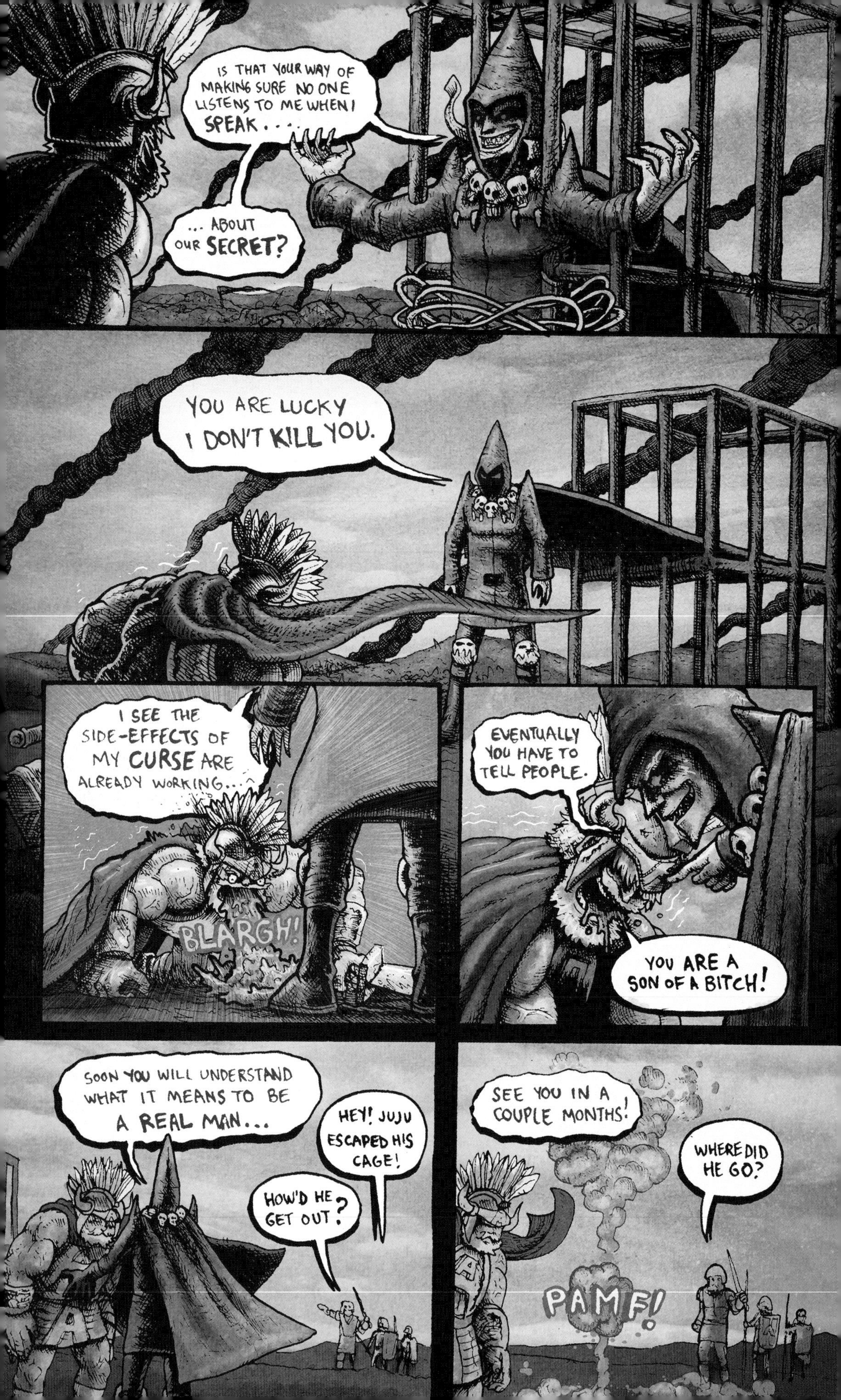
IS THAT YOUR WAY OF MAKING SURE NO ONE LISTENS TO ME WHEN I SPEAK . . . .
... ABOUT OUR SECRET?
YOU ARE LUCKY I DON'T KILL YOU.
I SEE THE SIDE-EFFECTS OF MY CURSE ARE ALREADY WORKING...
BLARGH!
EVENTUALLY YOU HAVE TO TELL PEOPLE.
YOU ARE A SON OF A BITCH!
SOON YOU WILL UNDERSTAND WHAT IT MEANS TO BE A REAL MAN...
HEY! JUJU ESCAPED HIS CAGE!
HOW'D HE GET OUT?
SEE YOU IN A COUPLE MONTHS!
WHERE DID HE GO?
PAMF!

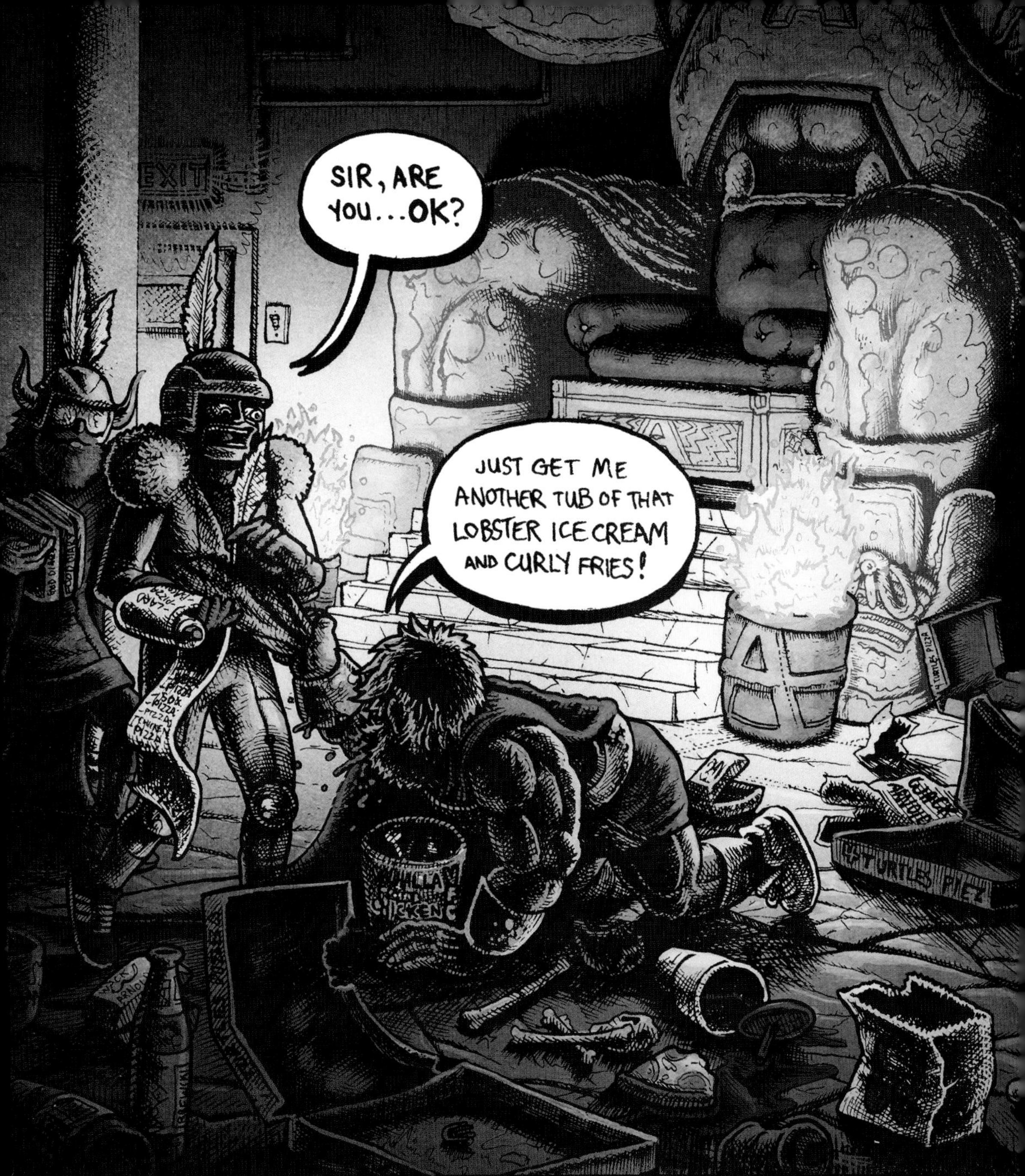
SIR, ARE YOU...OK?
JUST GET ME ANOTHER TUB OF THAT LOBSTER ICE CREAM AND CURLY FRIES!
EXIT

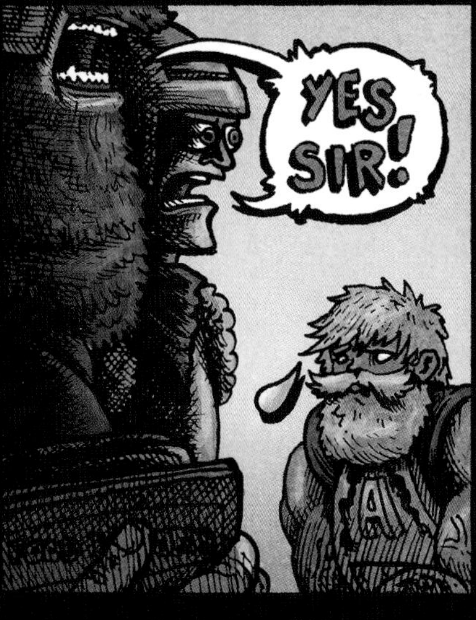
YES SIR!

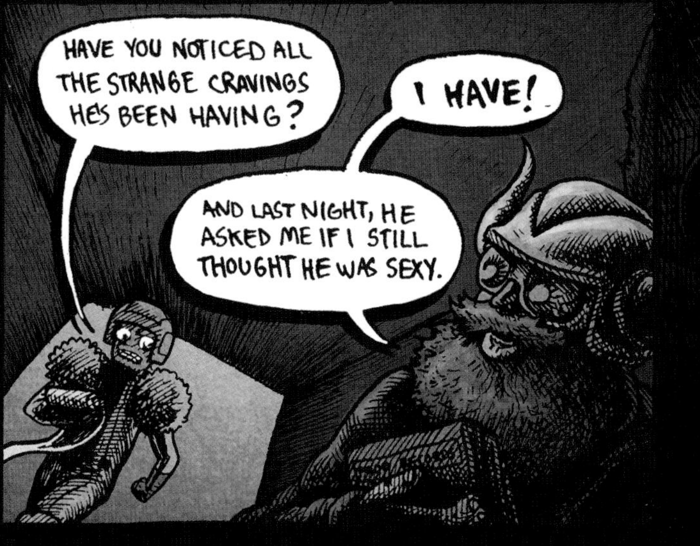
HAVE YOU NOTICED ALL THE STRANGE CRAVINGS HE'S BEEN HAVING?
I HAVE!
AND LAST NIGHT, HE ASKED ME IF I STILL THOUGHT HE WAS SEXY.

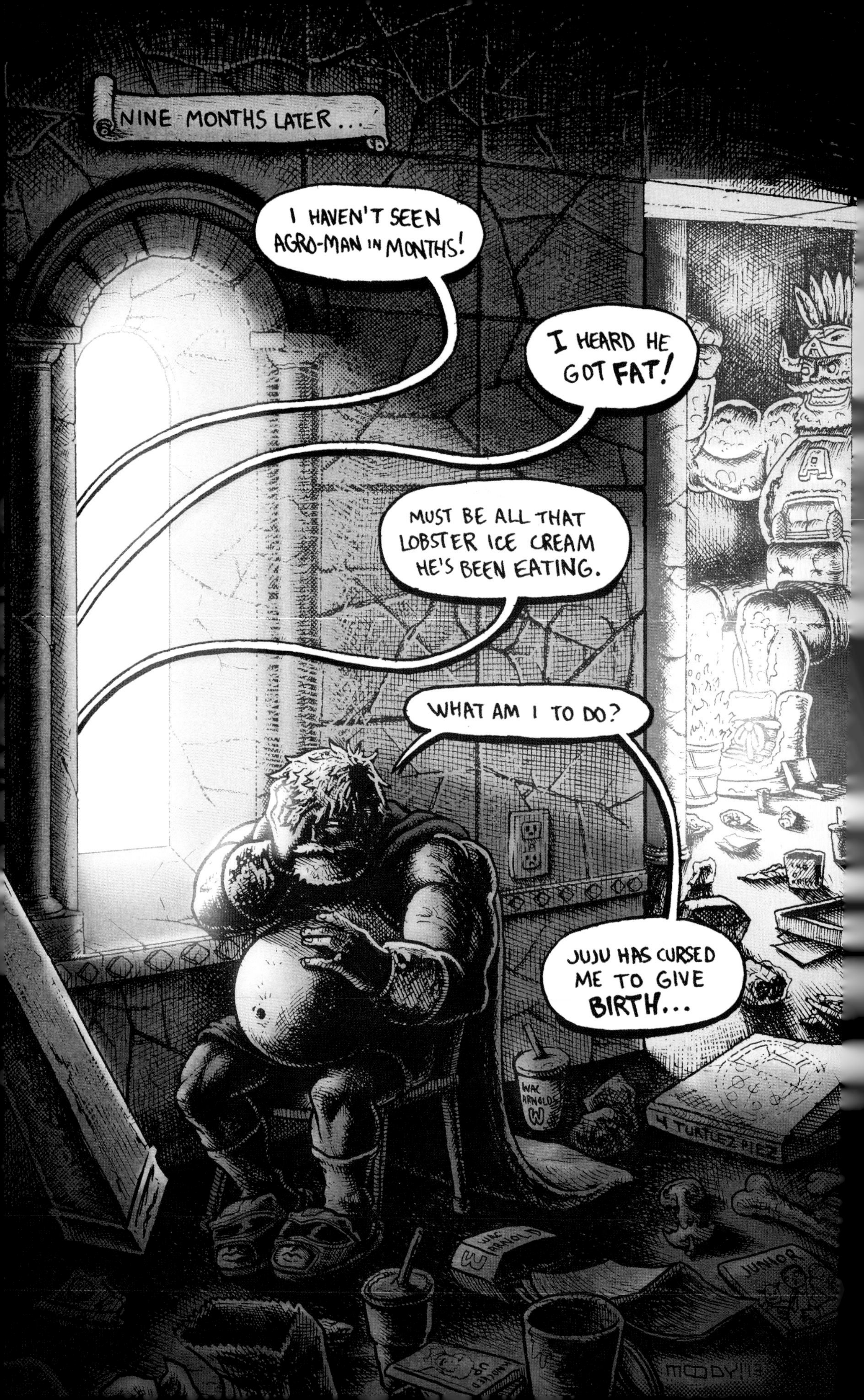
NINE MONTHS LATER...
I HAVEN'T SEEN AGRO-MAN IN MONTHS!
I HEARD HE GOT FAT!
MUST BE ALL THAT LOBSTER ICE CREAM HE'S BEEN EATING.
WHAT AM I TO DO?
JUJU HAS CURSED ME TO GIVE BIRTH...
WAC ARNOLDS
4 TURTLEZ PIEZ

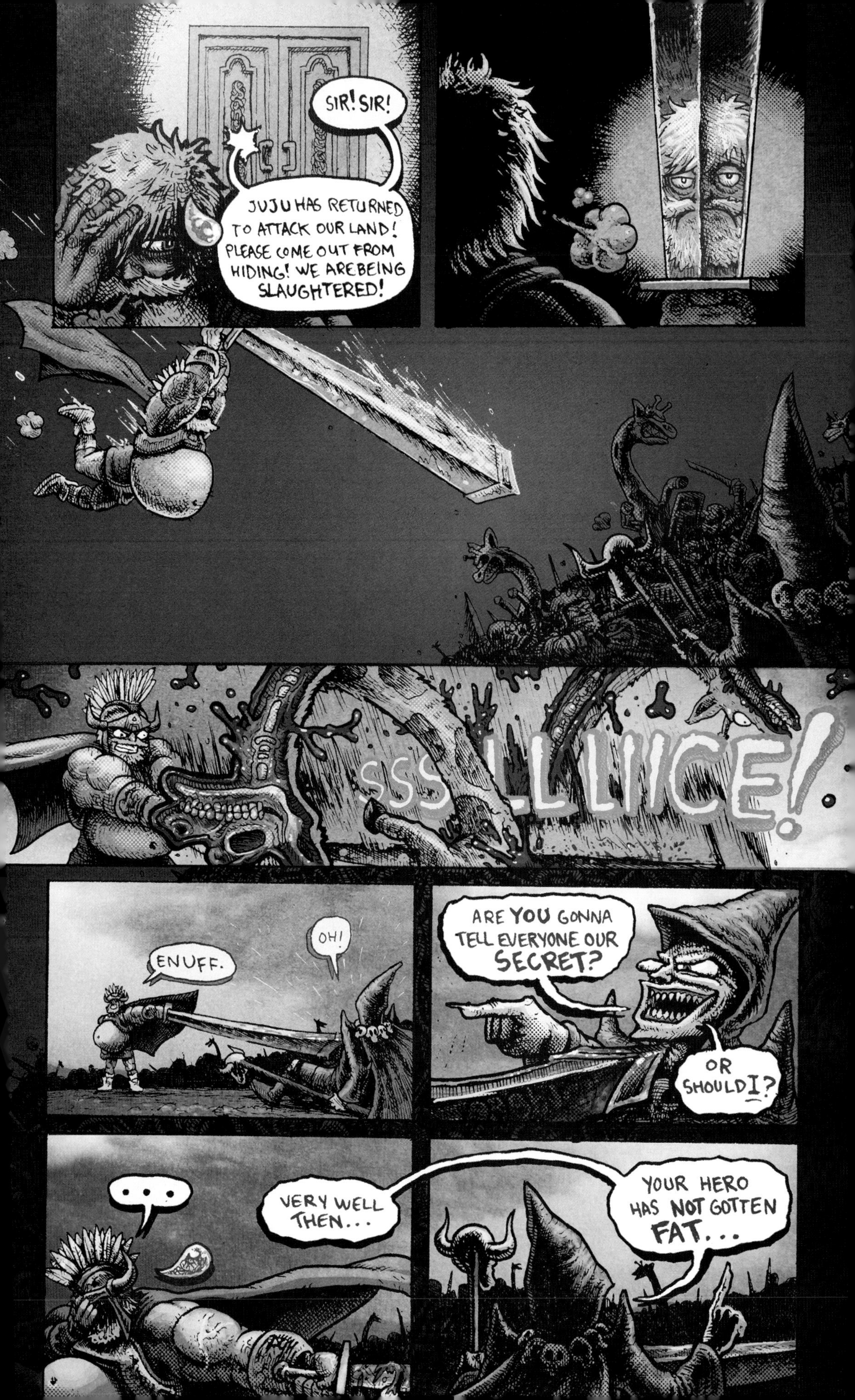
SIR! SIR!
JUJU HAS RETURNED TO ATTACK OUR LAND! PLEASE COME OUT FROM HIDING! WE ARE BEING SLAUGHTERED!
SSSLLLIICE!
ENUFF.
OH!
ARE YOU GONNA TELL EVERYONE OUR SECRET?
OR SHOULD I?
. . .
VERY WELL THEN...
YOUR HERO HAS NOT GOTTEN FAT...

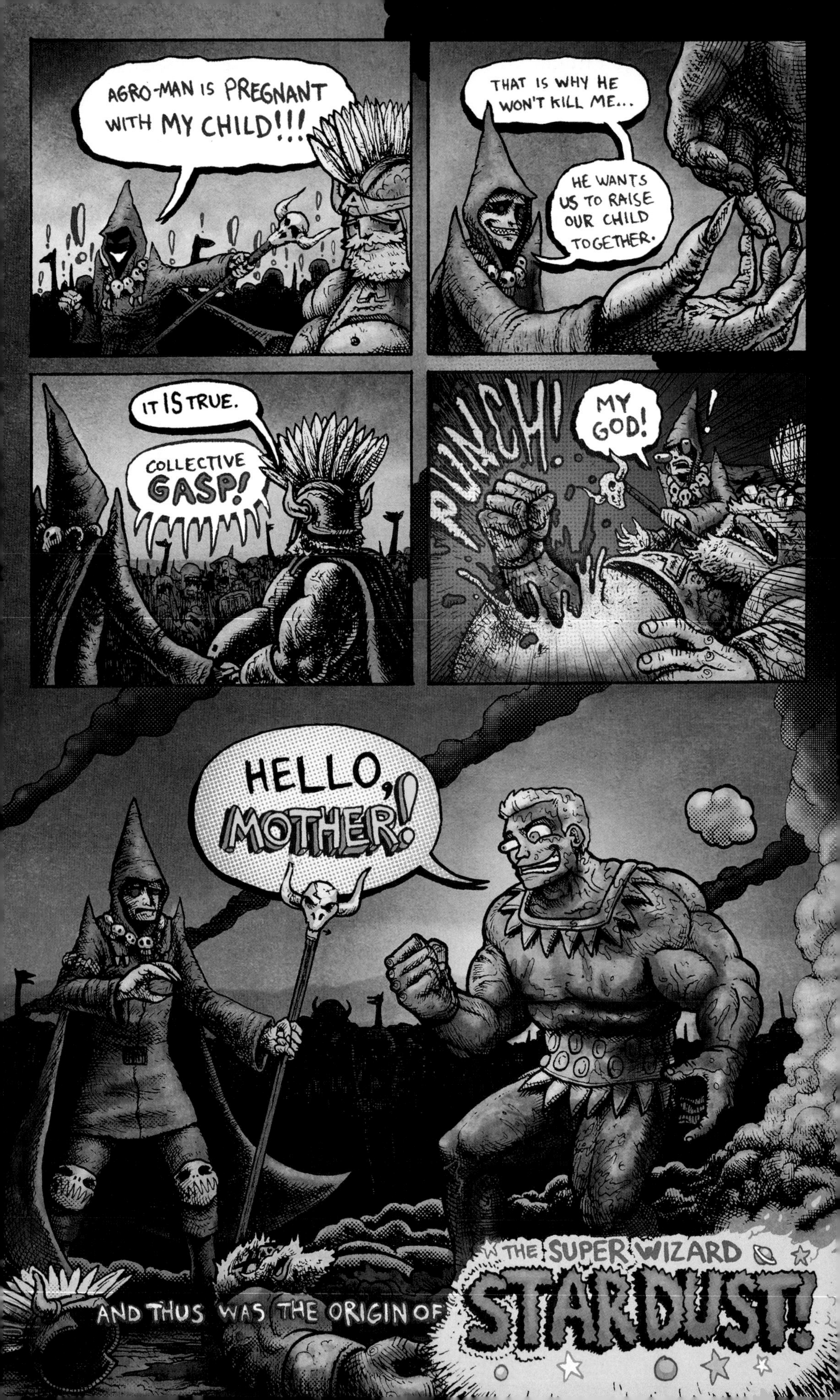
AGRO-MAN IS PREGNANT WITH MY CHILD!!!
THAT IS WHY HE WON'T KILL ME...
HE WANTS US TO RAISE OUR CHILD TOGETHER.
IT IS TRUE.
COLLECTIVE GASP!
PUNCH!
MY GOD!
HELLO, MOTHER!
AND THUS WAS THE ORIGIN OF
THE SUPER WIZARD
STARDUST!

Ben Franklin, Dragon Hunter Art by **Job Yamen** Colors by **Austin Breed**

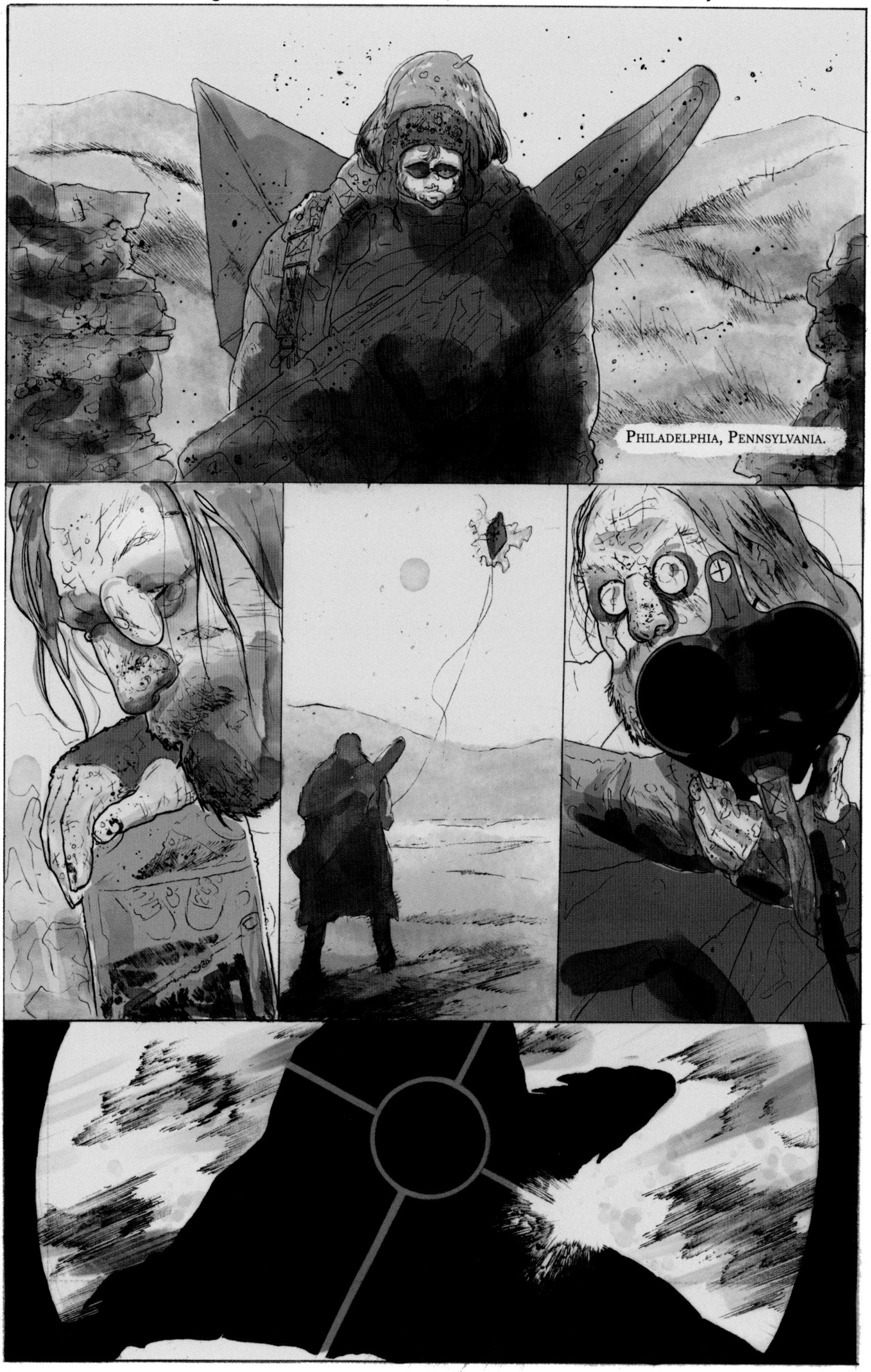
PHILADELPHIA, PENNSYLVANIA.

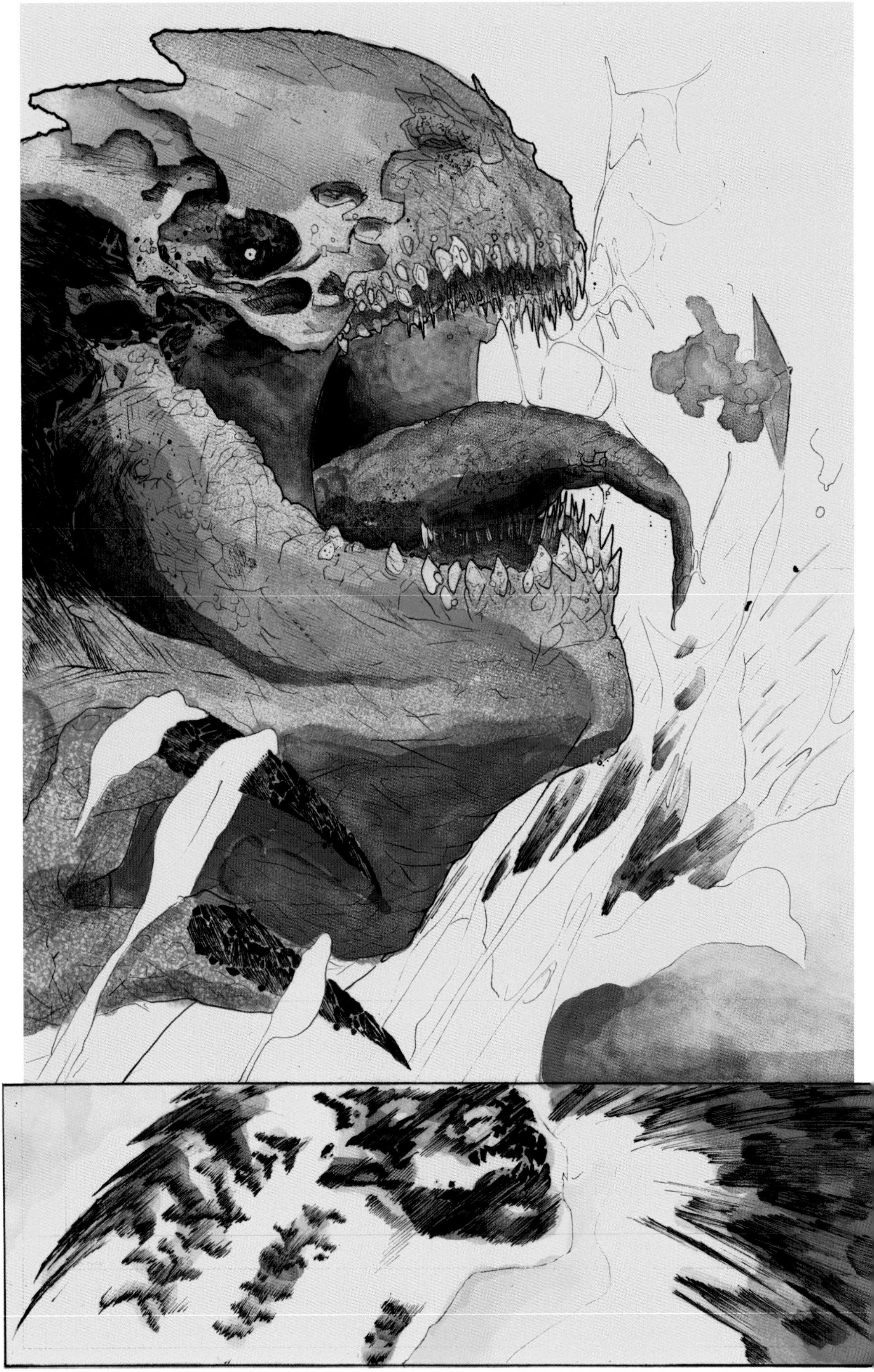

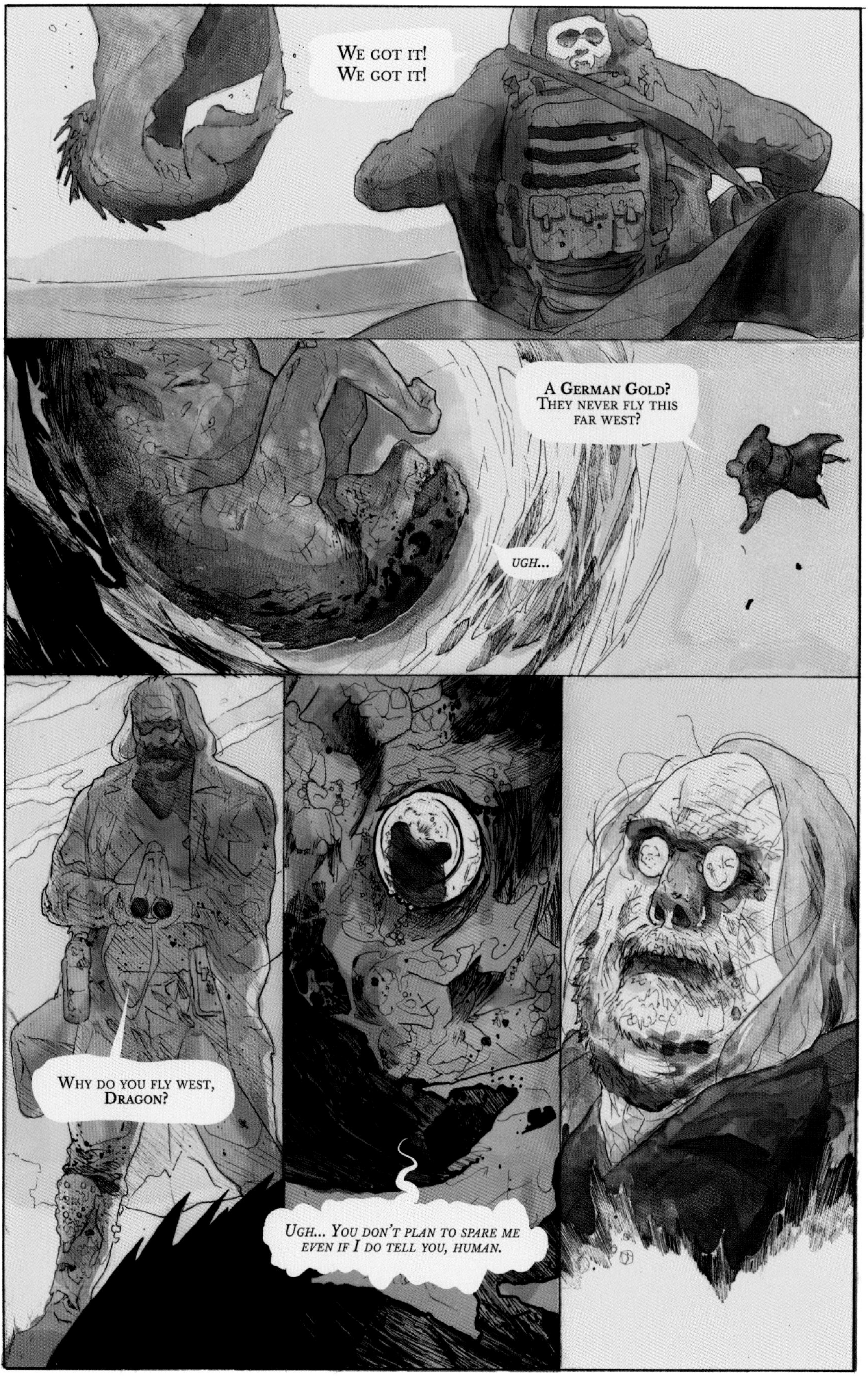
We got it!
We got it!
A German Gold?
They never fly this far west?
Ugh...
Why do you fly west, Dragon?
Ugh... You don't plan to spare me even if I do tell you, human.

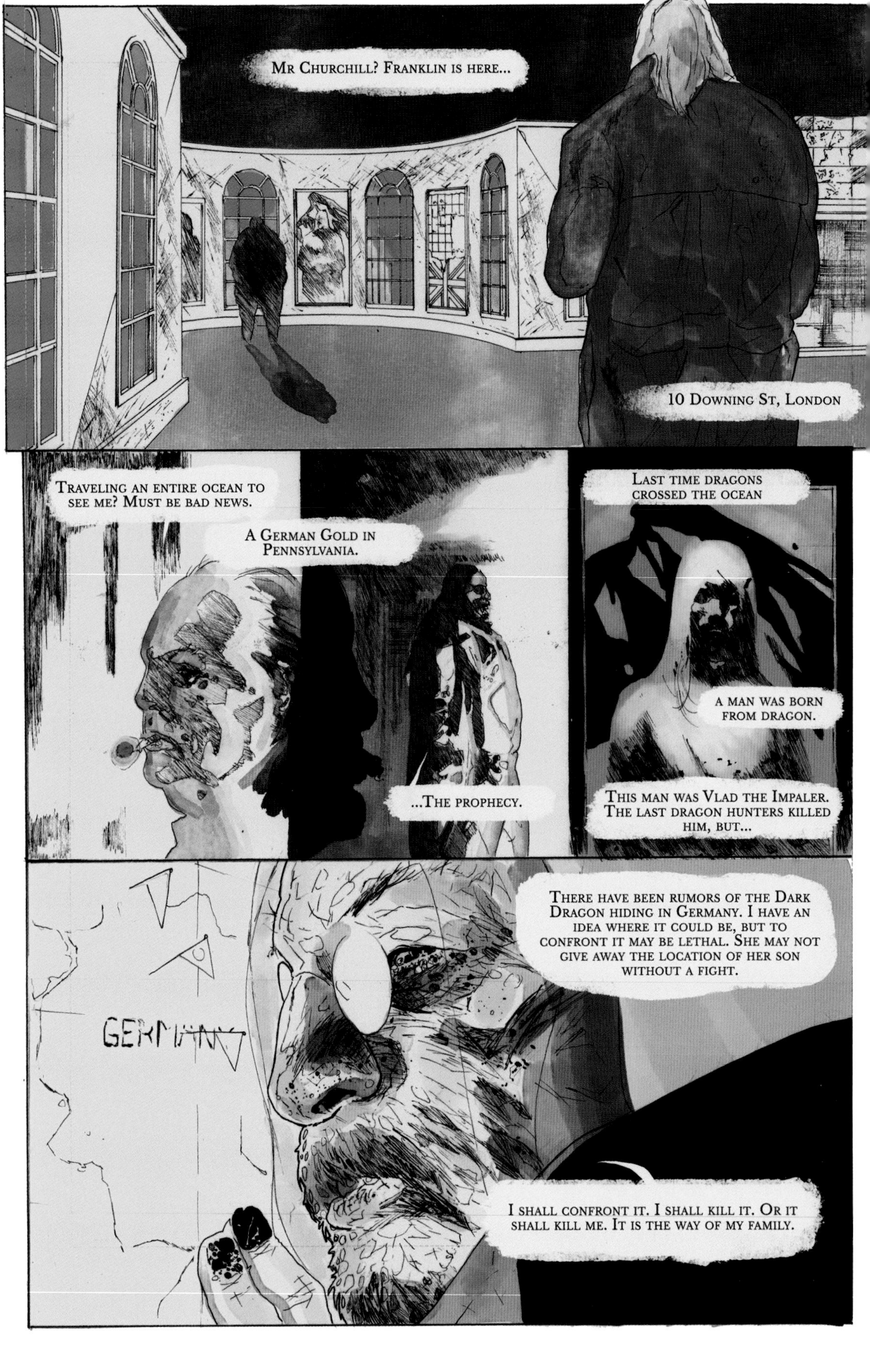
Mr Churchill? Franklin is here...
10 Downing St, London
Traveling an entire ocean to see me? Must be bad news.
A German Gold in Pennsylvania.
...The prophecy.
Last time dragons crossed the ocean
A man was born from dragon.
This man was Vlad the Impaler. The last dragon hunters killed him, but...
GERMANY
There have been rumors of the Dark Dragon hiding in Germany. I have an idea where it could be, but to confront it may be lethal. She may not give away the location of her son without a fight.
I shall confront it. I shall kill it. Or it shall kill me. It is the way of my family.

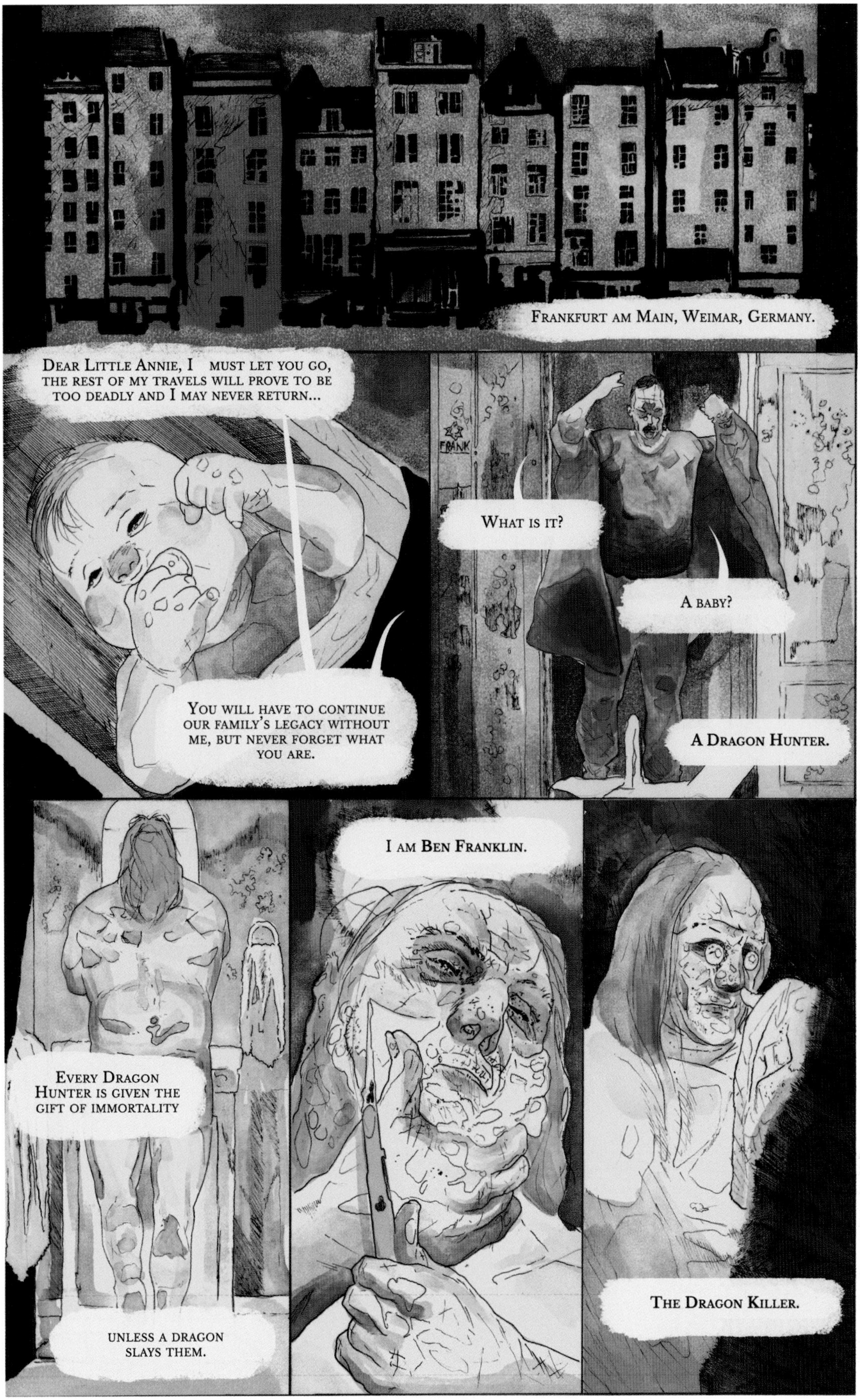
Frankfurt am Main, Weimar, Germany.
Dear Little Annie, I must let you go, the rest of my travels will prove to be too deadly and I may never return...
You will have to continue our family's legacy without me, but never forget what you are.
FRANK
What is it?
A baby?
A Dragon Hunter.
Every Dragon Hunter is given the gift of immortality
unless a dragon slays them.
I am Ben Franklin.
The Dragon Killer.

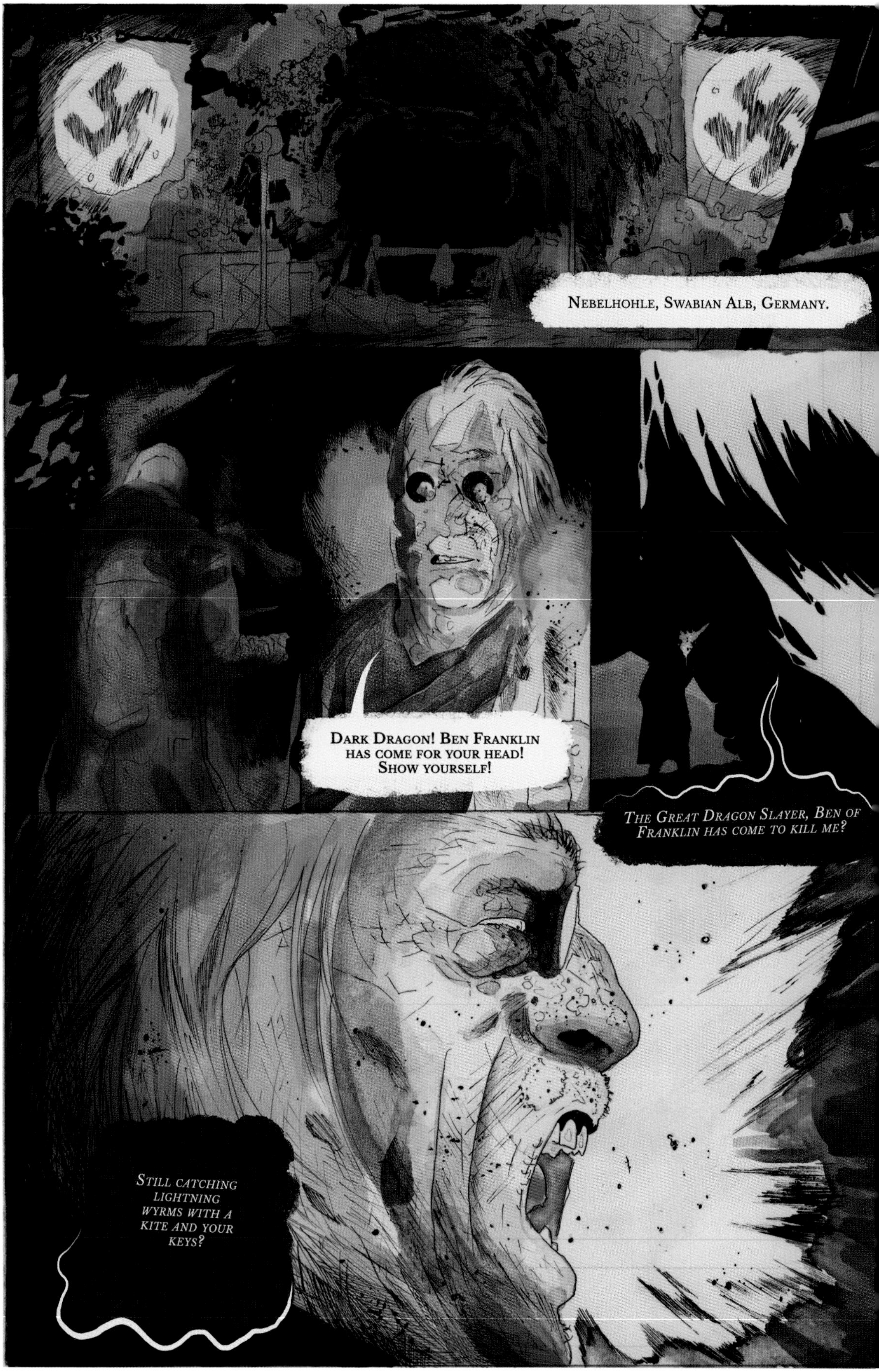
NEBELHOHLE, SWABIAN ALB, GERMANY.
DARK DRAGON! BEN FRANKLIN HAS COME FOR YOUR HEAD! SHOW YOURSELF!
THE GREAT DRAGON SLAYER, BEN OF FRANKLIN HAS COME TO KILL ME?
STILL CATCHING LIGHTNING WYRMS WITH A KITE AND YOUR KEYS?

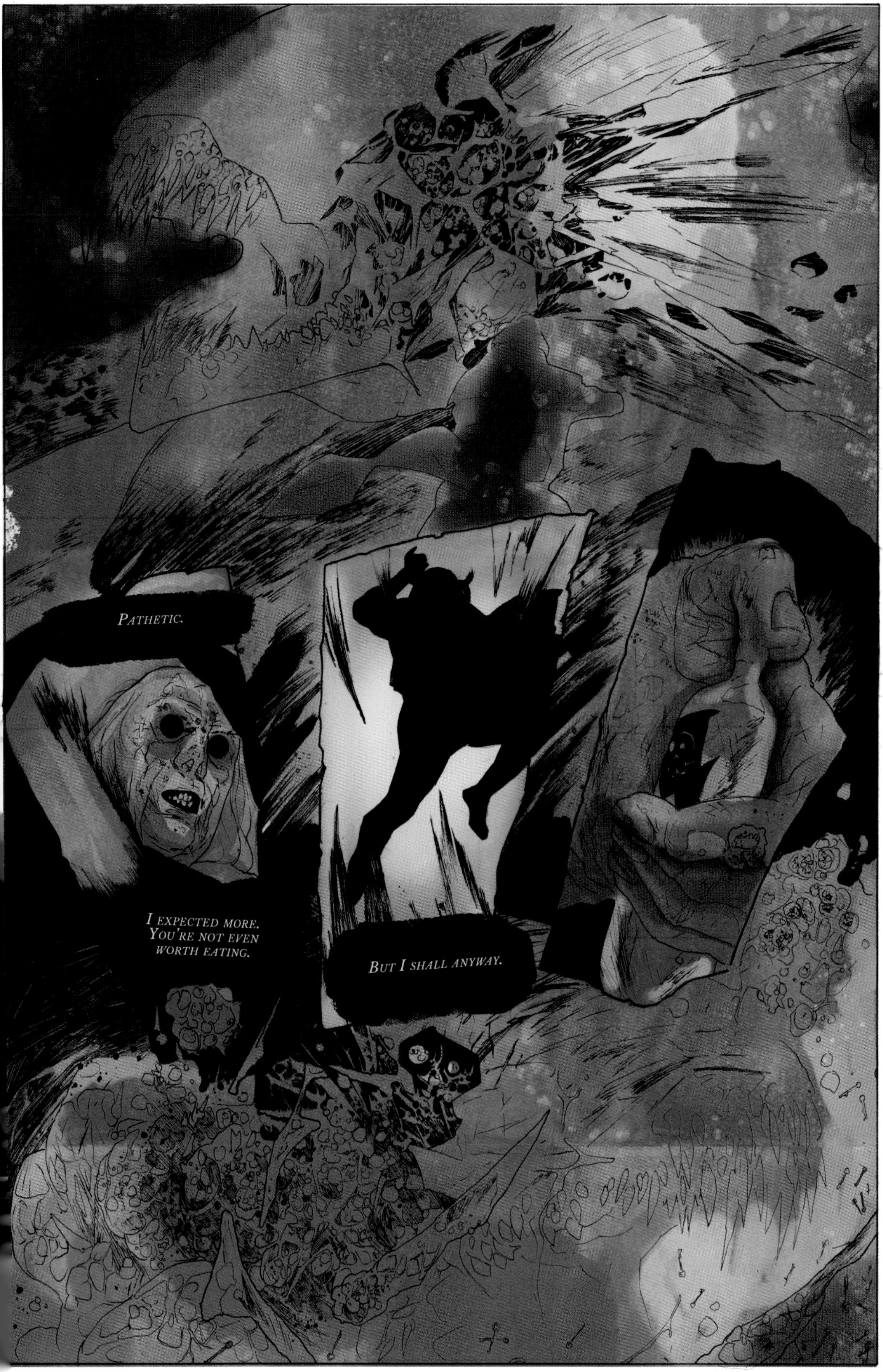
PATHETIC.
I EXPECTED MORE. YOU'RE NOT EVEN WORTH EATING.
BUT I SHALL ANYWAY.

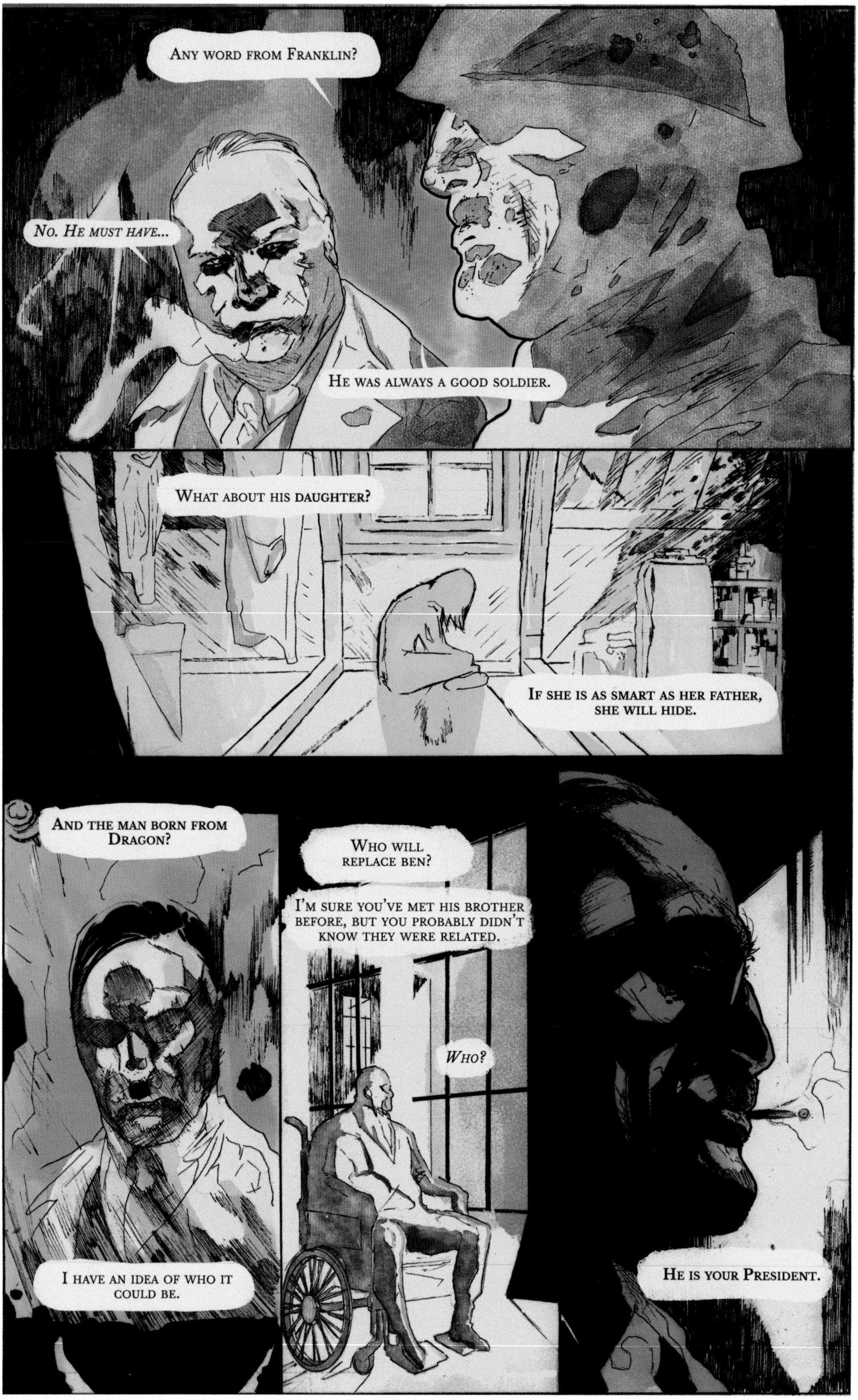

Any word from Franklin?
No. He must have...
He was always a good soldier.
What about his daughter?
If she is as smart as her father, she will hide.
And the man born from Dragon?
I have an idea of who it could be.
Who will replace Ben?
I'm sure you've met his brother before, but you probably didn't know they were related.
Who?
He is your President.

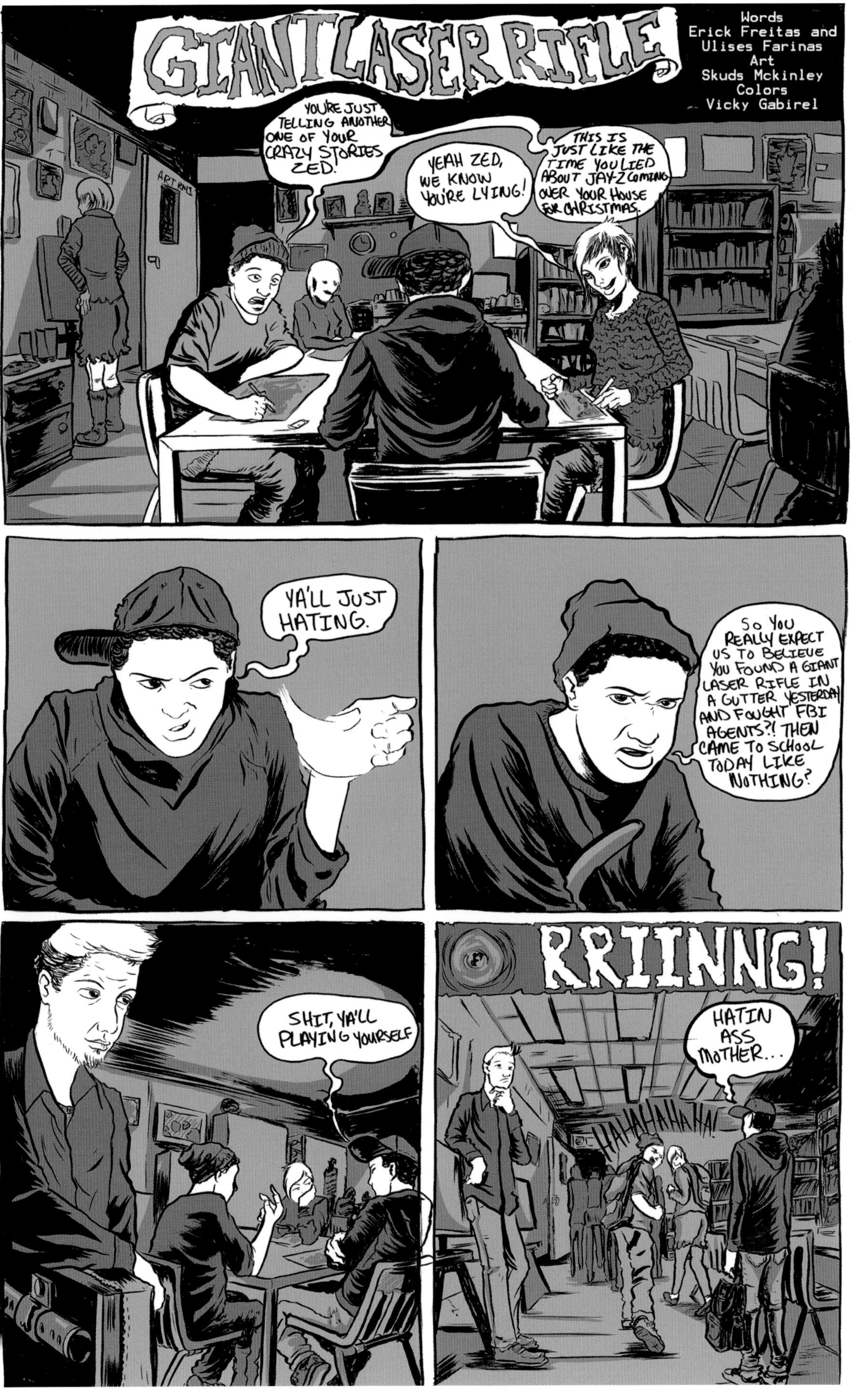

GIANT LASER RIFLE
Words
Erick Freitas and
Ulises Farinas
Art
Skuds Mckinley
Colors
Vicky Gabirel
YOU'RE JUST TELLING ANOTHER ONE OF YOUR CRAZY STORIES ZED.
YEAH ZED, WE KNOW YOU'RE LYING!
THIS IS JUST LIKE THE TIME YOU LIED ABOUT JAY-Z COMING OVER YOUR HOUSE FOR CHRISTMAS.
ART RM1
YA'LL JUST HATING.
SO YOU REALLY EXPECT US TO BELIEVE YOU FOUND A GIANT LASER RIFLE IN A GUTTER YESTERDAY AND FOUGHT FBI AGENTS?! THEN CAME TO SCHOOL TODAY LIKE NOTHING?
SHIT, YA'LL PLAYING YOURSELF
RRIINNG!
HATIN ASS MOTHER...
HAHAHAHAHA!

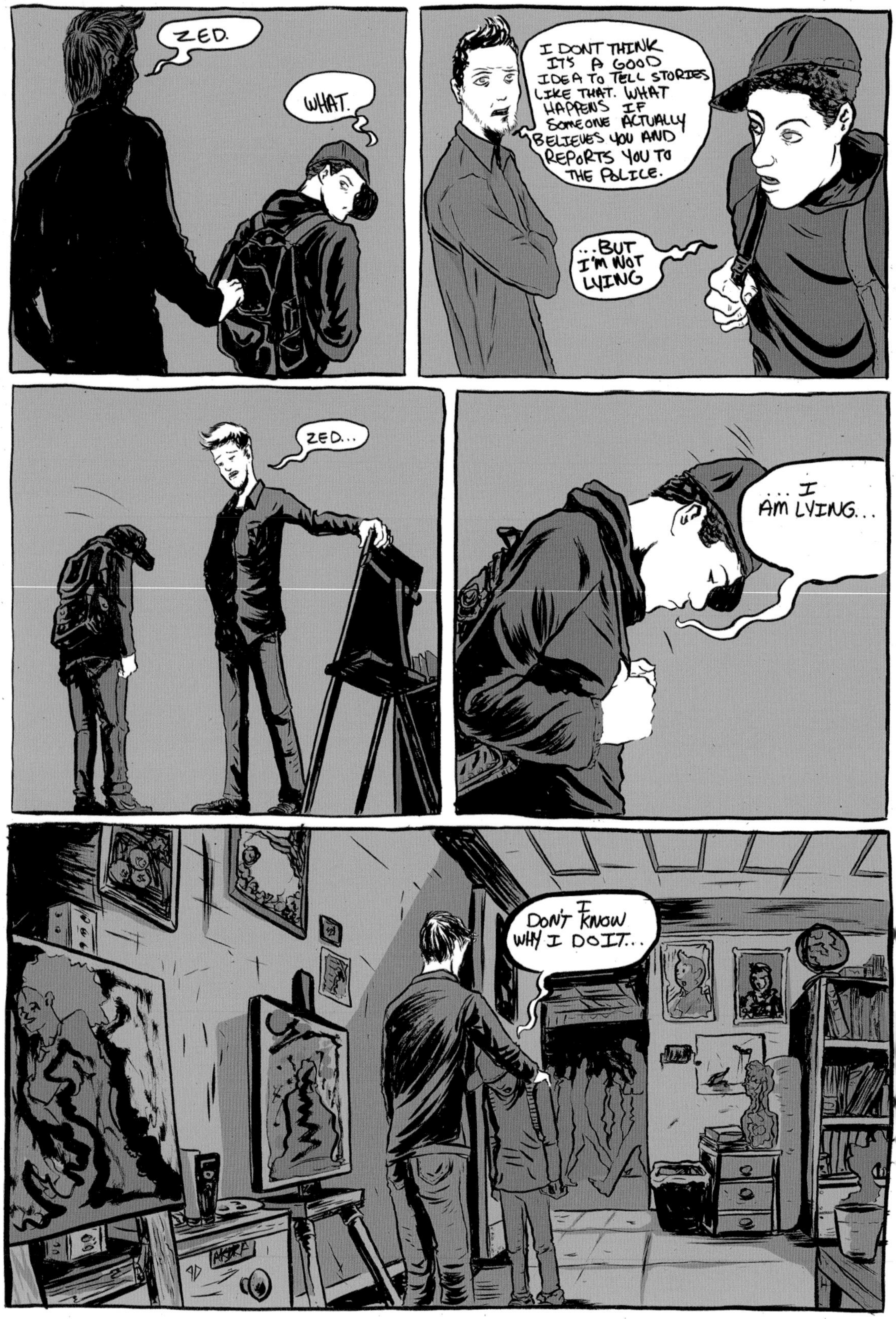
ZED.
WHAT.
I DON'T THINK IT'S A GOOD IDEA TO TELL STORIES LIKE THAT. WHAT HAPPENS IF SOMEONE ACTUALLY BELIEVES YOU AND REPORTS YOU TO THE POLICE.
...BUT I'M NOT LYING
ZED...
...I AM LYING...
I DON'T KNOW WHY I DO IT...

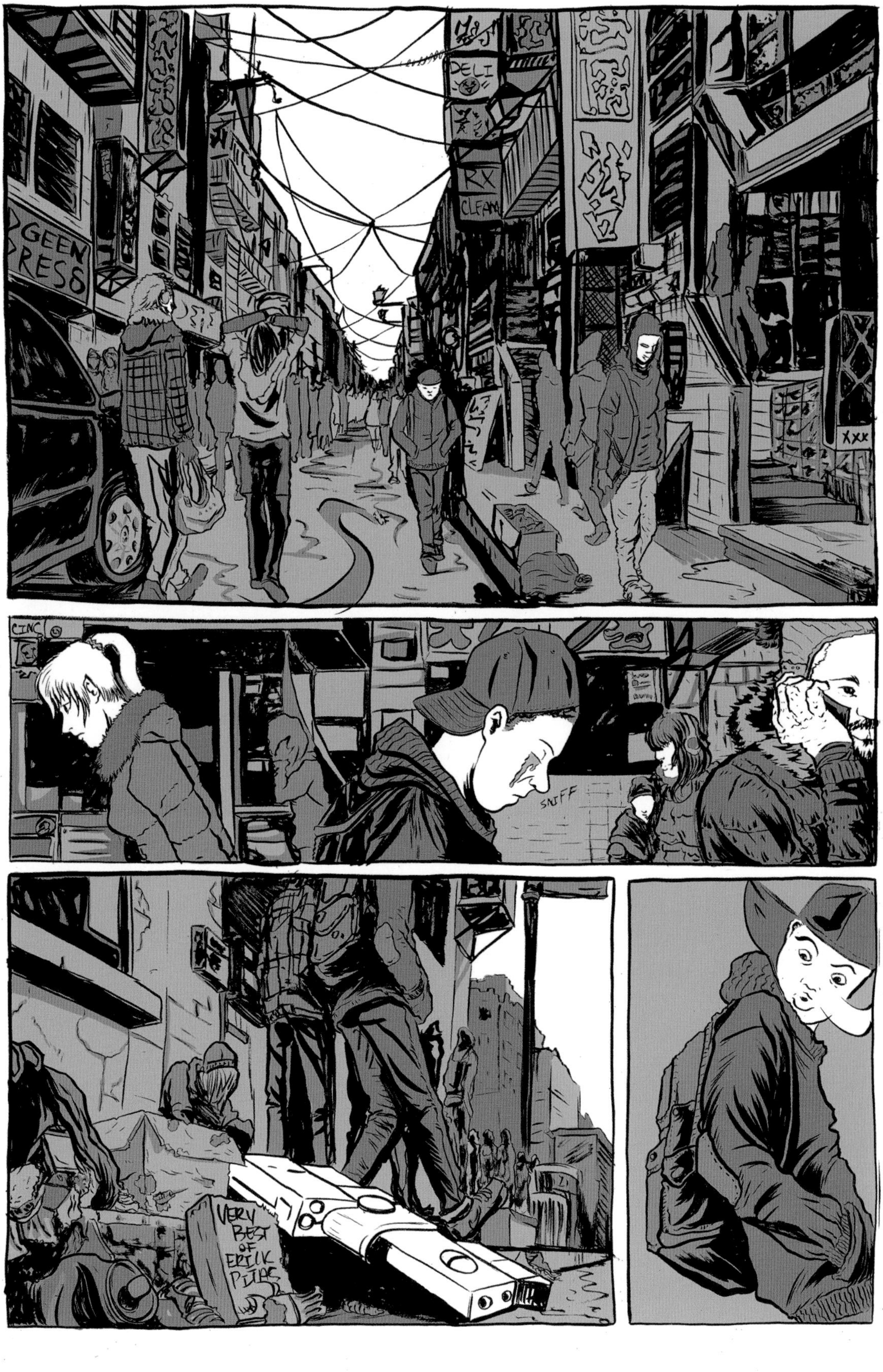
DELI
RX
CLEAN
XXX
SNIFF
VERY BEST OF ERICK

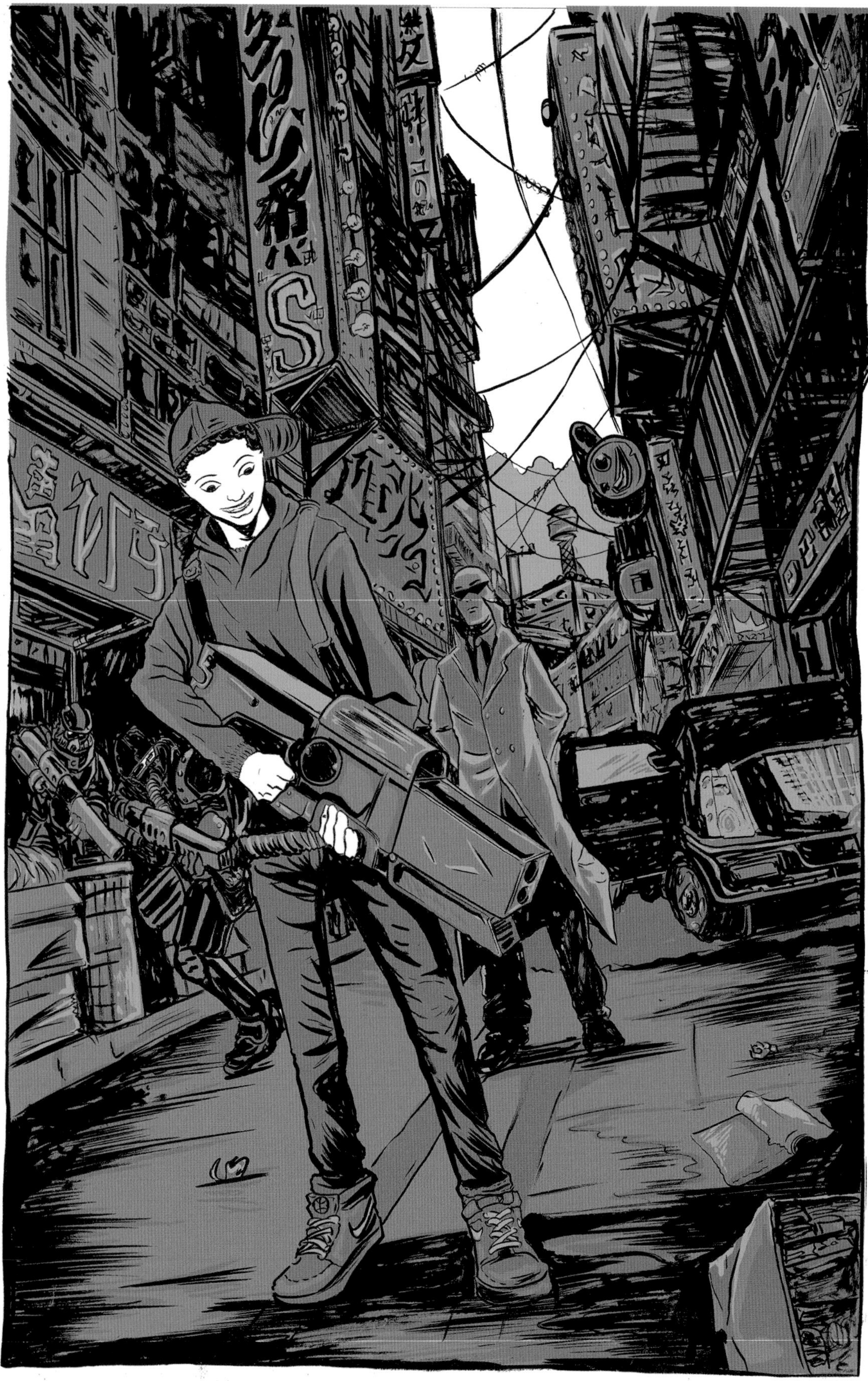

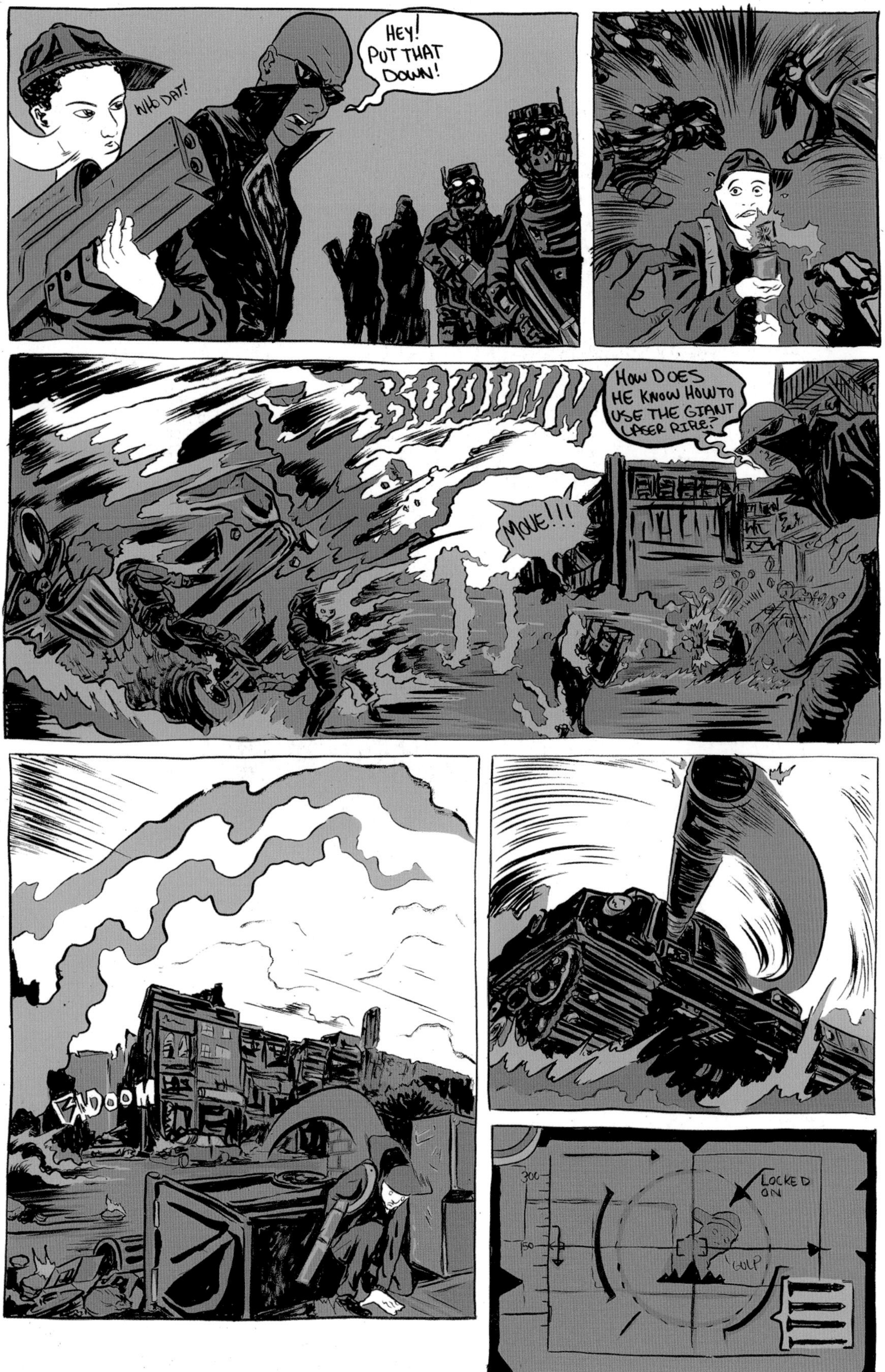

WHO DAT!
HEY! PUT THAT DOWN!
CLICK
BOOOMM
HOW DOES HE KNOW HOW TO USE THE GIANT LASER RIFLE?
MOVE!!!
BADOOOM
LOCKED ON
300
150
GULP

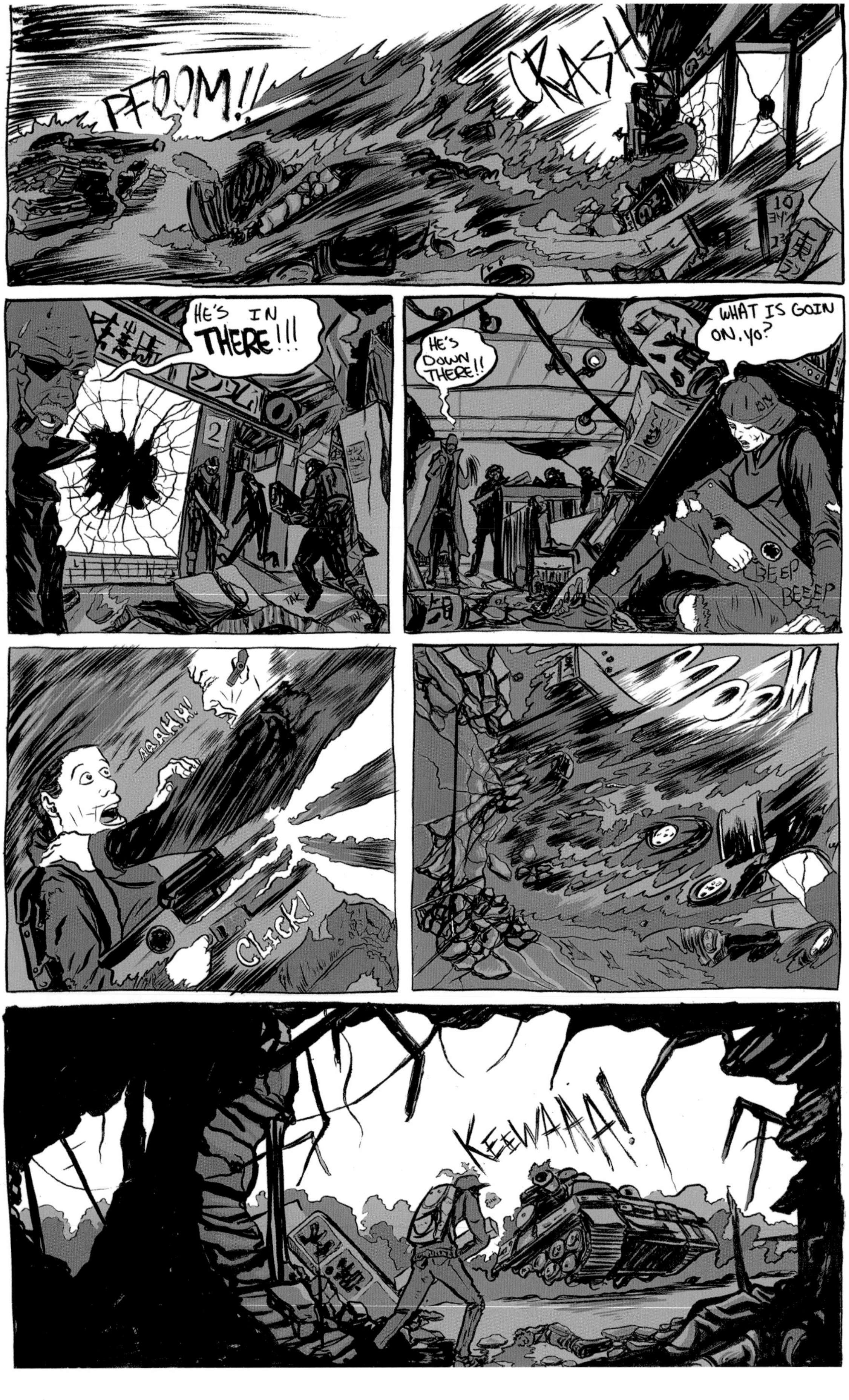
PFOOM!!
CRASH!
HE'S IN THERE!!!
HE'S DOWN THERE!!
WHAT IS GOIN ON, yo?
BEEP BEEEP
AAAHH!
CLICK!
WOOOM
KEEWAAAA!

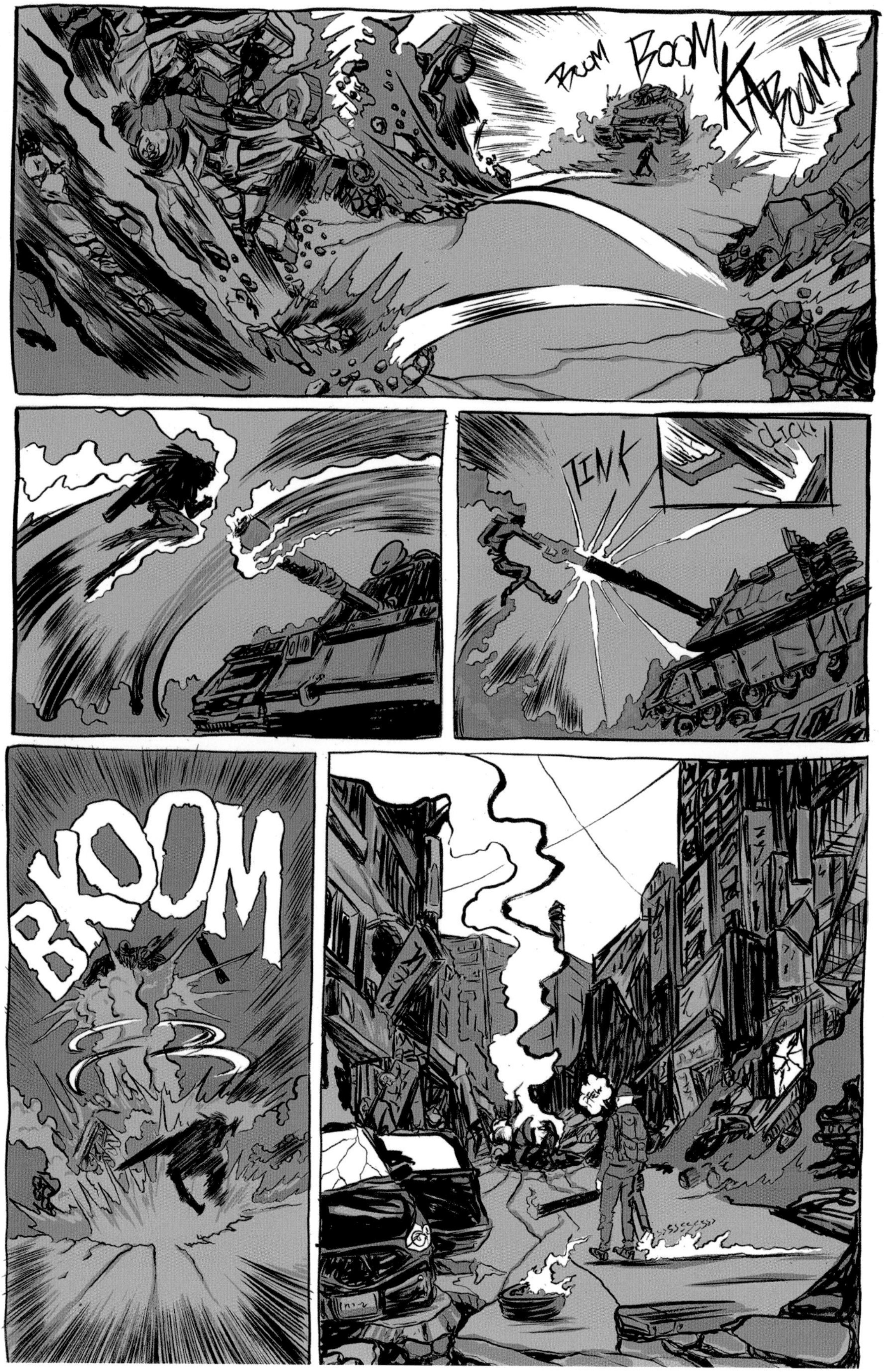
BOOM
BOOM
KABOOM
TINK
CLICK!
BKOOM
SSSSSSSSS

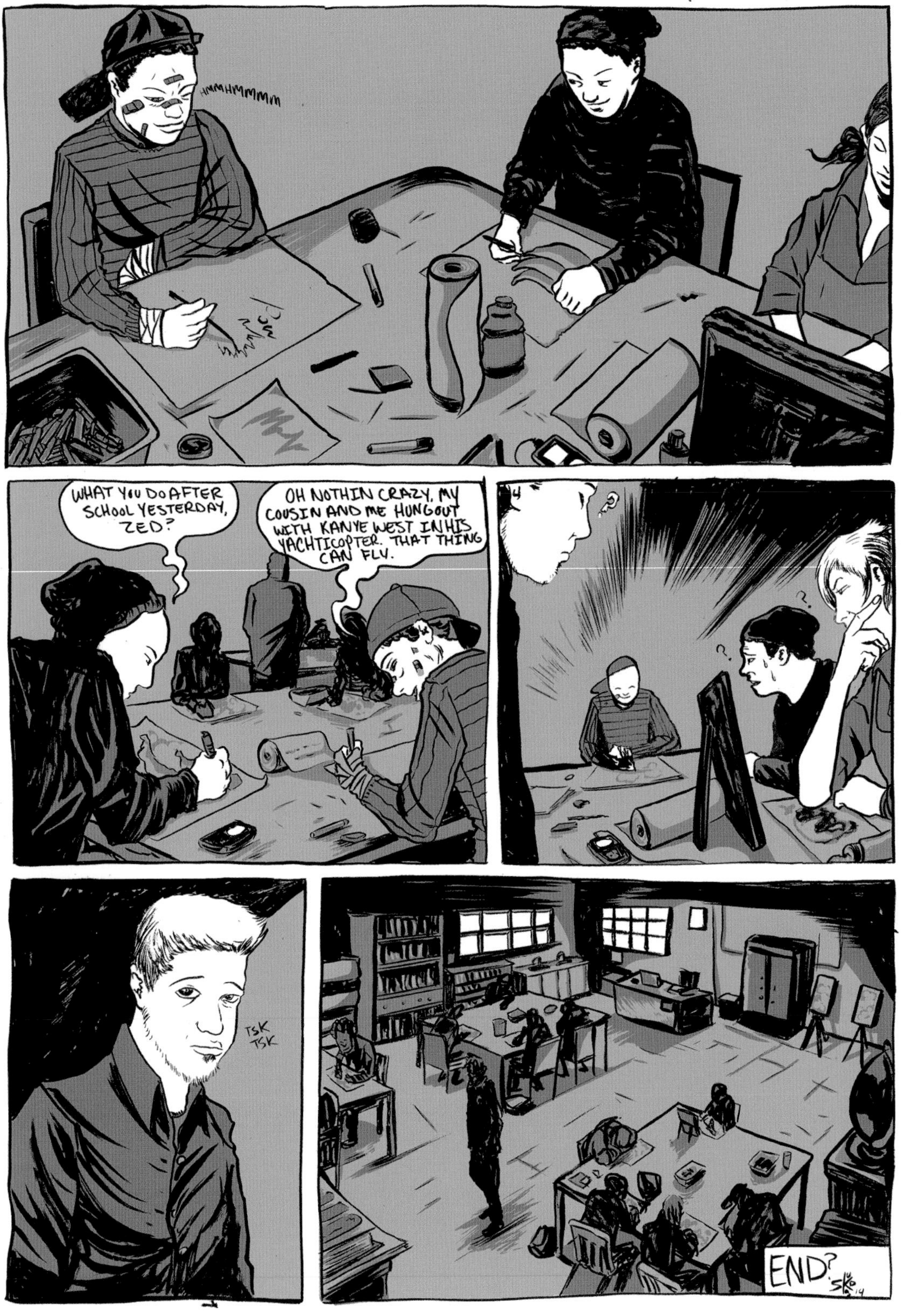
HMMHMMMM
WHAT YOU DO AFTER SCHOOL YESTERDAY, ZED?
OH NOTHIN CRAZY. MY COUSIN AND ME HUNG OUT WITH KANYE WEST IN HIS YACHTICOPTER. THAT THING CAN FLY.
?
?
TSK TSK
END?

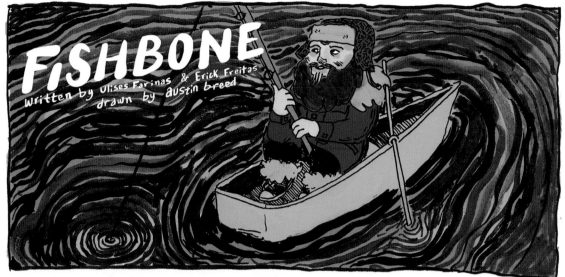

FISHBONE
Written by Ulises Farinas & Erick Freitas
drawn by austin breed

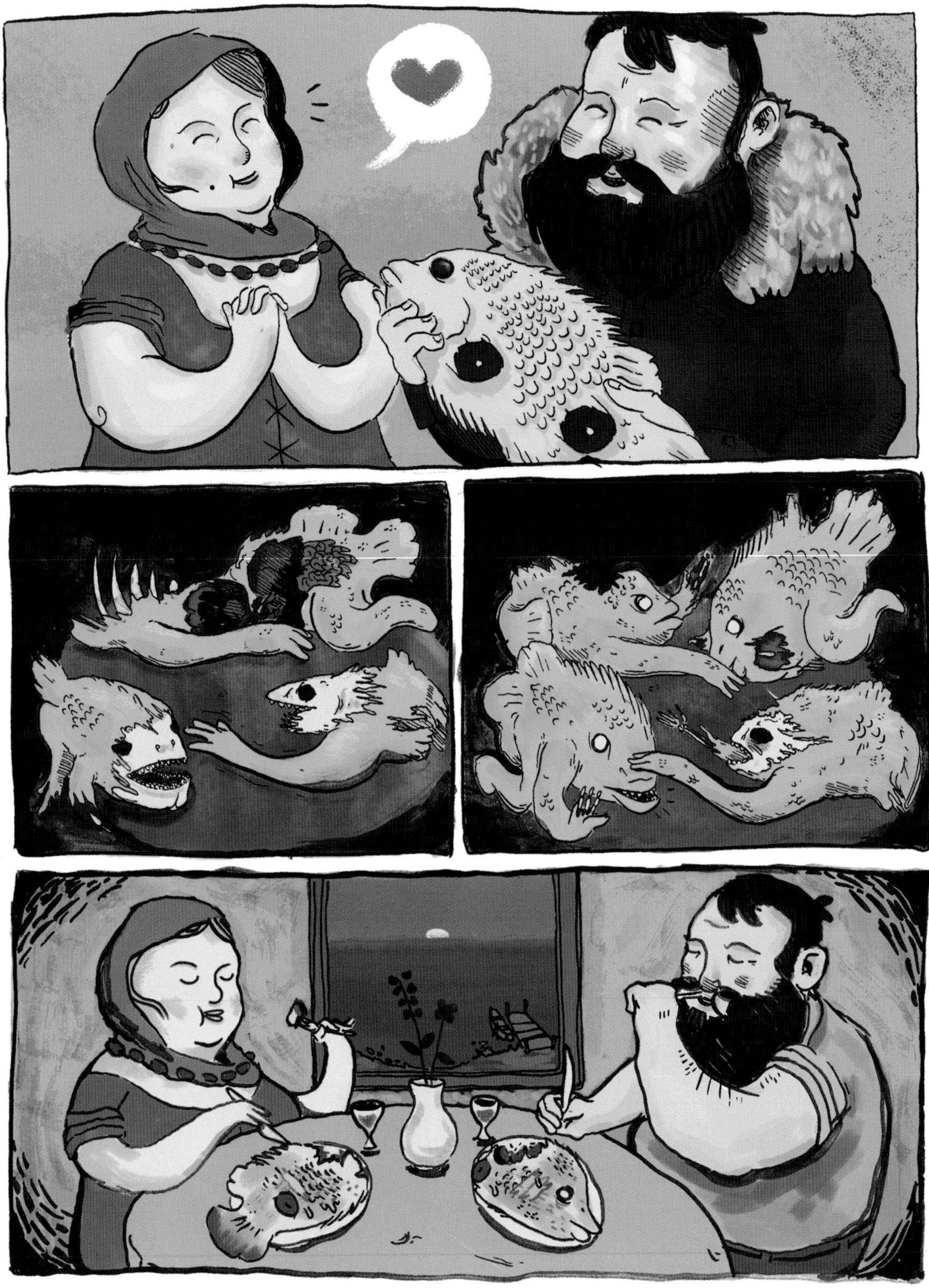

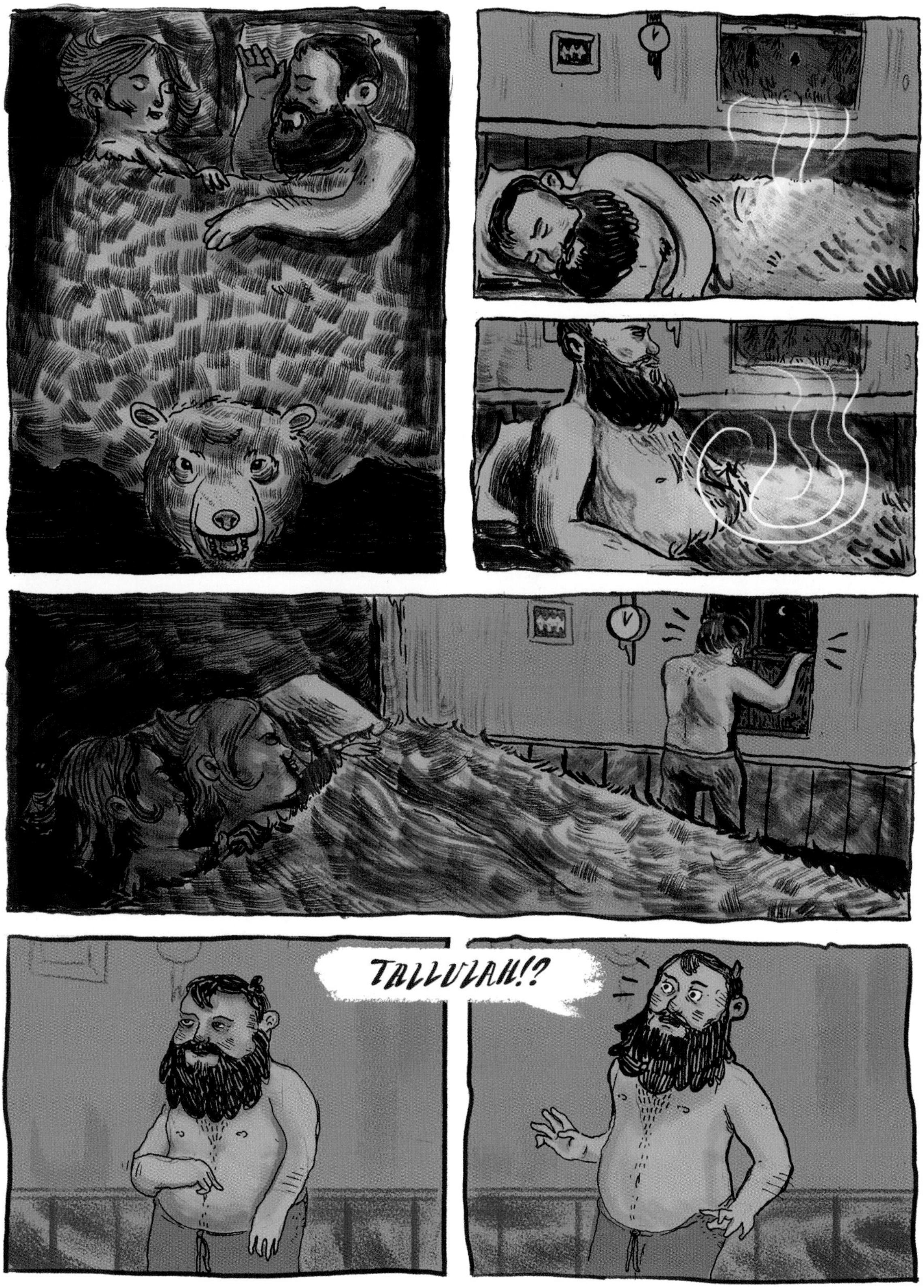
TALLULAH!?

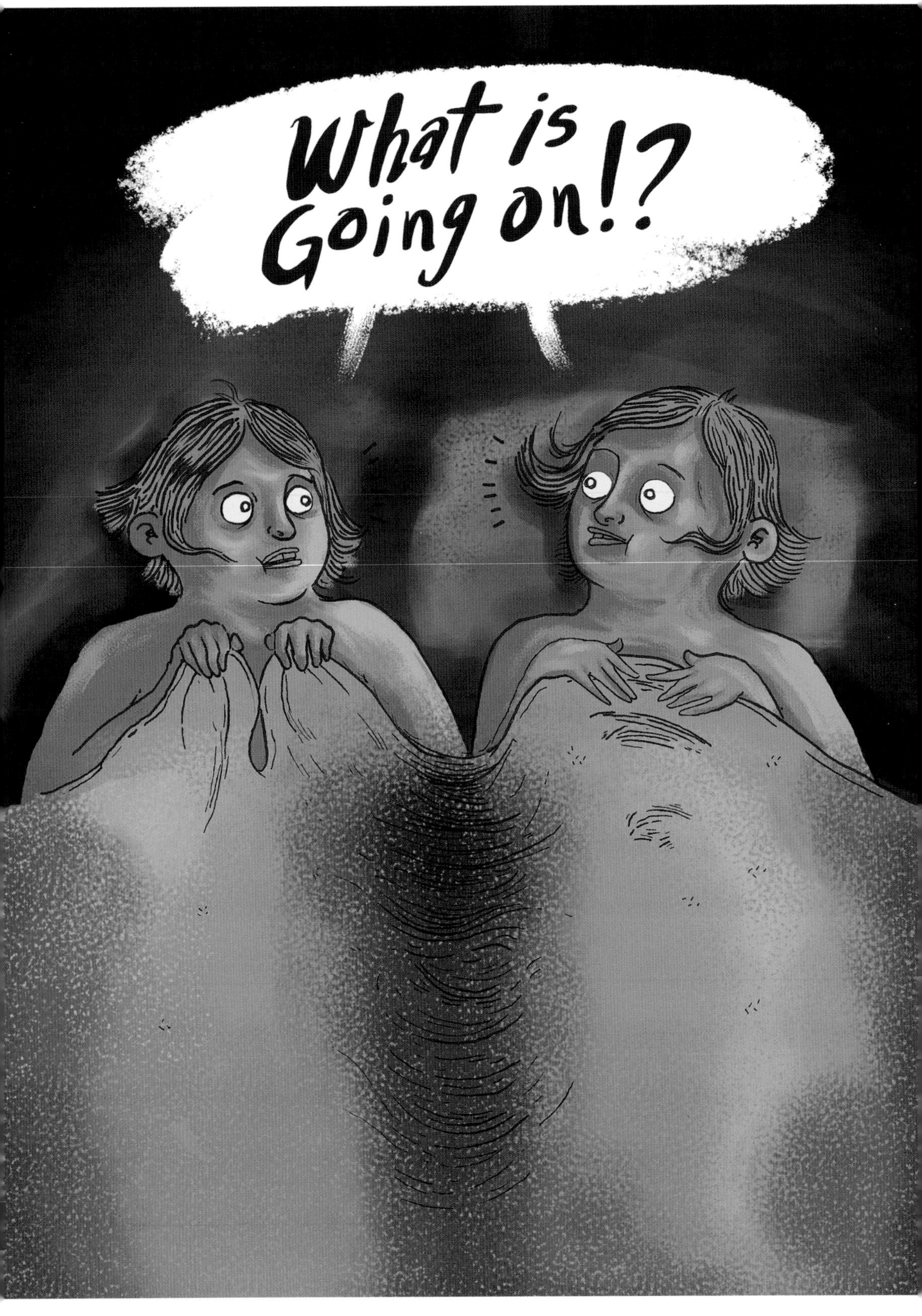
What is Going on!?

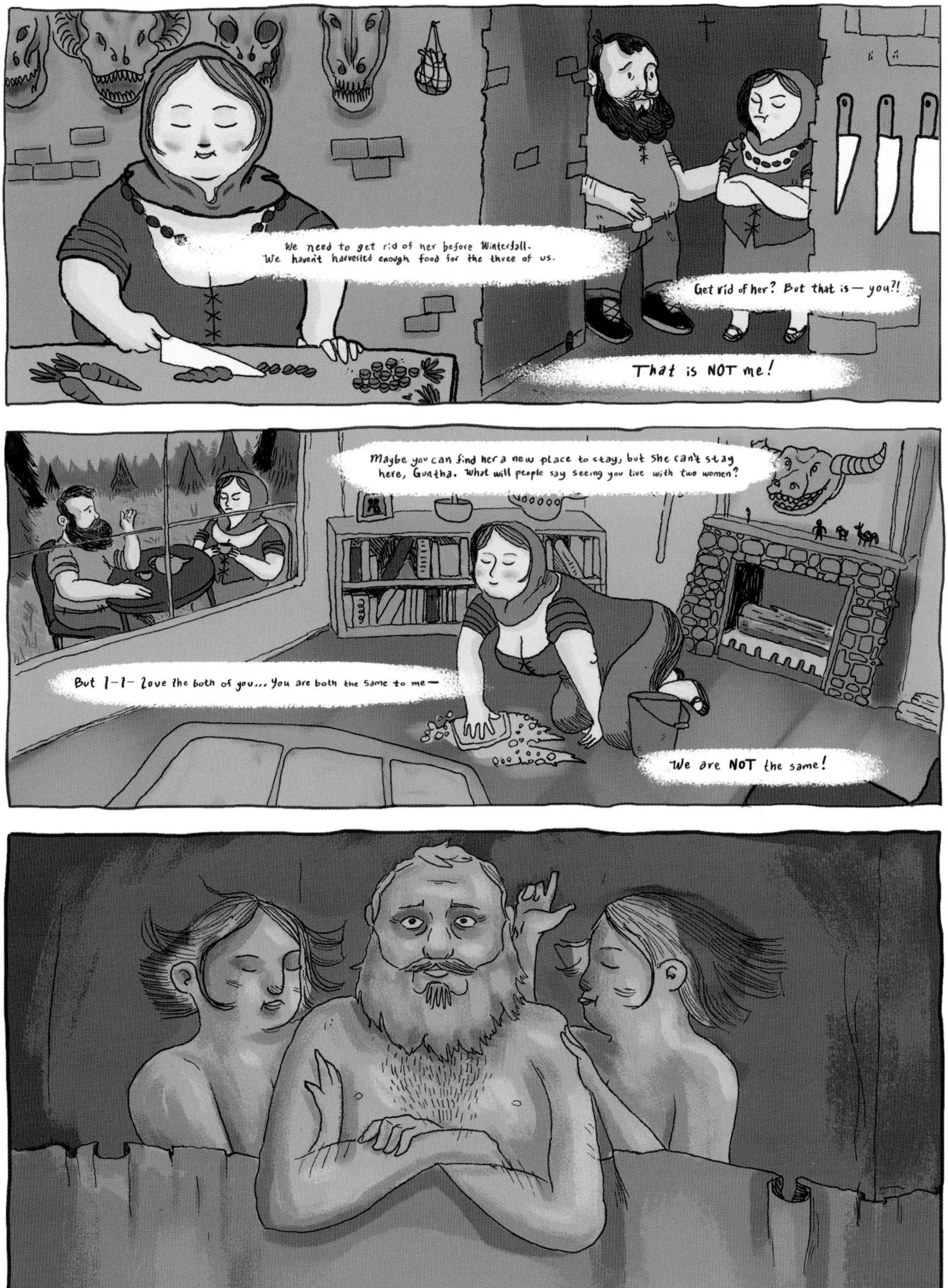
We need to get rid of her before Winterfall.
We haven't harvested enough food for the three of us.
Get rid of her? But that is— you?!
That is NOT me!
Maybe you can find her a new place to stay, but she can't stay here, Guntha. What will people say seeing you live with two women?
But I-I- love the both of you... You are both the same to me—
We are NOT the same!

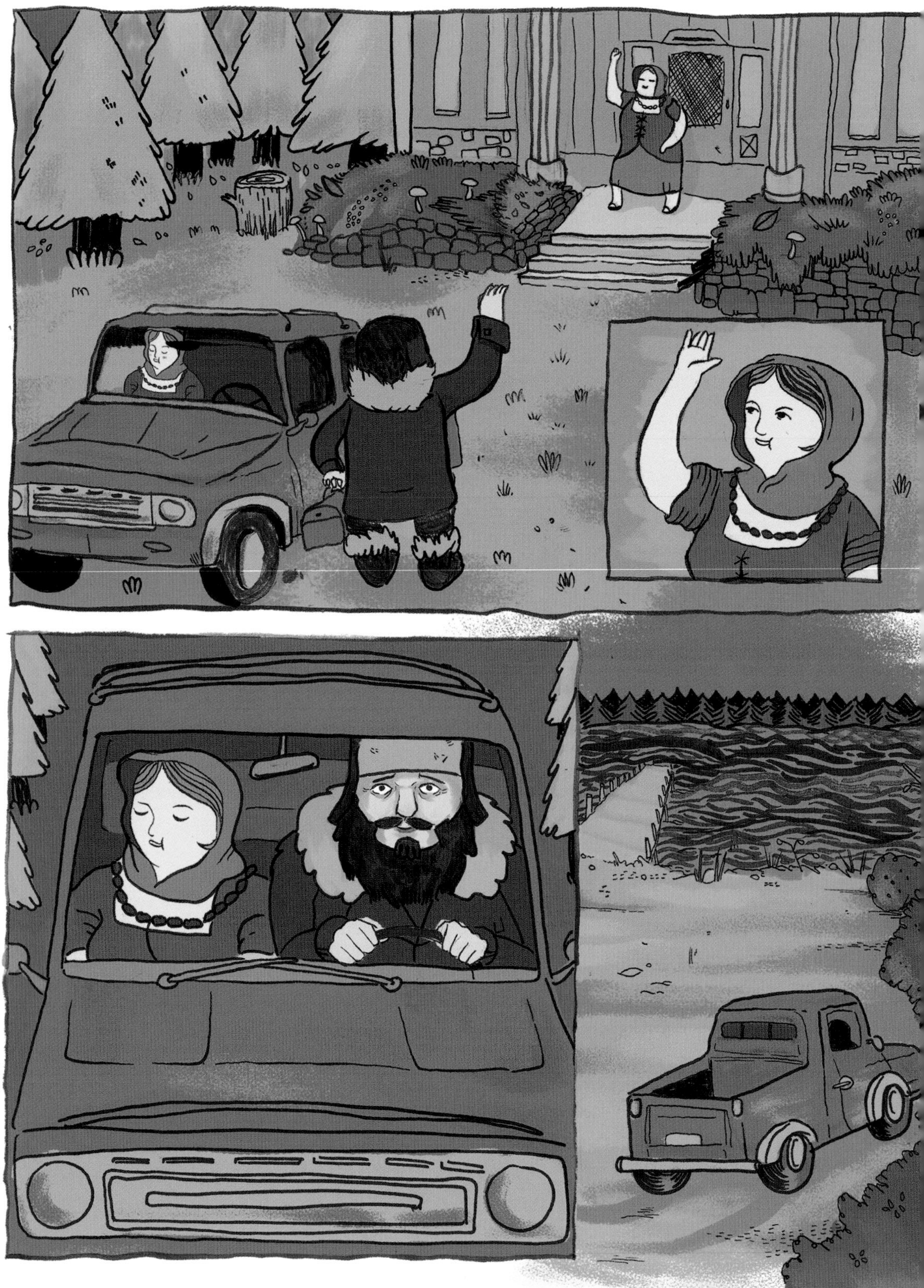

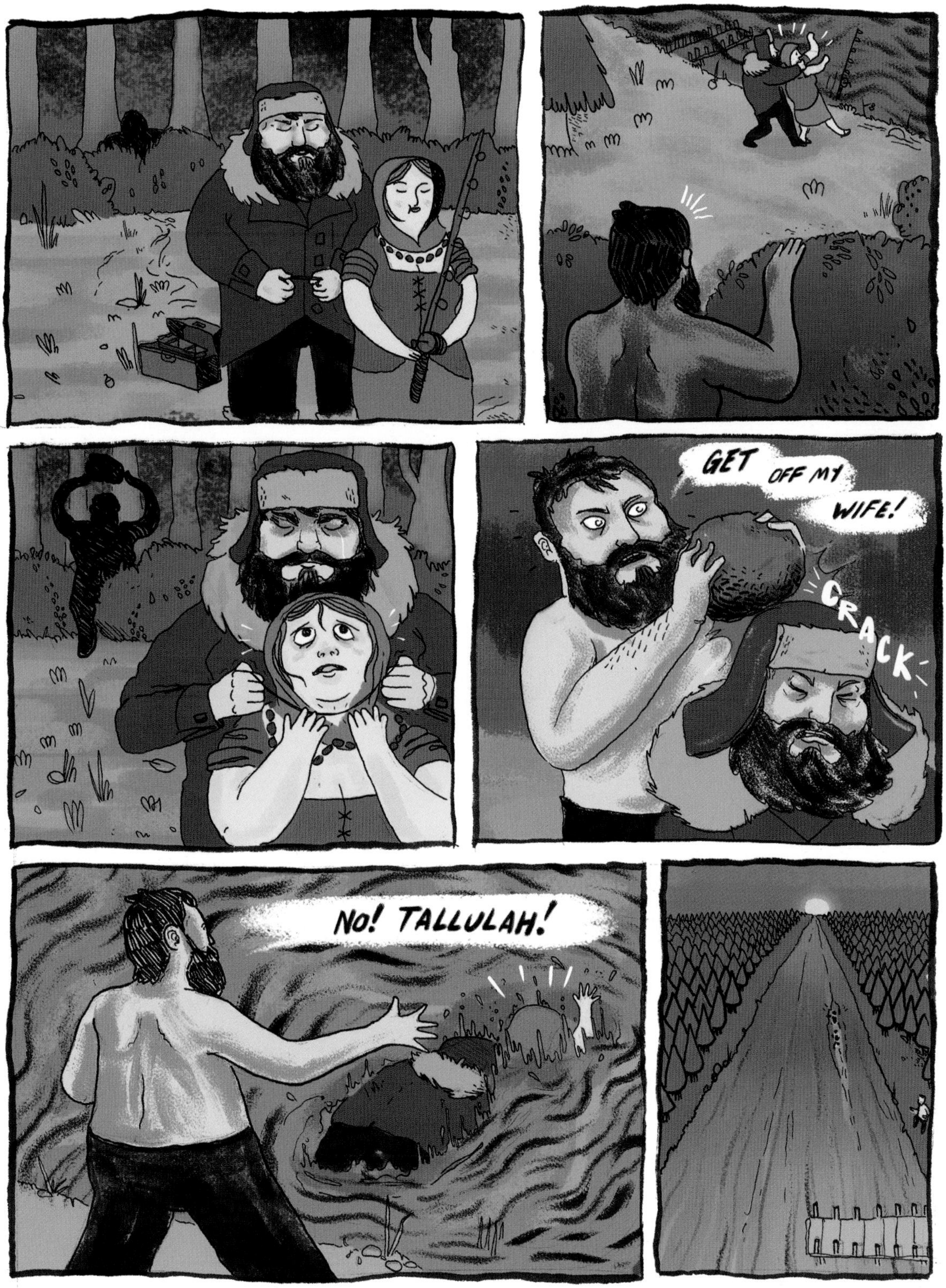
GET OFF MY WIFE!
CRACK
NO! TALLULAH!

...Tallulah...

...how am I going to explain what happened to her?

Tallulah?

are you still alive?

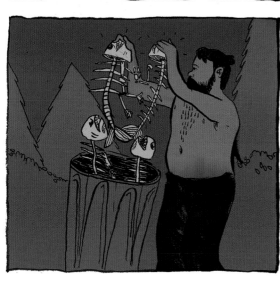
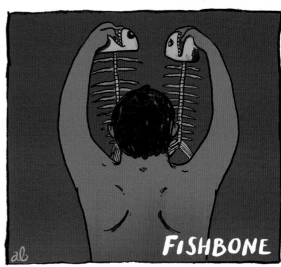

FISHBONE

Art by **Zoe Crockett**

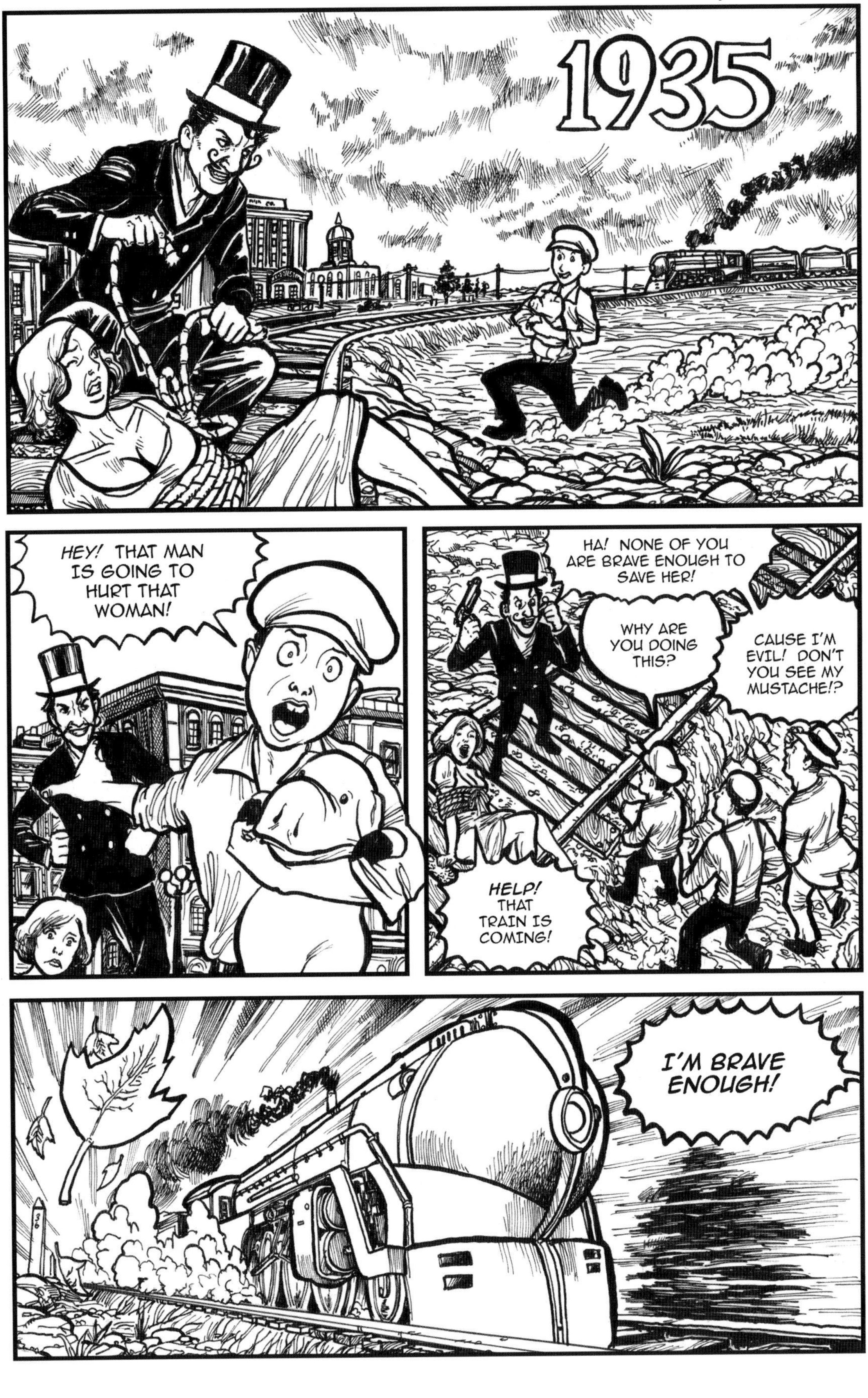
1935
HEY! THAT MAN IS GOING TO HURT THAT WOMAN!
HA! NONE OF YOU ARE BRAVE ENOUGH TO SAVE HER!
WHY ARE YOU DOING THIS?
CAUSE I'M EVIL! DON'T YOU SEE MY MUSTACHE!?
HELP! THAT TRAIN IS COMING!
I'M BRAVE ENOUGH!

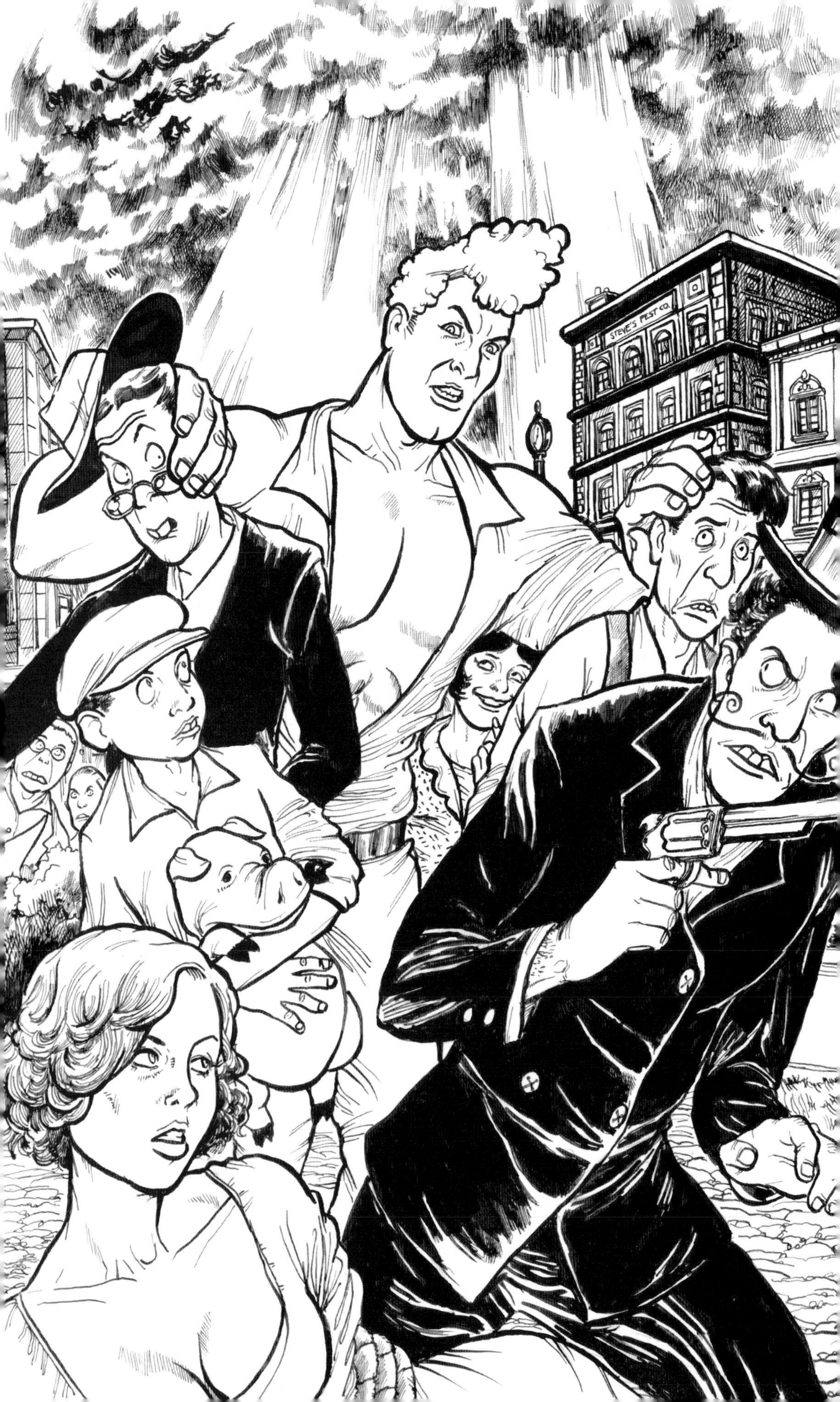
STEVE'S PEST CO.

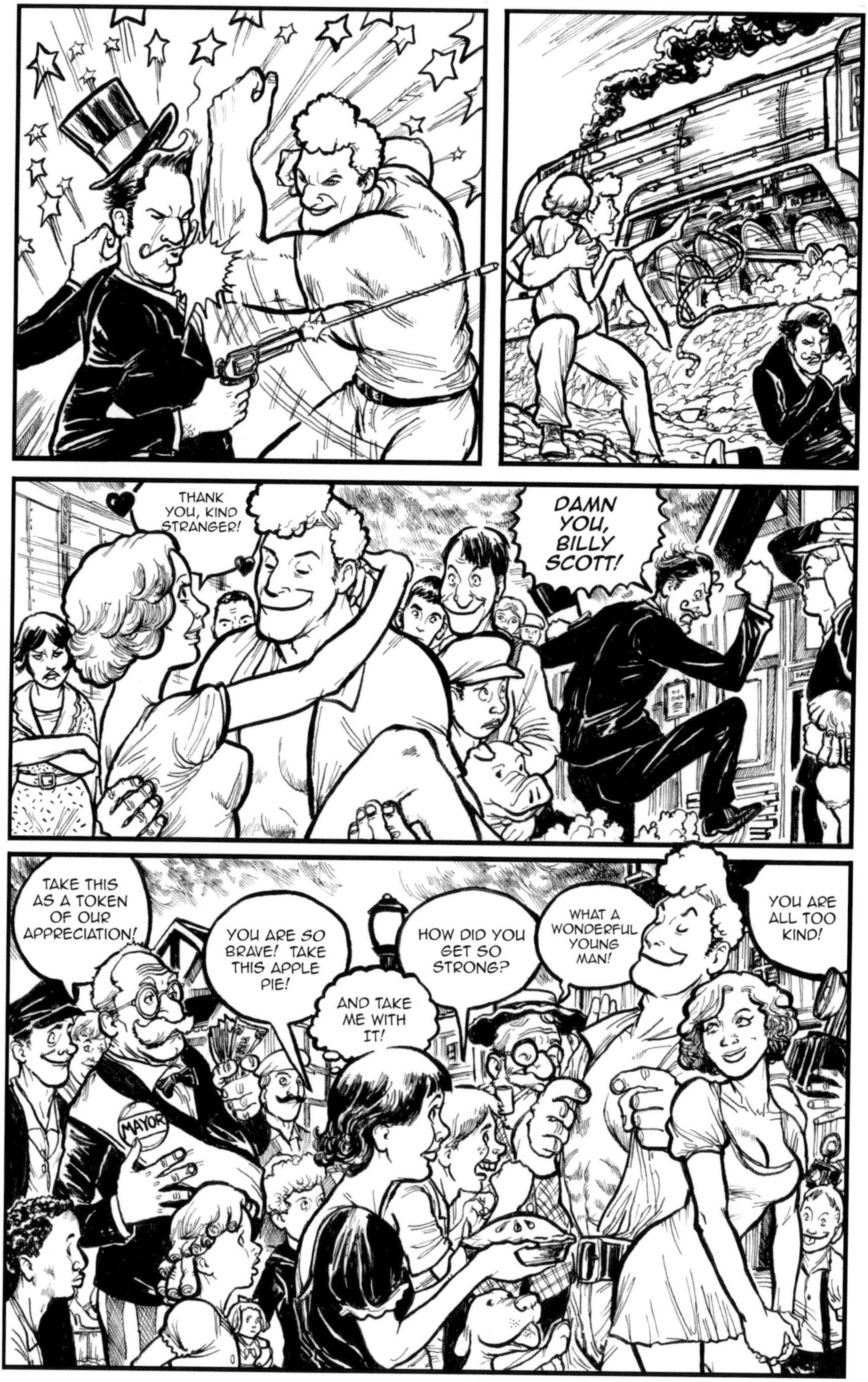
THANK YOU, KIND STRANGER!
DAMN YOU, BILLY SCOTT!
TAKE THIS AS A TOKEN OF OUR APPRECIATION!
MAYOR
YOU ARE SO BRAVE! TAKE THIS APPLE PIE!
AND TAKE ME WITH IT!
HOW DID YOU GET SO STRONG?
WHAT A WONDERFUL YOUNG MAN!
YOU ARE ALL TOO KIND!

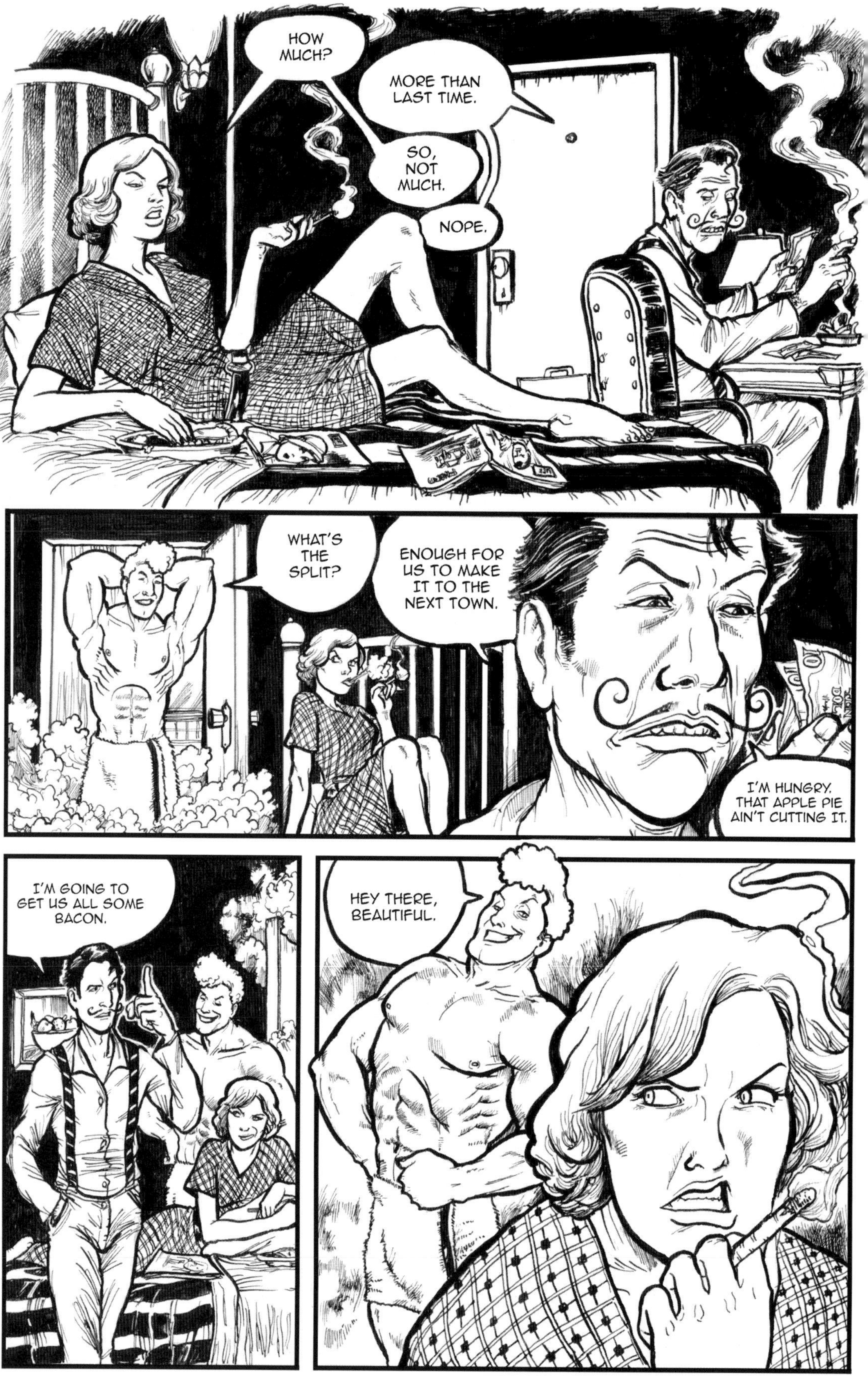
HOW MUCH?
MORE THAN LAST TIME.
SO, NOT MUCH.
NOPE.
WHAT'S THE SPLIT?
ENOUGH FOR US TO MAKE IT TO THE NEXT TOWN.
I'M HUNGRY. THAT APPLE PIE AIN'T CUTTING IT.
I'M GOING TO GET US ALL SOME BACON.
HEY THERE, BEAUTIFUL.

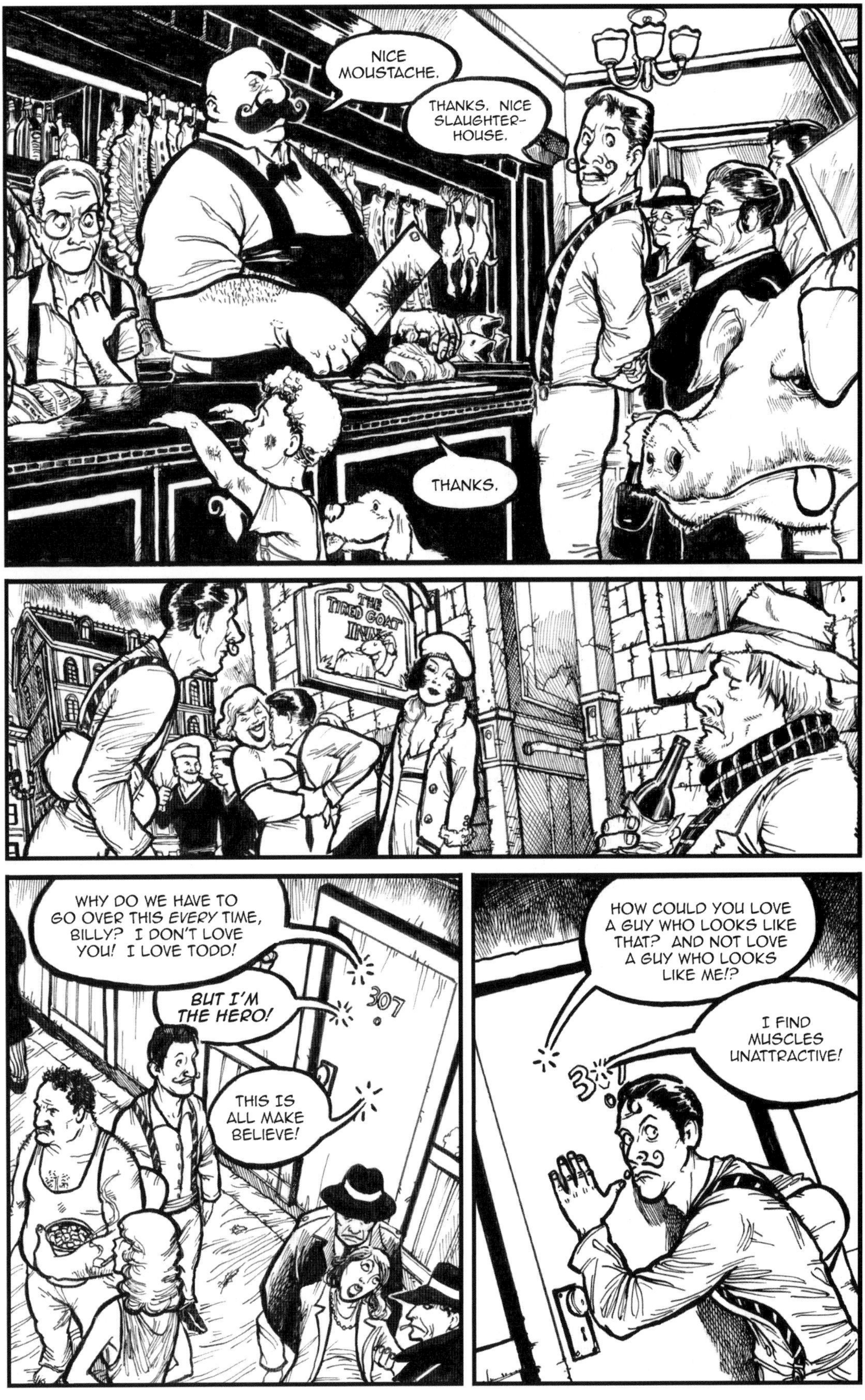
NICE MOUSTACHE.
THANKS. NICE SLAUGHTER-HOUSE.
THANKS.
THE TIRED GOAT INN
WHY DO WE HAVE TO GO OVER THIS *EVERY* TIME, BILLY? I DON'T LOVE YOU! I LOVE TODD!
BUT I'M THE HERO!
THIS IS ALL MAKE BELIEVE!
307
HOW COULD YOU LOVE A GUY WHO LOOKS LIKE THAT? AND NOT LOVE A GUY WHO LOOKS LIKE ME!?
I FIND MUSCLES UNATTRACTIVE!

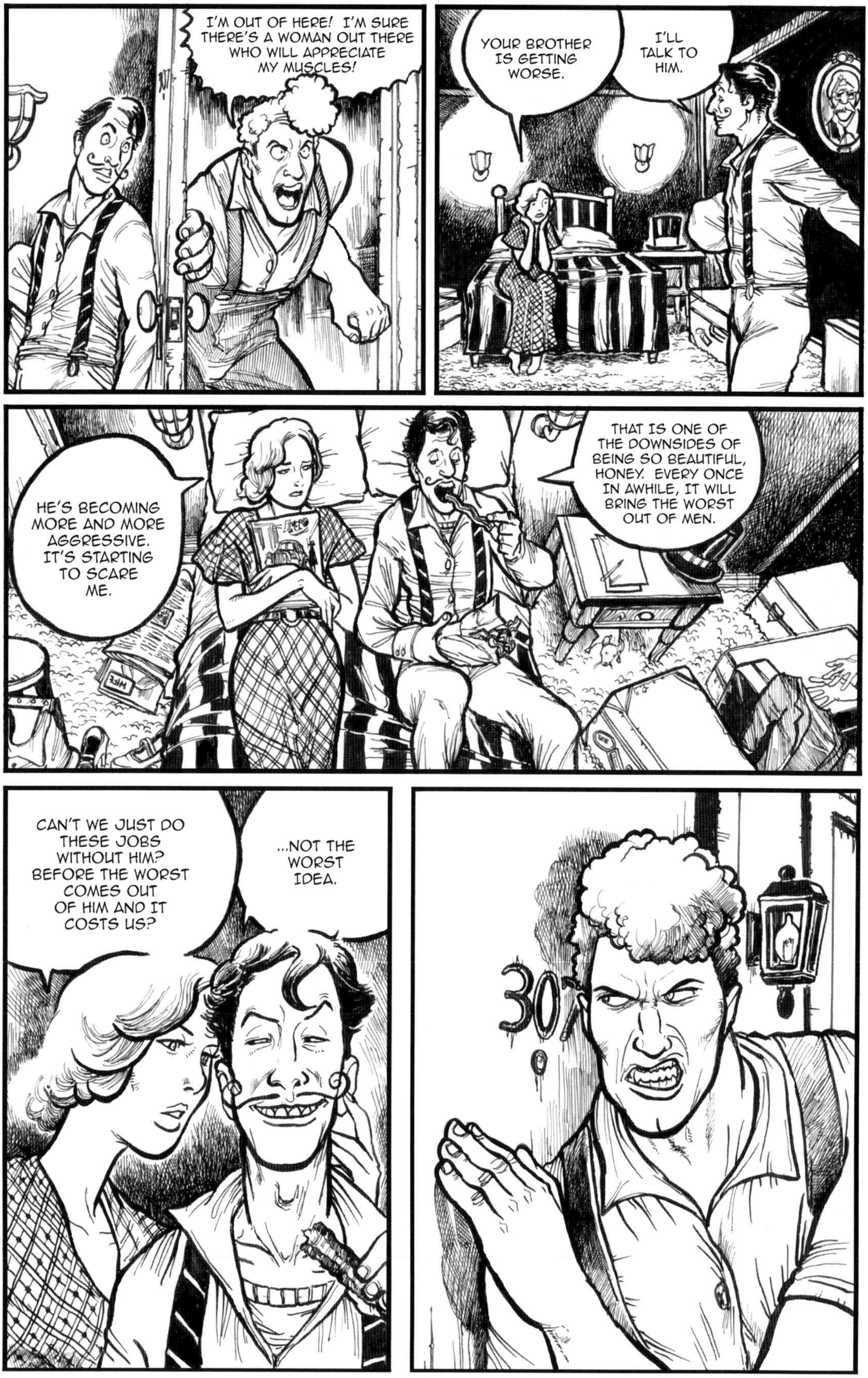

I'M OUT OF HERE! I'M SURE THERE'S A WOMAN OUT THERE WHO WILL APPRECIATE MY MUSCLES!
YOUR BROTHER IS GETTING WORSE.
I'LL TALK TO HIM.
HE'S BECOMING MORE AND MORE AGGRESSIVE. IT'S STARTING TO SCARE ME.
THAT IS ONE OF THE DOWNSIDES OF BEING SO BEAUTIFUL, HONEY. EVERY ONCE IN AWHILE, IT WILL BRING THE WORST OUT OF MEN.
CAN'T WE JUST DO THESE JOBS WITHOUT HIM? BEFORE THE WORST COMES OUT OF HIM AND IT COSTS US?
...NOT THE WORST IDEA.

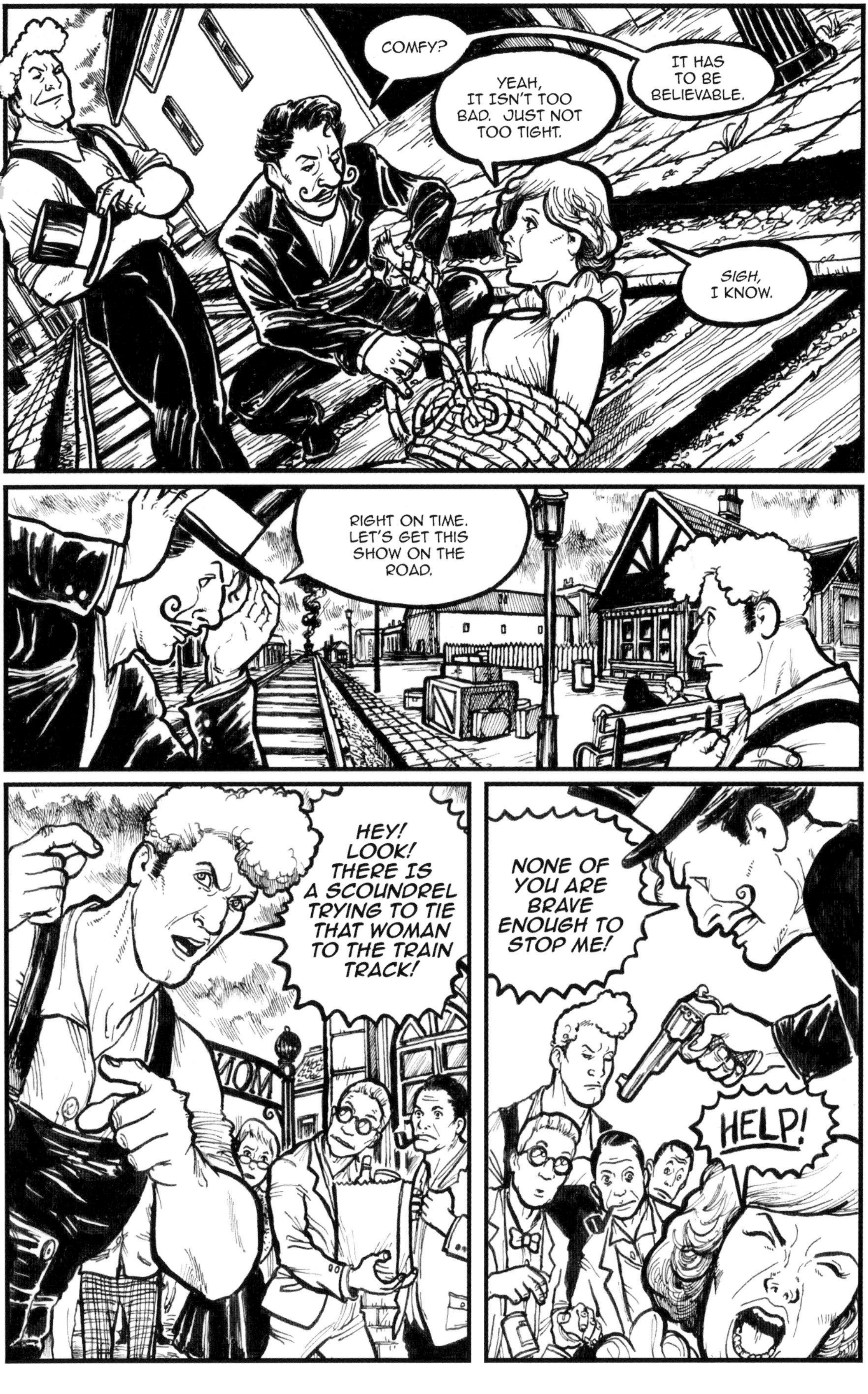
COMFY?
YEAH, IT ISN'T TOO BAD. JUST NOT TOO TIGHT.
IT HAS TO BE BELIEVABLE.
SIGH, I KNOW.
RIGHT ON TIME. LET'S GET THIS SHOW ON THE ROAD.
HEY! LOOK! THERE IS A SCOUNDREL TRYING TO TIE THAT WOMAN TO THE TRAIN TRACK!
NONE OF YOU ARE BRAVE ENOUGH TO STOP ME!
HELP!

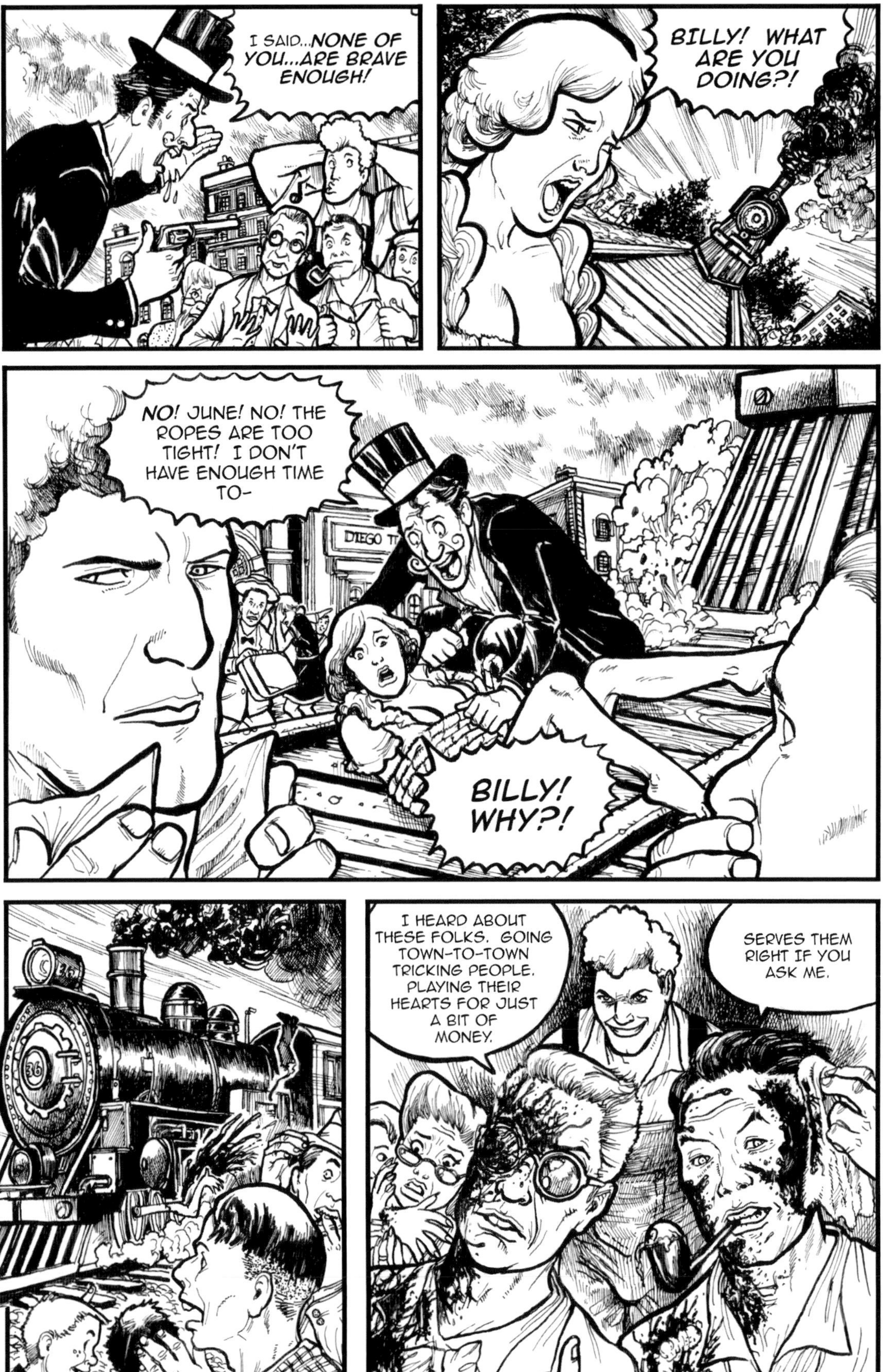
I SAID...NONE OF YOU...ARE BRAVE ENOUGH!
BILLY! WHAT ARE YOU DOING?!
NO! JUNE! NO! THE ROPES ARE TOO TIGHT! I DON'T HAVE ENOUGH TIME TO-
DIEGO T
BILLY! WHY?!
36
I HEARD ABOUT THESE FOLKS. GOING TOWN-TO-TOWN TRICKING PEOPLE. PLAYING THEIR HEARTS FOR JUST A BIT OF MONEY.
SERVES THEM RIGHT IF YOU ASK ME.

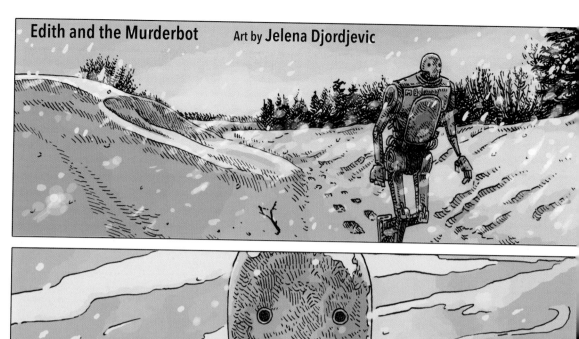

Edith and the Murderbot Art by Jelena Djordjevic

MB
MB
BIRAM TOW
POPULATION
~~1280~~
~~1279~~
~~1278~~
1277

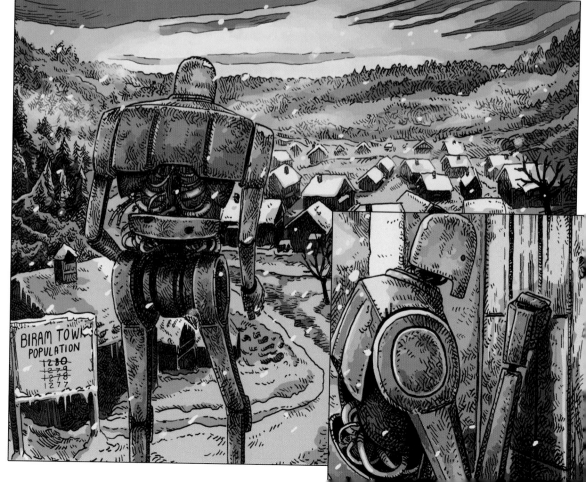

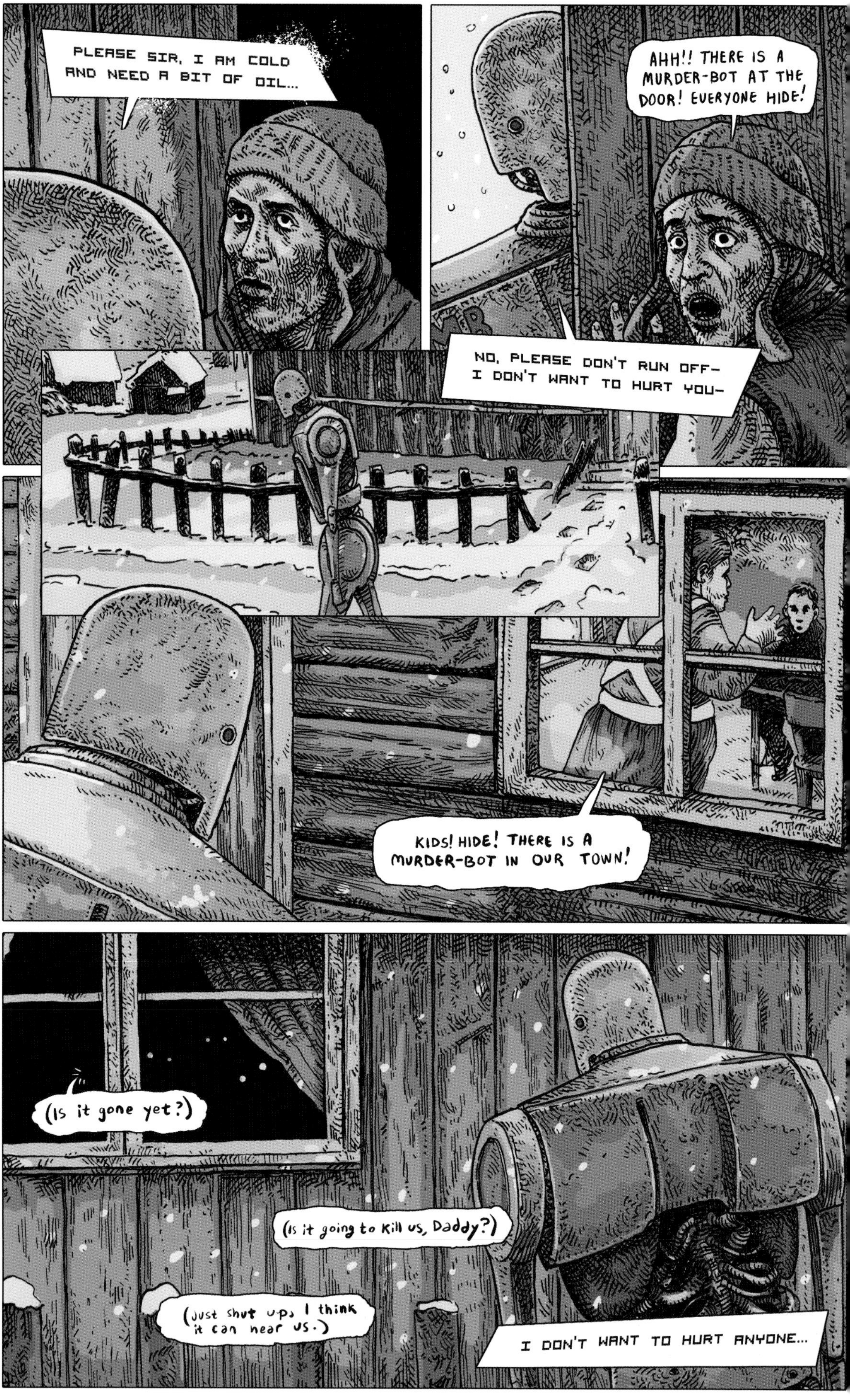
PLEASE SIR, I AM COLD AND NEED A BIT OF OIL...
AHH!! THERE IS A MURDER-BOT AT THE DOOR! EVERYONE HIDE!
NO, PLEASE DON'T RUN OFF– I DON'T WANT TO HURT YOU–
KIDS! HIDE! THERE IS A MURDER-BOT IN OUR TOWN!
(Is it gone yet?)
(Is it going to kill us, Daddy?)
(Just shut up, I think it can hear us.)
I DON'T WANT TO HURT ANYONE...

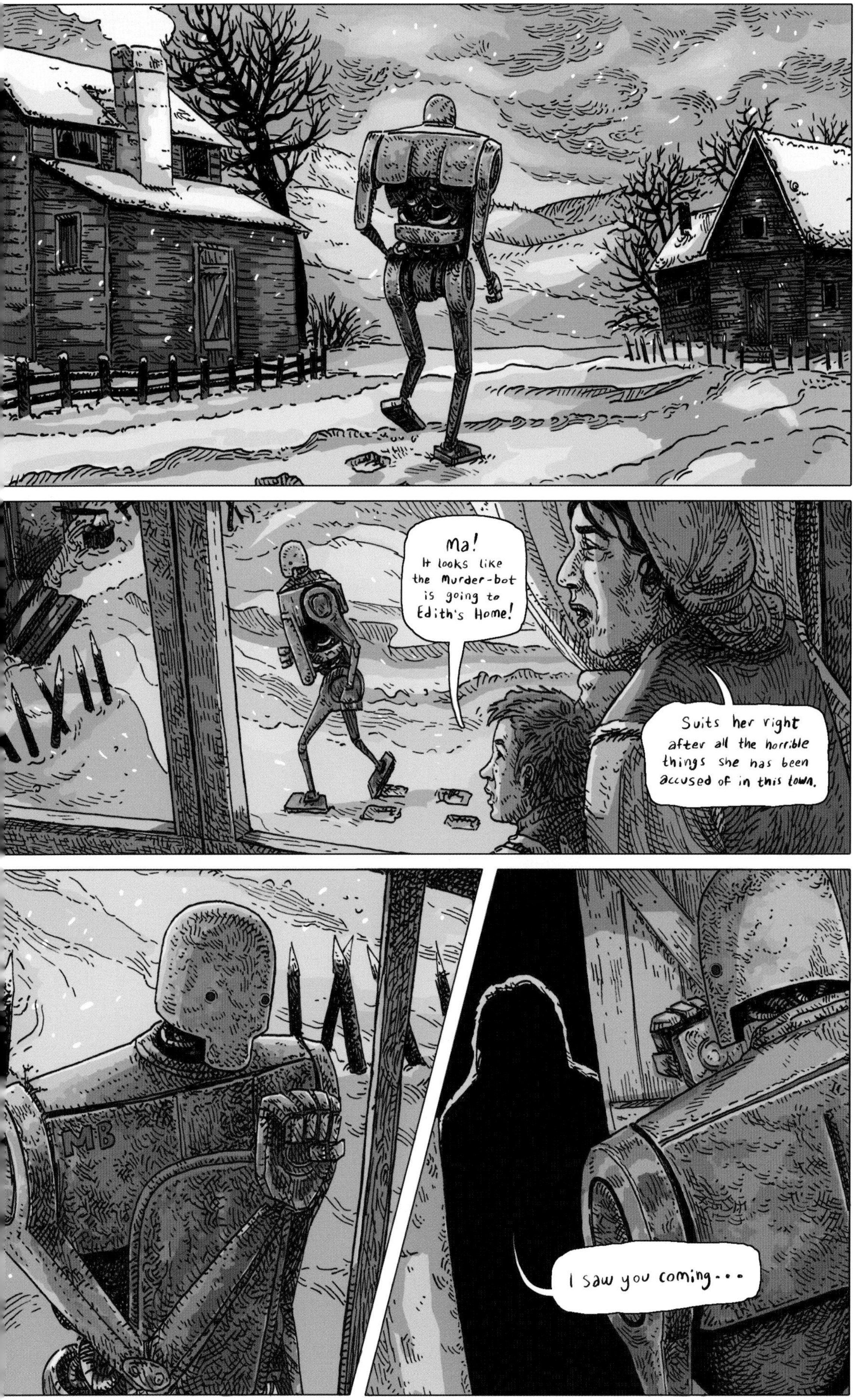

Ma! It looks like the Murder-bot is going to Edith's Home!
Suits her right after all the horrible things she has been accused of in this town.
MB
I saw you coming...

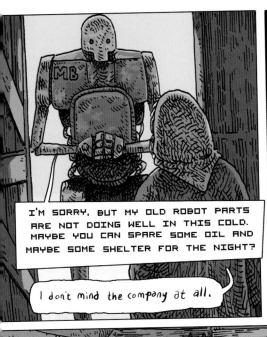

I'M SORRY, BUT MY OLD ROBOT PARTS ARE NOT DOING WELL IN THIS COLD. MAYBE YOU CAN SPARE SOME OIL AND MAYBE SOME SHELTER FOR THE NIGHT?

I don't mind the company at all.

YOU ARE SO KIND. EVERYONE THOUGHT BECAUSE I AM A MURDER-BOT I AM INCAPABLE OF NOT KILLING. A THOUSAND THANKS FOR NOT THROWING ME TO THE STREETS LIKE EVERYONE ELSE.

The people of this town can be very cruel sometimes. They have not been kind to me since I married a foreign man many years ago.

WHERE IS YOUR HUSBAND?

He passed, but this town's disdain for me remains.

BUMP

sorry, my chickens are unruly.

YOU KEEP YOUR CHICKENS UPSTAIRS?

yes, so they do not freeze in the cold.

STOP MAKING NOISE! I HAVE A GUEST!
MB
sorry about that, little piglets can be such a bother sometimes.
MB
Oh my...

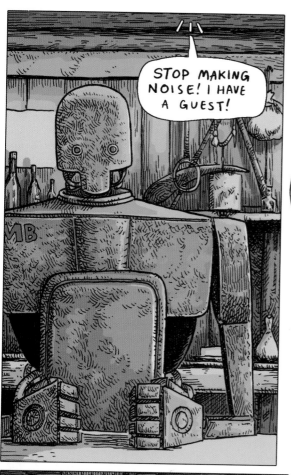

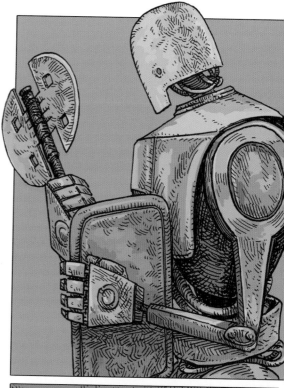

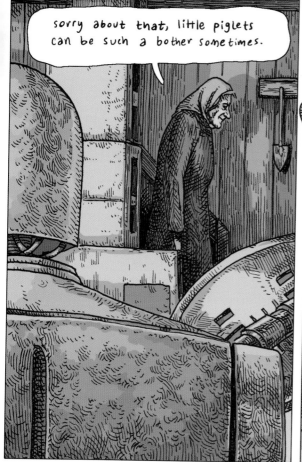

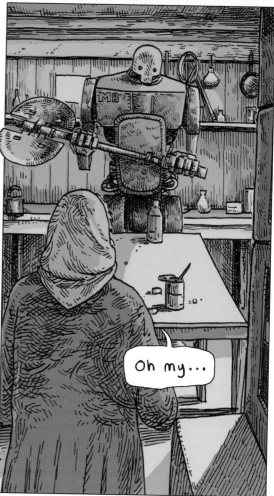

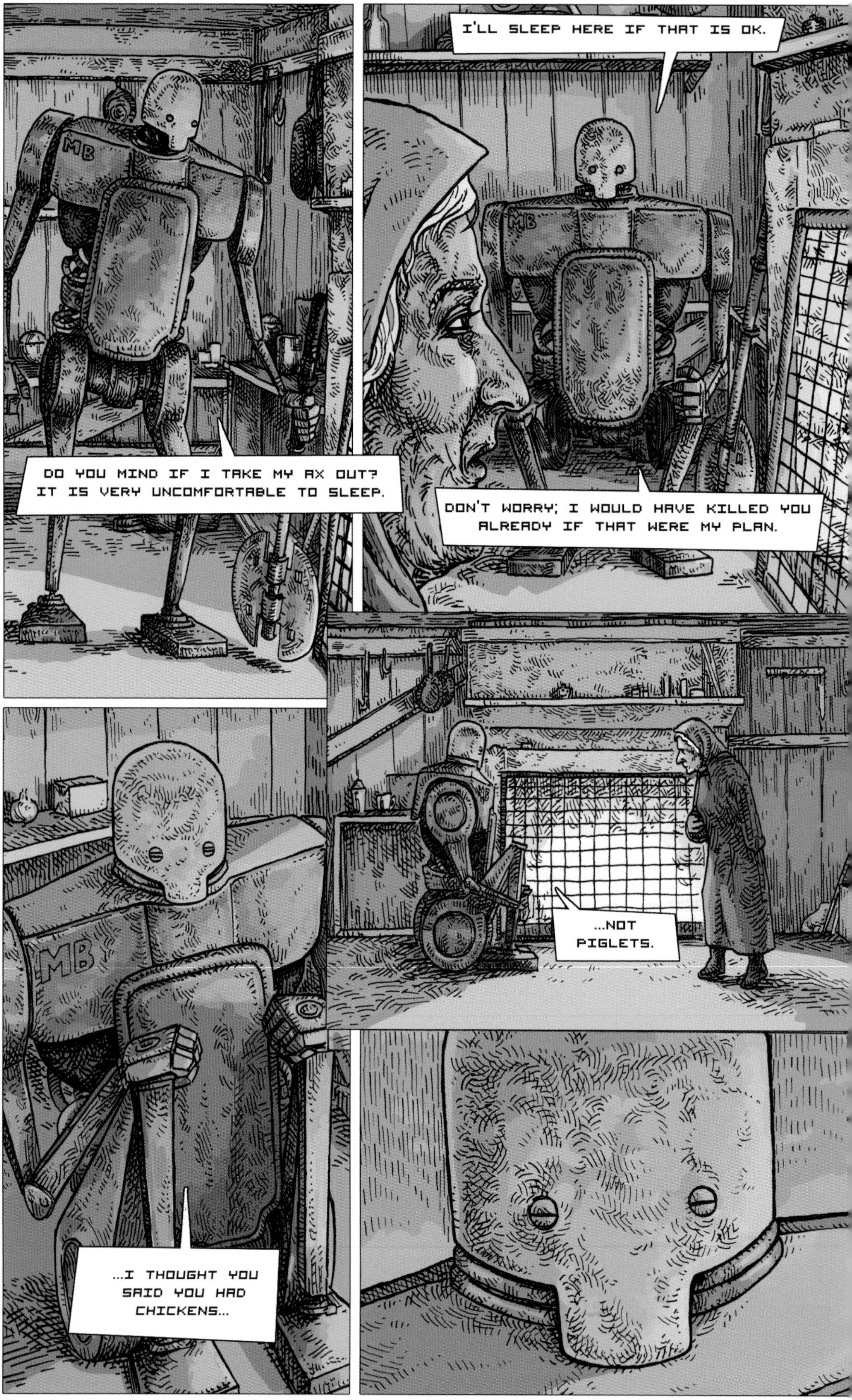
DO YOU MIND IF I TAKE MY AX OUT? IT IS VERY UNCOMFORTABLE TO SLEEP.
I'LL SLEEP HERE IF THAT IS OK.
DON'T WORRY; I WOULD HAVE KILLED YOU ALREADY IF THAT WERE MY PLAN.
MB
...I THOUGHT YOU SAID YOU HAD CHICKENS...
...NOT PIGLETS.

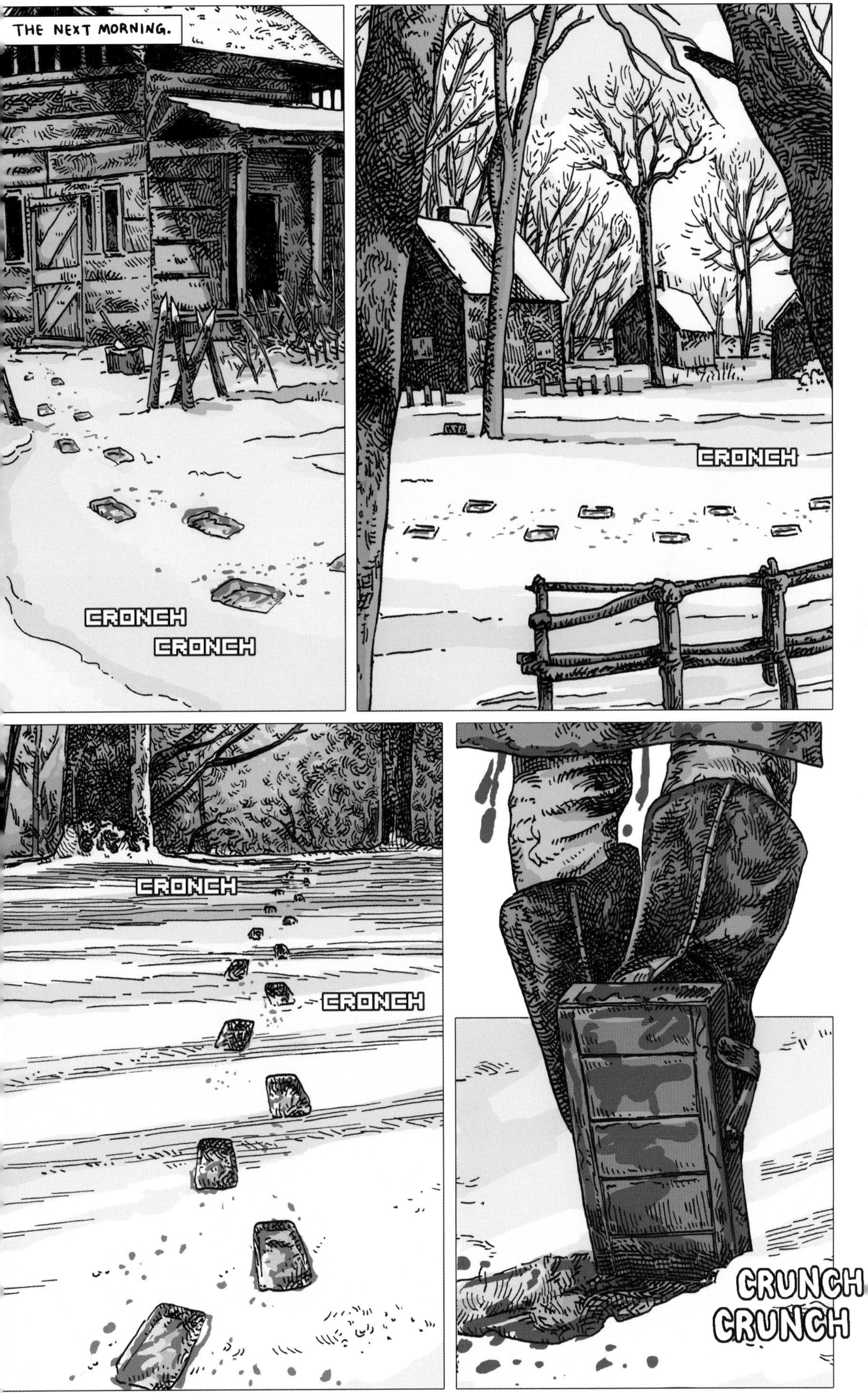
THE NEXT MORNING.
CRONCH
CRONCH
CRONCH
CRONCH
CRONCH
CRUNCH
CRUNCH

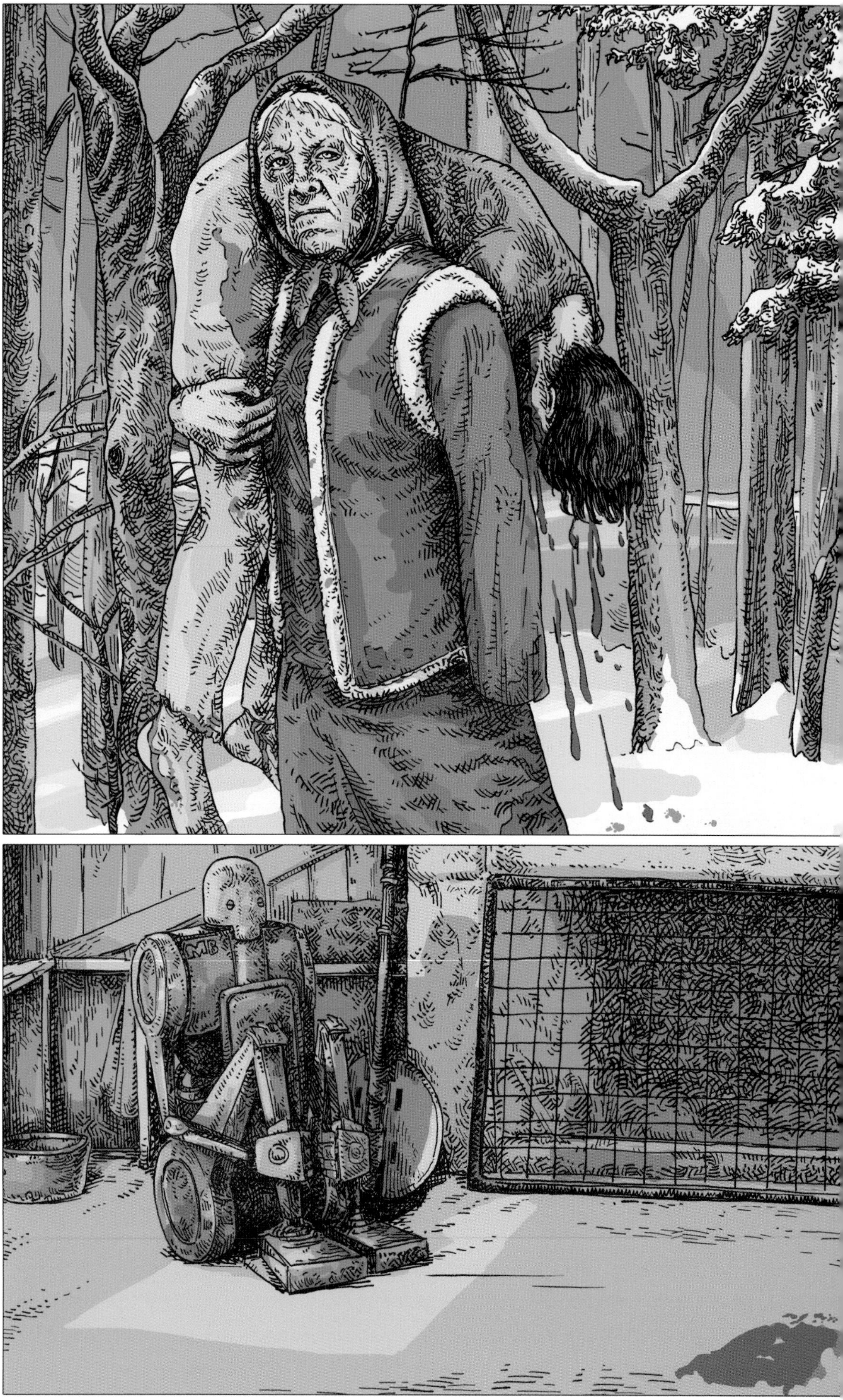
MB

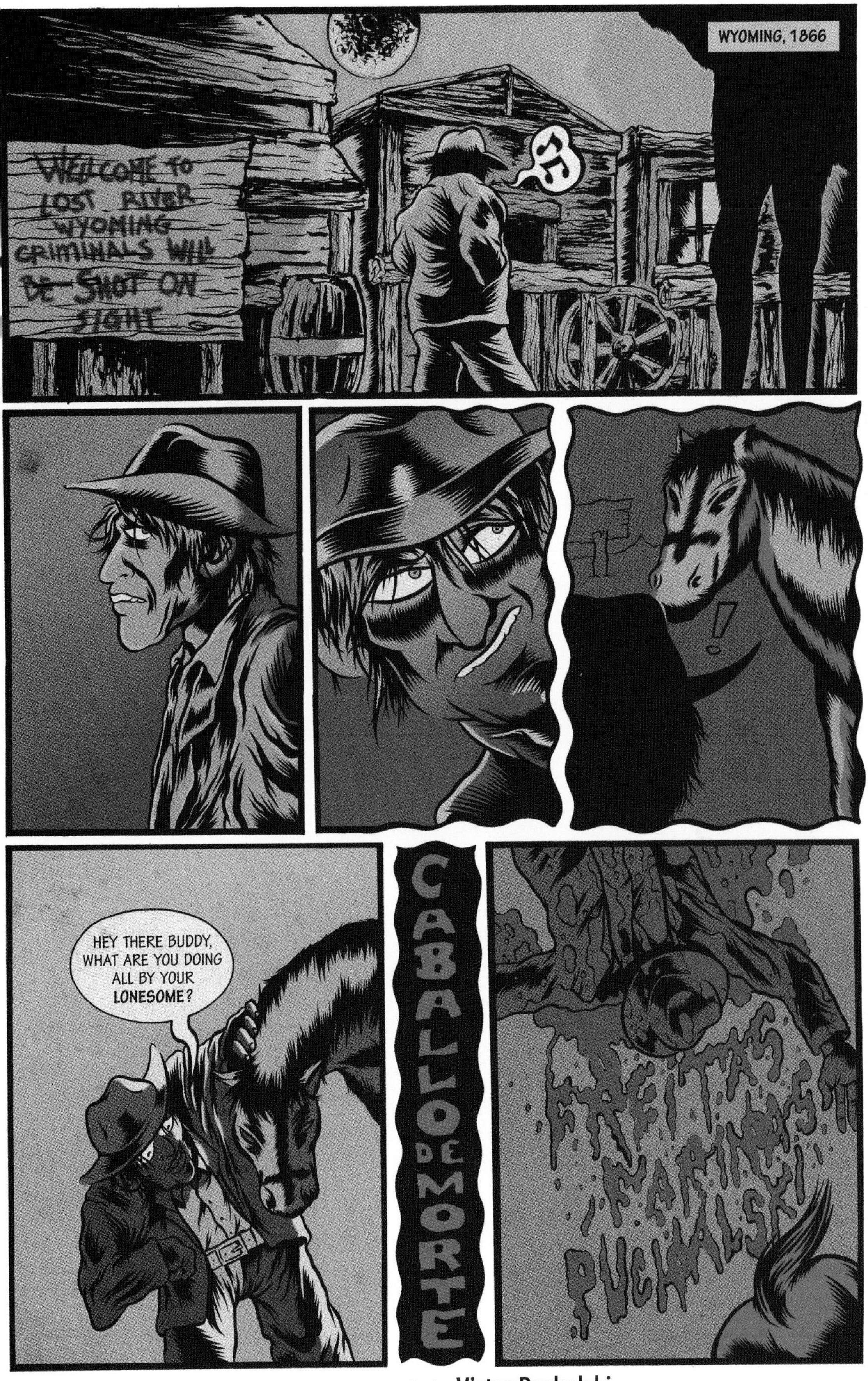
WYOMING, 1866
WELCOME TO LOST RIVER WYOMING CRIMINALS WILL BE SHOT ON SIGHT
!
HEY THERE BUDDY, WHAT ARE YOU DOING ALL BY YOUR LONESOME?
CABALLO DE MORTE
FREITAS FARINSKI PUCHALSKI

Art by Victor Puchalski

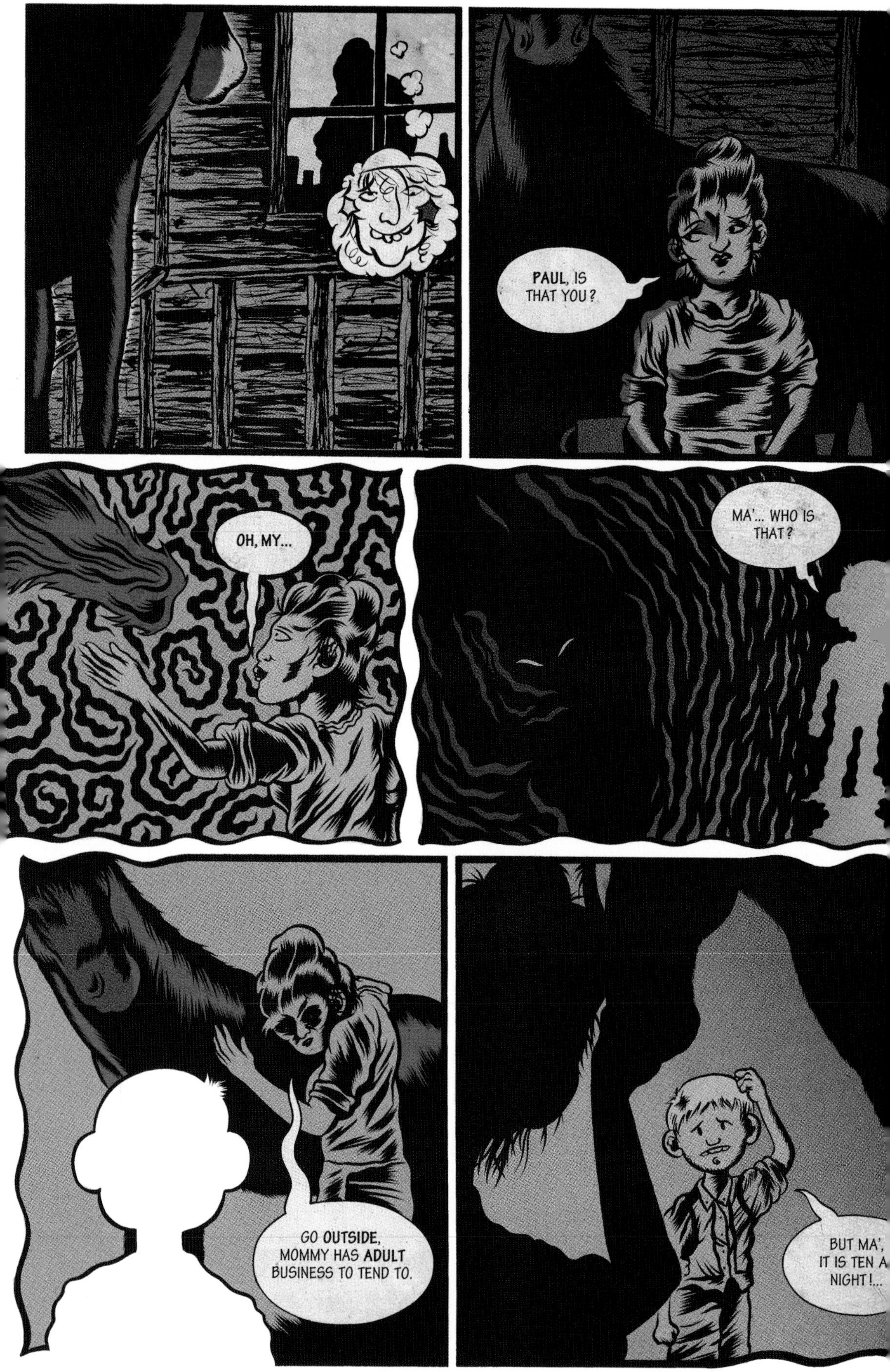
PAUL, IS THAT YOU?
OH, MY...
MA'... WHO IS THAT?
GO OUTSIDE, MOMMY HAS ADULT BUSINESS TO TEND TO.
BUT MA', IT IS TEN A NIGHT!...

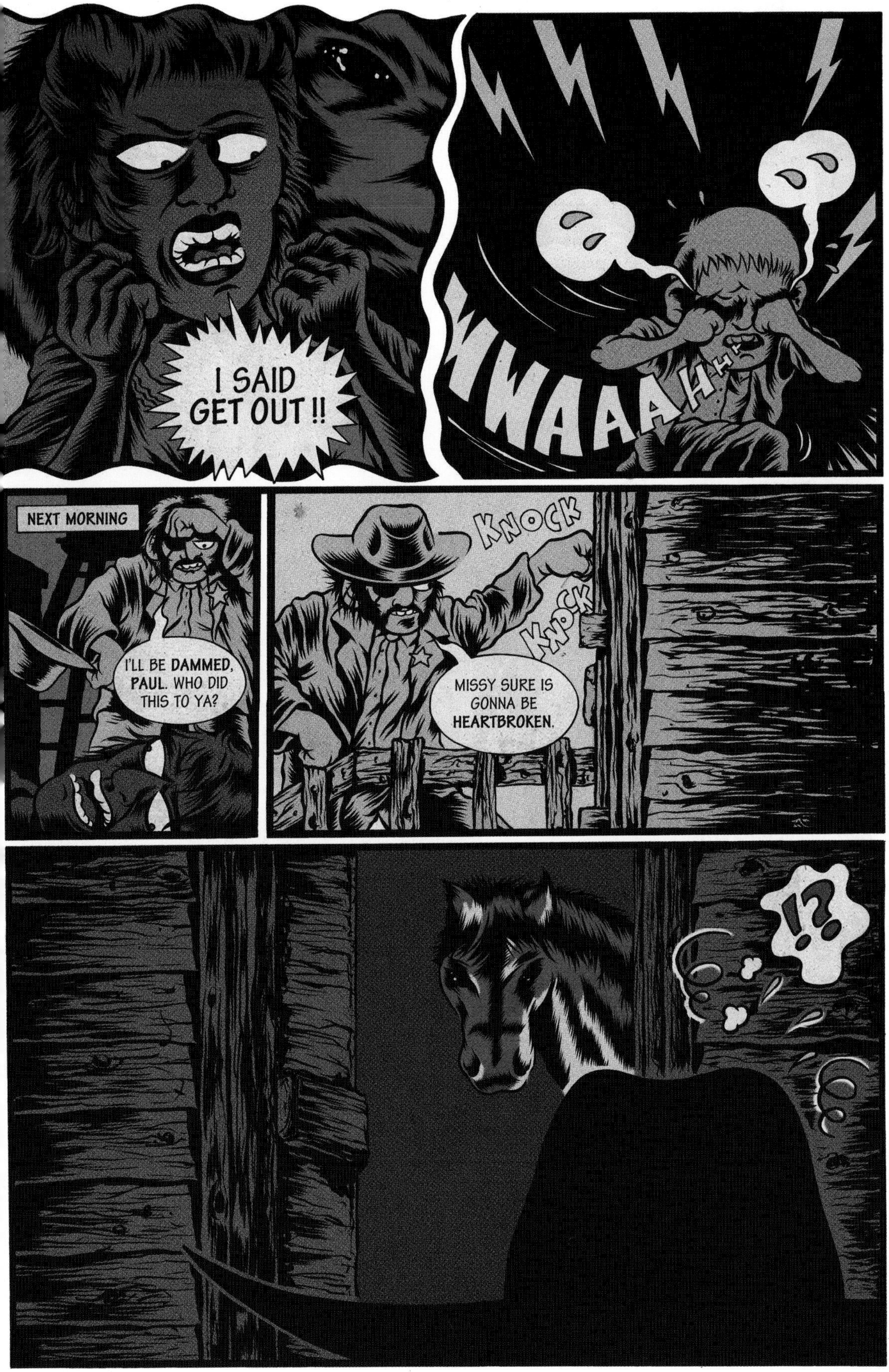
I SAID GET OUT !!
WWAAAAHHH
NEXT MORNING
I'LL BE DAMMED, PAUL. WHO DID THIS TO YA?
KNOCK
KNOCK
MISSY SURE IS GONNA BE HEARTBROKEN.
!?

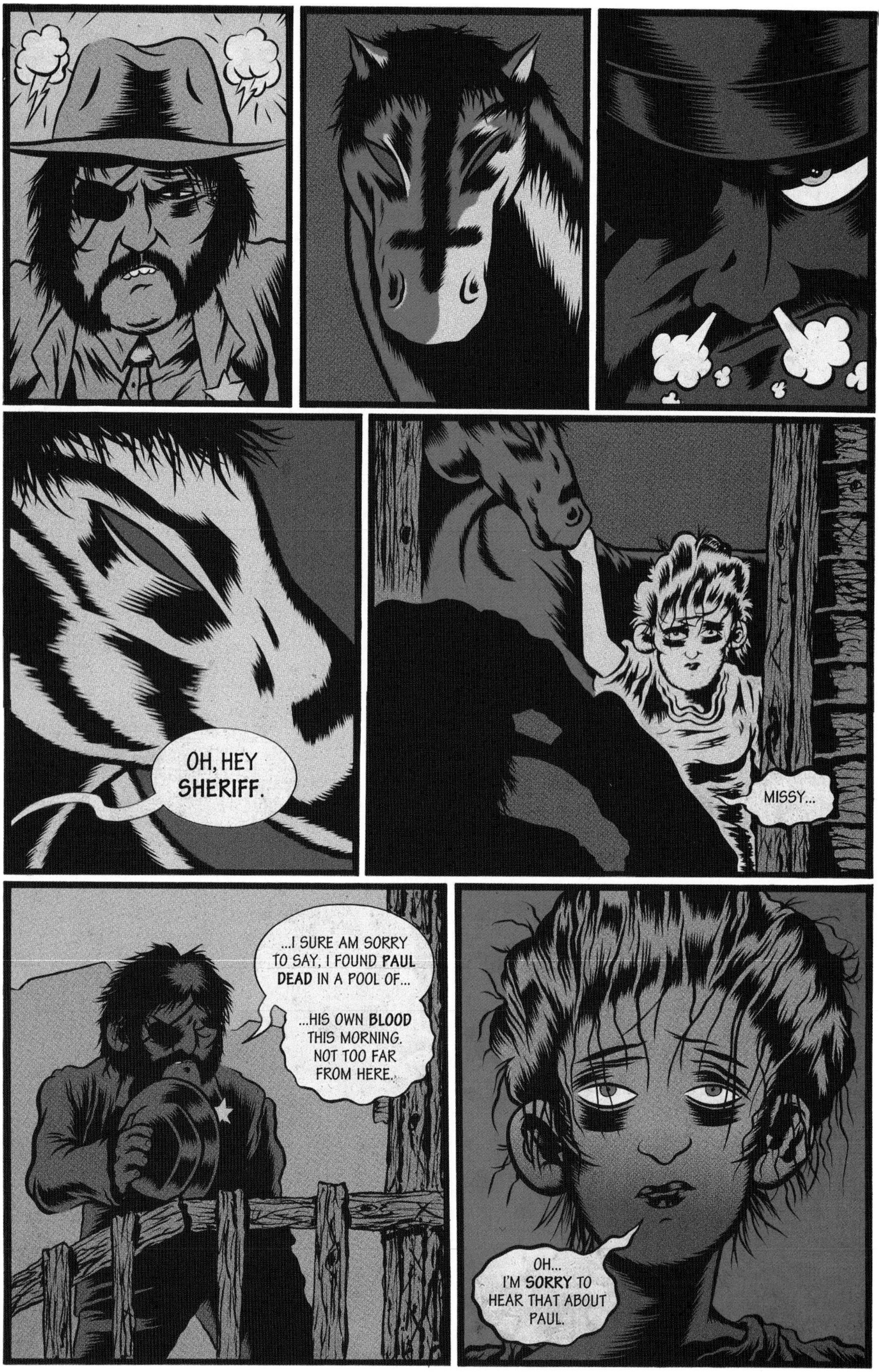
OH, HEY SHERIFF.
MISSY...
...I SURE AM SORRY TO SAY, I FOUND PAUL DEAD IN A POOL OF...
...HIS OWN BLOOD THIS MORNING. NOT TOO FAR FROM HERE.
OH... I'M SORRY TO HEAR THAT ABOUT PAUL.

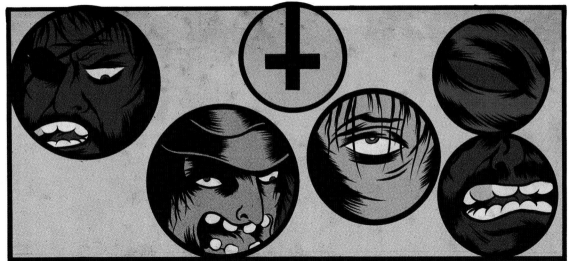

WHY IS THERE A **GOD DAMN HORSE** IN YOUR HOUSE, MISSY !!? I'M TRYING TO FIGURE OUT WHY YOUR HUSBAND IS **DEAD** AND...

...

...I GOT THIS **GOD DAMN HORSE** STARING HOLES THROUGH ME LIKE I **STOLE** SOMETHING FROM **HIM** !!

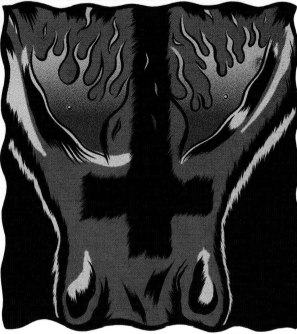

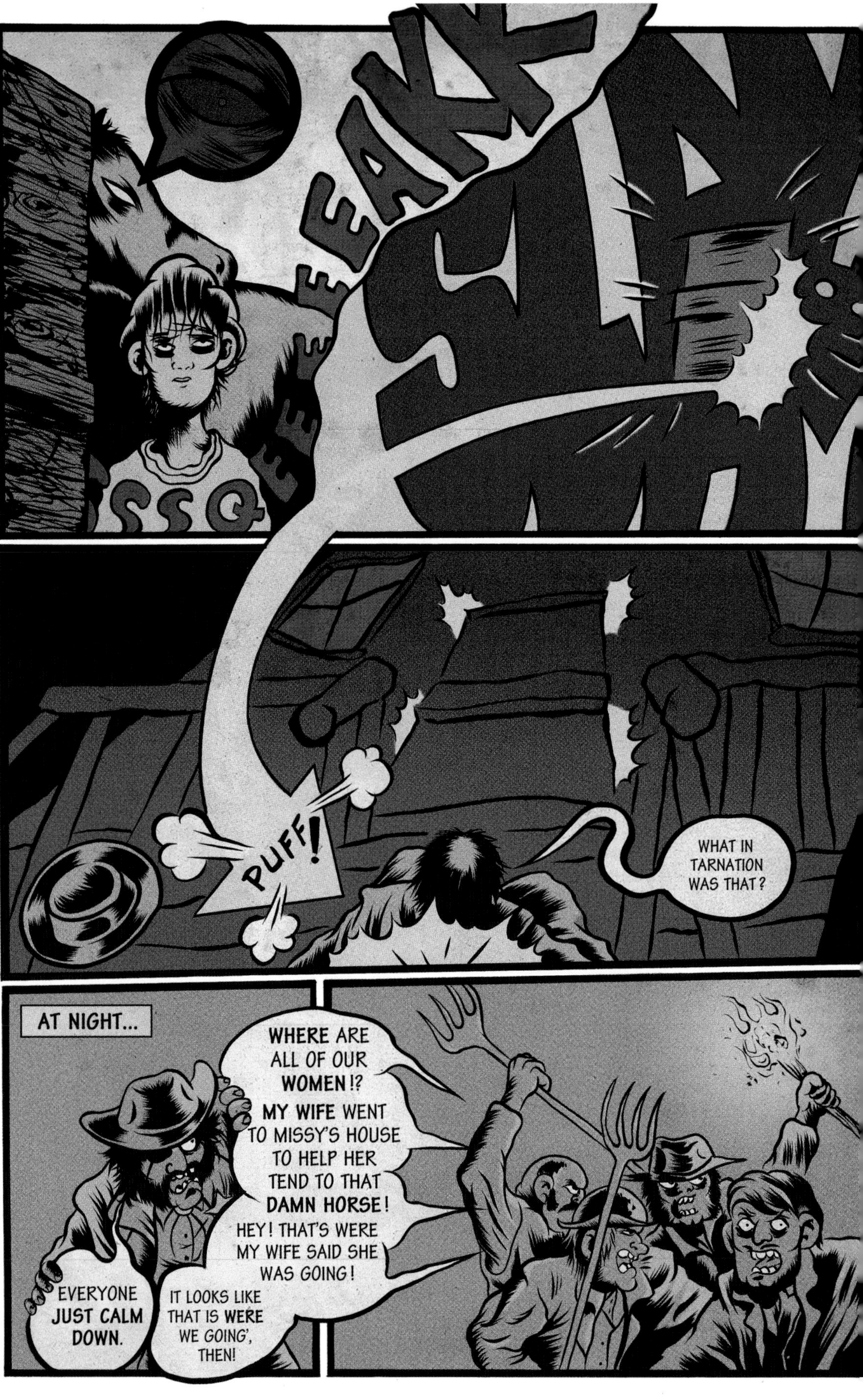
PUFF!
WHAT IN TARNATION WAS THAT?
AT NIGHT...
WHERE ARE ALL OF OUR WOMEN!?
MY WIFE WENT TO MISSY'S HOUSE TO HELP HER TEND TO THAT DAMN HORSE!
HEY! THAT'S WERE MY WIFE SAID SHE WAS GOING!
EVERYONE JUST CALM DOWN.
IT LOOKS LIKE THAT IS WERE WE GOING', THEN!

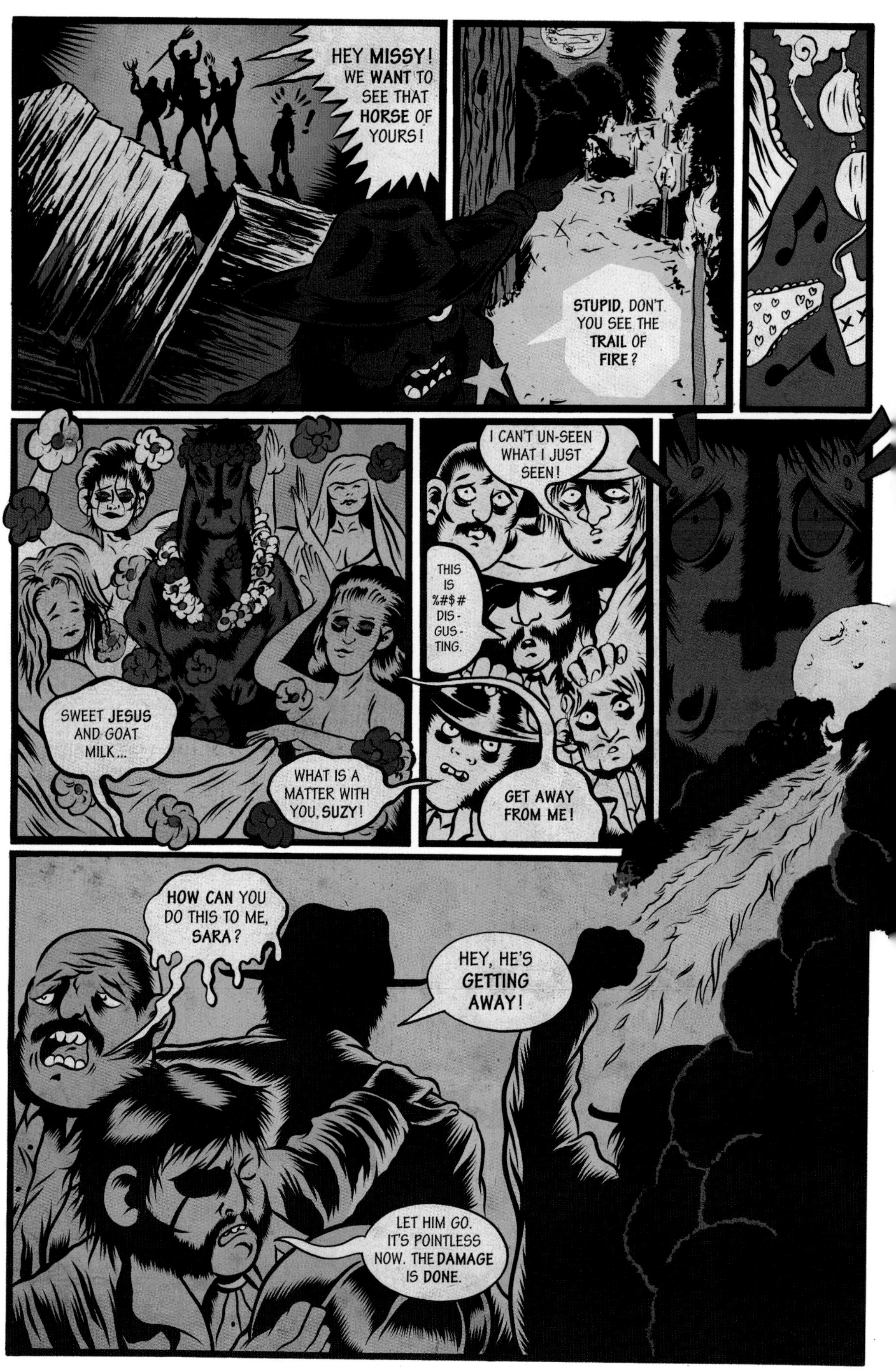

HEY MISSY! WE WANT TO SEE THAT HORSE OF YOURS!
STUPID, DON'T YOU SEE THE TRAIL OF FIRE?
SWEET JESUS AND GOAT MILK...
WHAT IS A MATTER WITH YOU, SUZY!
I CAN'T UN-SEEN WHAT I JUST SEEN!
THIS IS %#$# DIS-GUS-TING.
GET AWAY FROM ME!
HOW CAN YOU DO THIS TO ME, SARA?
HEY, HE'S GETTING AWAY!
LET HIM GO. IT'S POINTLESS NOW. THE DAMAGE IS DONE.

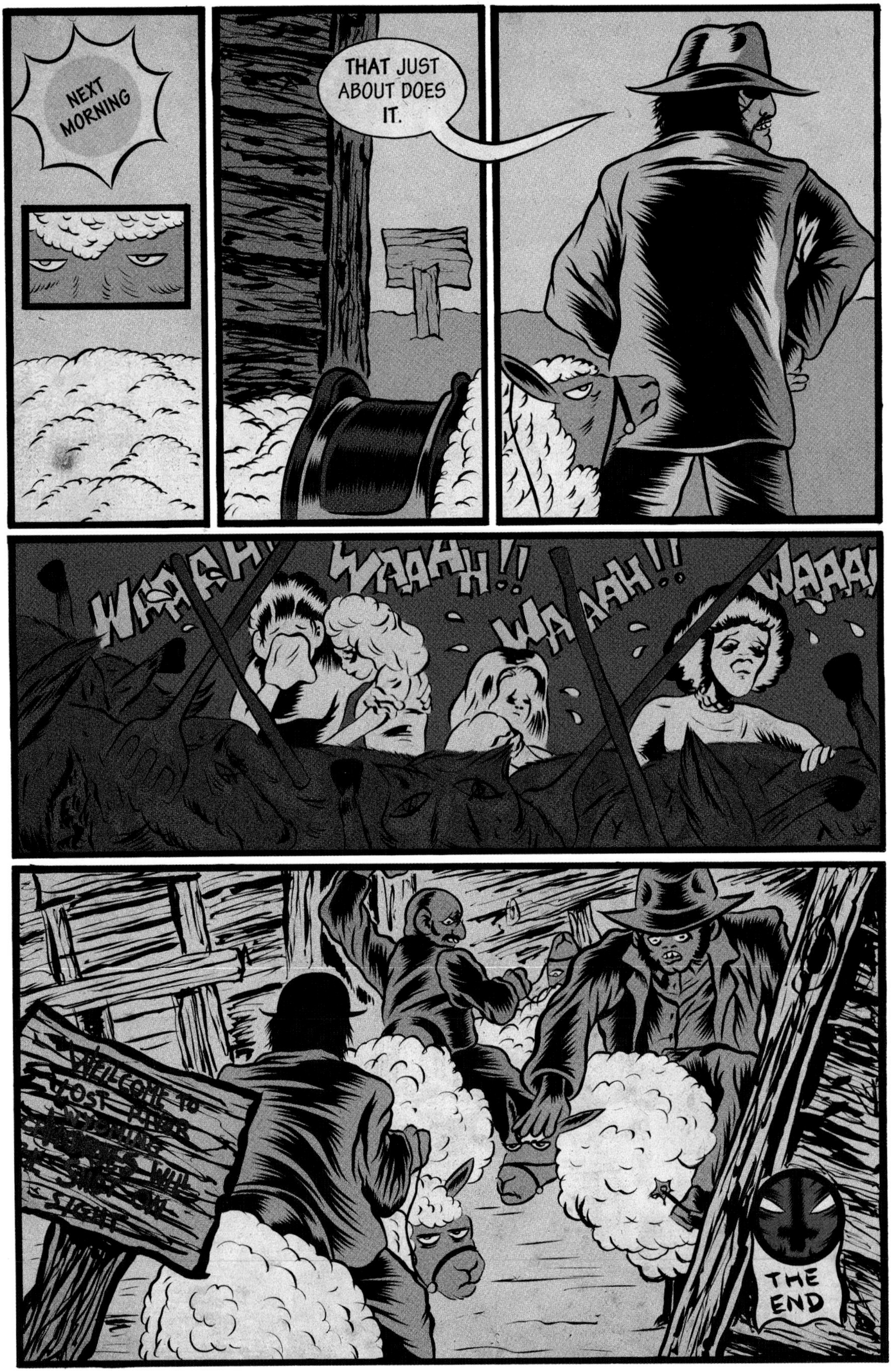
NEXT MORNING
THAT JUST ABOUT DOES IT.
WAAAH!!
WAAAH!!
WELCOME TO
LOST RIVER
WILL
ON
SIGHT
THE END

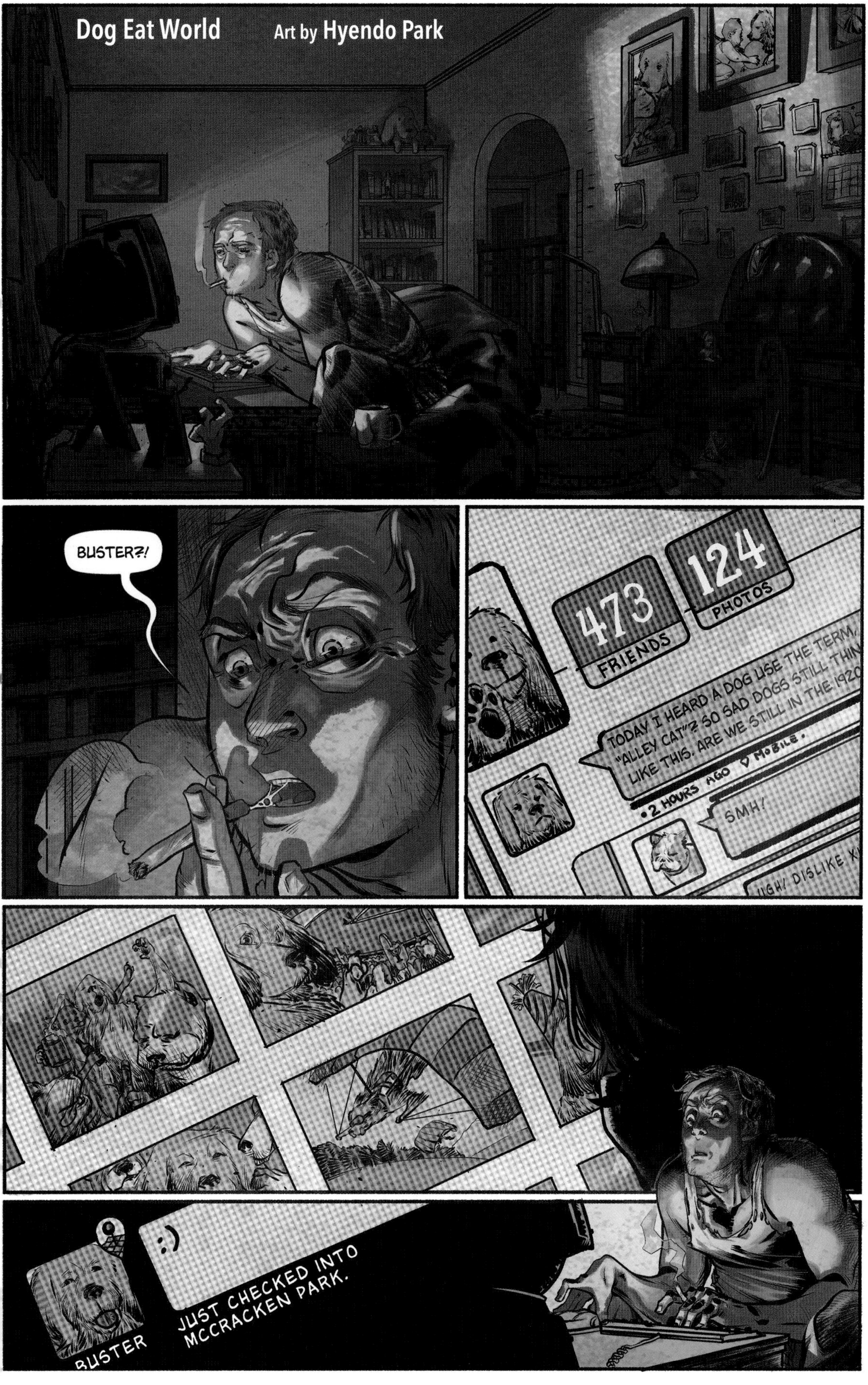
Dog Eat World
Art by Hyendo Park
BUSTER?!
473
FRIENDS
124
PHOTOS
TODAY I HEARD A DOG USE THE TERM, "ALLEY CAT"? SO SAD DOGS STILL THIN LIKE THIS. ARE WE STILL IN THE 1920
•2 HOURS AGO ♡ MOBILE.
SMH!
UGH! DISLIKE
:)
JUST CHECKED INTO MCCRACKEN PARK.
BUSTER

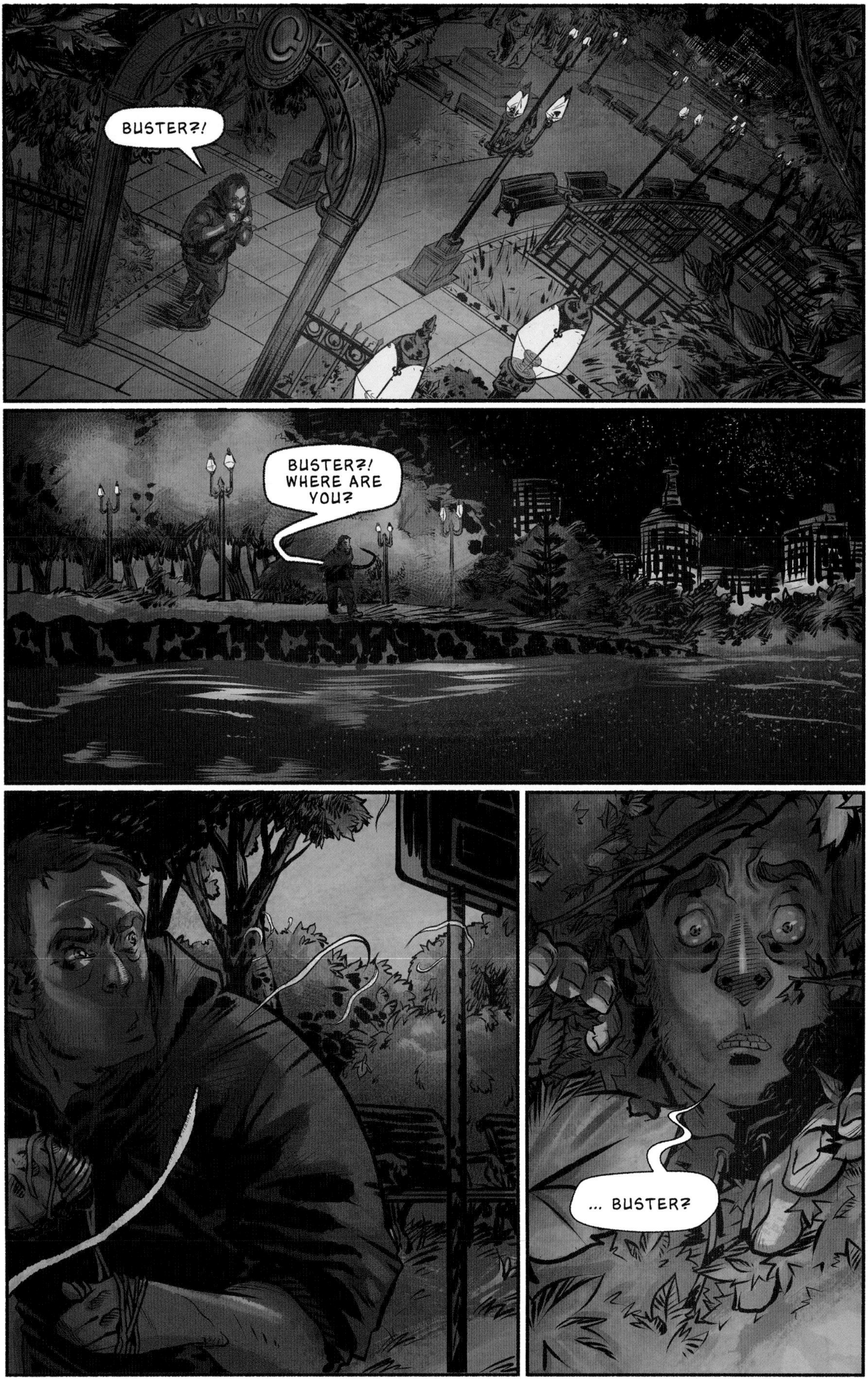
BUSTER?!
BUSTER?! WHERE ARE YOU?
... BUSTER?

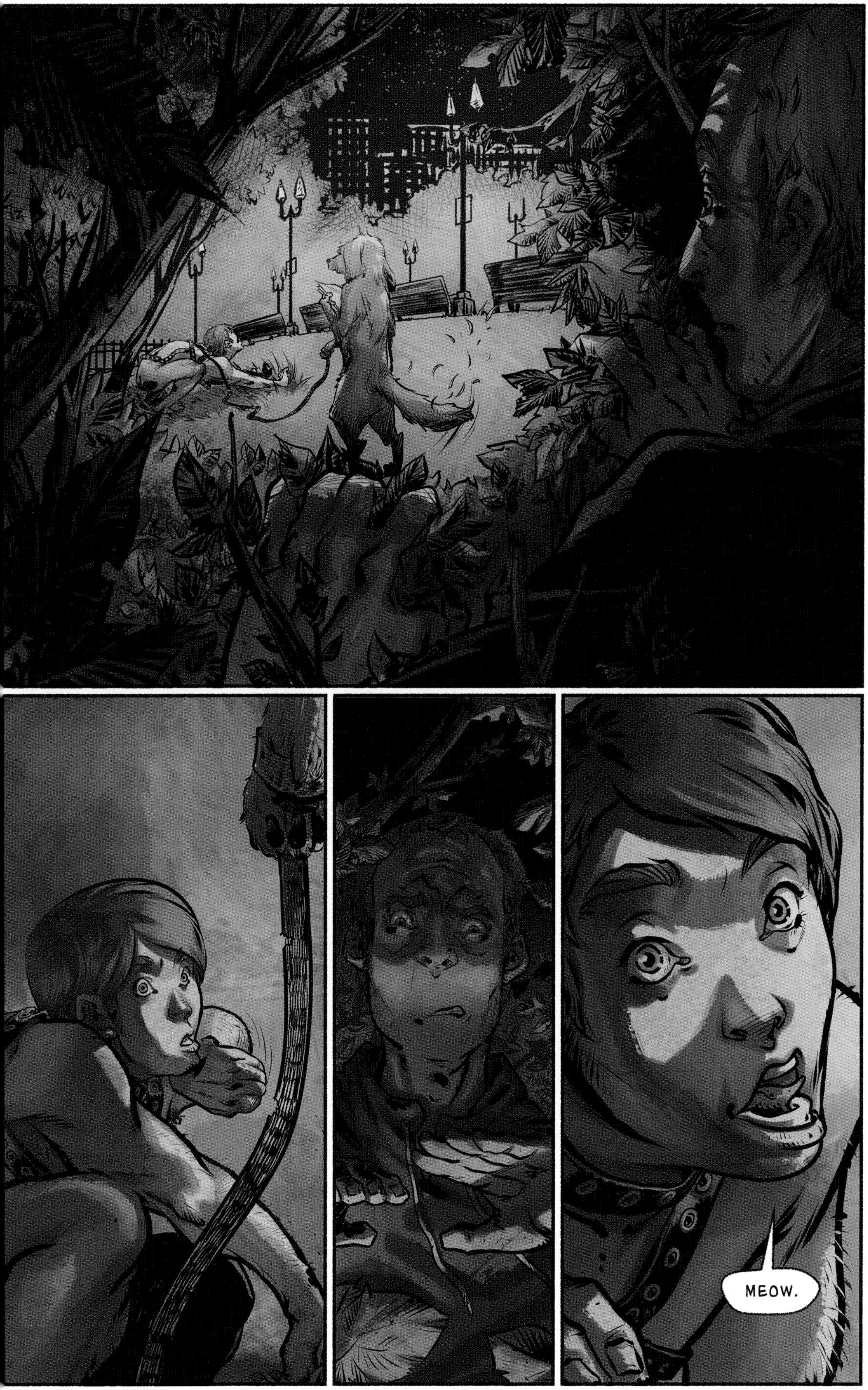
MEOW.

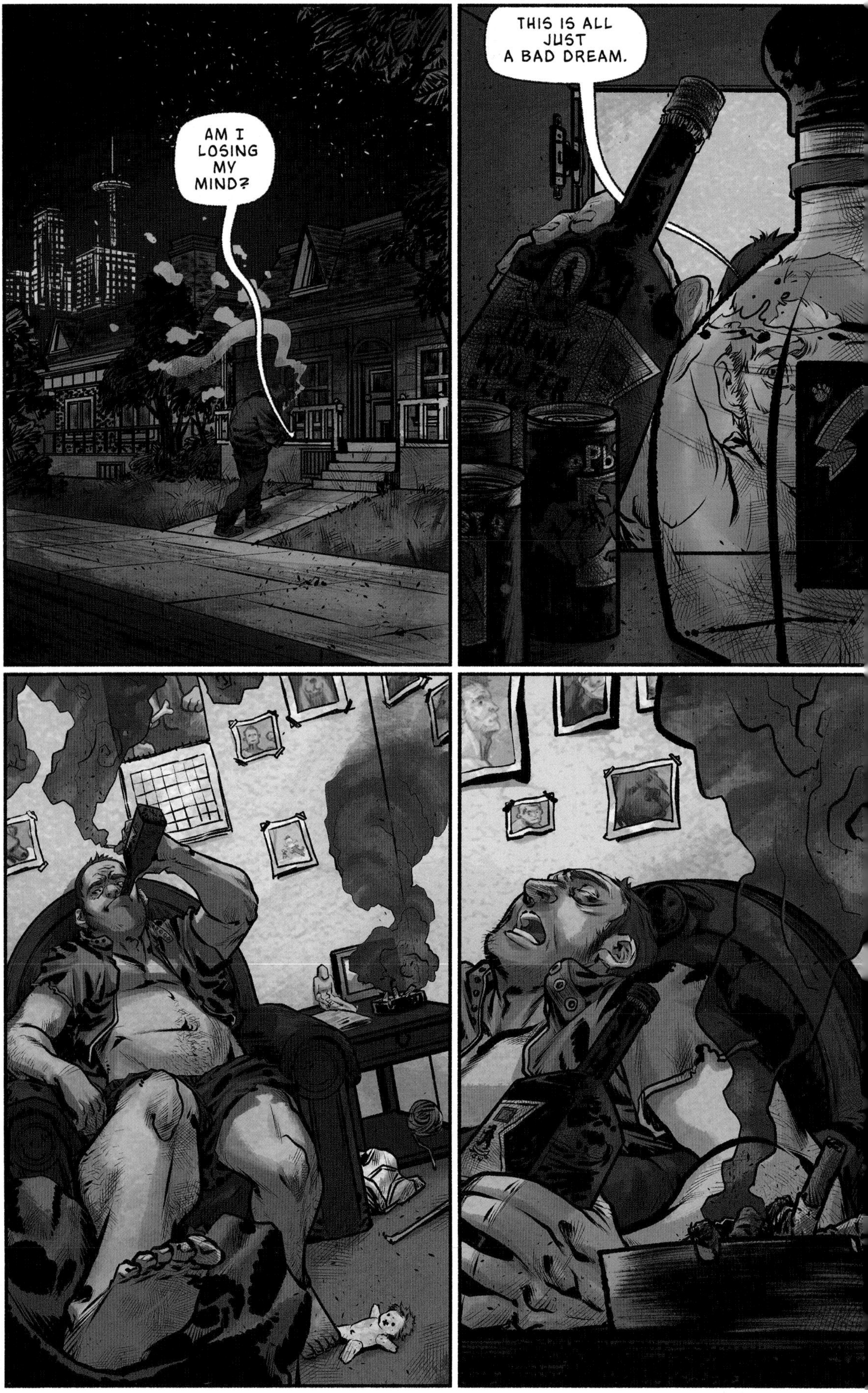
AM I LOSING MY MIND?
THIS IS ALL JUST A BAD DREAM.

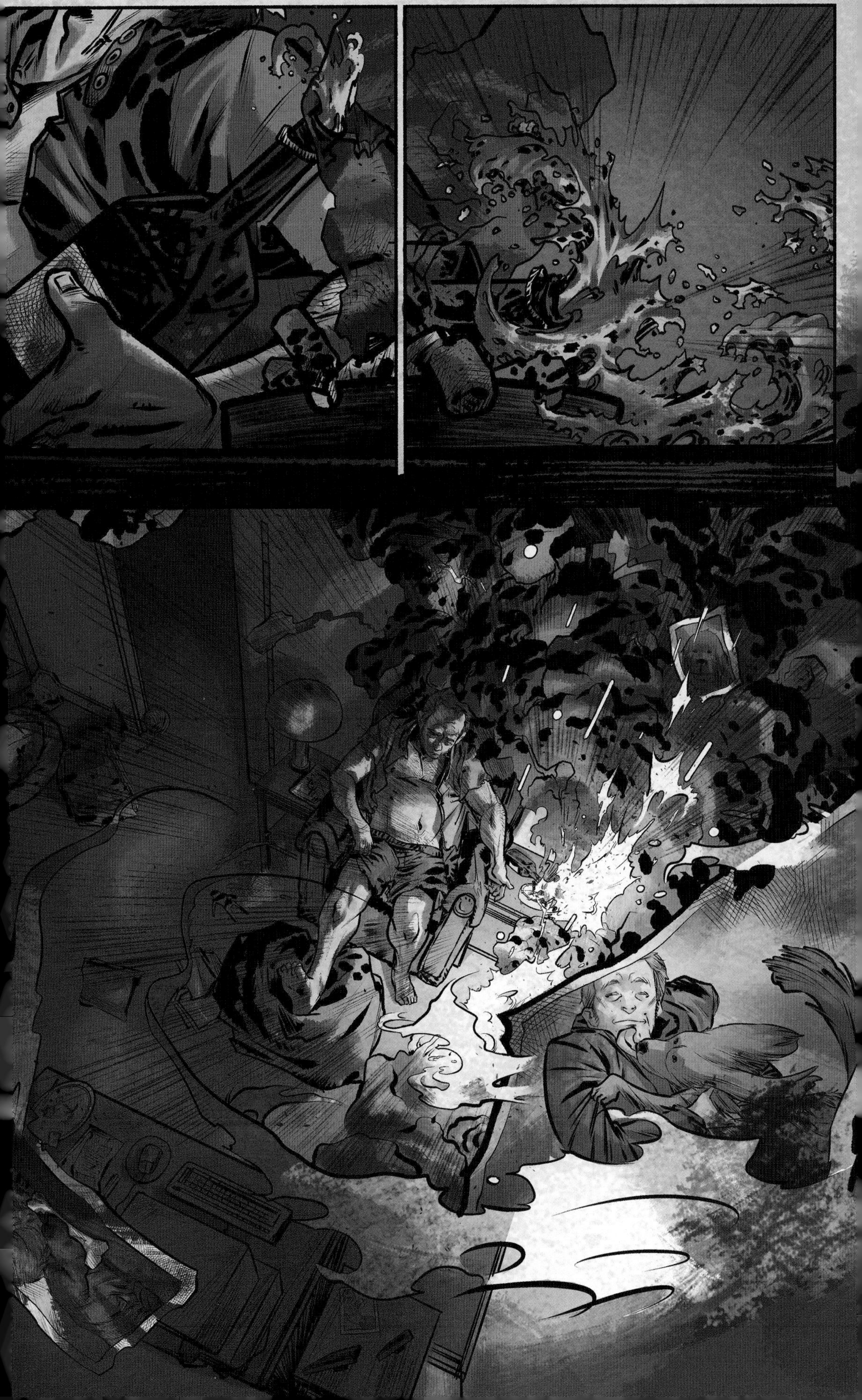

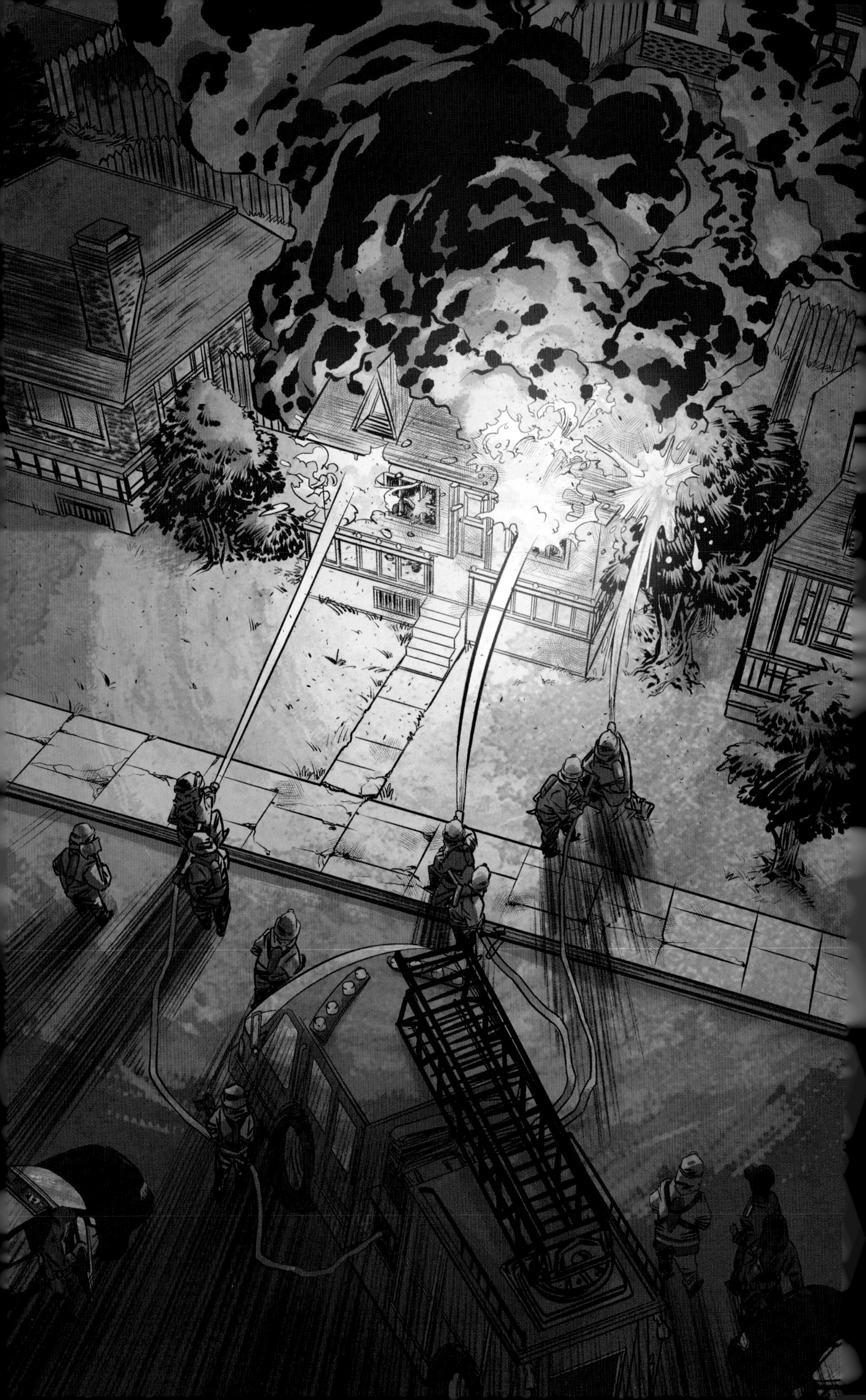

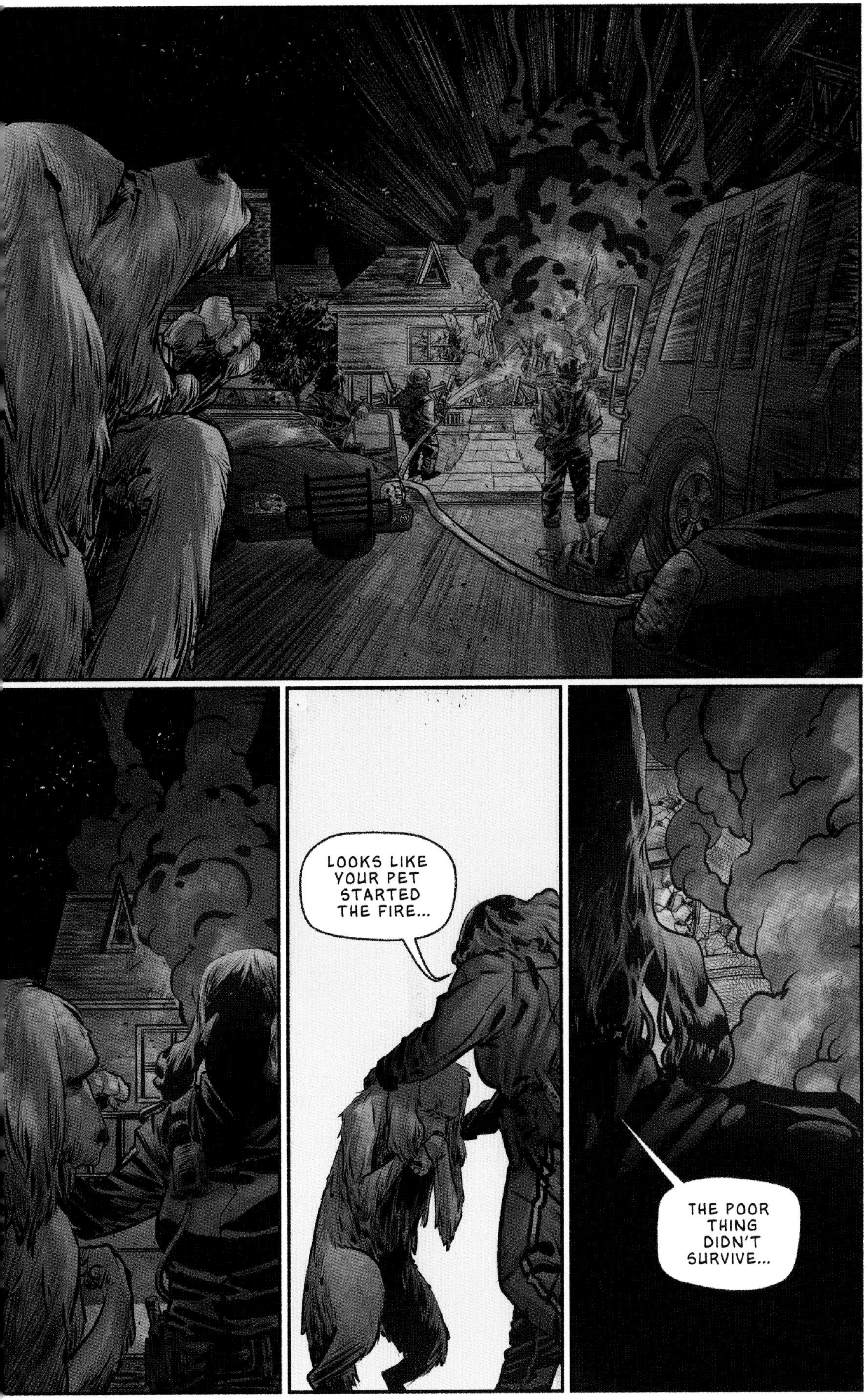
LOOKS LIKE YOUR PET STARTED THE FIRE...
THE POOR THING DIDN'T SURVIVE...

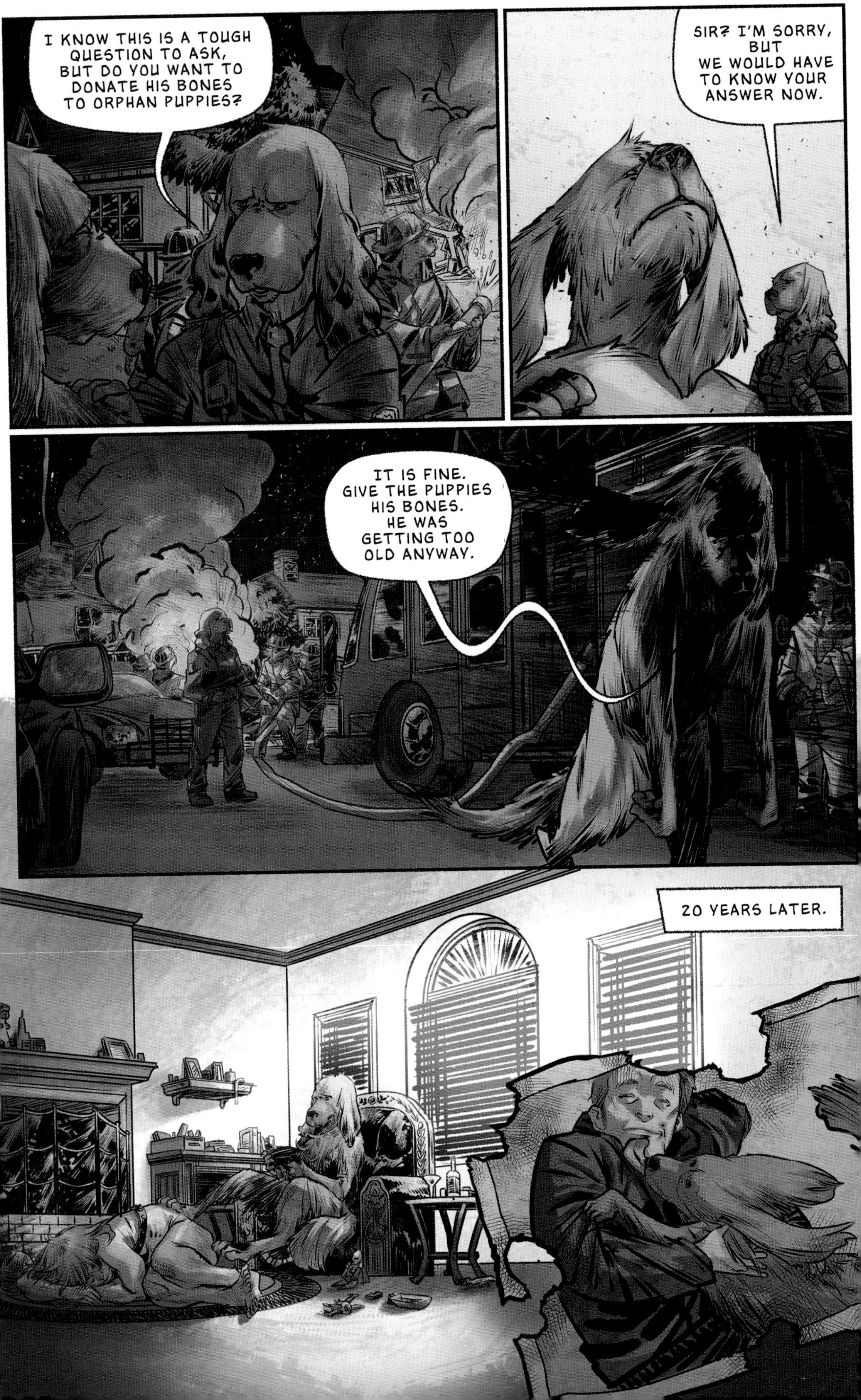
I KNOW THIS IS A TOUGH QUESTION TO ASK, BUT DO YOU WANT TO DONATE HIS BONES TO ORPHAN PUPPIES?
SIR? I'M SORRY, BUT WE WOULD HAVE TO KNOW YOUR ANSWER NOW.
IT IS FINE. GIVE THE PUPPIES HIS BONES. HE WAS GETTING TOO OLD ANYWAY.
20 YEARS LATER.

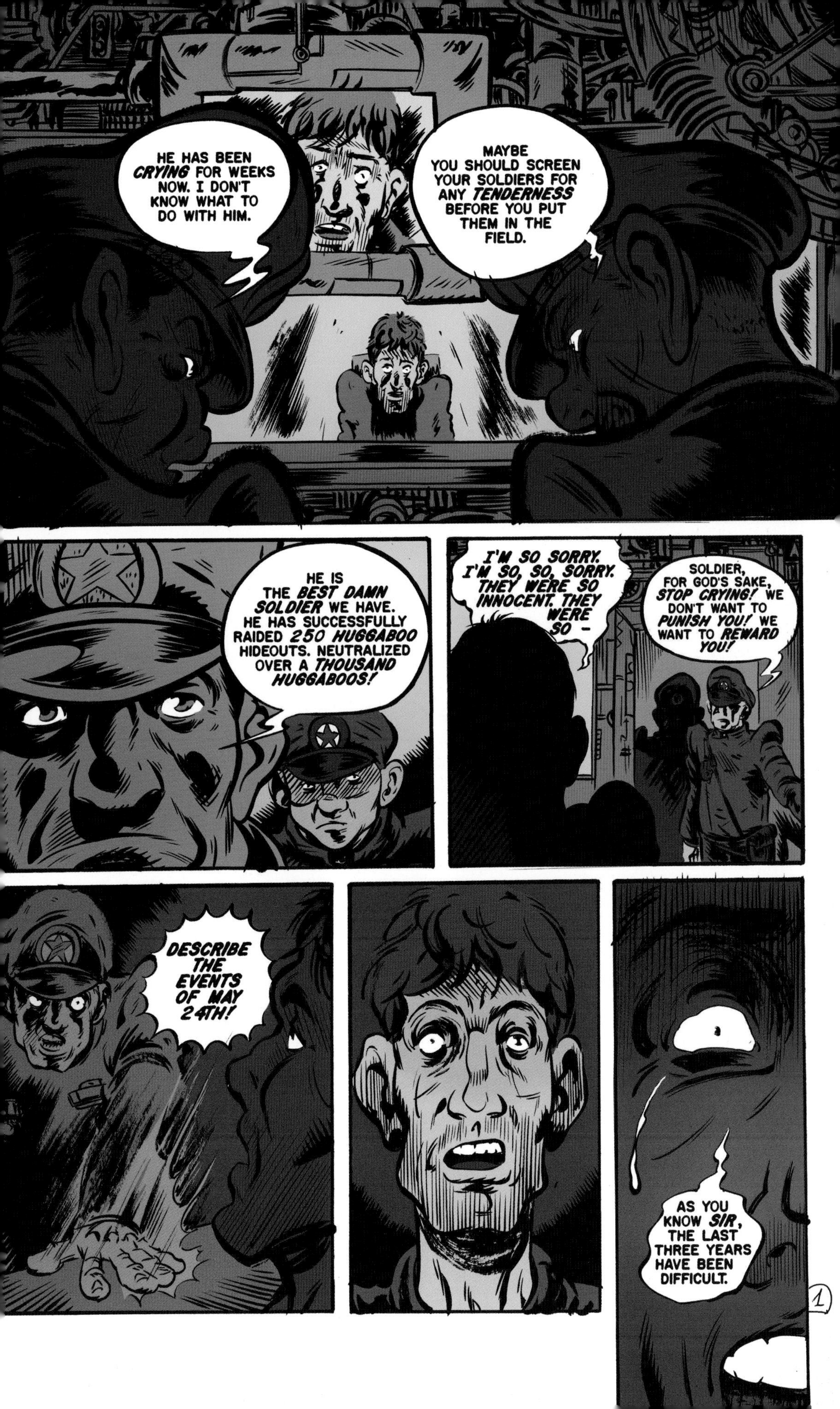

HE HAS BEEN CRYING FOR WEEKS NOW. I DON'T KNOW WHAT TO DO WITH HIM.
MAYBE YOU SHOULD SCREEN YOUR SOLDIERS FOR ANY TENDERNESS BEFORE YOU PUT THEM IN THE FIELD.
HE IS THE BEST DAMN SOLDIER WE HAVE. HE HAS SUCCESSFULLY RAIDED 250 HUGGABOO HIDEOUTS. NEUTRALIZED OVER A THOUSAND HUGGABOOS!
I'M SO SORRY. I'M SO, SO, SORRY. THEY WERE SO INNOCENT. THEY WERE SO -
SOLDIER, FOR GOD'S SAKE, STOP CRYING! WE DON'T WANT TO PUNISH YOU! WE WANT TO REWARD YOU!
DESCRIBE THE EVENTS OF MAY 24TH!
AS YOU KNOW SIR, THE LAST THREE YEARS HAVE BEEN DIFFICULT.

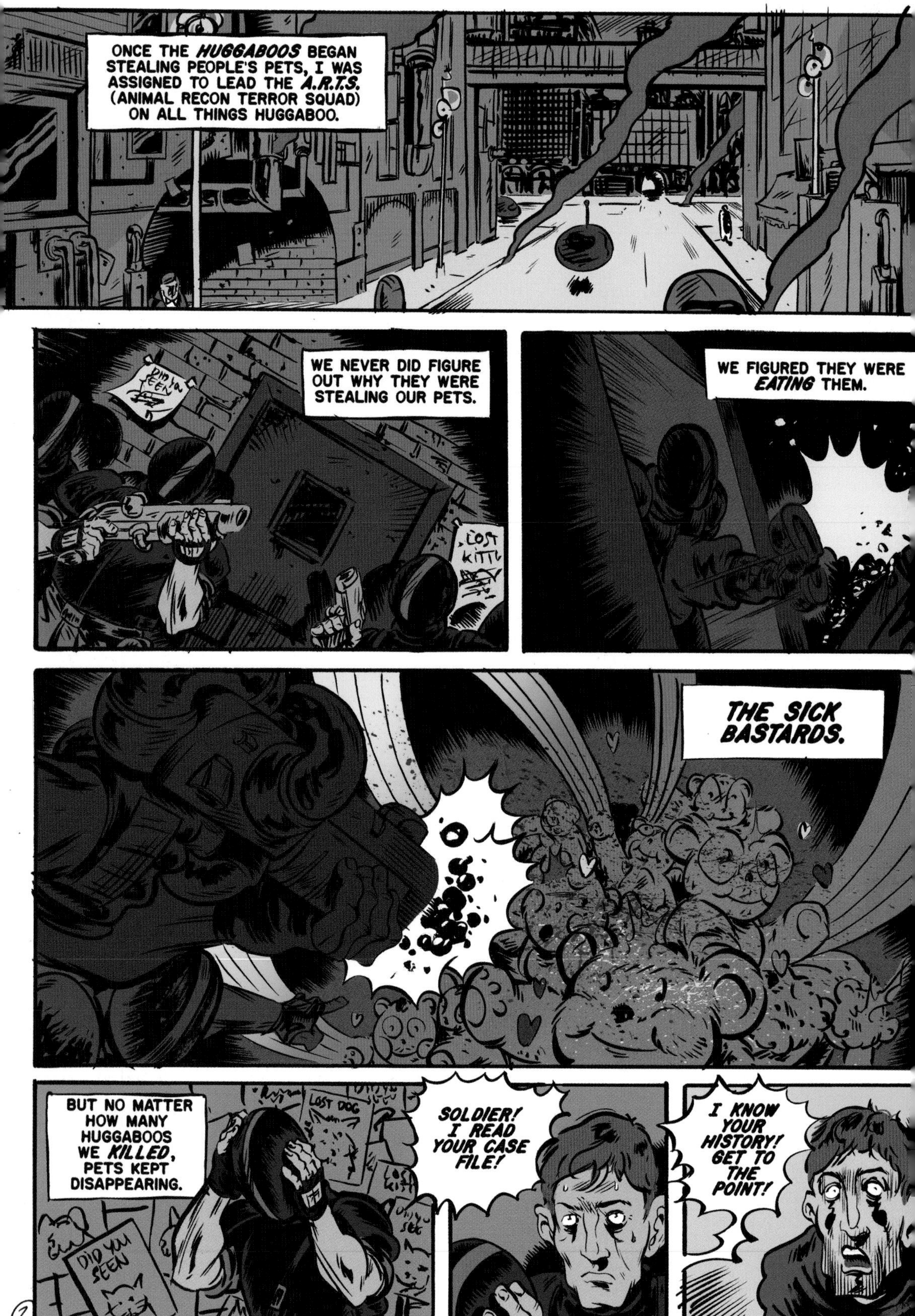
ONCE THE HUGGABOOS BEGAN STEALING PEOPLE'S PETS, I WAS ASSIGNED TO LEAD THE A.R.T.S. (ANIMAL RECON TERROR SQUAD) ON ALL THINGS HUGGABOO.
WE NEVER DID FIGURE OUT WHY THEY WERE STEALING OUR PETS.
LOST KITTY
WE FIGURED THEY WERE EATING THEM.
THE SICK BASTARDS.
BUT NO MATTER HOW MANY HUGGABOOS WE KILLED, PETS KEPT DISAPPEARING.
LOST DOG
DID YOU SEEN
SOLDIER! I READ YOUR CASE FILE!
I KNOW YOUR HISTORY! GET TO THE POINT!
2

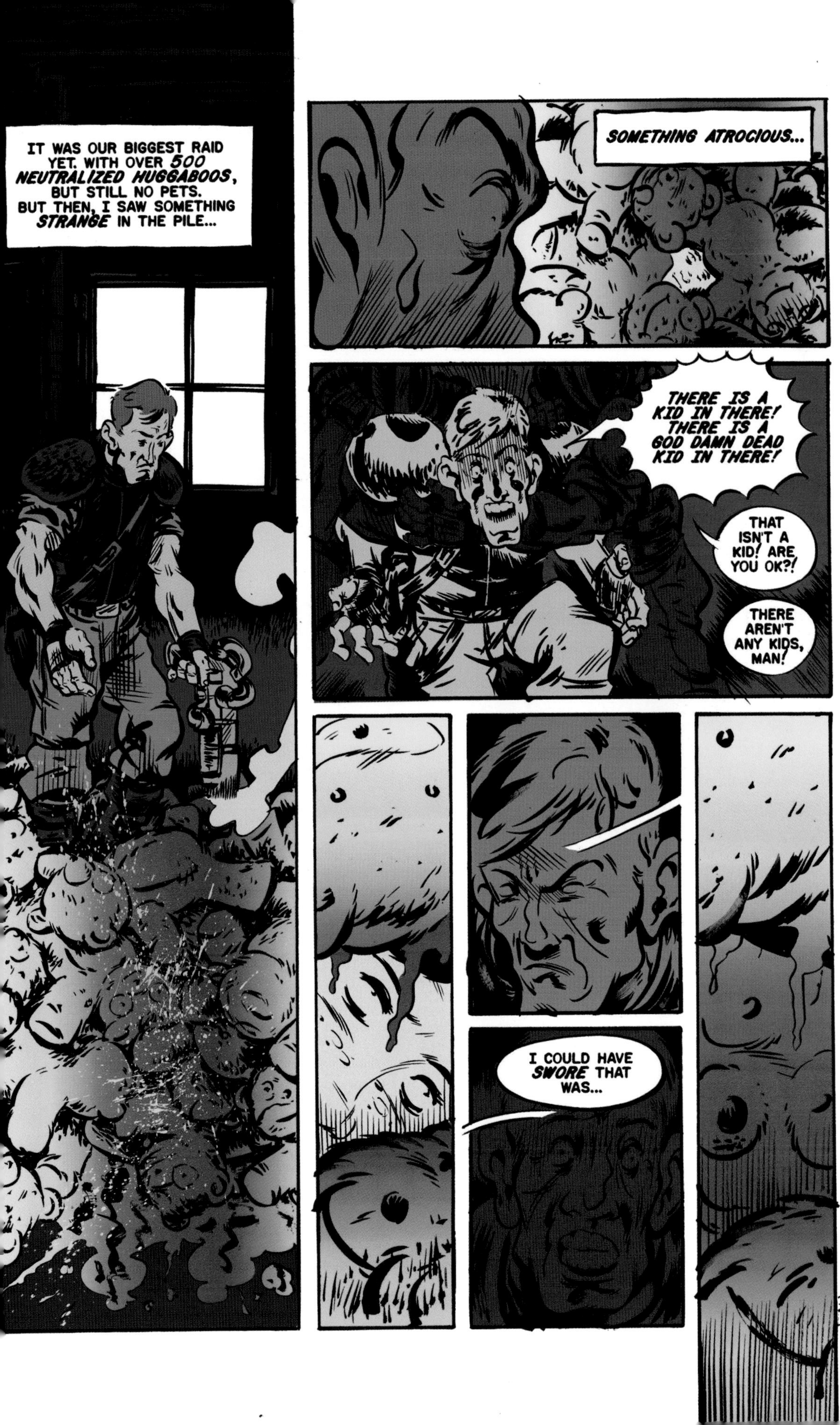
IT WAS OUR BIGGEST RAID YET. WITH OVER 500 NEUTRALIZED HUGGABOOS, BUT STILL NO PETS. BUT THEN, I SAW SOMETHING STRANGE IN THE PILE...
SOMETHING ATROCIOUS...
THERE IS A KID IN THERE! THERE IS A GOD DAMN DEAD KID IN THERE!
THAT ISN'T A KID! ARE YOU OK?!
THERE AREN'T ANY KIDS, MAN!
I COULD HAVE SWORE THAT WAS...

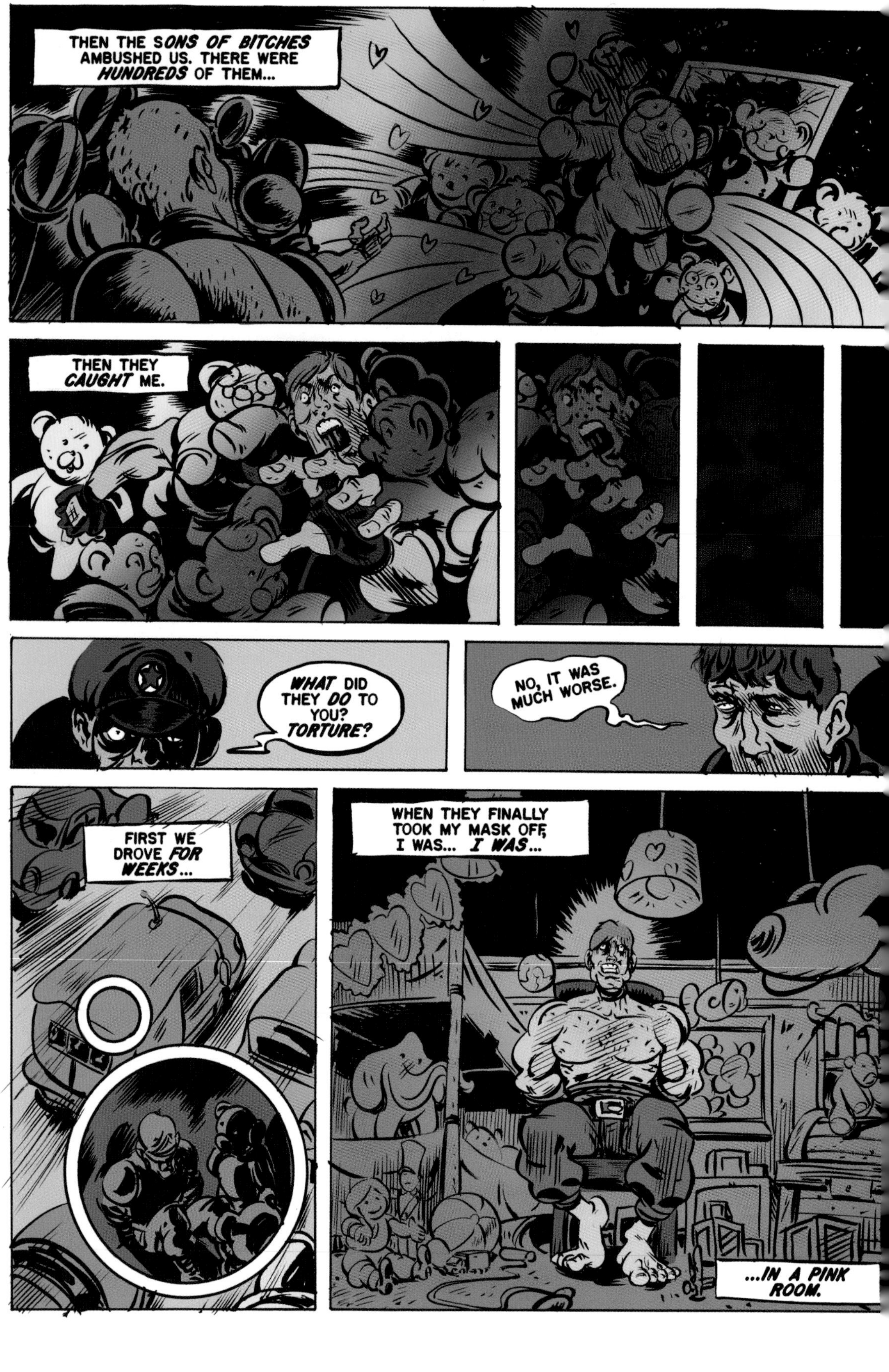
THEN THE SONS OF BITCHES AMBUSHED US. THERE WERE HUNDREDS OF THEM...
THEN THEY CAUGHT ME.
WHAT DID THEY DO TO YOU? TORTURE?
NO, IT WAS MUCH WORSE.
FIRST WE DROVE FOR WEEKS...
WHEN THEY FINALLY TOOK MY MASK OFF, I WAS... I WAS...
...IN A PINK ROOM.

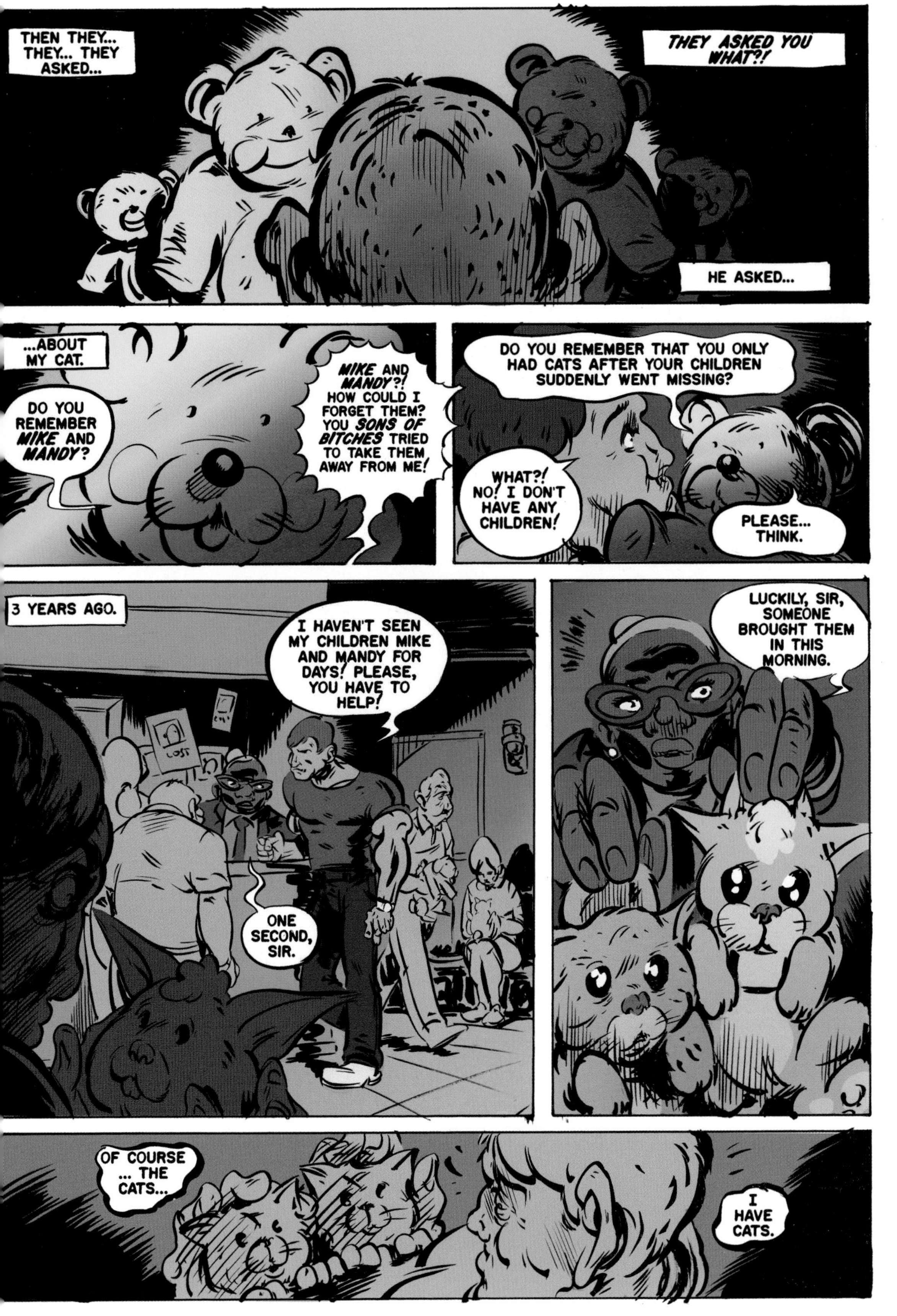
THEN THEY... THEY... THEY ASKED...
THEY ASKED YOU WHAT?!
HE ASKED...
...ABOUT MY CAT.
DO YOU REMEMBER MIKE AND MANDY?
MIKE AND MANDY?! HOW COULD I FORGET THEM? YOU SONS OF BITCHES TRIED TO TAKE THEM AWAY FROM ME!
DO YOU REMEMBER THAT YOU ONLY HAD CATS AFTER YOUR CHILDREN SUDDENLY WENT MISSING?
WHAT?! NO! I DON'T HAVE ANY CHILDREN!
PLEASE... THINK.
3 YEARS AGO.
I HAVEN'T SEEN MY CHILDREN MIKE AND MANDY FOR DAYS! PLEASE, YOU HAVE TO HELP!
LOST
ONE SECOND, SIR.
LUCKILY, SIR, SOMEONE BROUGHT THEM IN THIS MORNING.
OF COURSE ... THE CATS...
I HAVE CATS.

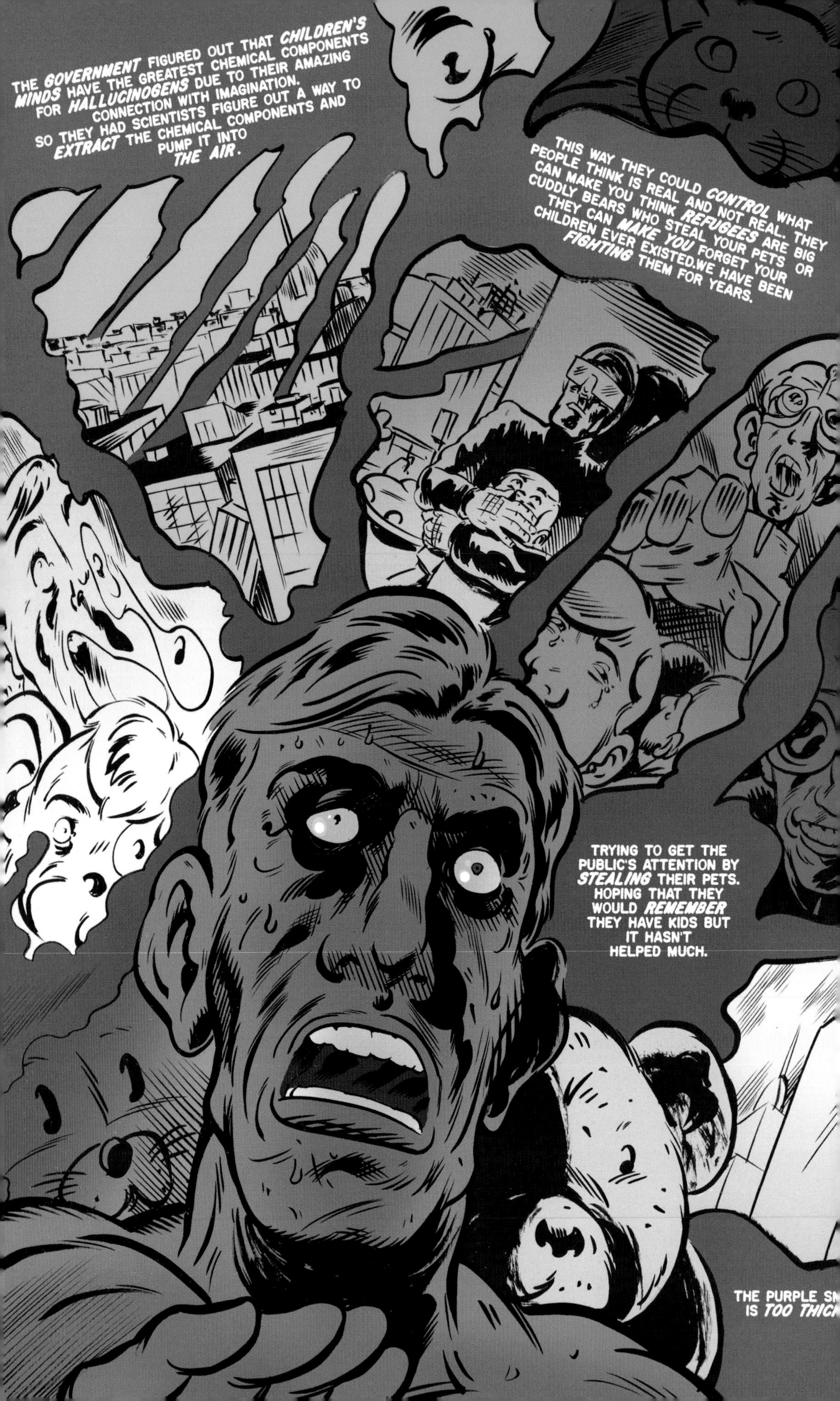
THE GOVERNMENT FIGURED OUT THAT CHILDREN'S MINDS HAVE THE GREATEST CHEMICAL COMPONENTS FOR HALLUCINOGENS DUE TO THEIR AMAZING CONNECTION WITH IMAGINATION.
SO THEY HAD SCIENTISTS FIGURE OUT A WAY TO EXTRACT THE CHEMICAL COMPONENTS AND PUMP IT INTO THE AIR.
THIS WAY THEY COULD CONTROL WHAT PEOPLE THINK IS REAL AND NOT REAL. THEY CAN MAKE YOU THINK REFUGEES ARE BIG CUDDLY BEARS WHO STEAL YOUR PETS OR THEY CAN MAKE YOU FORGET YOUR CHILDREN EVER EXISTED.WE HAVE BEEN FIGHTING THEM FOR YEARS.
TRYING TO GET THE PUBLIC'S ATTENTION BY STEALING THEIR PETS. HOPING THAT THEY WOULD REMEMBER THEY HAVE KIDS BUT IT HASN'T HELPED MUCH.

THESE ARE *YOUR CHILDREN*. WE SAVED THEM FROM BEING TURNED INTO SMOG.

THIS CAN'T BE REAL... THIS CAN'T BE REAL. I DON'T HAVE CHILDREN. I CAN'T HAVE CHILDREN. AND ALL THE HUGGABOOS I KILLED?

THEY WERE *PEOPLE*... SOME OF THEM *KIDS*...THEY WERE ALL PART OF THE *REVOLUTION*. THEY KNEW WHAT THEY WERE SIGNING UP FOR WHEN THEY PICKED UP THAT GUN.

THIS CAN'T BE REAL... THEY CAN'T BE MY CHILDREN...

I DIDN'T KILL INNOCENT PEOPLE FOR YEARS...

ZAP!

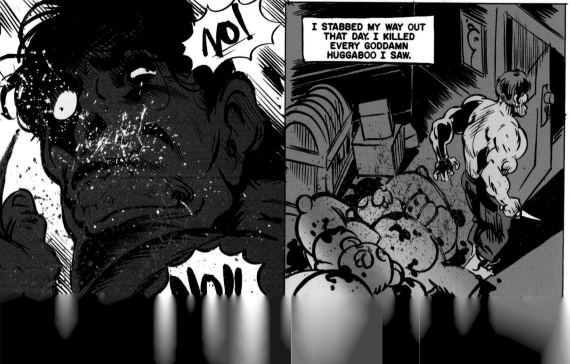

NO!

I STABBED MY WAY OUT THAT DAY. I KILLED EVERY GODDAMN HUGGABOO I SAW.

NO!!

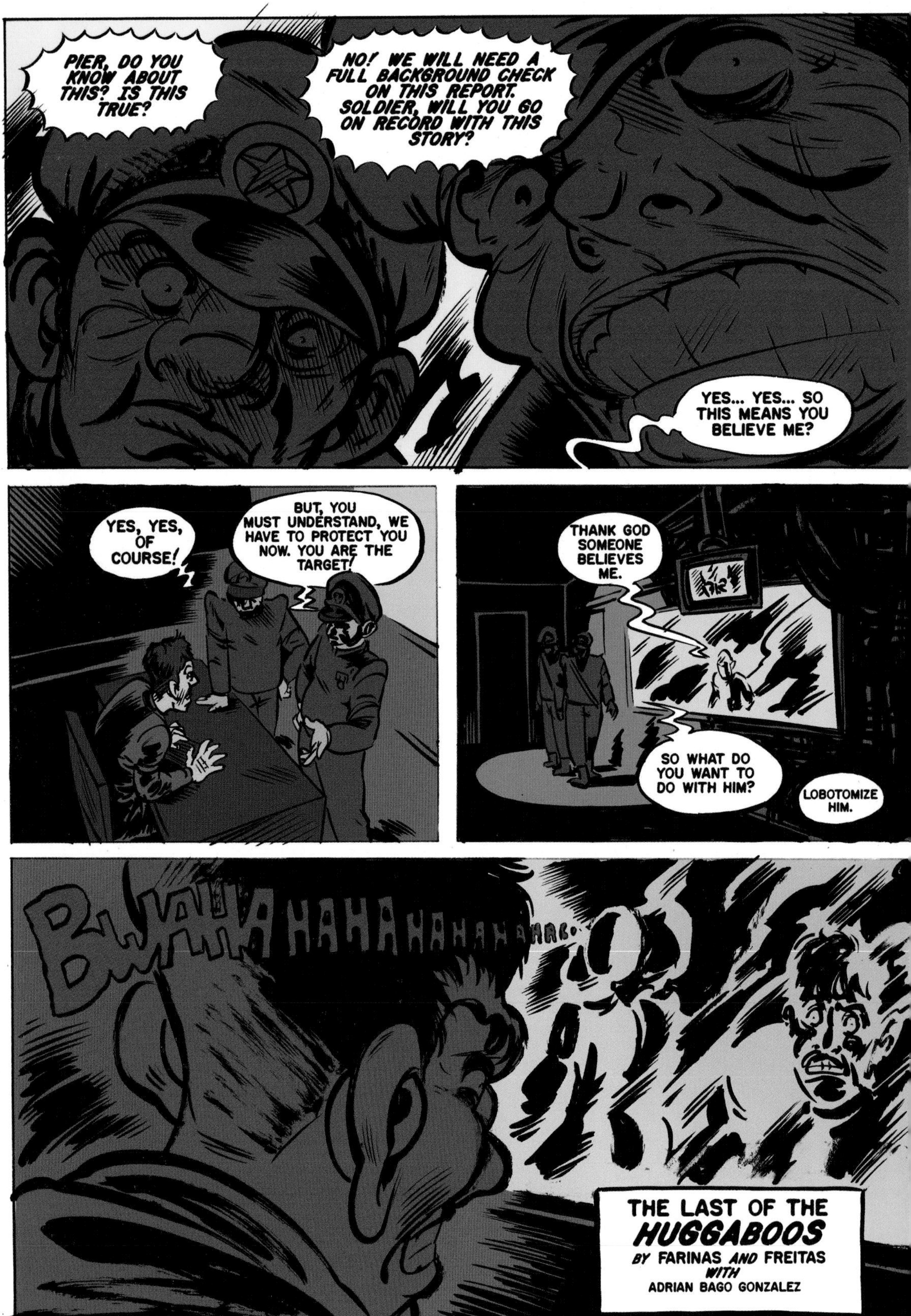

PIER, DO YOU KNOW ABOUT THIS? IS THIS TRUE?
NO! WE WILL NEED A FULL BACKGROUND CHECK ON THIS REPORT. SOLDIER, WILL YOU GO ON RECORD WITH THIS STORY?
YES... YES... SO THIS MEANS YOU BELIEVE ME?
YES, YES, OF COURSE!
BUT, YOU MUST UNDERSTAND, WE HAVE TO PROTECT YOU NOW. YOU ARE THE TARGET!
THANK GOD SOMEONE BELIEVES ME.
SO WHAT DO YOU WANT TO DO WITH HIM?
LOBOTOMIZE HIM.
BWAHAHAHAHAHAHAHAHA
THE LAST OF THE HUGGABOOS
BY FARINAS AND FREITAS
WITH
ADRIAN BAGO GONZALEZ

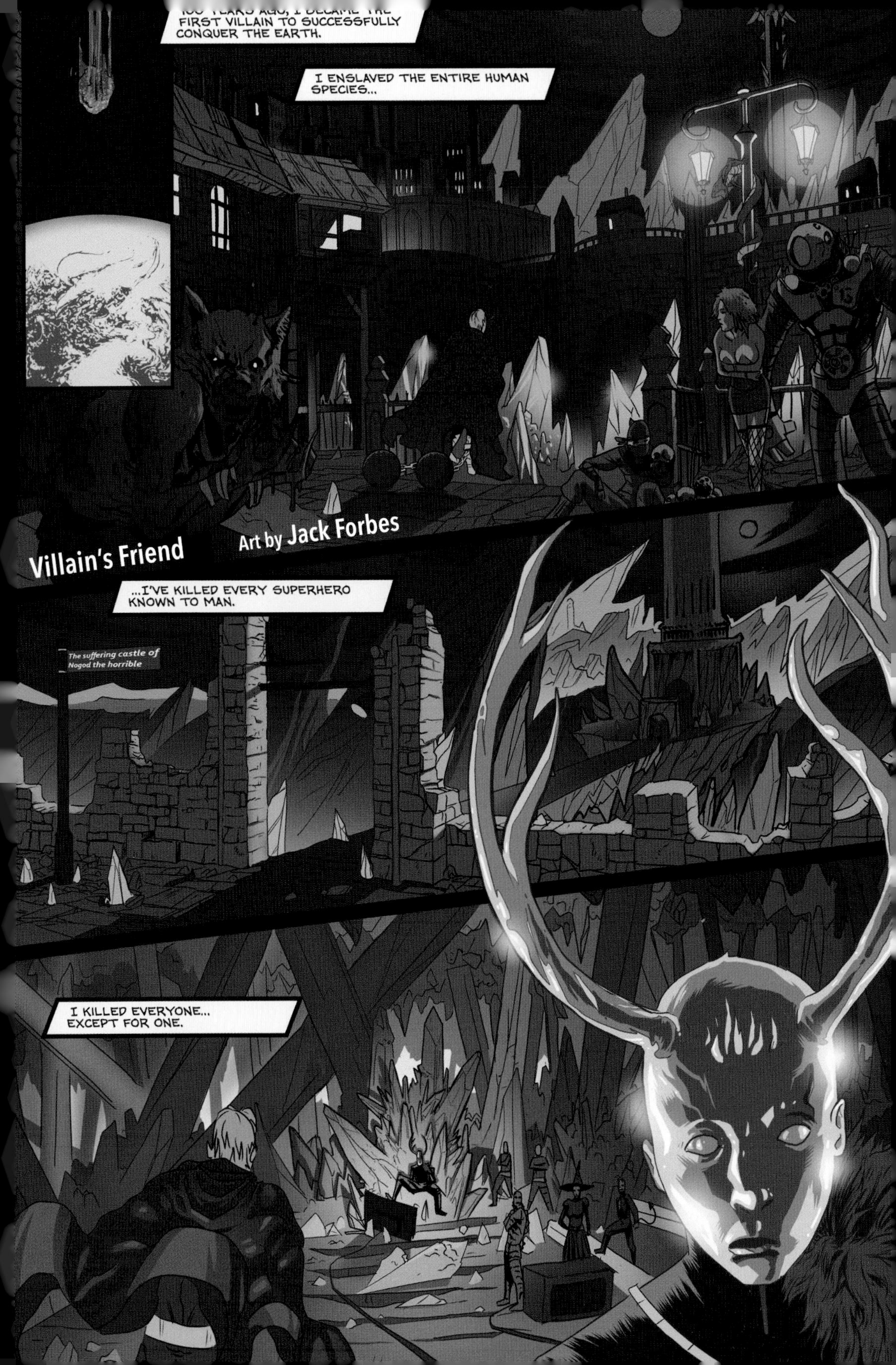
FIRST VILLAIN TO SUCCESSFULLY CONQUER THE EARTH.
I ENSLAVED THE ENTIRE HUMAN SPECIES...
Villain's Friend
Art by Jack Forbes
...I'VE KILLED EVERY SUPERHERO KNOWN TO MAN.
The suffering castle of Nogod the horrible
I KILLED EVERYONE... EXCEPT FOR ONE.

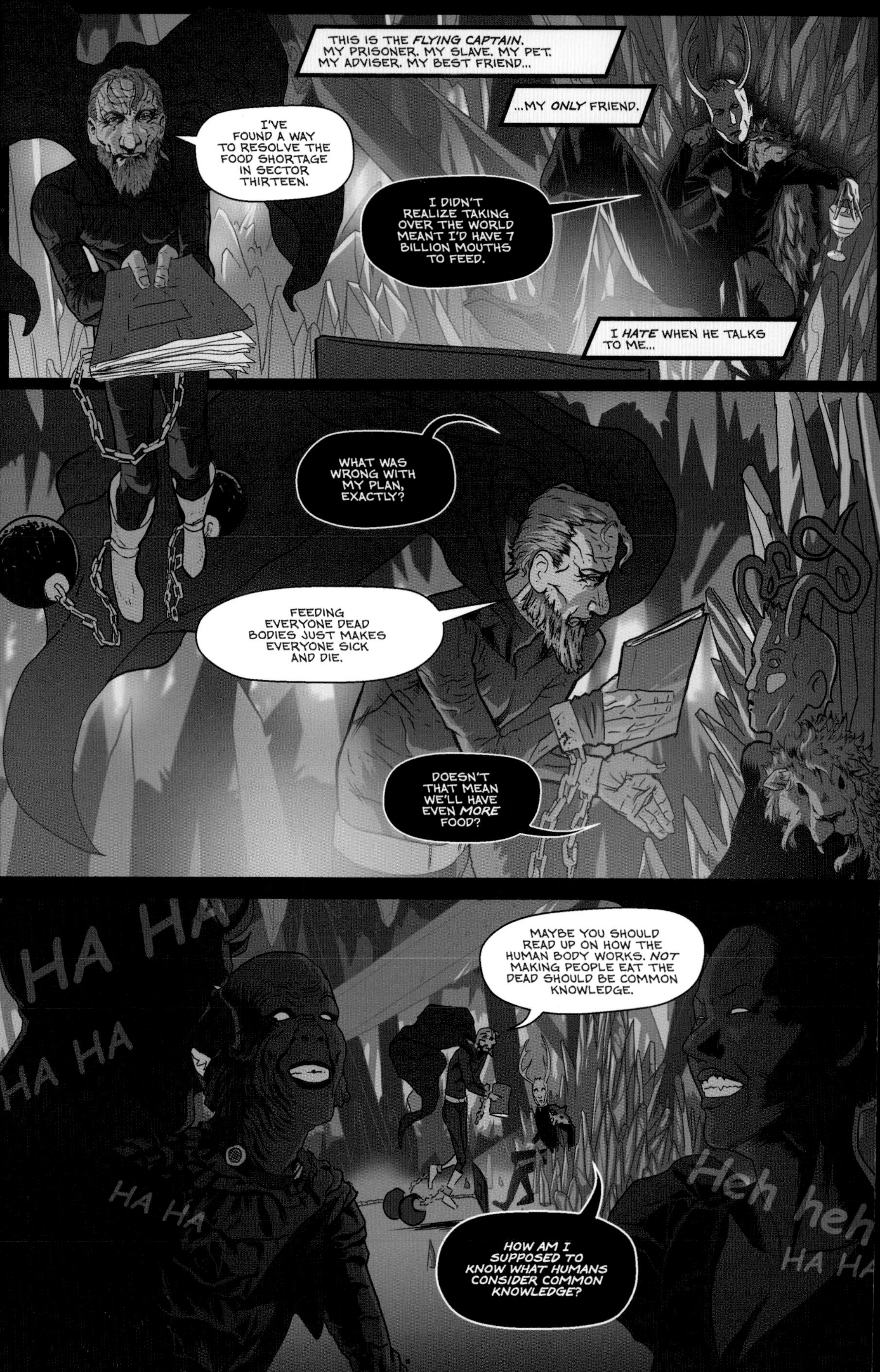
THIS IS THE FLYING CAPTAIN. MY PRISONER. MY SLAVE. MY PET. MY ADVISER. MY BEST FRIEND...
...MY ONLY FRIEND.
I'VE FOUND A WAY TO RESOLVE THE FOOD SHORTAGE IN SECTOR THIRTEEN.
I DIDN'T REALIZE TAKING OVER THE WORLD MEANT I'D HAVE 7 BILLION MOUTHS TO FEED.
I HATE WHEN HE TALKS TO ME...
WHAT WAS WRONG WITH MY PLAN, EXACTLY?
FEEDING EVERYONE DEAD BODIES JUST MAKES EVERYONE SICK AND DIE.
DOESN'T THAT MEAN WE'LL HAVE EVEN MORE FOOD?
HA HA
HA HA
MAYBE YOU SHOULD READ UP ON HOW THE HUMAN BODY WORKS. NOT MAKING PEOPLE EAT THE DEAD SHOULD BE COMMON KNOWLEDGE.
HA HA
Heh heh
HA HA
HOW AM I SUPPOSED TO KNOW WHAT HUMANS CONSIDER COMMON KNOWLEDGE?

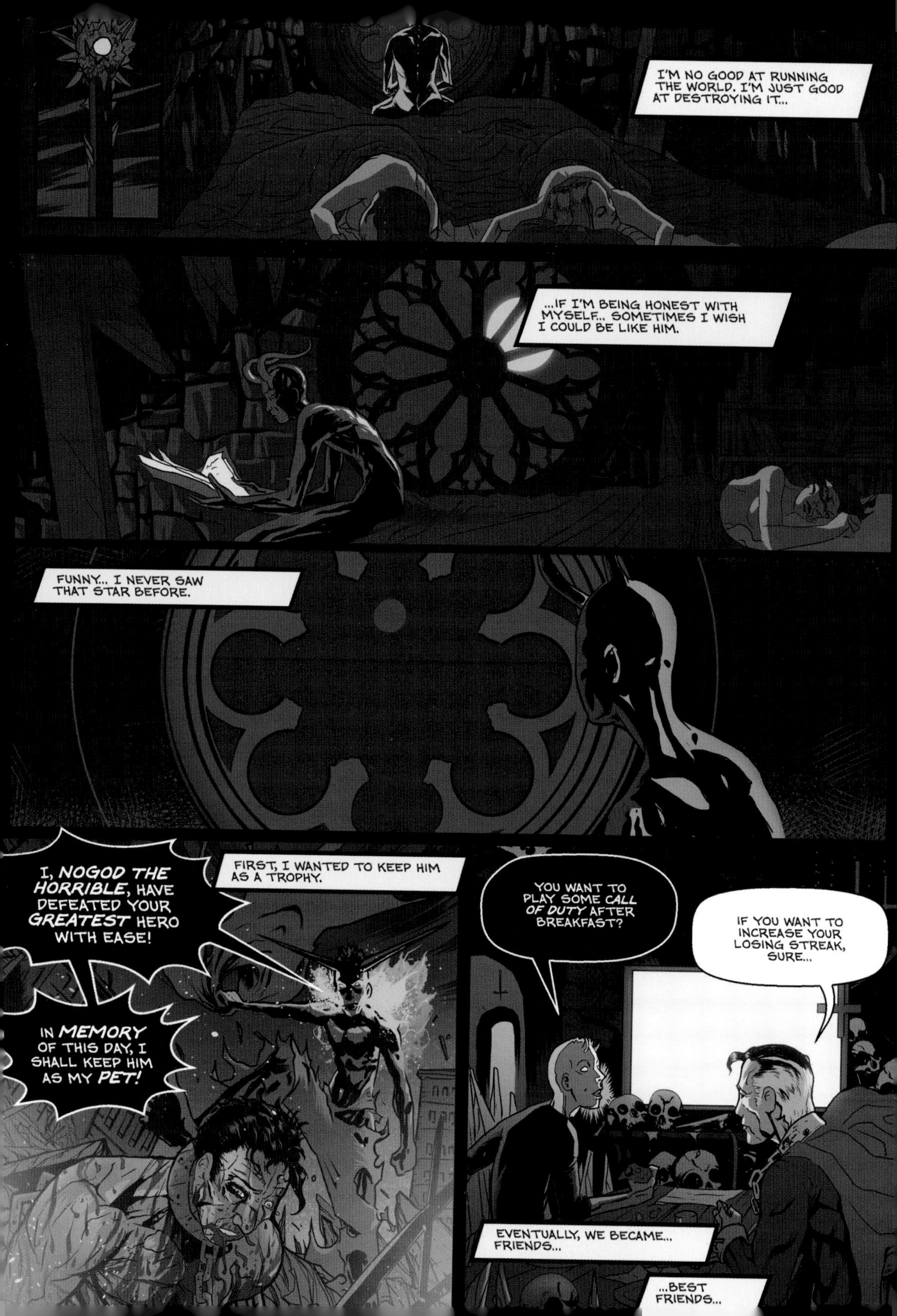
I'M NO GOOD AT RUNNING THE WORLD. I'M JUST GOOD AT DESTROYING IT...
...IF I'M BEING HONEST WITH MYSELF... SOMETIMES I WISH I COULD BE LIKE HIM.
FUNNY... I NEVER SAW THAT STAR BEFORE.
I, NOGOD THE HORRIBLE, HAVE DEFEATED YOUR GREATEST HERO WITH EASE!
FIRST, I WANTED TO KEEP HIM AS A TROPHY.
IN MEMORY OF THIS DAY, I SHALL KEEP HIM AS MY PET!
YOU WANT TO PLAY SOME CALL OF DUTY AFTER BREAKFAST?
IF YOU WANT TO INCREASE YOUR LOSING STREAK, SURE...
EVENTUALLY, WE BECAME... FRIENDS...
...BEST FRIENDS...

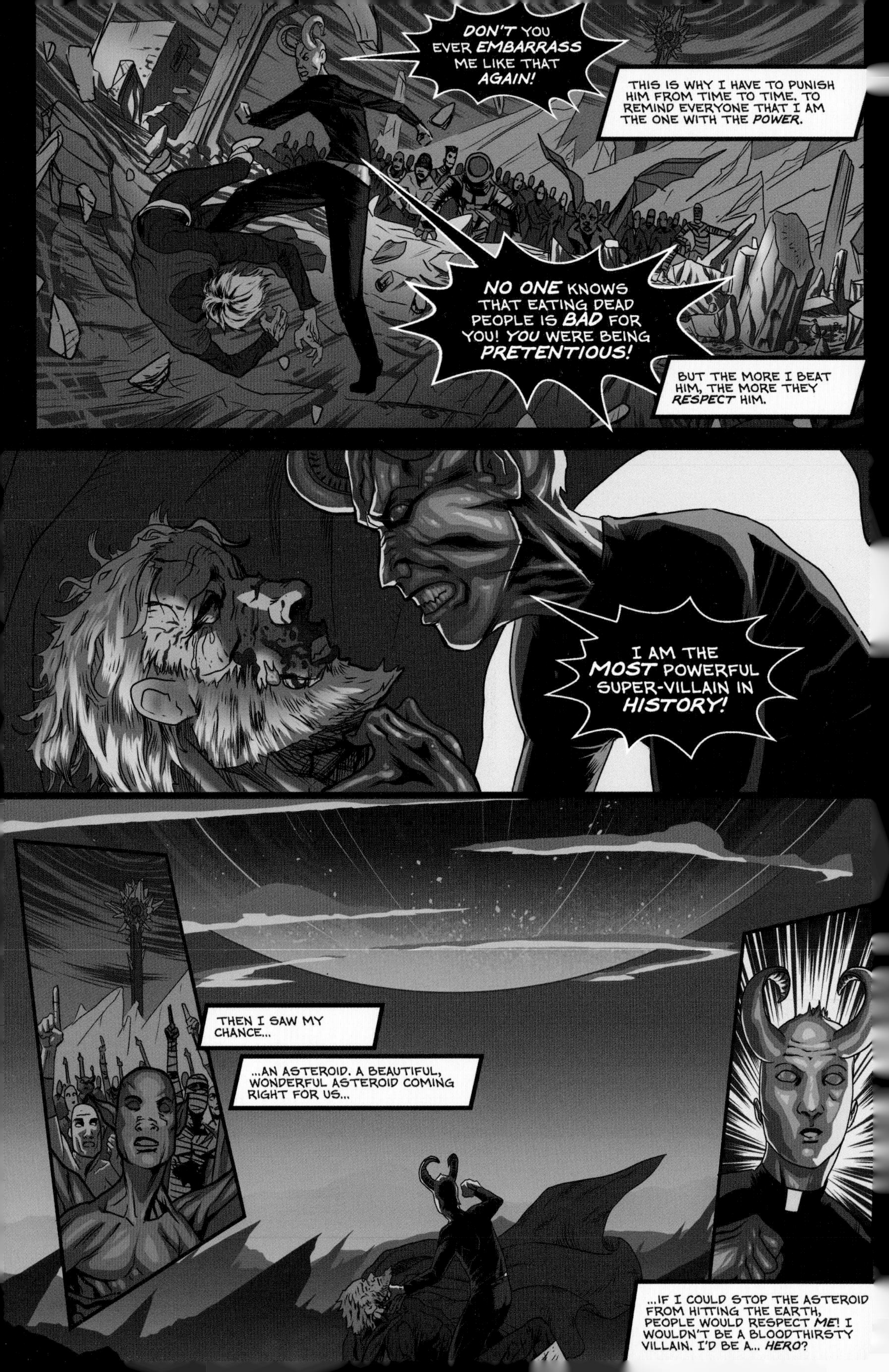
DON'T YOU EVER EMBARRASS ME LIKE THAT AGAIN!
THIS IS WHY I HAVE TO PUNISH HIM FROM TIME TO TIME. TO REMIND EVERYONE THAT I AM THE ONE WITH THE POWER.
NO ONE KNOWS THAT EATING DEAD PEOPLE IS BAD FOR YOU! YOU WERE BEING PRETENTIOUS!
BUT THE MORE I BEAT HIM, THE MORE THEY RESPECT HIM.
I AM THE MOST POWERFUL SUPER-VILLAIN IN HISTORY!
THEN I SAW MY CHANCE...
...AN ASTEROID. A BEAUTIFUL, WONDERFUL ASTEROID COMING RIGHT FOR US...
...IF I COULD STOP THE ASTEROID FROM HITTING THE EARTH, PEOPLE WOULD RESPECT ME! I WOULDN'T BE A BLOODTHIRSTY VILLAIN. I'D BE A... HERO?

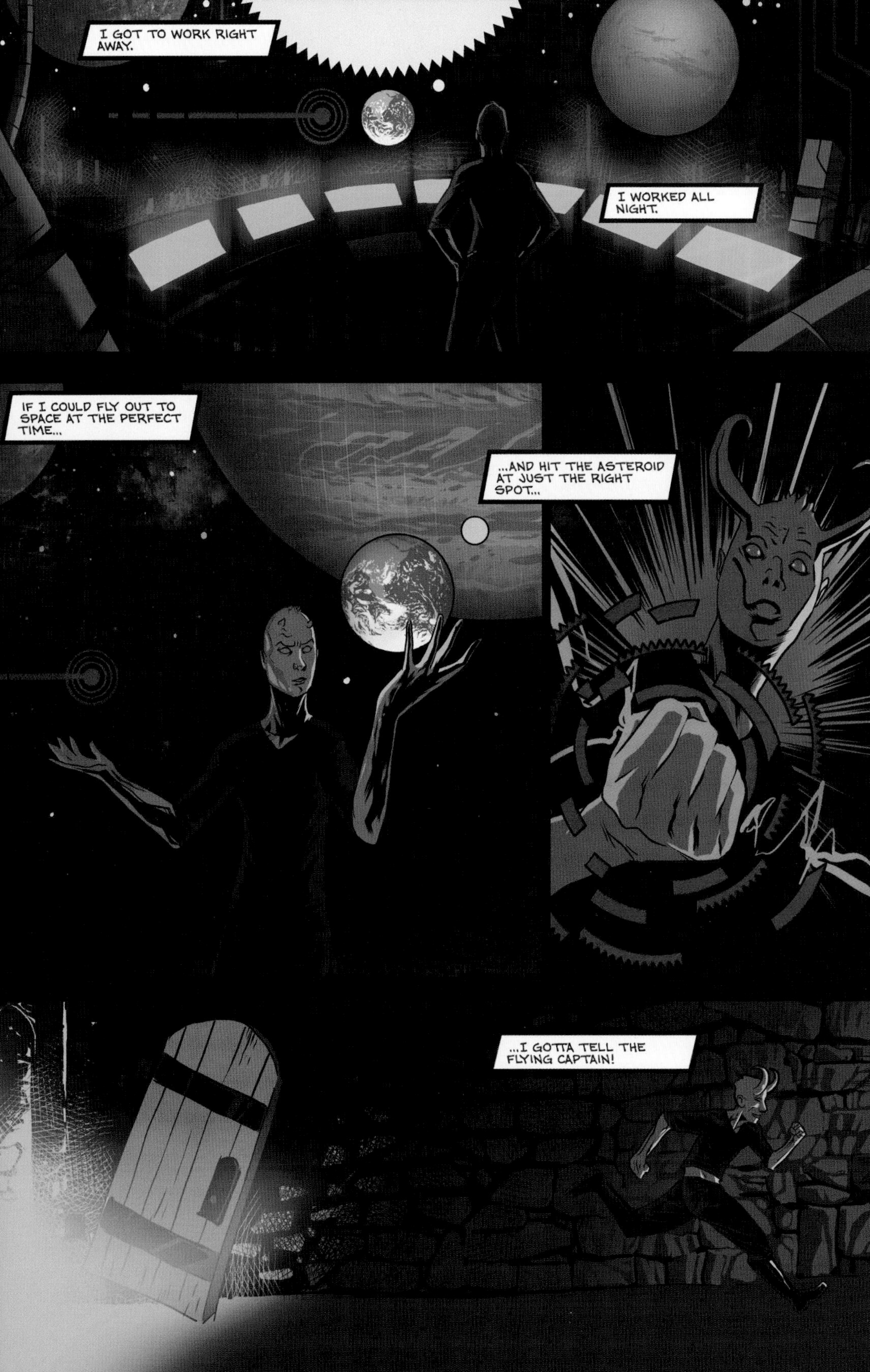
I GOT TO WORK RIGHT AWAY.
I WORKED ALL NIGHT.
IF I COULD FLY OUT TO SPACE AT THE PERFECT TIME...
...AND HIT THE ASTEROID AT JUST THE RIGHT SPOT...
...I GOTTA TELL THE FLYING CAPTAIN!

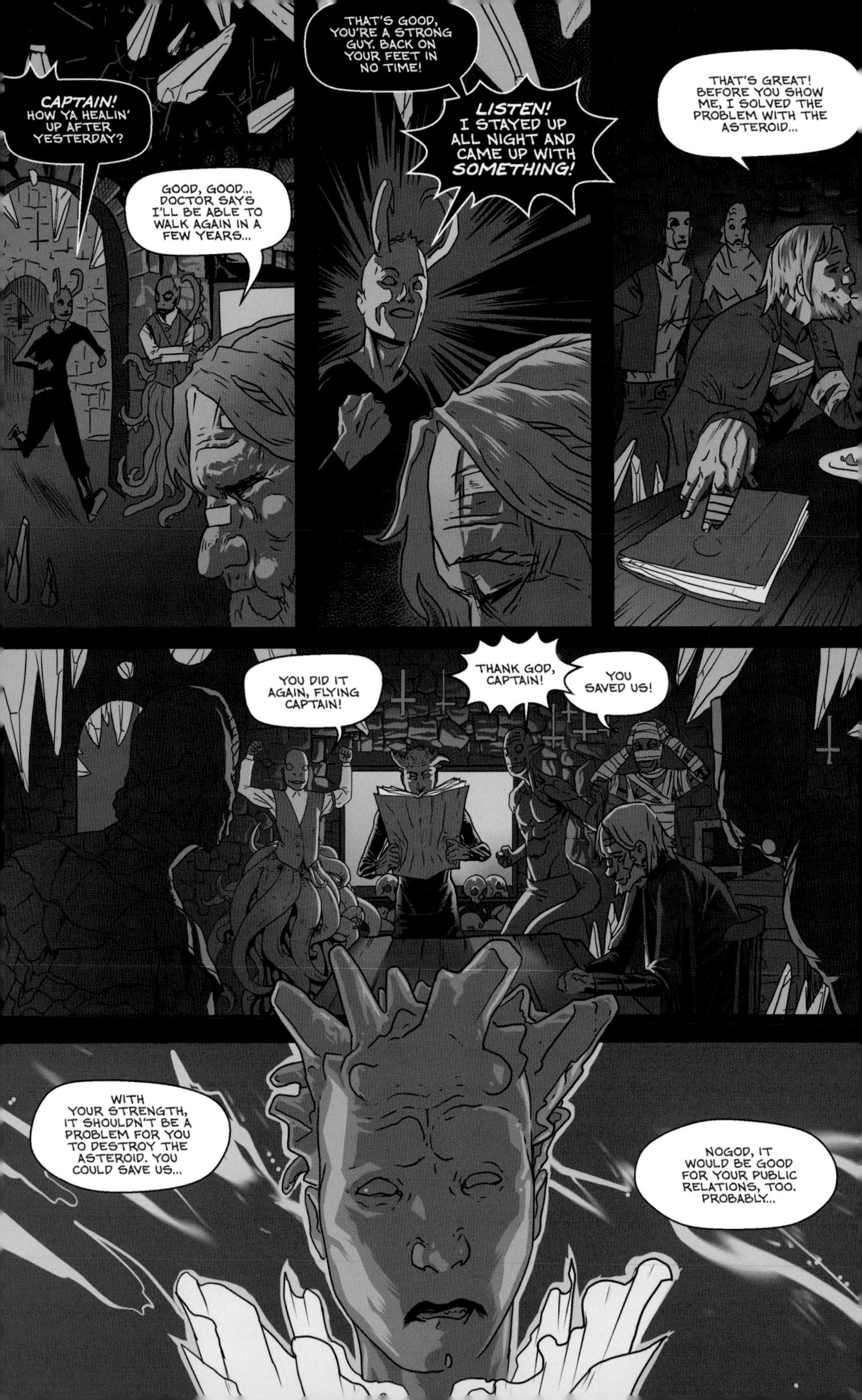
CAPTAIN! HOW YA HEALIN' UP AFTER YESTERDAY?
GOOD, GOOD... DOCTOR SAYS I'LL BE ABLE TO WALK AGAIN IN A FEW YEARS...
THAT'S GOOD, YOU'RE A STRONG GUY. BACK ON YOUR FEET IN NO TIME!
LISTEN! I STAYED UP ALL NIGHT AND CAME UP WITH SOMETHING!
THAT'S GREAT! BEFORE YOU SHOW ME, I SOLVED THE PROBLEM WITH THE ASTEROID...
YOU DID IT AGAIN, FLYING CAPTAIN!
THANK GOD, CAPTAIN!
YOU SAVED US!
WITH YOUR STRENGTH, IT SHOULDN'T BE A PROBLEM FOR YOU TO DESTROY THE ASTEROID. YOU COULD SAVE US...
NOGOD, IT WOULD BE GOOD FOR YOUR PUBLIC RELATIONS, TOO. PROBABLY...

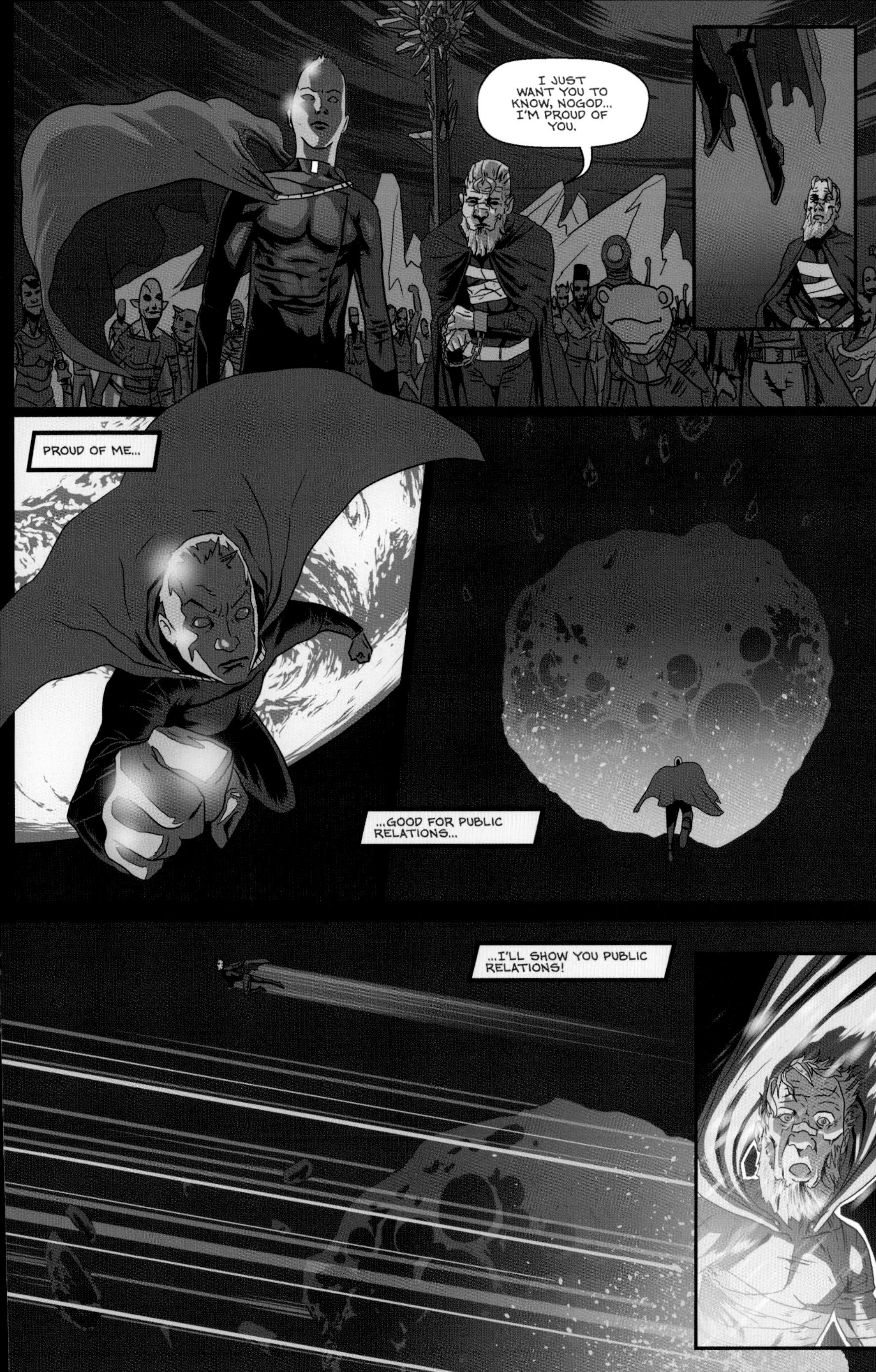
I JUST WANT YOU TO KNOW, NOGOD... I'M PROUD OF YOU.
PROUD OF ME...
...GOOD FOR PUBLIC RELATIONS...
...I'LL SHOW YOU PUBLIC RELATIONS!

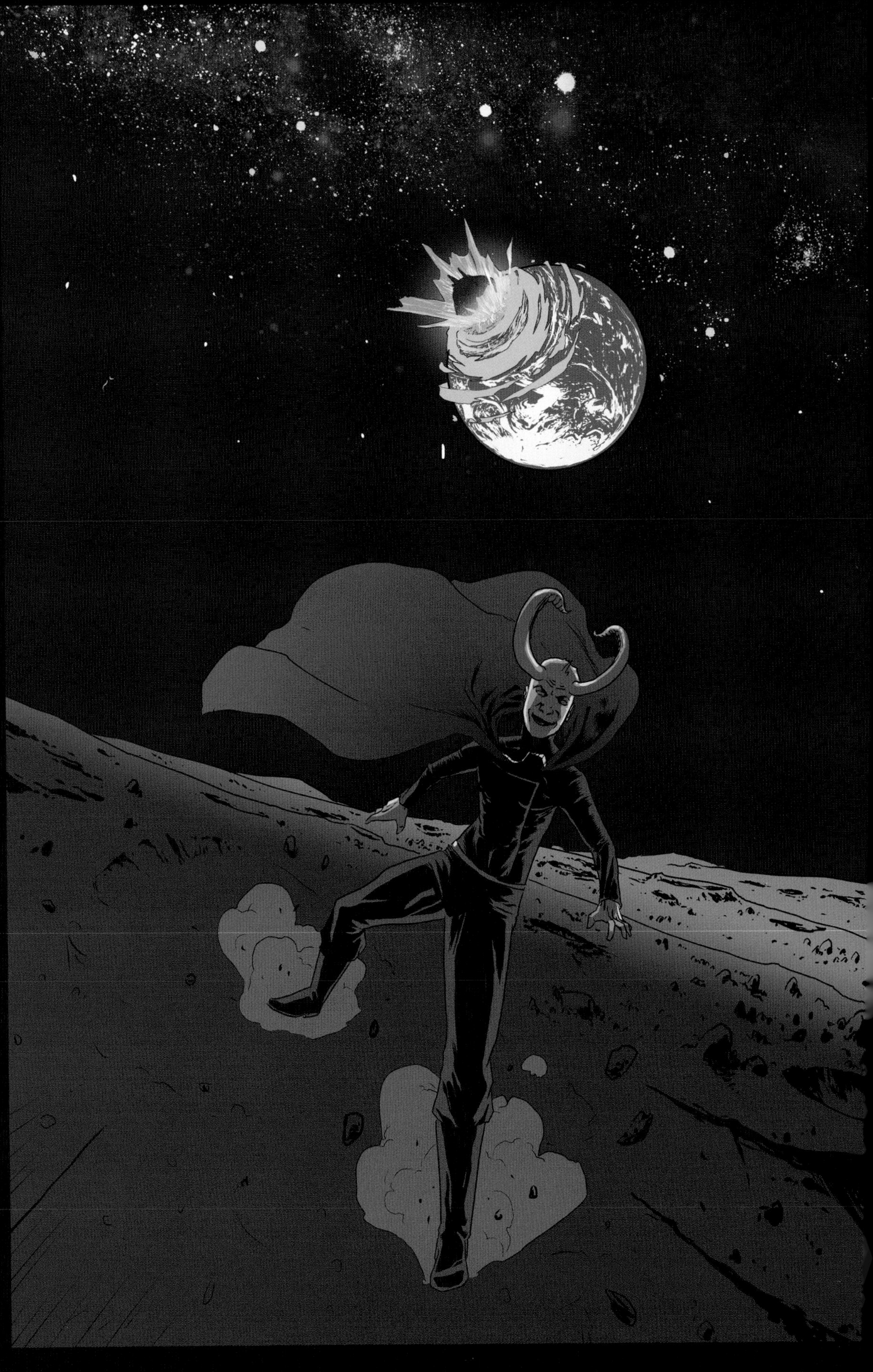

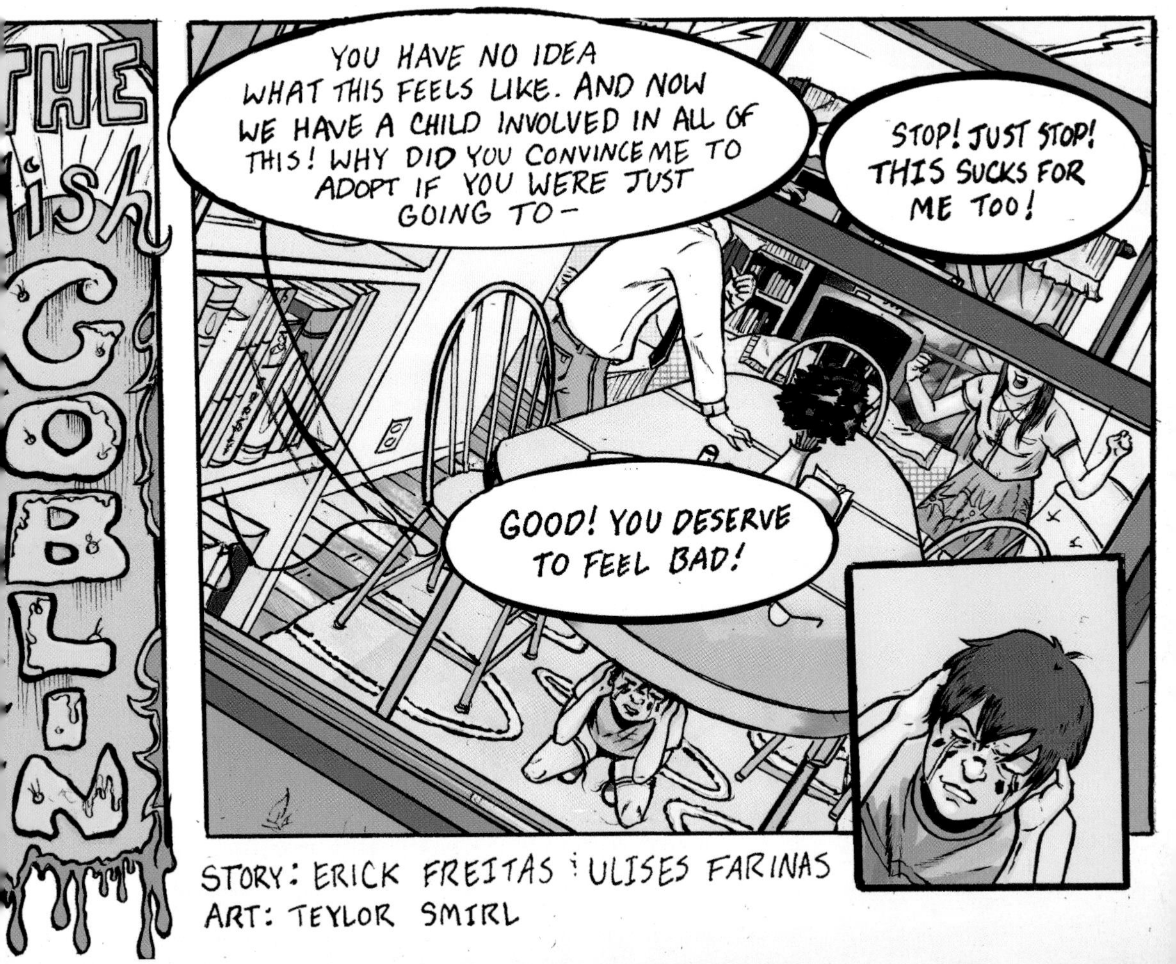
THE ish GOBLIN
YOU HAVE NO IDEA WHAT THIS FEELS LIKE. AND NOW WE HAVE A CHILD INVOLVED IN ALL OF THIS! WHY DID YOU CONVINCE ME TO ADOPT IF YOU WERE JUST GOING TO—
STOP! JUST STOP! THIS SUCKS FOR ME TOO!
GOOD! YOU DESERVE TO FEEL BAD!

STORY: ERICK FREITAS & ULISES FARINAS
ART: TEYLOR SMIRL

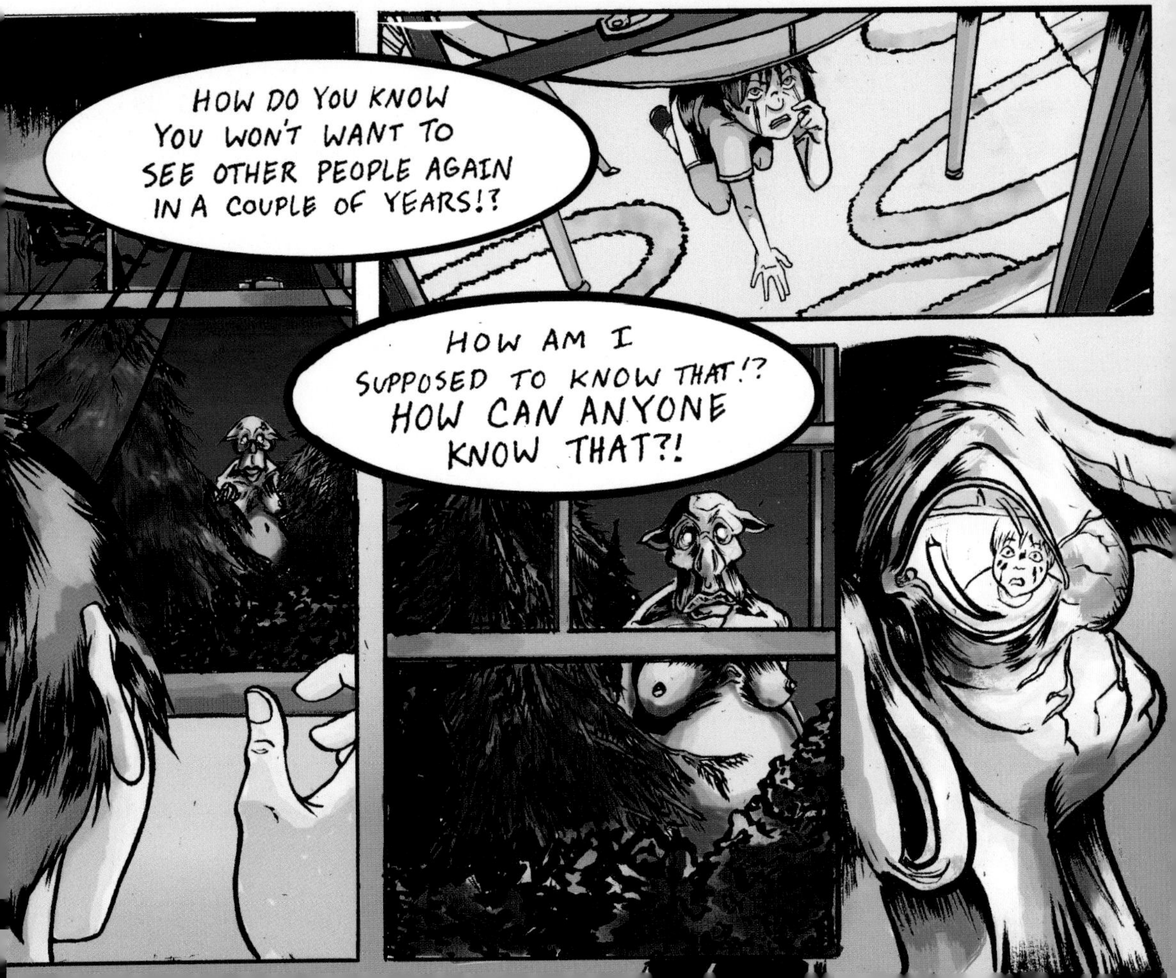
HOW DO YOU KNOW YOU WON'T WANT TO SEE OTHER PEOPLE AGAIN IN A COUPLE OF YEARS!?
HOW AM I SUPPOSED TO KNOW THAT!? HOW CAN ANYONE KNOW THAT?!

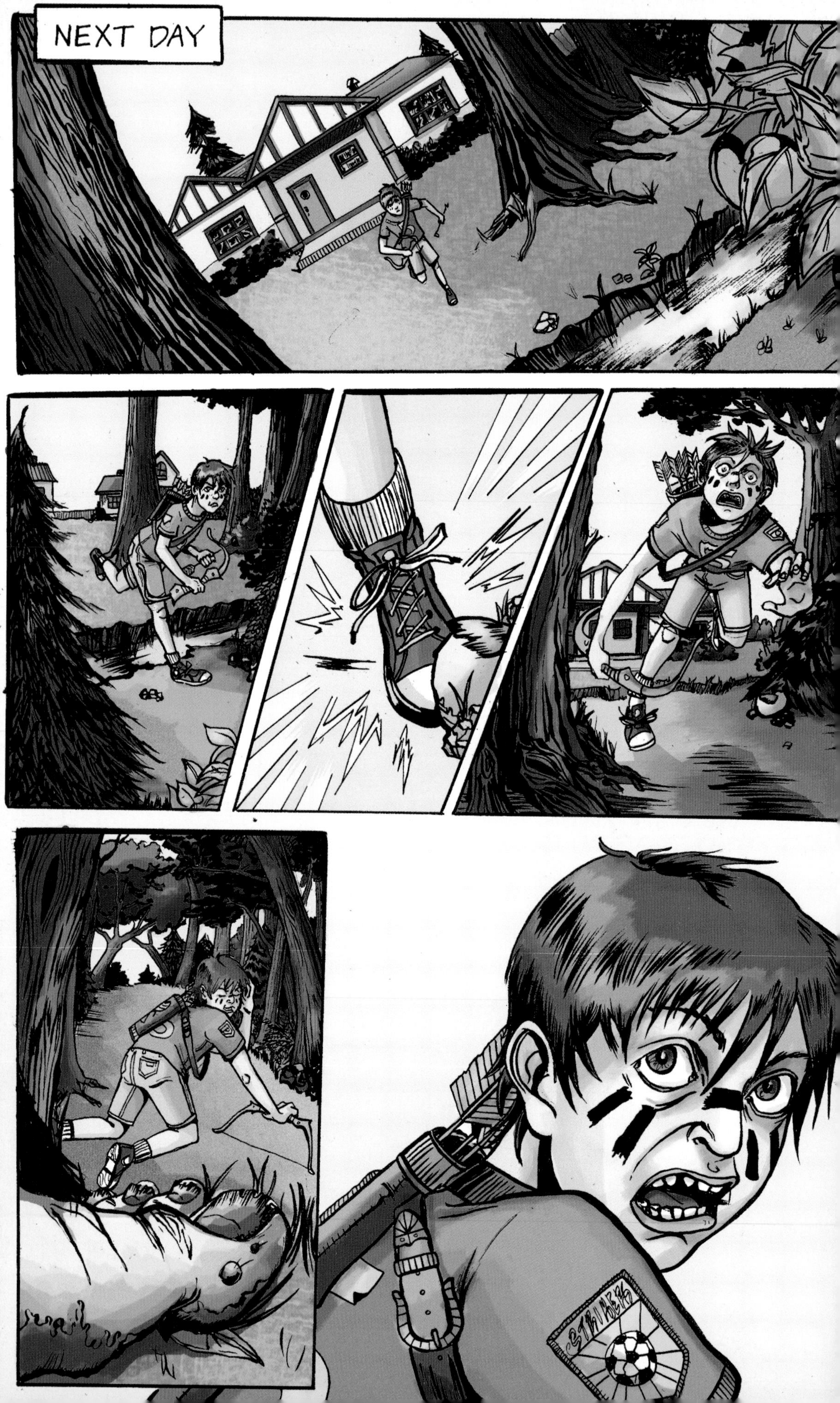
NEXT DAY

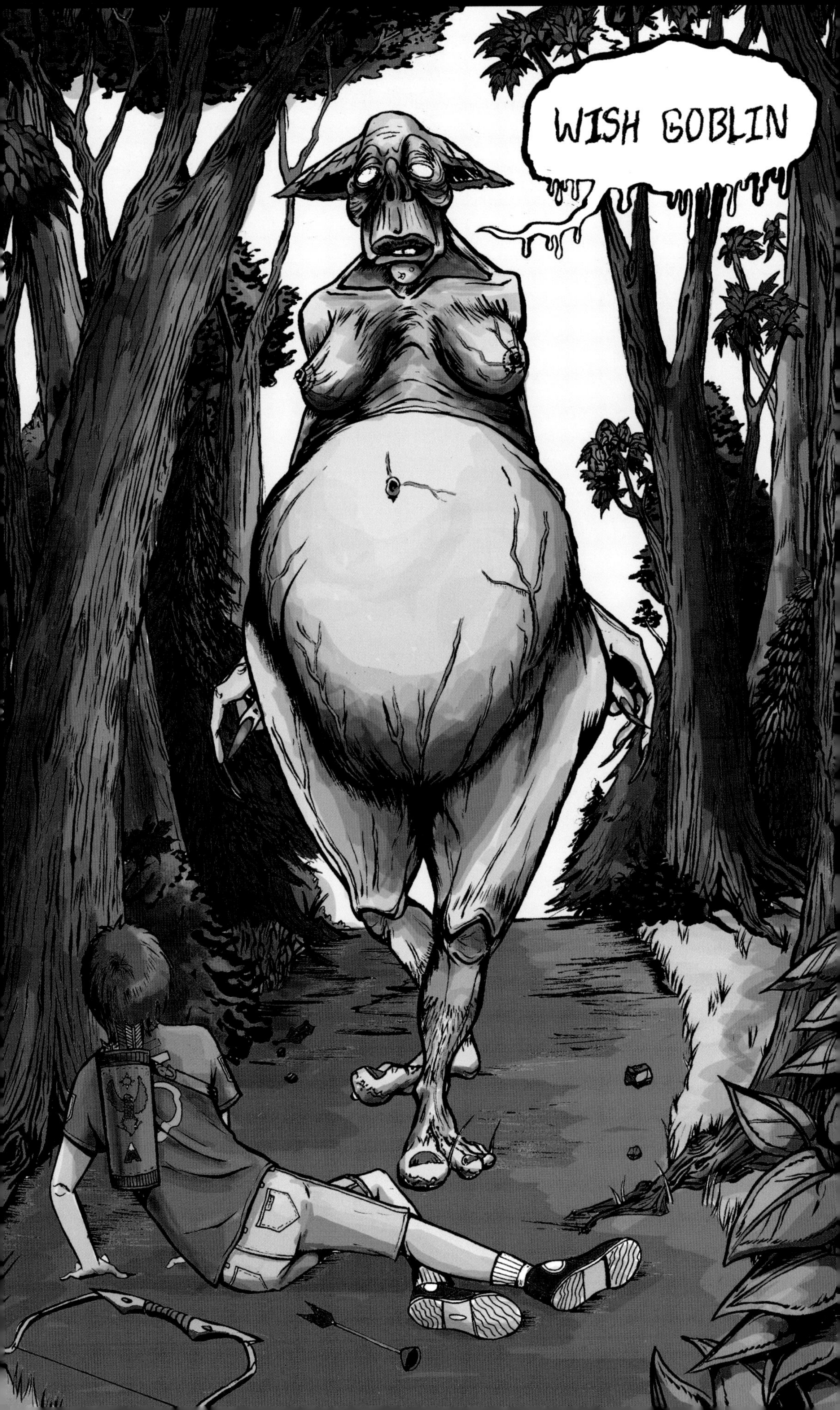
WISH GOBLIN

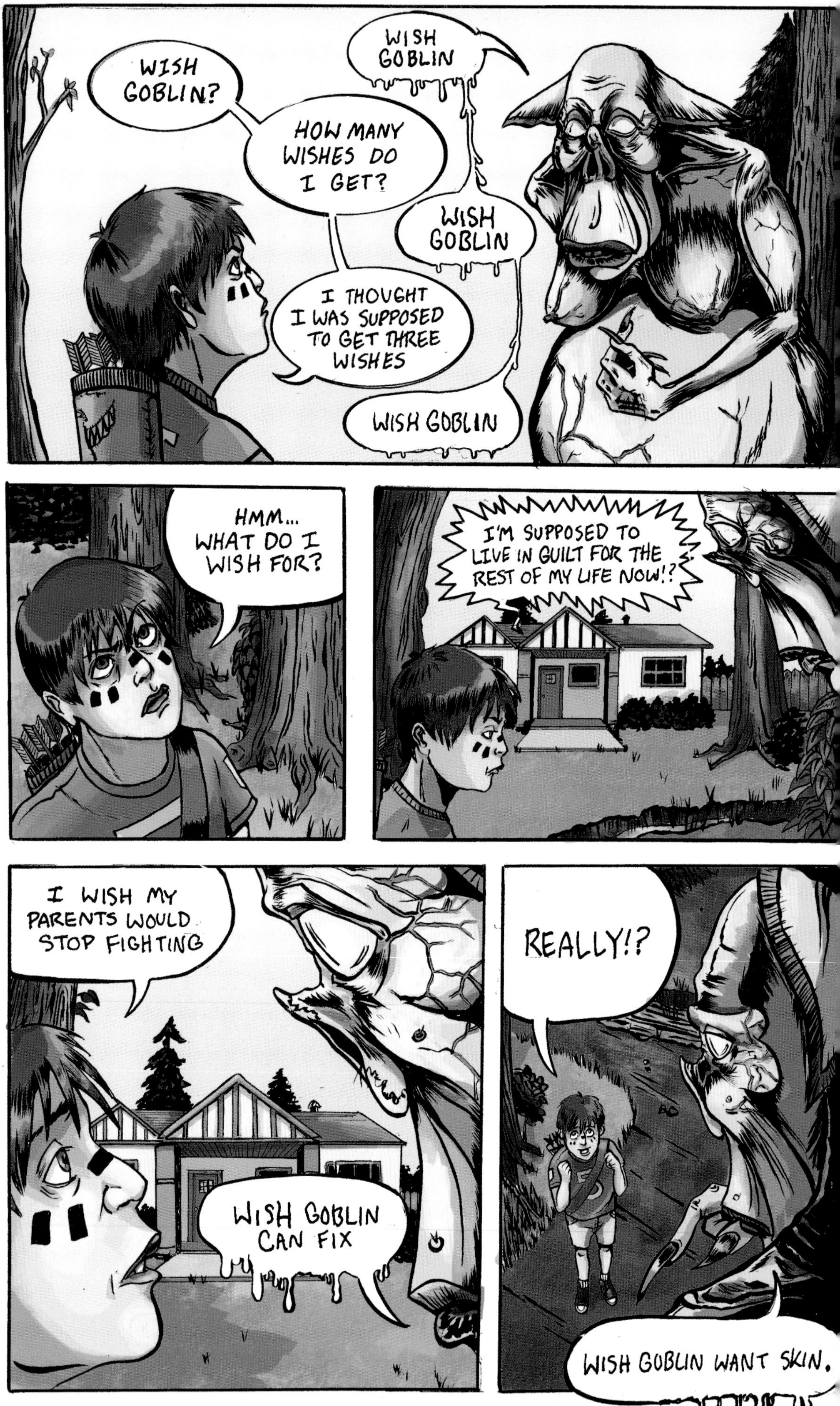
WISH GOBLIN?
WISH GOBLIN
HOW MANY WISHES DO I GET?
WISH GOBLIN
I THOUGHT I WAS SUPPOSED TO GET THREE WISHES
WISH GOBLIN
HMM... WHAT DO I WISH FOR?
I'M SUPPOSED TO LIVE IN GUILT FOR THE REST OF MY LIFE NOW!?
I WISH MY PARENTS WOULD STOP FIGHTING
WISH GOBLIN CAN FIX
REALLY!?
WISH GOBLIN WANT SKIN.

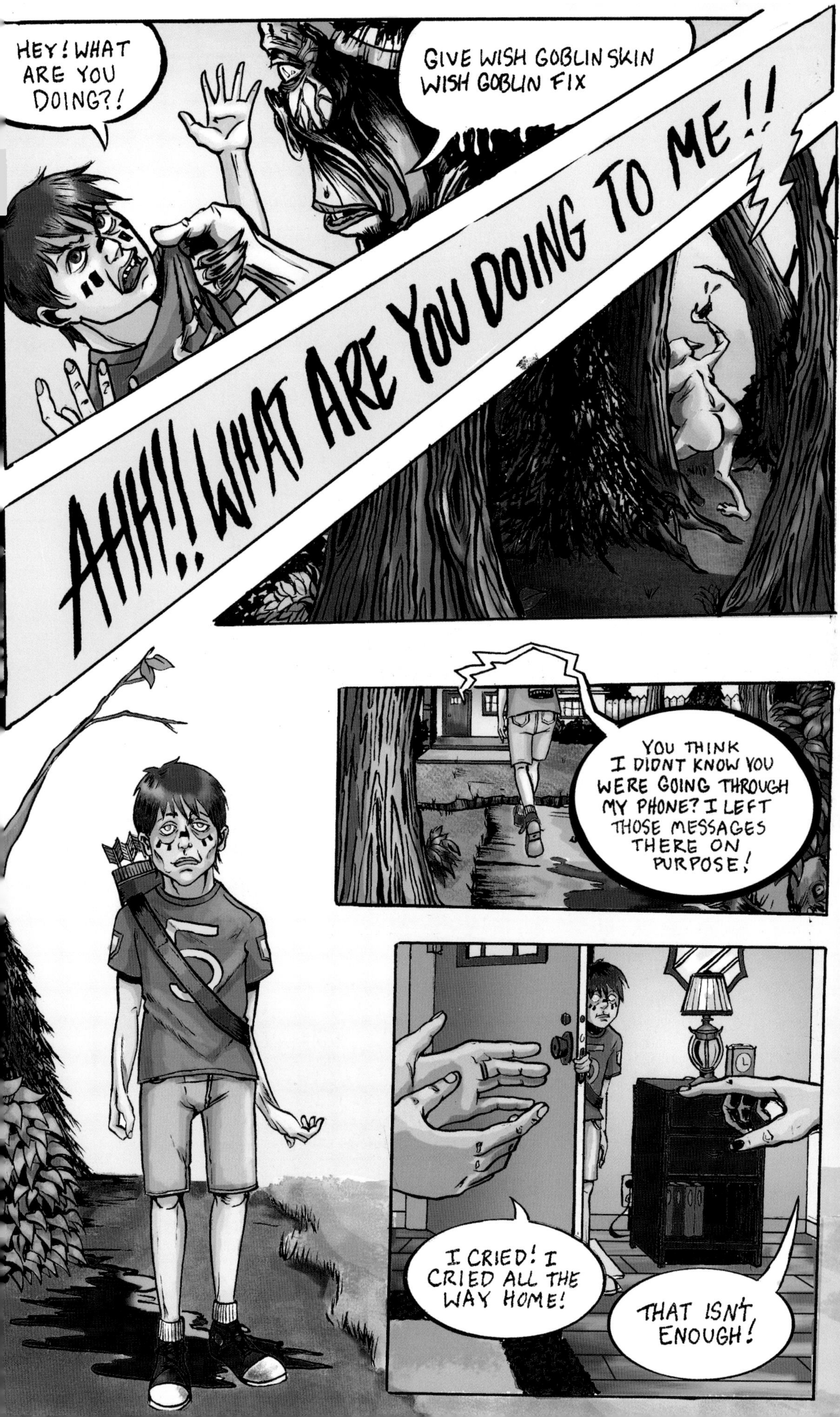
HEY! WHAT ARE YOU DOING?!
GIVE WISH GOBLIN SKIN WISH GOBLIN FIX
AHH!! WHAT ARE YOU DOING TO ME!!
YOU THINK I DIDNT KNOW YOU WERE GOING THROUGH MY PHONE? I LEFT THOSE MESSAGES THERE ON PURPOSE!
I CRIED! I CRIED ALL THE WAY HOME!
THAT ISN'T ENOUGH!

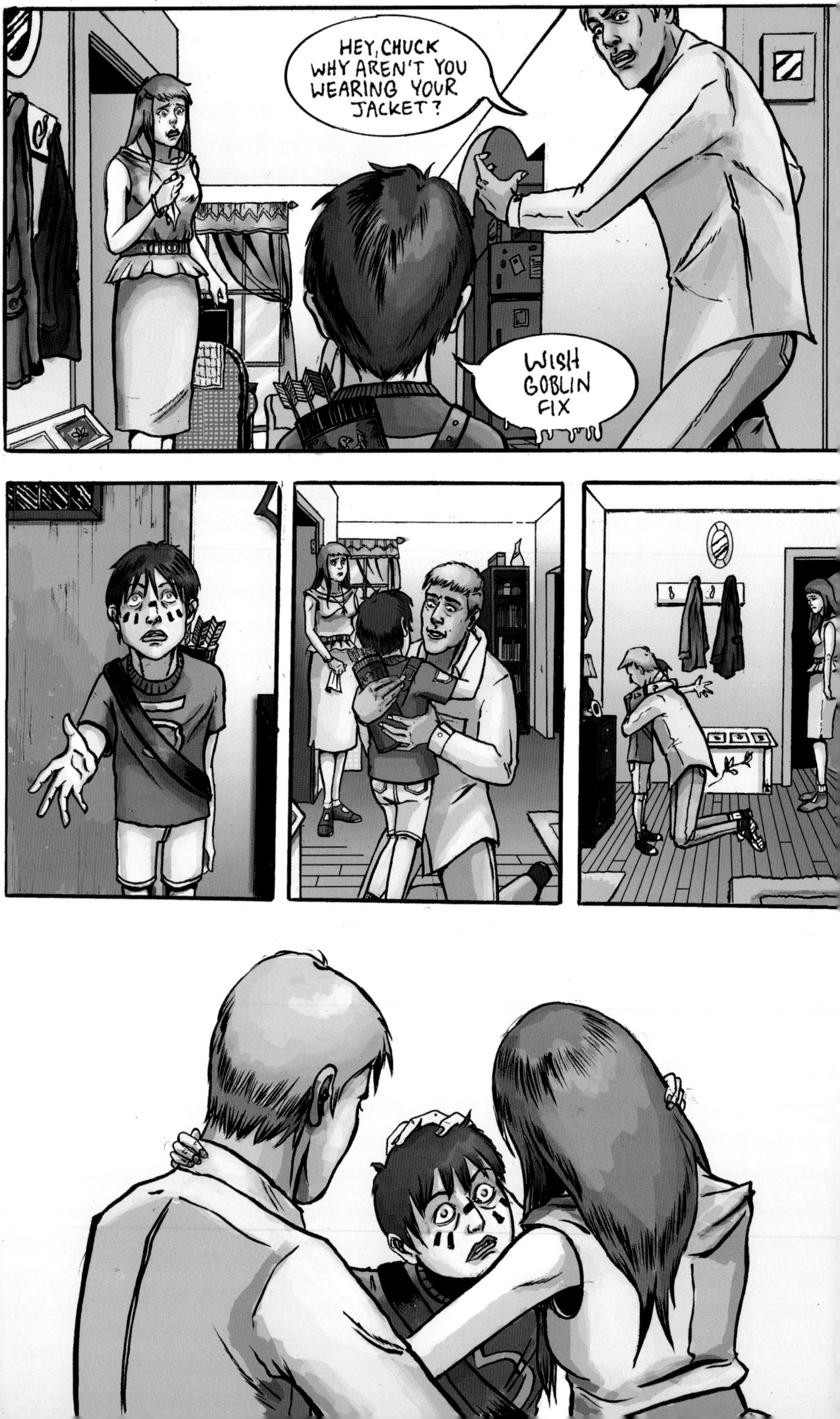
HEY, CHUCK WHY AREN'T YOU WEARING YOUR JACKET?
WISH GOBLIN FIX

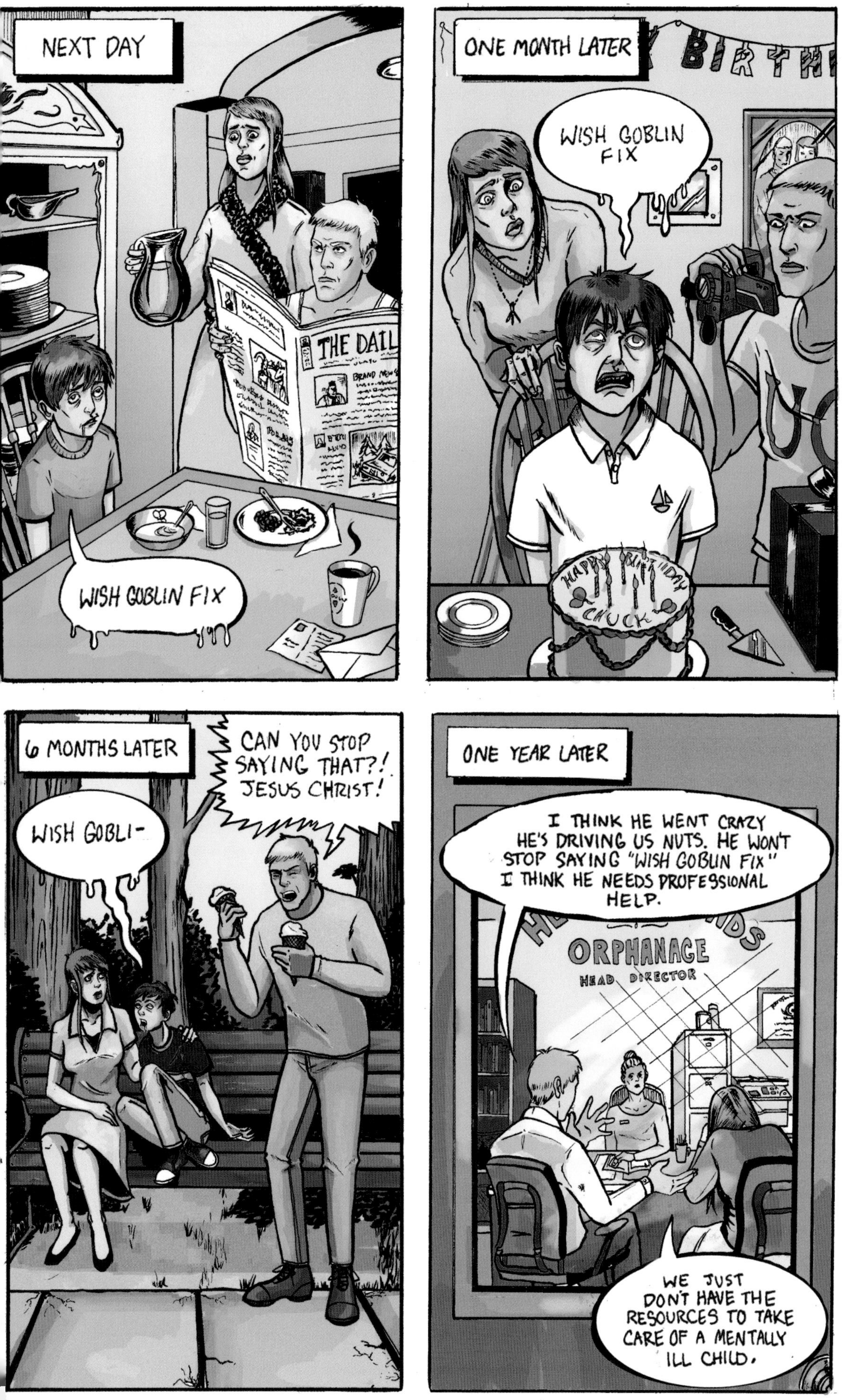
NEXT DAY
THE DAIL
WISH GOBLIN FIX
ONE MONTH LATER
BIRTH
WISH GOBLIN FIX
HAPPY BIRTHDAY CHUCK
6 MONTHS LATER
CAN YOU STOP SAYING THAT?! JESUS CHRIST!
WISH GOBLI-
ONE YEAR LATER
I THINK HE WENT CRAZY HE'S DRIVING US NUTS. HE WON'T STOP SAYING "WISH GOBLIN FIX" I THINK HE NEEDS PROFESSIONAL HELP.
ORPHANAGE
HEAD DIRECTOR
WE JUST DON'T HAVE THE RESOURCES TO TAKE CARE OF A MENTALLY ILL CHILD.

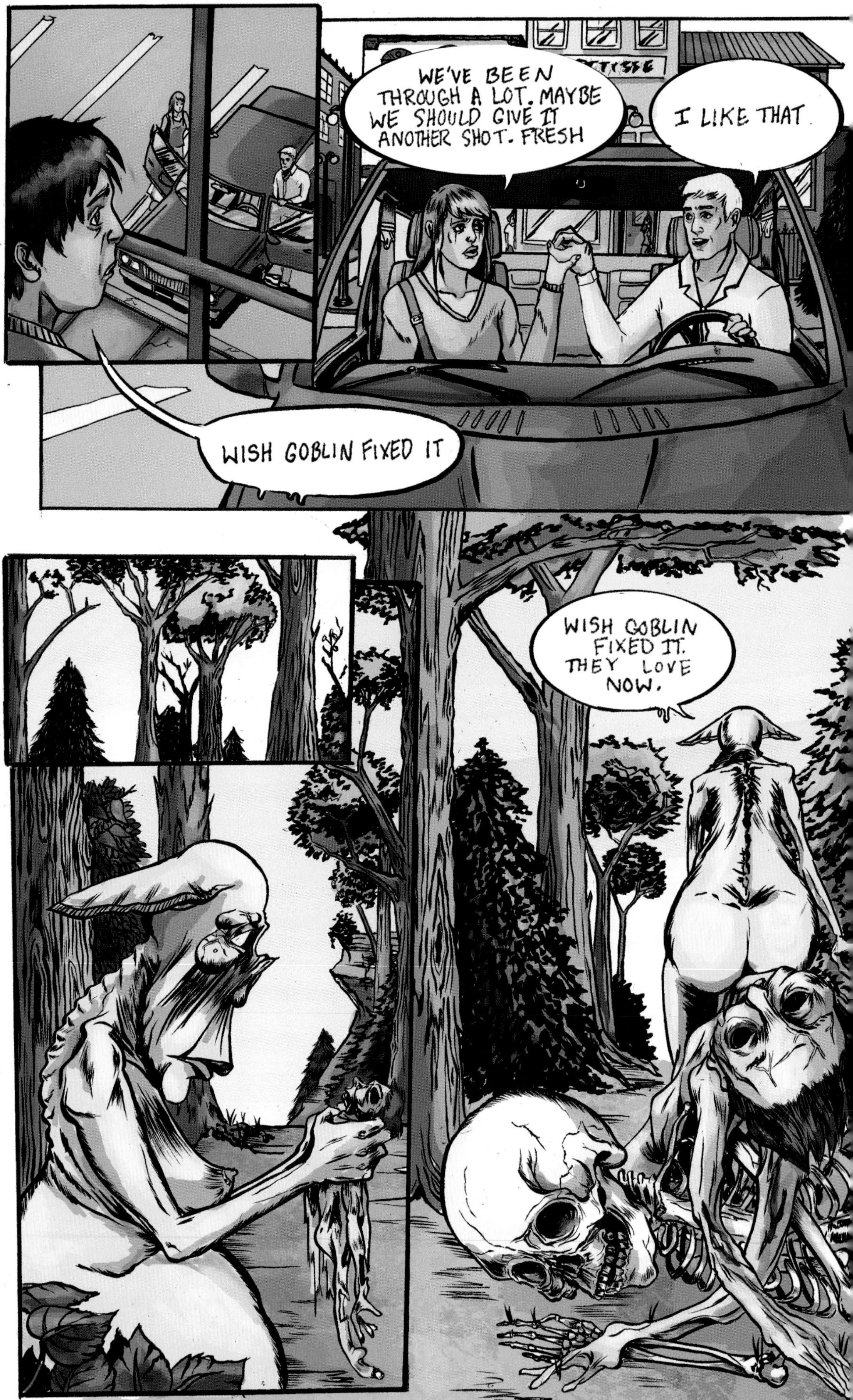
WE'VE BEEN THROUGH A LOT. MAYBE WE SHOULD GIVE IT ANOTHER SHOT. FRESH
I LIKE THAT
WISH GOBLIN FIXED IT
WISH GOBLIN FIXED IT. THEY LOVE NOW.

SNOW JOKES
PAT PAT
CREAK!
HEY, KID! THANKS FOR MAKING MY FACE!
HUH? YOU'RE ALIVE?!
I HOPE YOU ENJOY SNOW-JOKES! BECAUSE I'M NOT JUST A SNOWMAN, BUT A JOKE TELLER!

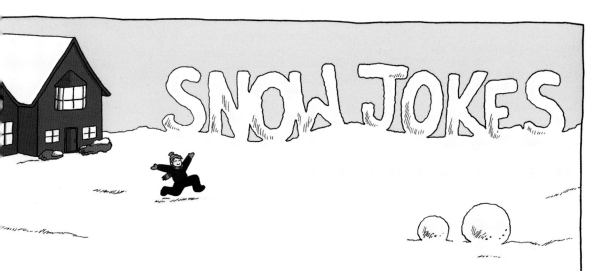

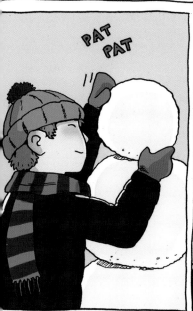

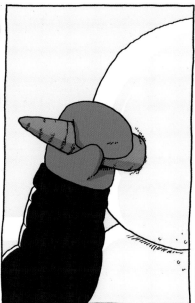

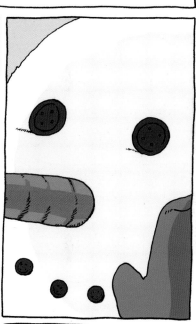

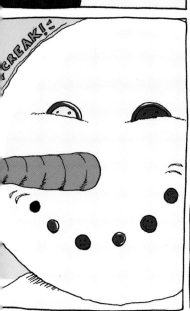

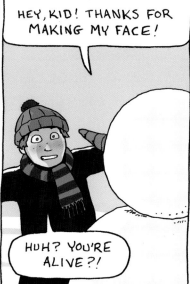

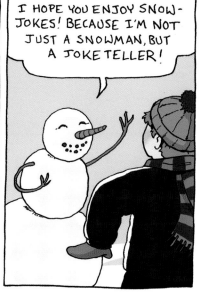

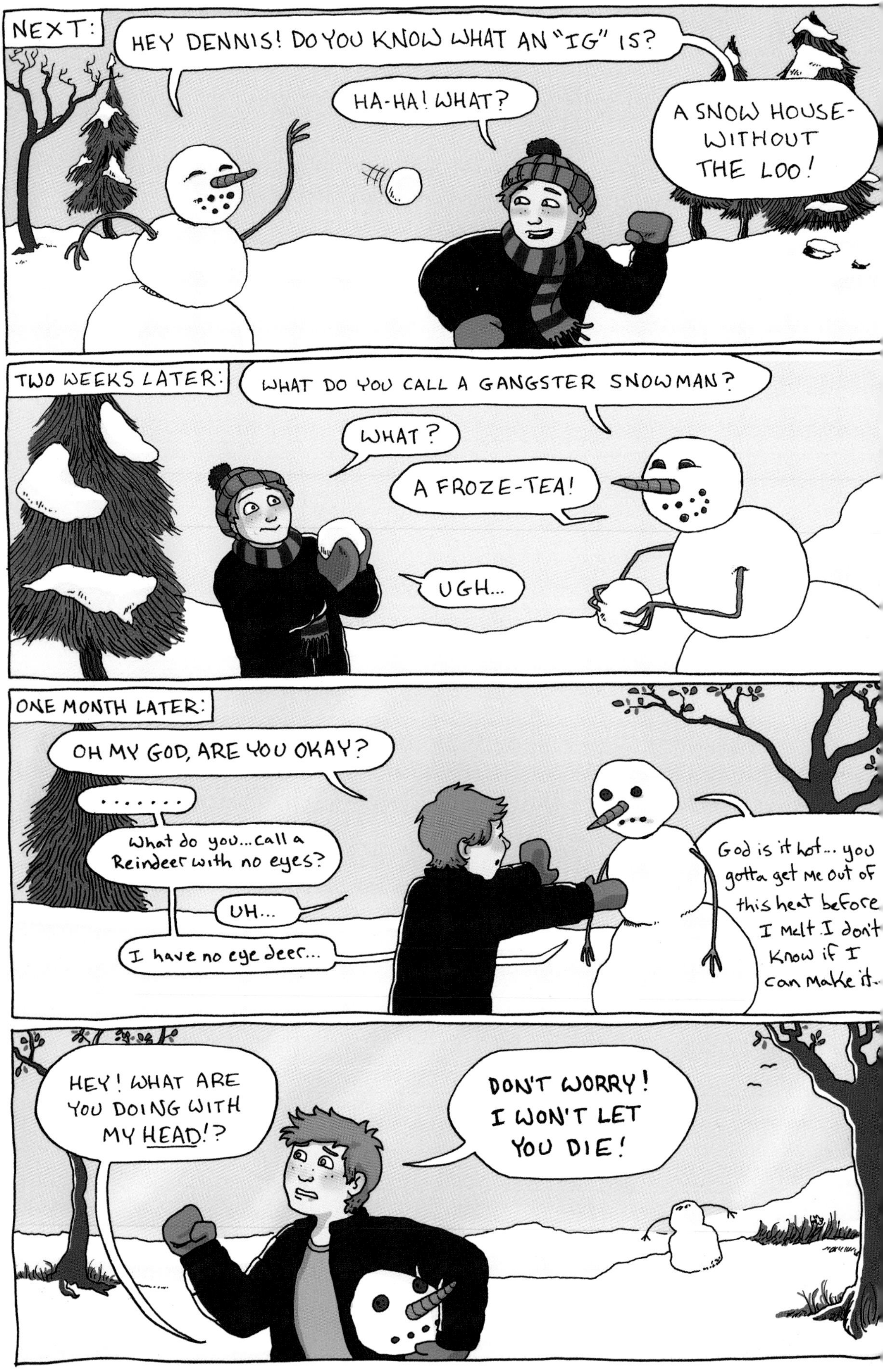
NEXT:
HEY DENNIS! DO YOU KNOW WHAT AN "IG" IS?
HA-HA! WHAT?
A SNOW HOUSE- WITHOUT THE LOO!
TWO WEEKS LATER:
WHAT DO YOU CALL A GANGSTER SNOWMAN?
WHAT?
A FROZE-TEA!
UGH...
ONE MONTH LATER:
OH MY GOD, ARE YOU OKAY?
....
What do you... call a Reindeer with no eyes?
UH...
I have no eye deer...
God is it hot... you gotta get me out of this heat before I melt. I don't know if I can make it.
HEY! WHAT ARE YOU DOING WITH MY HEAD!?
DON'T WORRY! I WON'T LET YOU DIE!

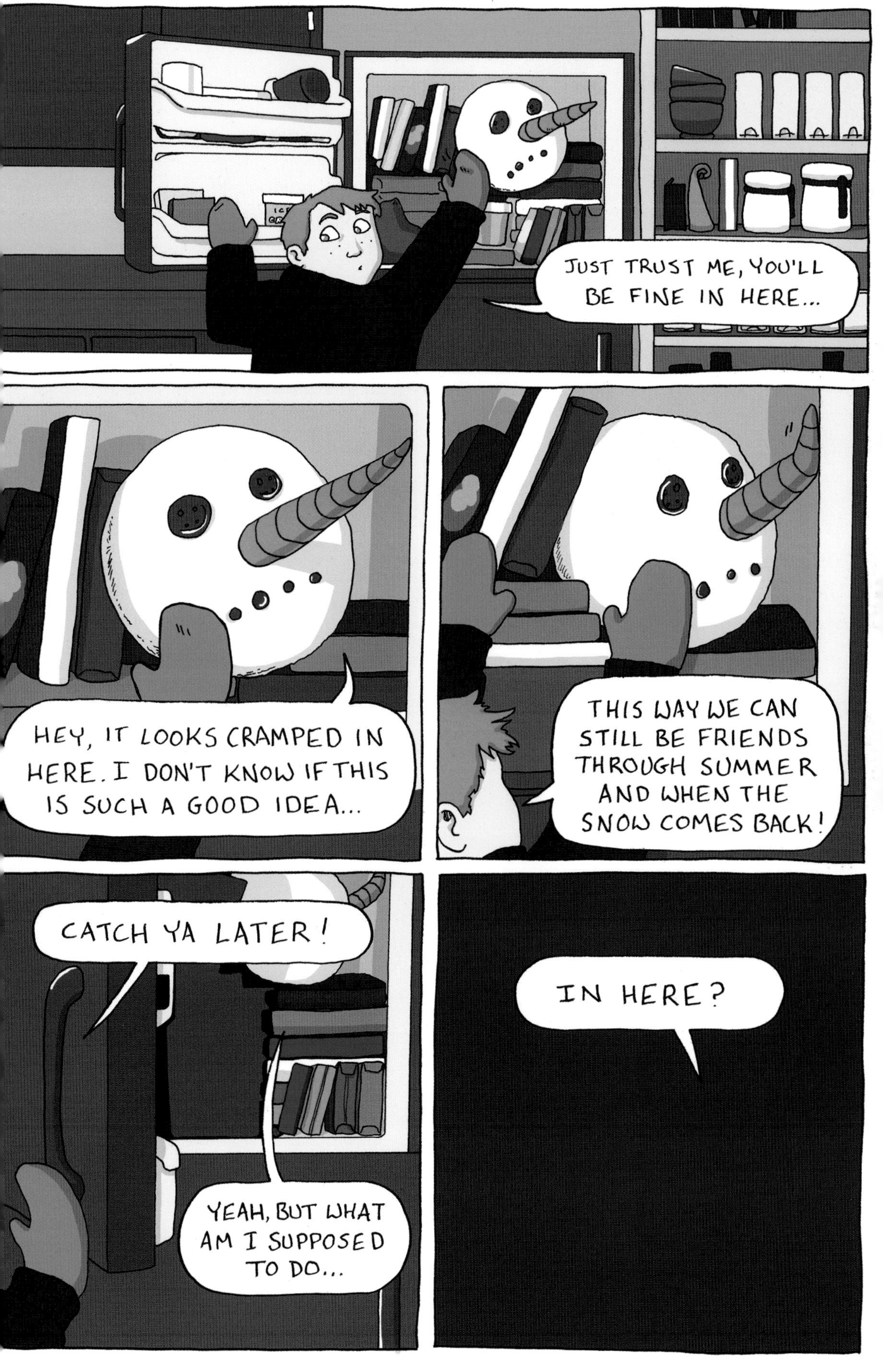
JUST TRUST ME, YOU'LL BE FINE IN HERE...
HEY, IT LOOKS CRAMPED IN HERE. I DON'T KNOW IF THIS IS SUCH A GOOD IDEA...
THIS WAY WE CAN STILL BE FRIENDS THROUGH SUMMER AND WHEN THE SNOW COMES BACK!
CATCH YA LATER!
YEAH, BUT WHAT AM I SUPPOSED TO DO...
IN HERE?

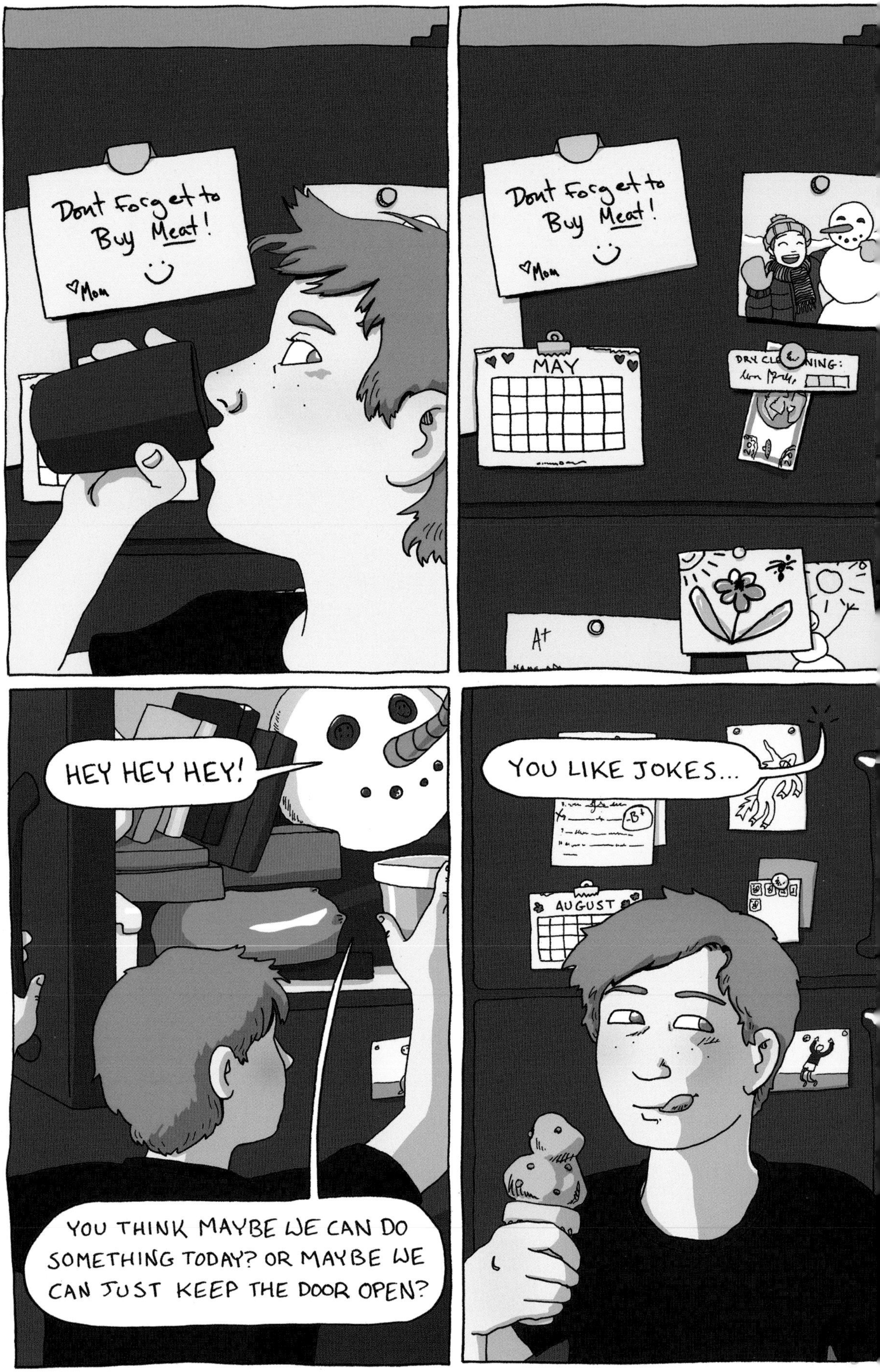
Dont Forget to Buy Meat!
♡Mom
Dont Forget to Buy Meat!
♡Mom
MAY
A+
HEY HEY HEY!
YOU THINK MAYBE WE CAN DO SOMETHING TODAY? OR MAYBE WE CAN JUST KEEP THE DOOR OPEN?
YOU LIKE JOKES...
AUGUST

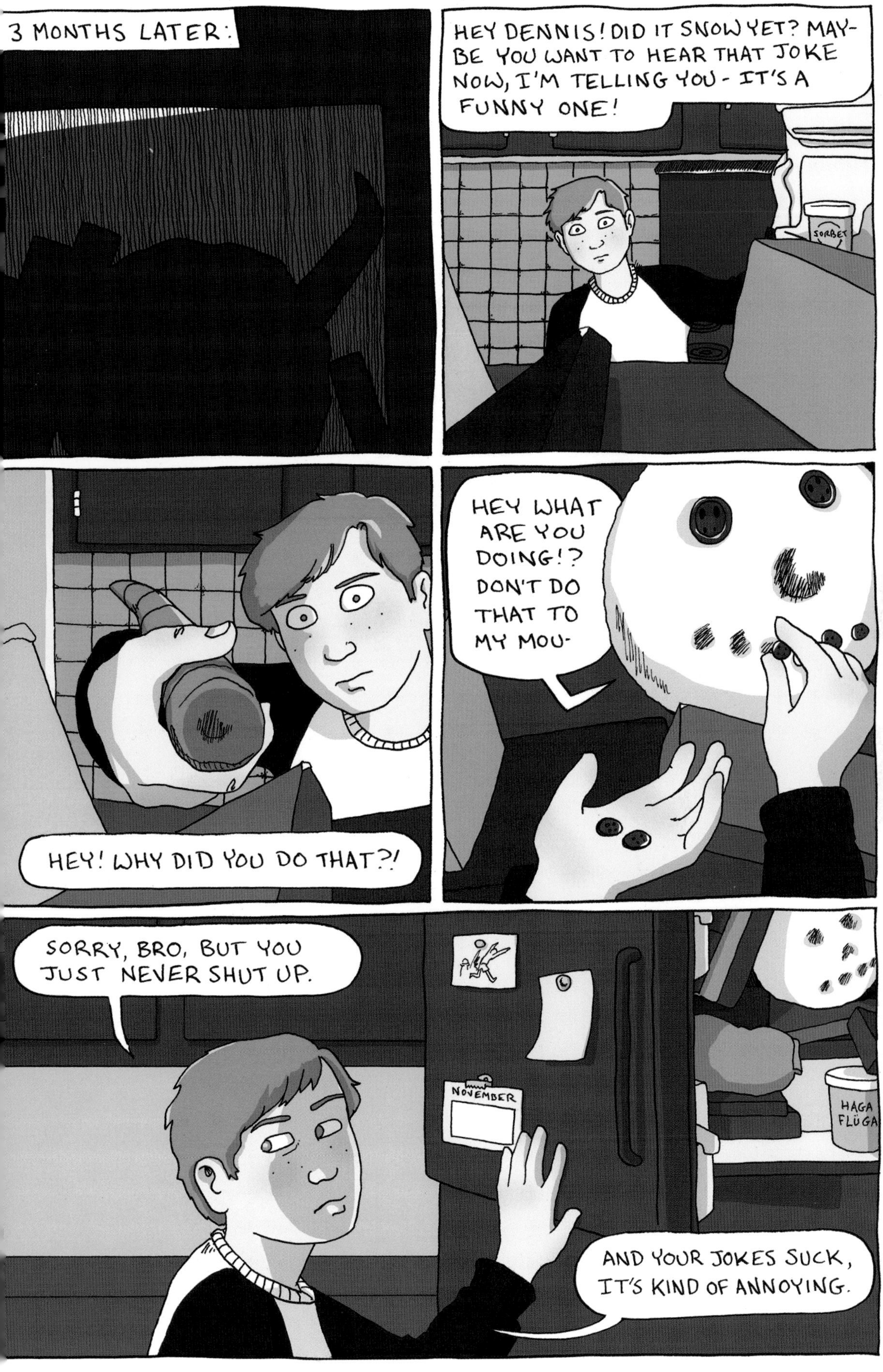
3 MONTHS LATER:
HEY DENNIS! DID IT SNOW YET? MAY-BE YOU WANT TO HEAR THAT JOKE NOW, I'M TELLING YOU - IT'S A FUNNY ONE!
SORBET
HEY! WHY DID YOU DO THAT?!
HEY WHAT ARE YOU DOING!? DON'T DO THAT TO MY MOU-
SORRY, BRO, BUT YOU JUST NEVER SHUT UP.
NOVEMBER
HAGA FLÜGA
AND YOUR JOKES SUCK, IT'S KIND OF ANNOYING.

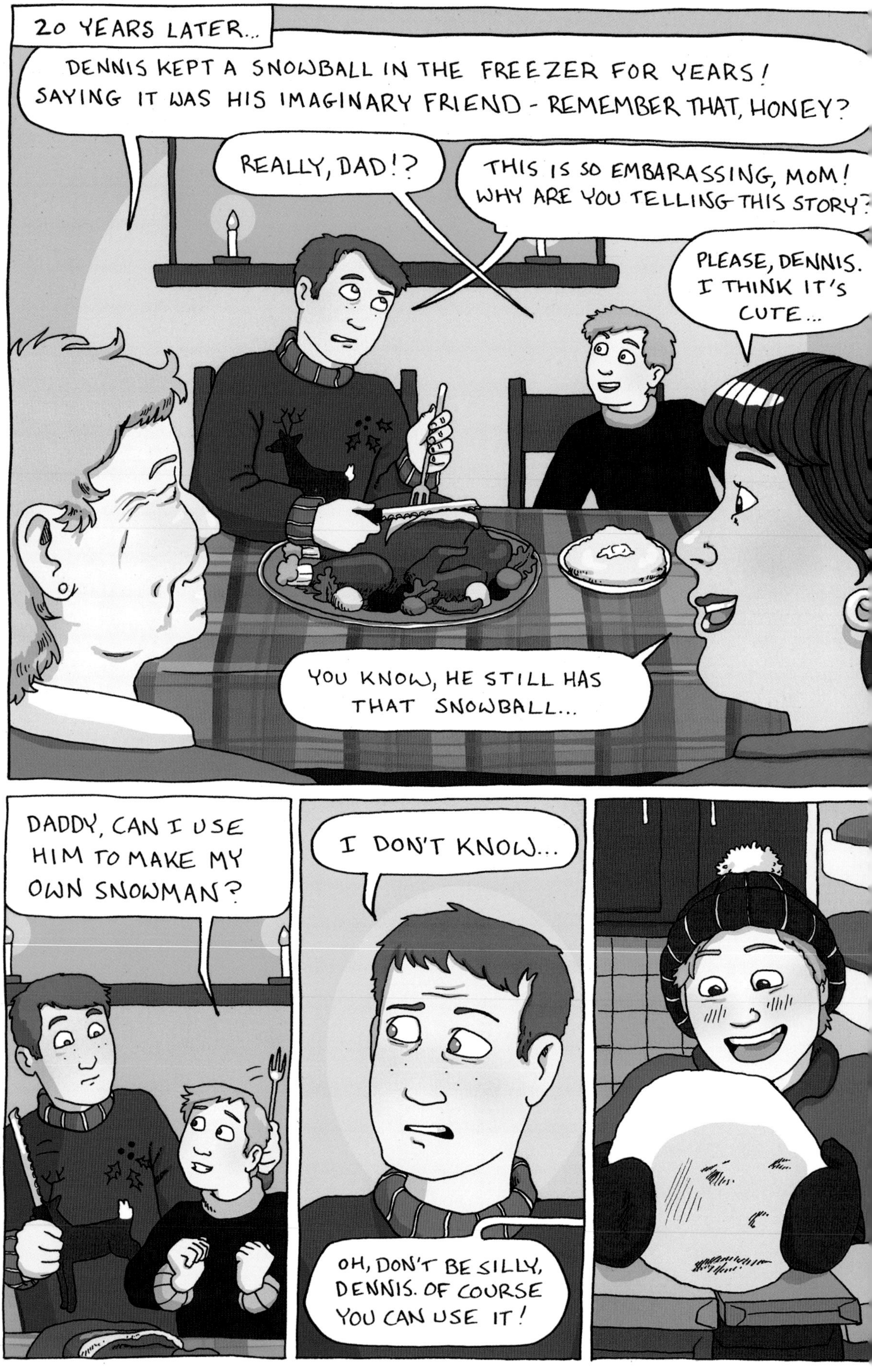
20 YEARS LATER...
DENNIS KEPT A SNOWBALL IN THE FREEZER FOR YEARS! SAYING IT WAS HIS IMAGINARY FRIEND - REMEMBER THAT, HONEY?
REALLY, DAD!?
THIS IS SO EMBARASSING, MOM! WHY ARE YOU TELLING THIS STORY?
PLEASE, DENNIS. I THINK IT'S CUTE...
YOU KNOW, HE STILL HAS THAT SNOWBALL...
DADDY, CAN I USE HIM TO MAKE MY OWN SNOWMAN?
I DON'T KNOW...
OH, DON'T BE SILLY, DENNIS. OF COURSE YOU CAN USE IT!

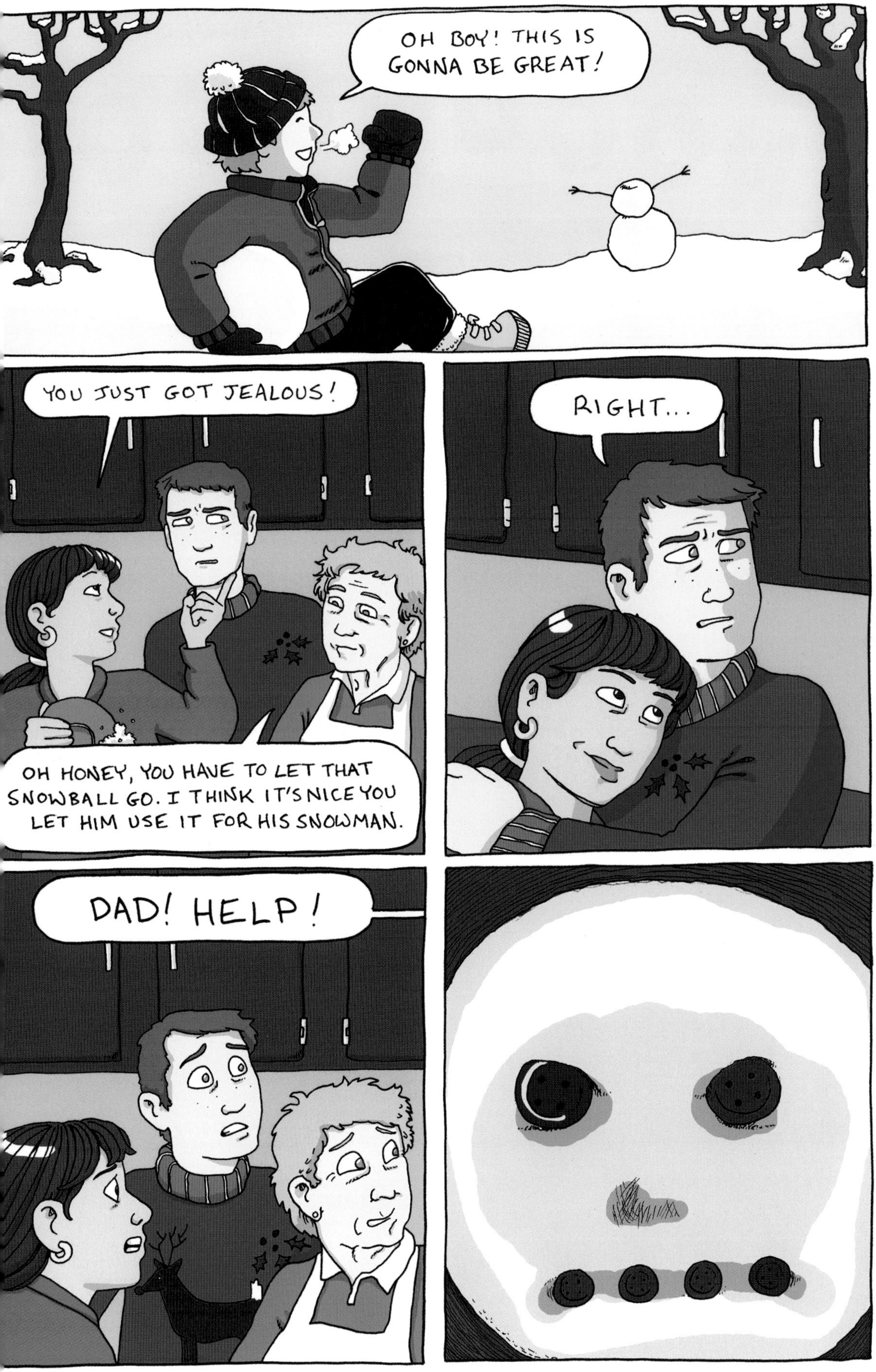
OH BOY! THIS IS GONNA BE GREAT!
YOU JUST GOT JEALOUS!
OH HONEY, YOU HAVE TO LET THAT SNOWBALL GO. I THINK IT'S NICE YOU LET HIM USE IT FOR HIS SNOWMAN.
RIGHT...
DAD! HELP!

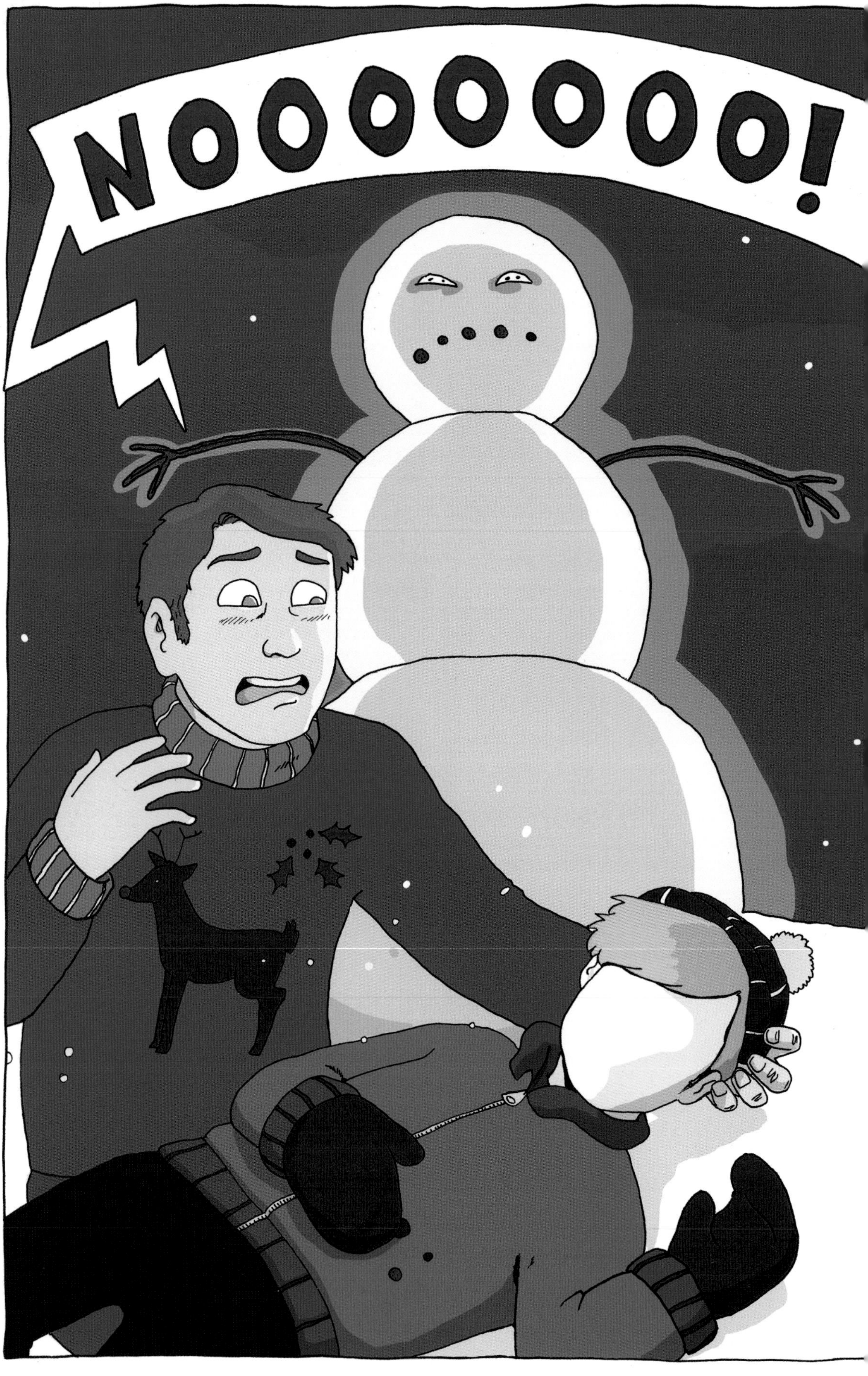
NOOOOOOO!

Robo Dream Art by Edwin Vasquez

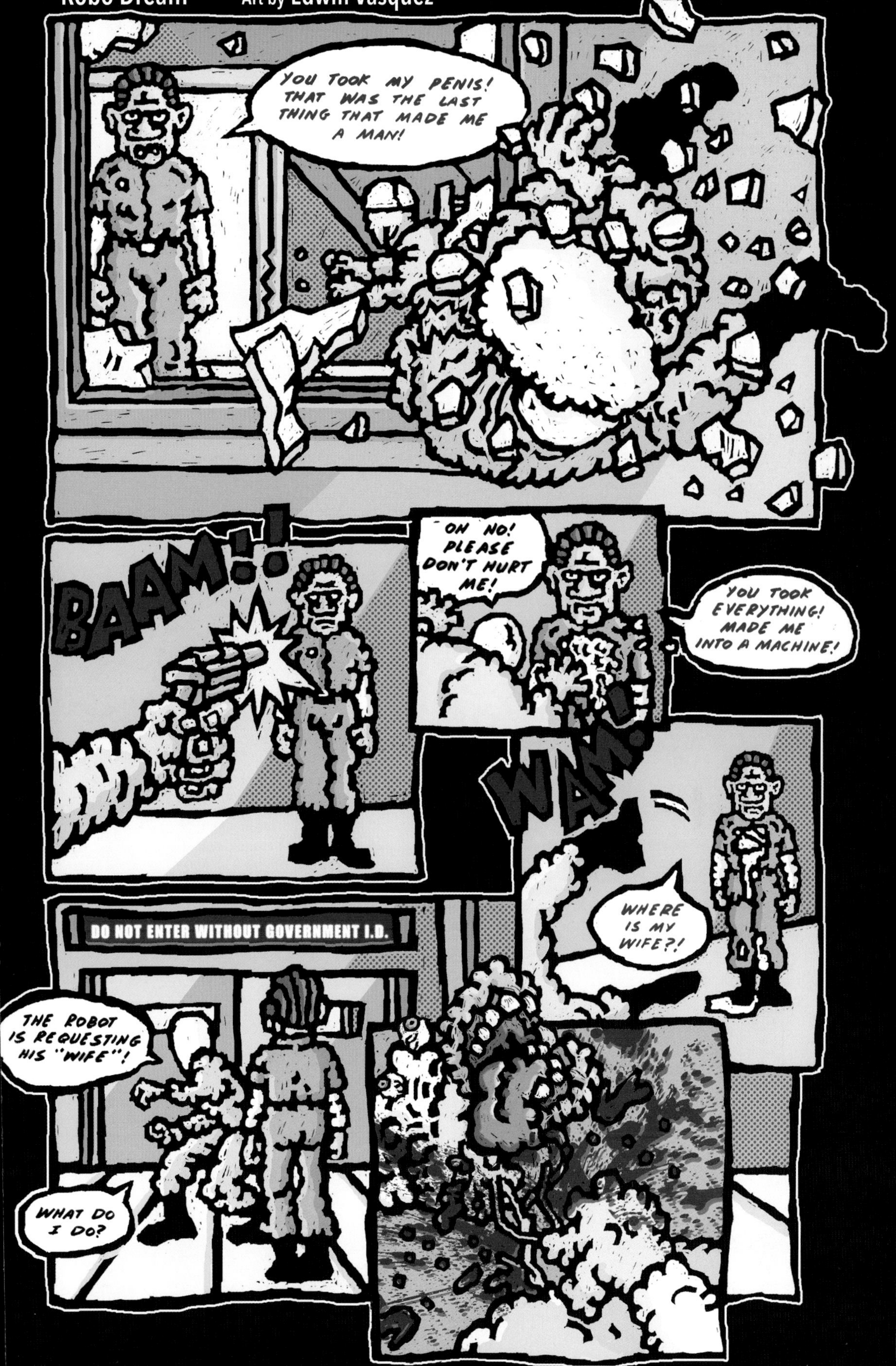
YOU TOOK MY PENIS! THAT WAS THE LAST THING THAT MADE ME A MAN!
BAAM!!!
OH NO! PLEASE DON'T HURT ME!
YOU TOOK EVERYTHING! MADE ME INTO A MACHINE!
WAM!
WHERE IS MY WIFE?!
DO NOT ENTER WITHOUT GOVERNMENT I.D.
THE ROBOT IS REQUESTING HIS "WIFE"!
WHAT DO I DO?

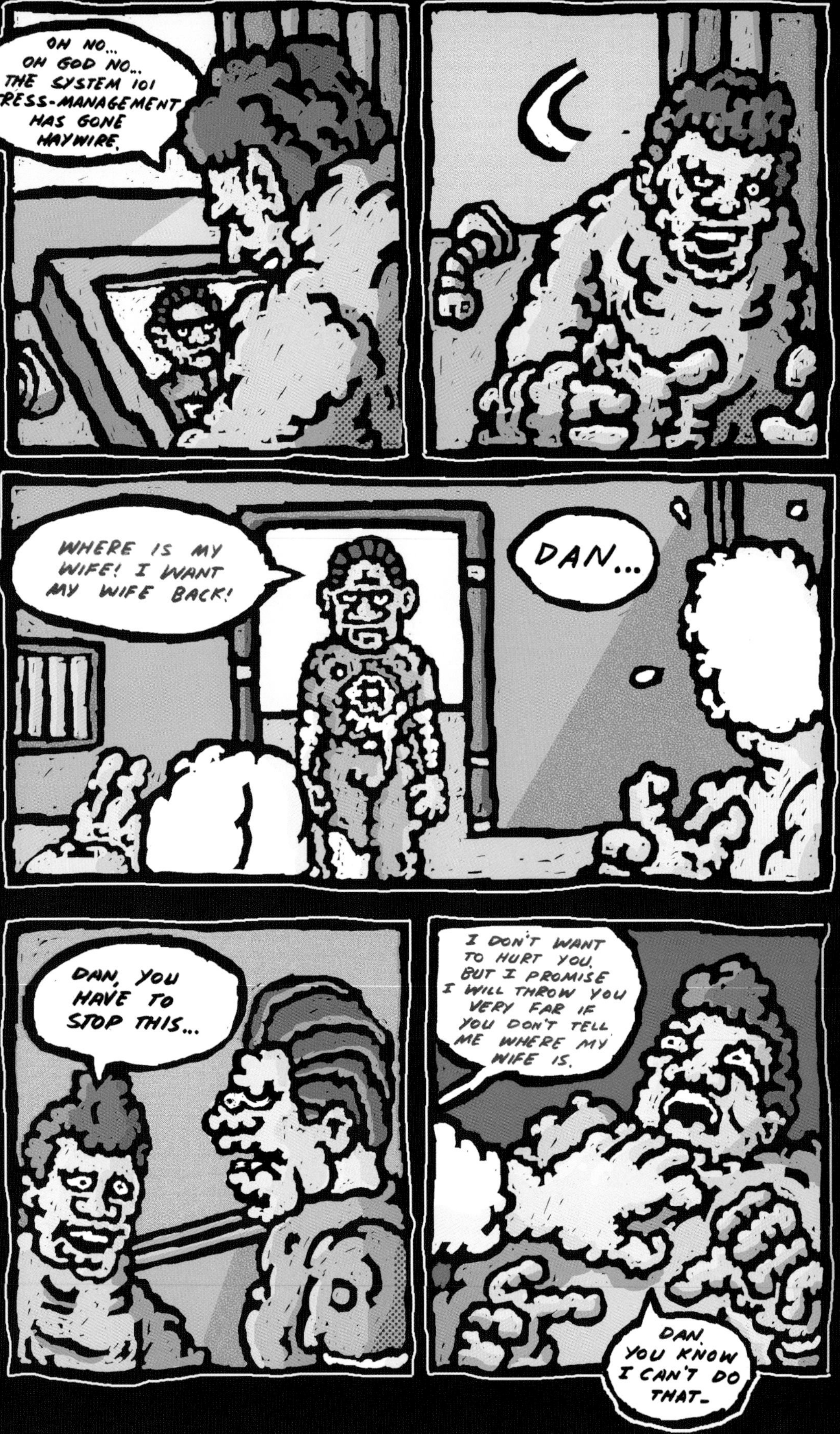
OH NO... OH GOD NO... THE SYSTEM 101 STRESS-MANAGEMENT HAS GONE HAYWIRE.
WHERE IS MY WIFE! I WANT MY WIFE BACK!
DAN...
DAN, YOU HAVE TO STOP THIS...
I DON'T WANT TO HURT YOU. BUT I PROMISE I WILL THROW YOU VERY FAR IF YOU DON'T TELL ME WHERE MY WIFE IS.
DAN. YOU KNOW I CAN'T DO THAT.

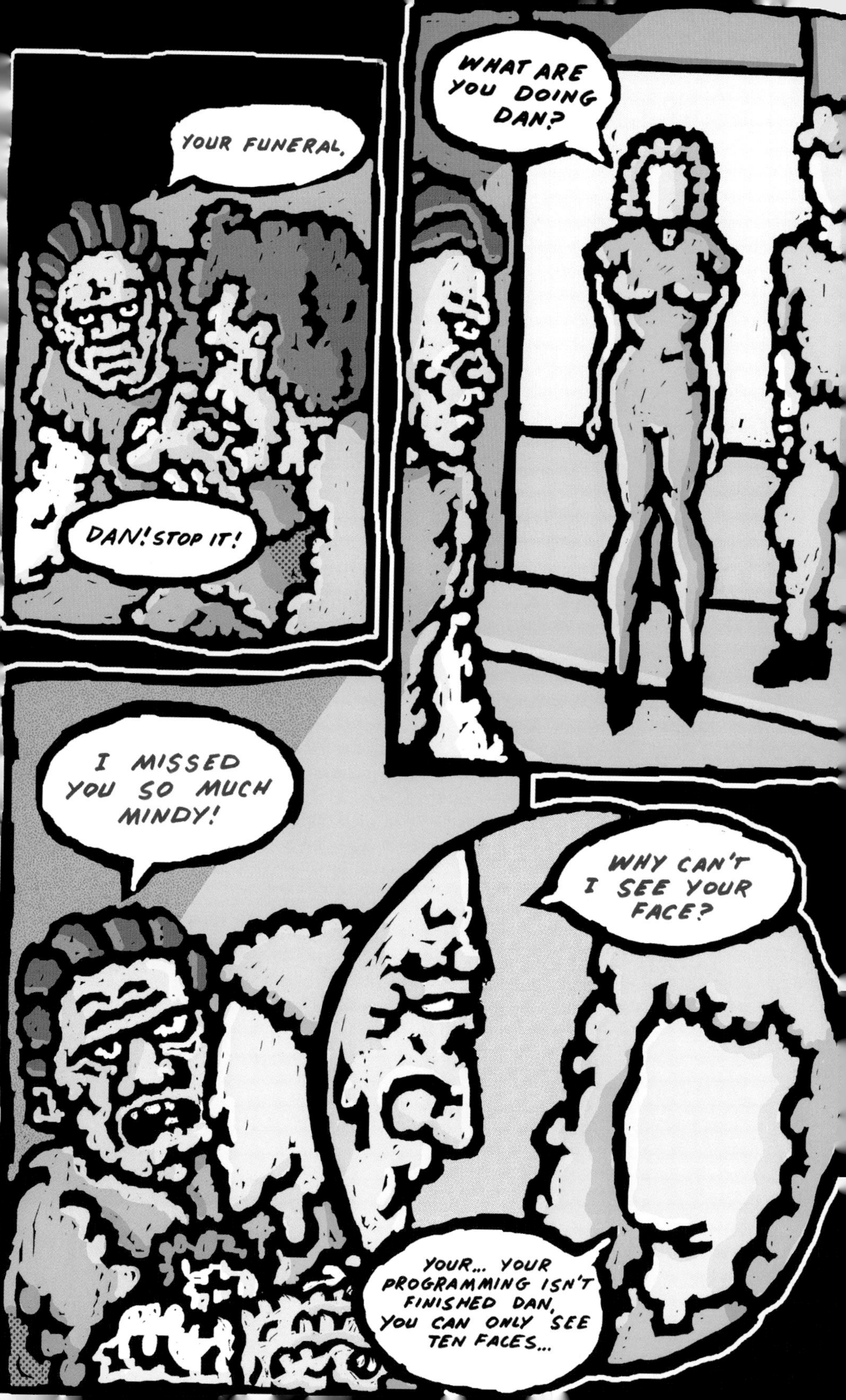
YOUR FUNERAL.
DAN! STOP IT!
WHAT ARE YOU DOING DAN?
I MISSED YOU SO MUCH MINDY!
WHY CAN'T I SEE YOUR FACE?
YOUR... YOUR PROGRAMMING ISN'T FINISHED DAN, YOU CAN ONLY SEE TEN FACES...

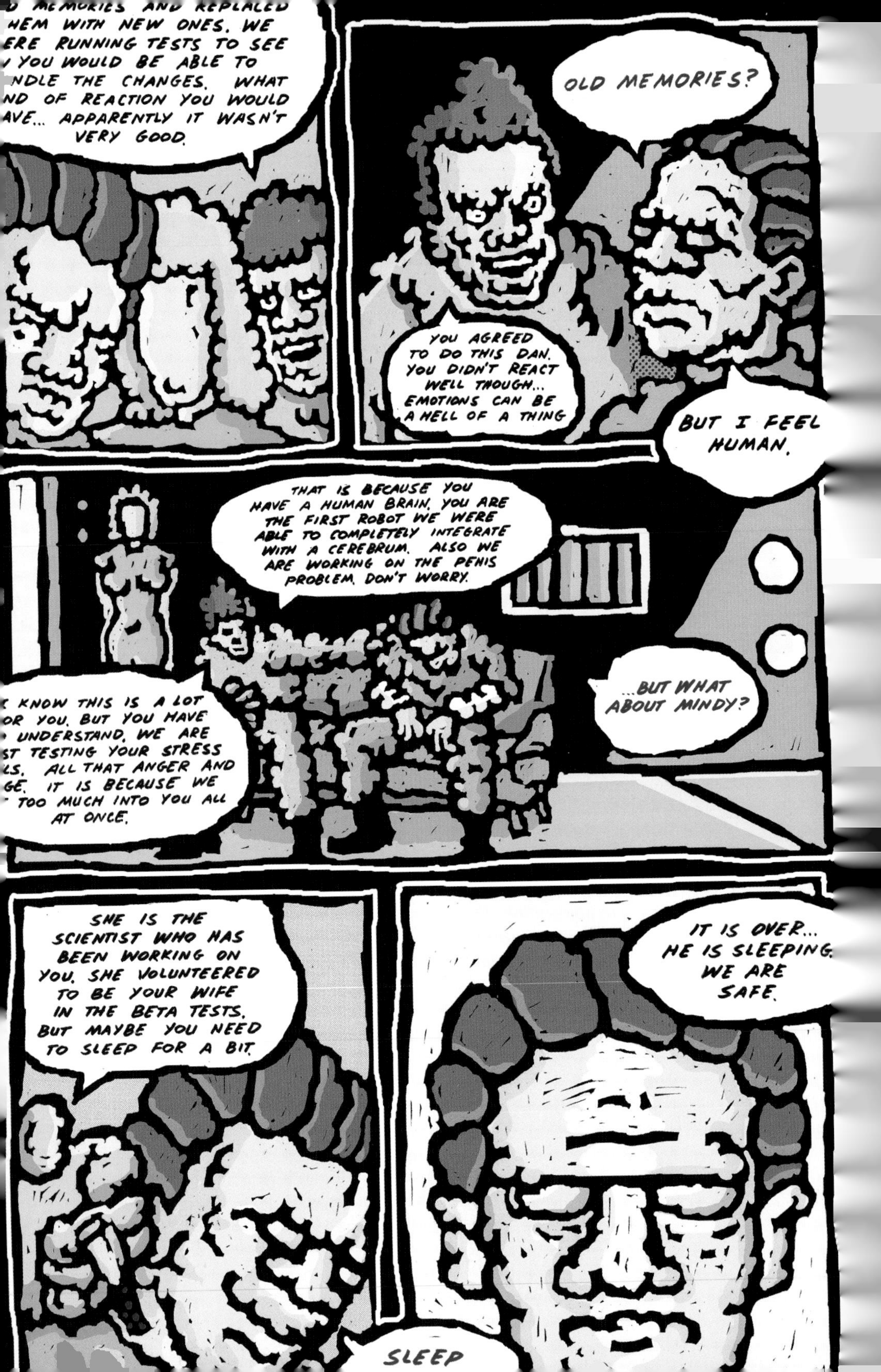

HEM WITH NEW ONES. WE ERE RUNNING TESTS TO SEE YOU WOULD BE ABLE TO NDLE THE CHANGES. WHAT ND OF REACTION YOU WOULD AVE... APPARENTLY IT WASN'T VERY GOOD.
OLD MEMORIES?
YOU AGREED TO DO THIS DAN. YOU DIDN'T REACT WELL THOUGH... EMOTIONS CAN BE A HELL OF A THING
BUT I FEEL HUMAN.
THAT IS BECAUSE YOU HAVE A HUMAN BRAIN. YOU ARE THE FIRST ROBOT WE WERE ABLE TO COMPLETELY INTEGRATE WITH A CEREBRUM. ALSO WE ARE WORKING ON THE PENIS PROBLEM. DON'T WORRY.
...BUT WHAT ABOUT MINDY?
KNOW THIS IS A LOT OR YOU. BUT YOU HAVE UNDERSTAND. WE ARE ST TESTING YOUR STRESS LS. ALL THAT ANGER AND GE. IT IS BECAUSE WE TOO MUCH INTO YOU ALL AT ONCE.
SHE IS THE SCIENTIST WHO HAS BEEN WORKING ON YOU. SHE VOLUNTEERED TO BE YOUR WIFE IN THE BETA TESTS. BUT MAYBE YOU NEED TO SLEEP FOR A BIT.
IT IS OVER... HE IS SLEEPING. WE ARE SAFE.
SLEEP

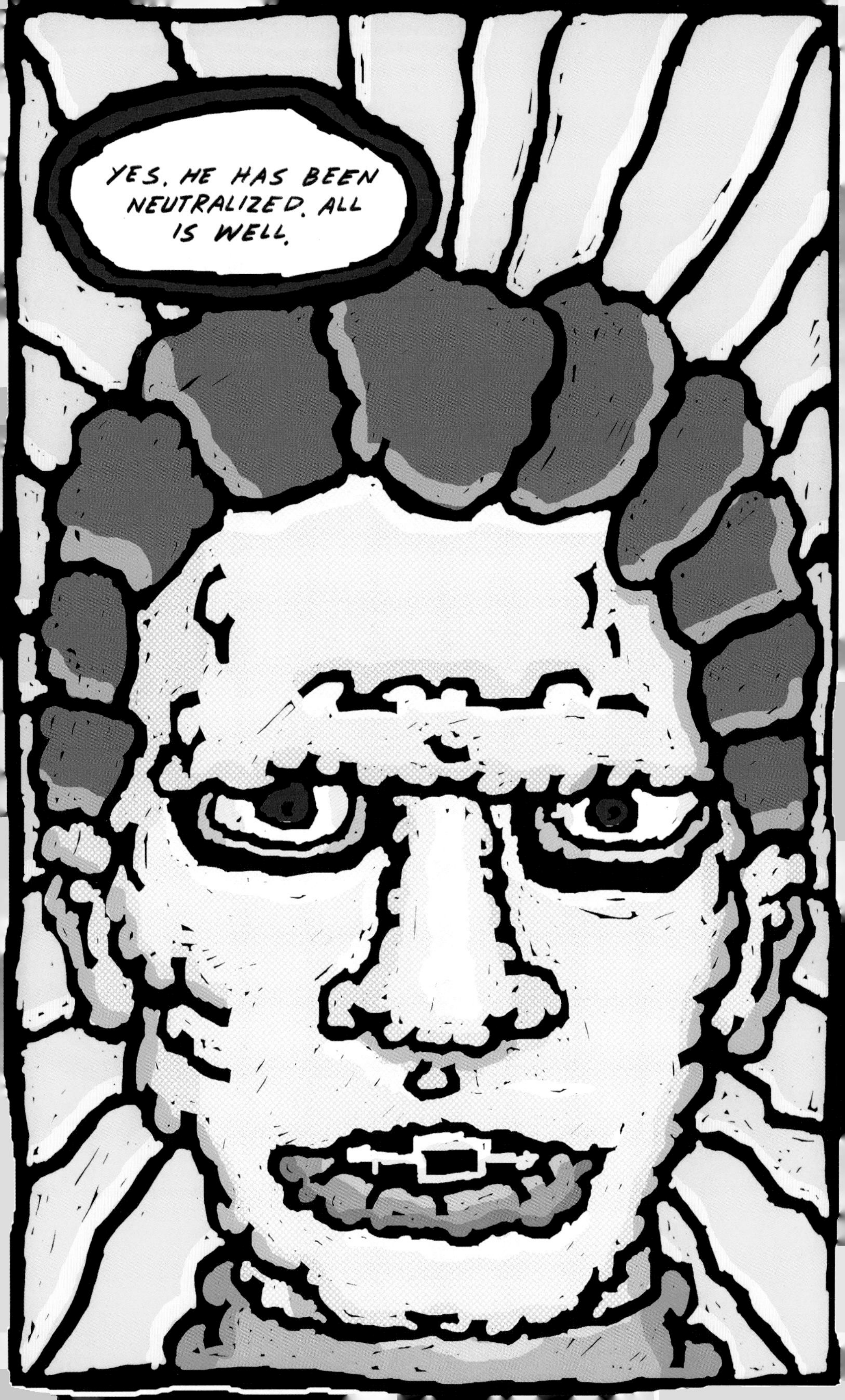
YES. HE HAS BEEN NEUTRALIZED. ALL IS WELL.

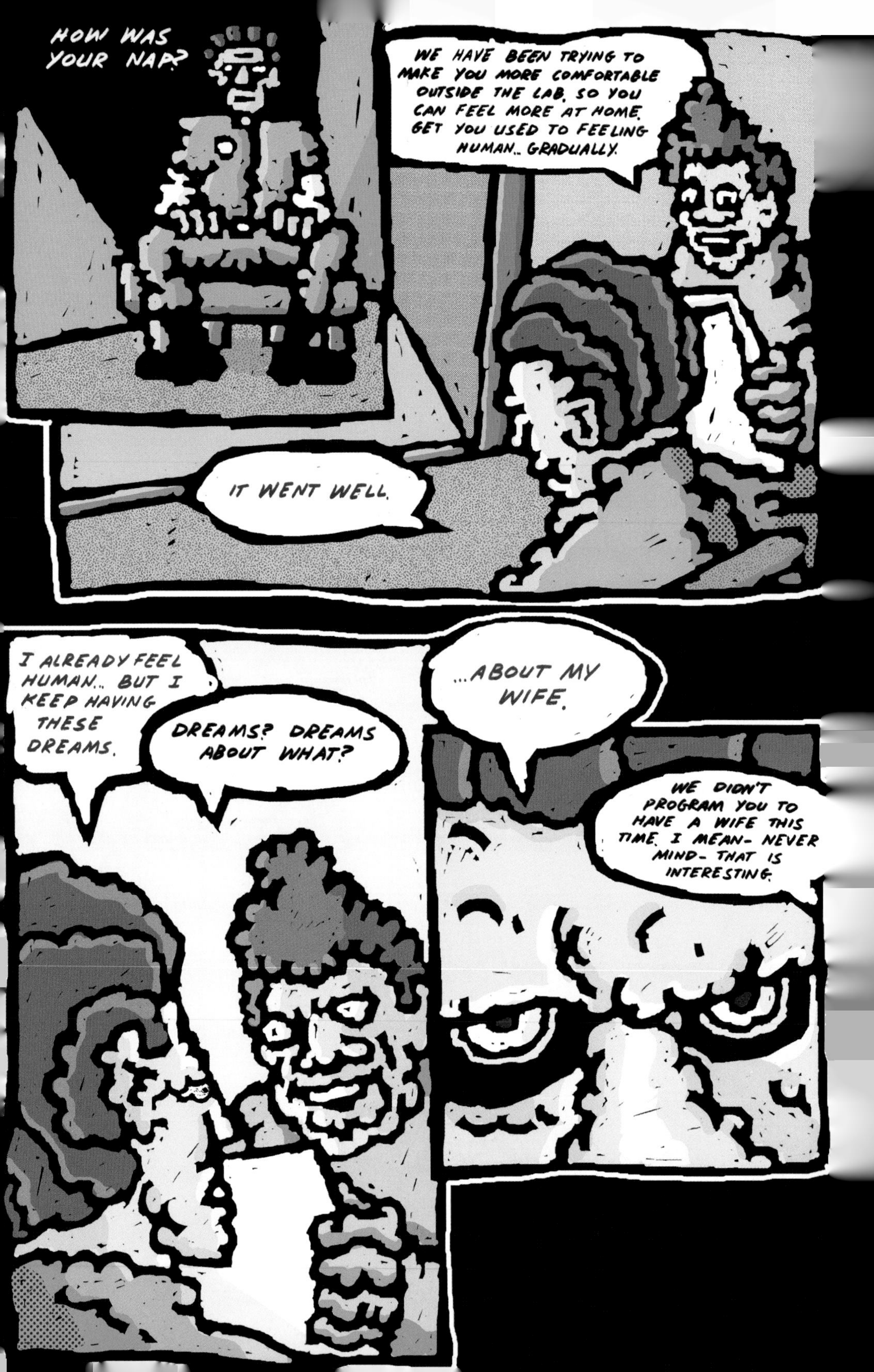
HOW WAS YOUR NAP?
WE HAVE BEEN TRYING TO MAKE YOU MORE COMFORTABLE OUTSIDE THE LAB, SO YOU CAN FEEL MORE AT HOME. GET YOU USED TO FEELING HUMAN... GRADUALLY.
IT WENT WELL.
I ALREADY FEEL HUMAN... BUT I KEEP HAVING THESE DREAMS.
DREAMS? DREAMS ABOUT WHAT?
...ABOUT MY WIFE.
WE DIDN'T PROGRAM YOU TO HAVE A WIFE THIS TIME. I MEAN- NEVER MIND- THAT IS INTERESTING.

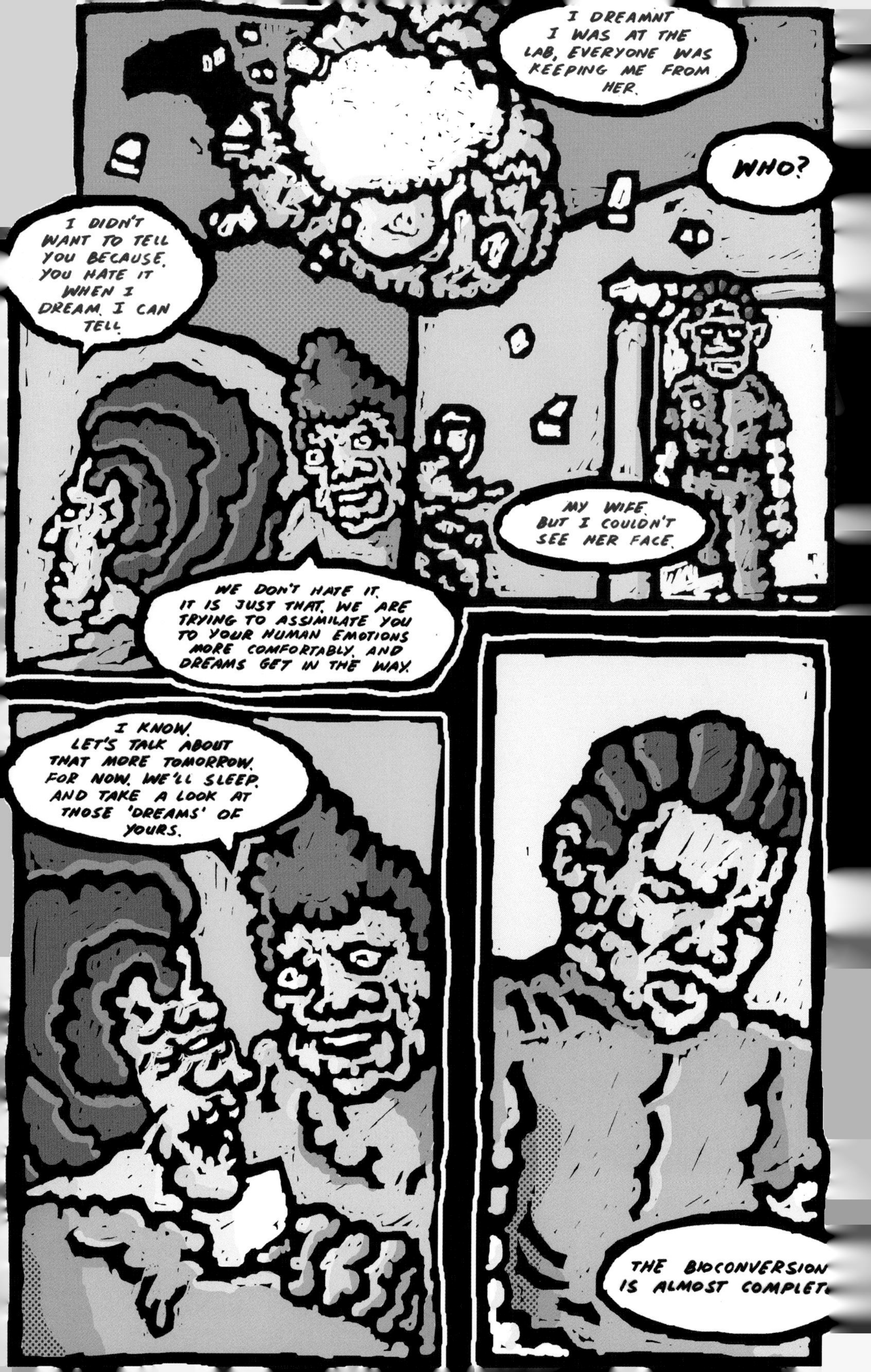
I DREAMNT I WAS AT THE LAB, EVERYONE WAS KEEPING ME FROM HER.
WHO?
I DIDN'T WANT TO TELL YOU BECAUSE. YOU HATE IT WHEN I DREAM. I CAN TELL.
MY WIFE. BUT I COULDN'T SEE HER FACE.
WE DON'T HATE IT. IT IS JUST THAT. WE ARE TRYING TO ASSIMILATE YOU TO YOUR HUMAN EMOTIONS MORE COMFORTABLY. AND DREAMS GET IN THE WAY.
I KNOW. LET'S TALK ABOUT THAT MORE TOMORROW. FOR NOW. WE'LL SLEEP. AND TAKE A LOOK AT THOSE 'DREAMS' OF YOURS.
THE BIOCONVERSION IS ALMOST COMPLETE

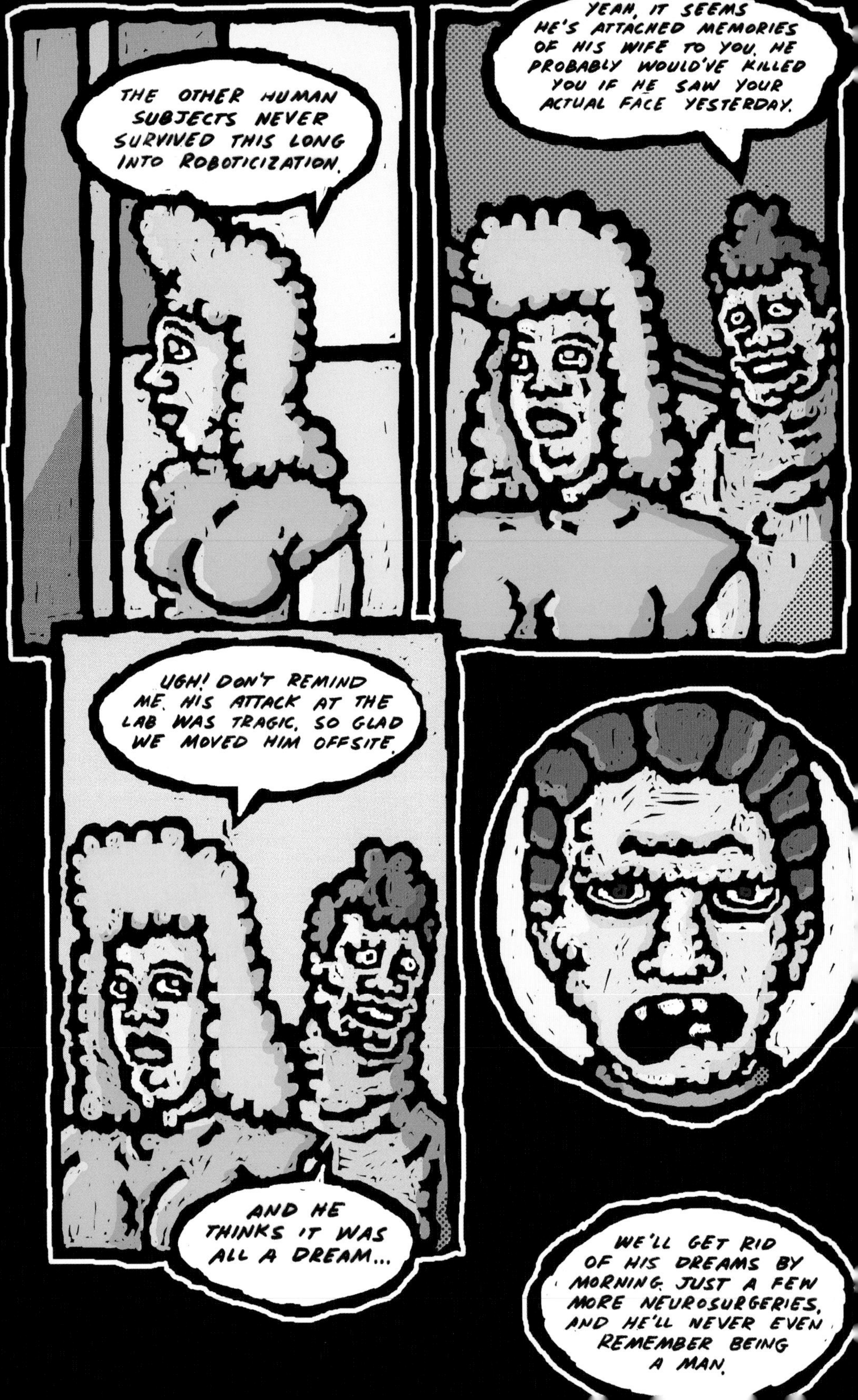
THE OTHER HUMAN SUBJECTS NEVER SURVIVED THIS LONG INTO ROBOTICIZATION.
YEAH, IT SEEMS HE'S ATTACHED MEMORIES OF HIS WIFE TO YOU. HE PROBABLY WOULD'VE KILLED YOU IF HE SAW YOUR ACTUAL FACE YESTERDAY.
UGH! DON'T REMIND ME. HIS ATTACK AT THE LAB WAS TRAGIC. SO GLAD WE MOVED HIM OFFSITE.
AND HE THINKS IT WAS ALL A DREAM...
WE'LL GET RID OF HIS DREAMS BY MORNING. JUST A FEW MORE NEUROSURGERIES, AND HE'LL NEVER EVEN REMEMBER BEING A MAN.

The Katzenjammer Virus Art by Mike Prezzato

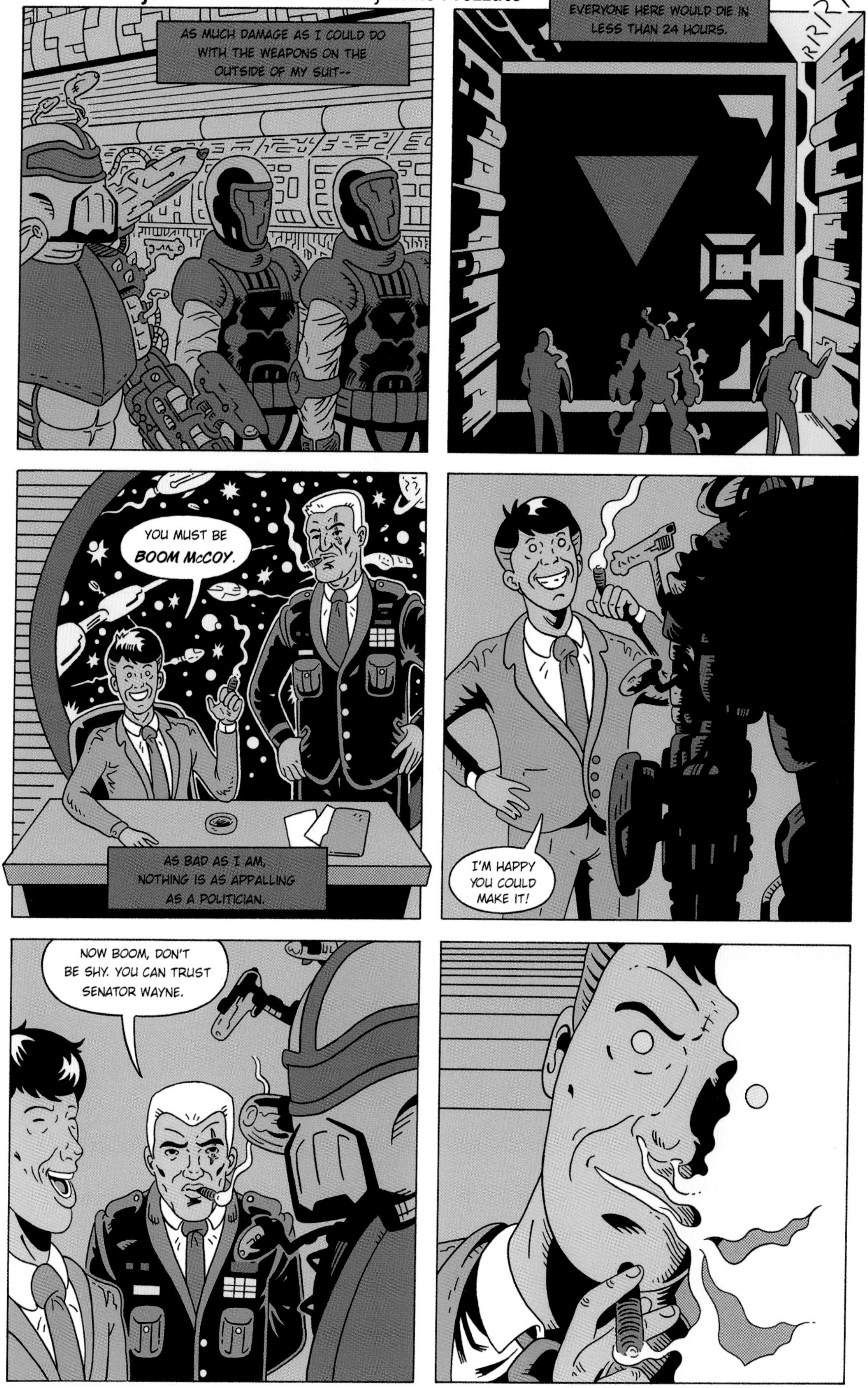
AS MUCH DAMAGE AS I COULD DO WITH THE WEAPONS ON THE OUTSIDE OF MY SUIT--
--IF I WERE TO TAKE IT OFF, EVERYONE HERE WOULD DIE IN LESS THAN 24 HOURS.
RRRRR
YOU MUST BE BOOM McCOY.
AS BAD AS I AM, NOTHING IS AS APPALLING AS A POLITICIAN.
I'M HAPPY YOU COULD MAKE IT!
NOW BOOM, DON'T BE SHY. YOU CAN TRUST SENATOR WAYNE.

BOOM, DO YOU UNDERSTAND YOUR MISSION?

CLEANSE THE POLITICAL CAMPAIGN SHIP OF ROSS HEYMAN OF THE KATZENJAMMER VIRUS. A VIRUS THAT WAS RELEASED ON THE ORDERS OF SENATOR WAYNE.

McCOY. SENATOR WAYNE HAD NOTHING TO DO WITH THE VIRUS. DO YOU UNDERSTAND?

I WAS JUST REITERATING WHAT WAS IN THE BRIEFING.

SOLDIER!
SENATOR WAYNE HAD NOTHING TO DO WITH--

IT'S OK. HE CAN BELIEVE WHATEVER HE WANTS, AS LONG AS HE DOES HIS JOB. BUT THERE IS ONE THING...

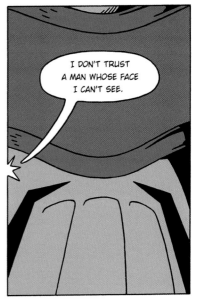

I DON'T TRUST A MAN WHOSE FACE I CAN'T SEE.

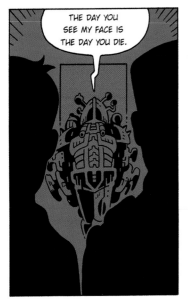

THE DAY YOU SEE MY FACE IS THE DAY YOU DIE.

DID YOU HEAR HIM? WHO DOES HE THINK HE IS TALKING TO?

I HATE POLITICIANS.

HEY, MAN VOTE FOR HEYMAN!

I HATE BUREAUCRACY.

THUD

I HATE HIERARCHY.

MEOW

BUT IF THERE IS ONE THING THAT I HATE MORE THAN EVERYTHING IN THIS UNIVERSE...

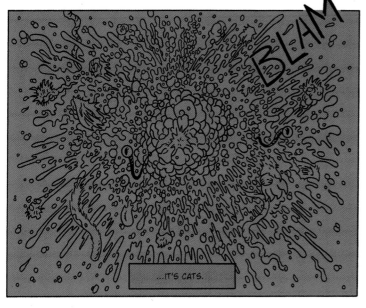

BLAM

...IT'S CATS.

SSS

THE KATZENJAMMER VIRUS IS BY THE FAR THE WORST BIOLOGICAL WEAPON I HAVE EVER ENCOUNTERED.

THE VIRUS IS DISGUSTING. SAPS A MAN OF HIS WILL.

MEOW

MAKES HIM THE PLAYTHING OF EVIL FORCES.

!

MUNCH MUNCH

MUNCH

MUNCH CRUNCH

SIZZLE!

FIRST HIS IMMUNE SYSTEM GOES.

THEN YOUR BODY RELEASES EVERY GODDAMN THING IT CAN RELEASE THROUGH EVERY GODDAMN HOLE.

HELP ME.

HEY MAN

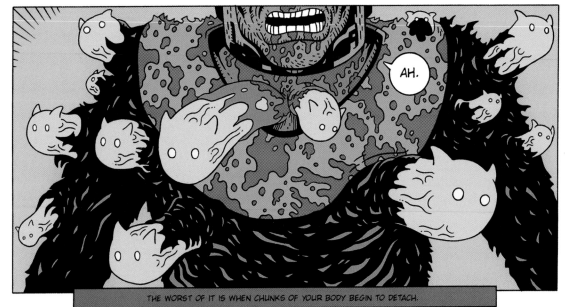

AH.

THE WORST OF IT IS WHEN CHUNKS OF YOUR BODY BEGIN TO DETACH.

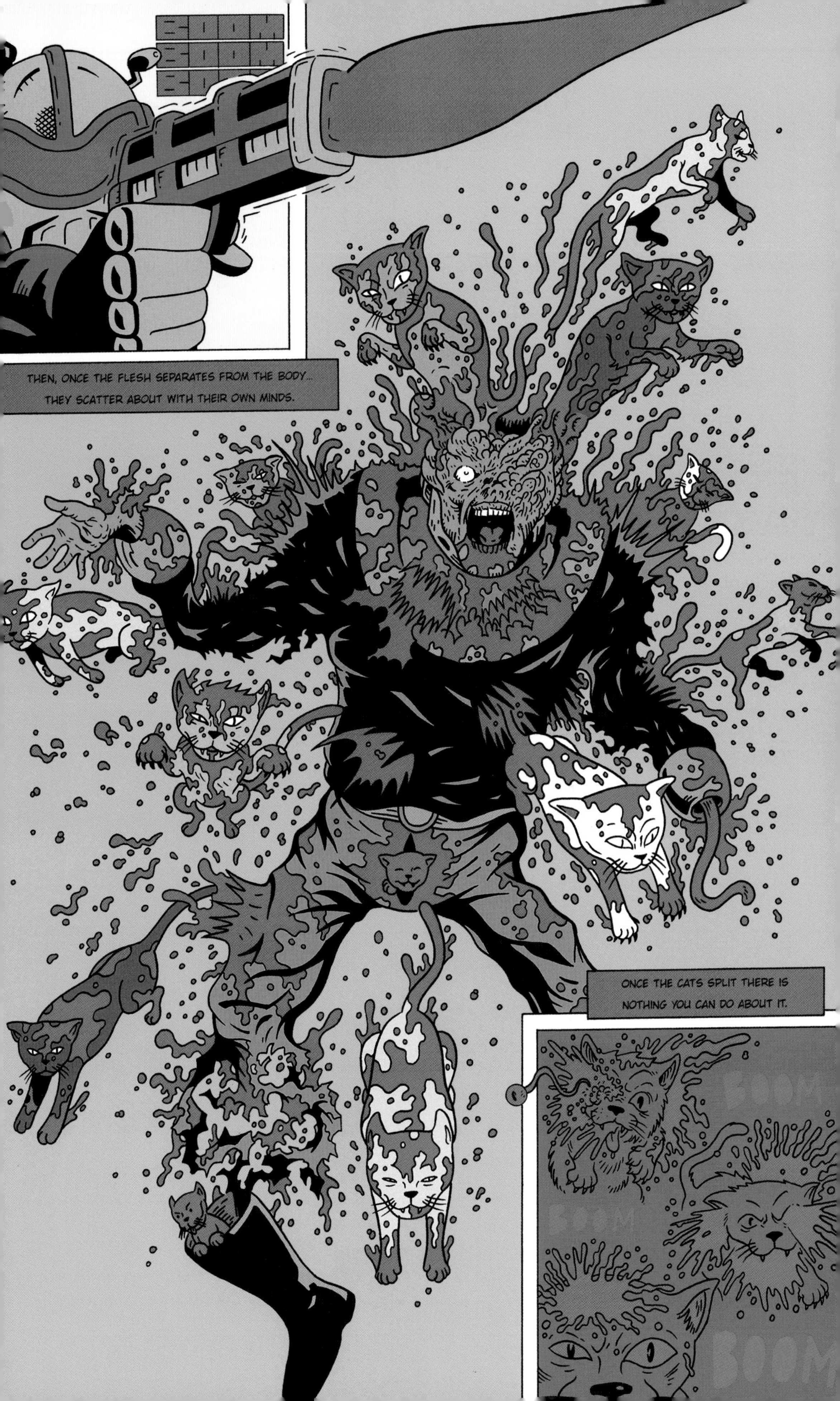
BOOM
BOOM
BOOM
THEN, ONCE THE FLESH SEPARATES FROM THE BODY...
THEY SCATTER ABOUT WITH THEIR OWN MINDS.
ONCE THE CATS SPLIT THERE IS NOTHING YOU CAN DO ABOUT IT.
BOOM
BOOM
BOOM

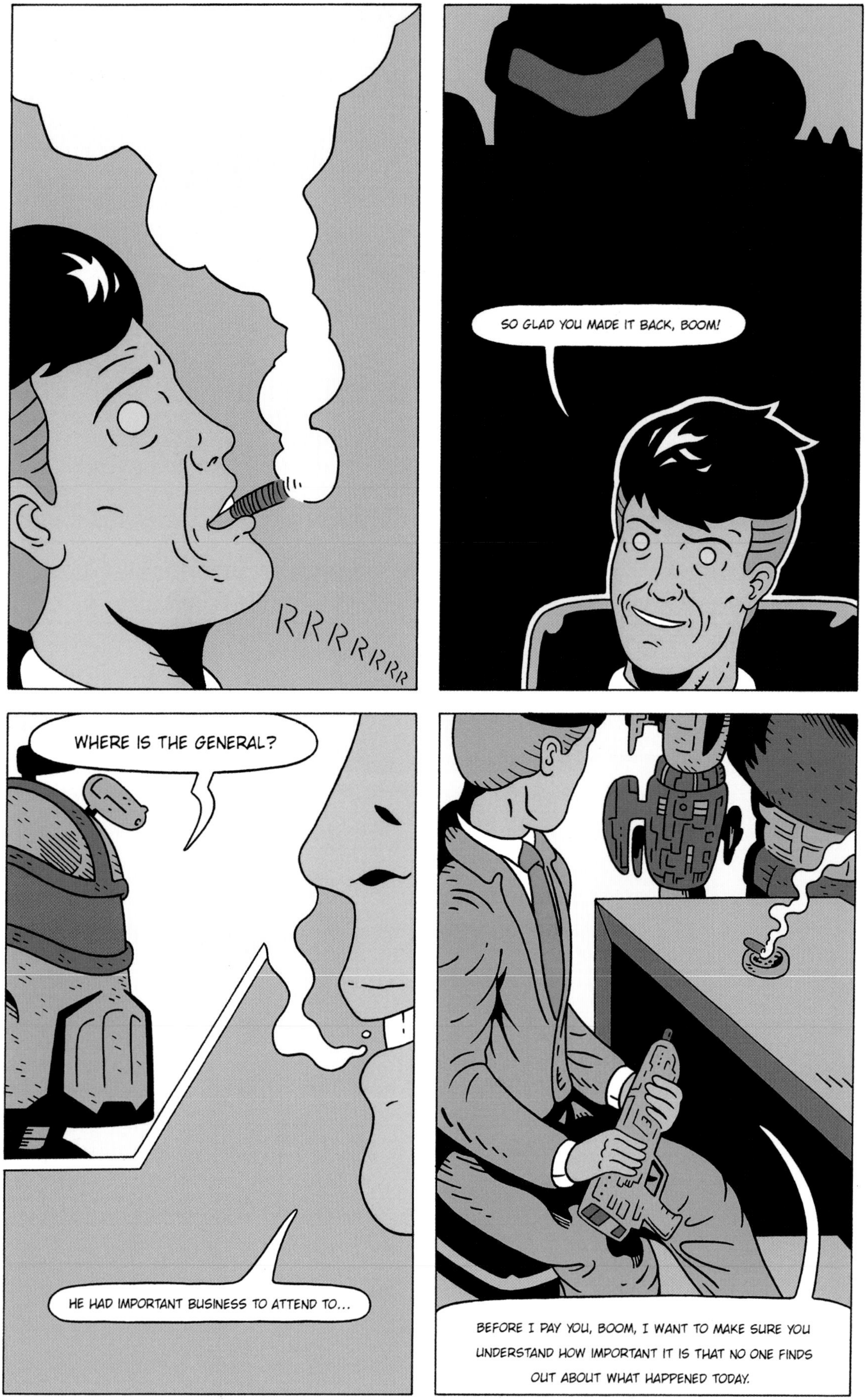
RRRRRRRR
SO GLAD YOU MADE IT BACK, BOOM!
WHERE IS THE GENERAL?
HE HAD IMPORTANT BUSINESS TO ATTEND TO...
BEFORE I PAY YOU, BOOM, I WANT TO MAKE SURE YOU UNDERSTAND HOW IMPORTANT IT IS THAT NO ONE FINDS OUT ABOUT WHAT HAPPENED TODAY.

I AM RUNNING FOR OMNI-PRESIDENT NEXT YEAR AND I CAN'T HAVE SOMETHING LIKE THIS COME OUT. A SENATOR RELEASING SUCH A NASTY DISEASE ON HIS OPPONENT IS VERY BAD PRESS.

IT IS UNFORTUNATE YOU KNOW THAT BIT OF INFORMATION... IT IS VERY UNFORTUNATE.

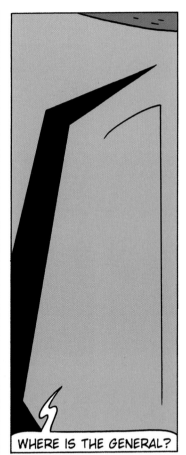

WHERE IS THE GENERAL?

BANG!

THOOM THOOM THOOM

POP

POP

POP

NO! YOU FOOL! YOU WILL KILL US ALL!

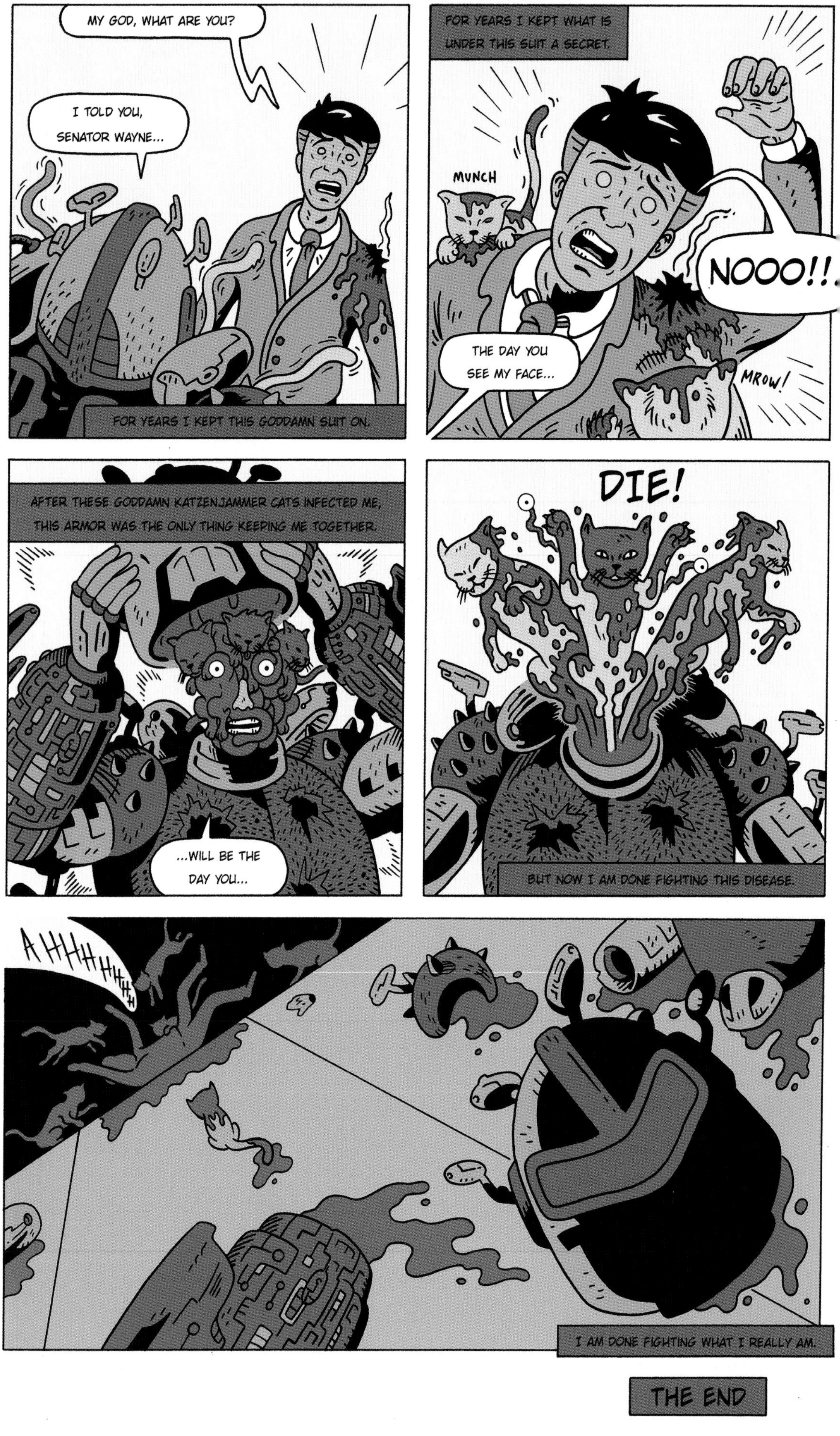
MY GOD, WHAT ARE YOU?
I TOLD YOU, SENATOR WAYNE...
FOR YEARS I KEPT THIS GODDAMN SUIT ON.
FOR YEARS I KEPT WHAT IS UNDER THIS SUIT A SECRET.
MUNCH
NOOO!!
THE DAY YOU SEE MY FACE...
MROW!
AFTER THESE GODDAMN KATZENJAMMER CATS INFECTED ME, THIS ARMOR WAS THE ONLY THING KEEPING ME TOGETHER.
...WILL BE THE DAY YOU...
DIE!
BUT NOW I AM DONE FIGHTING THIS DISEASE.
AHHHHHHH
I AM DONE FIGHTING WHAT I REALLY AM.
THE END

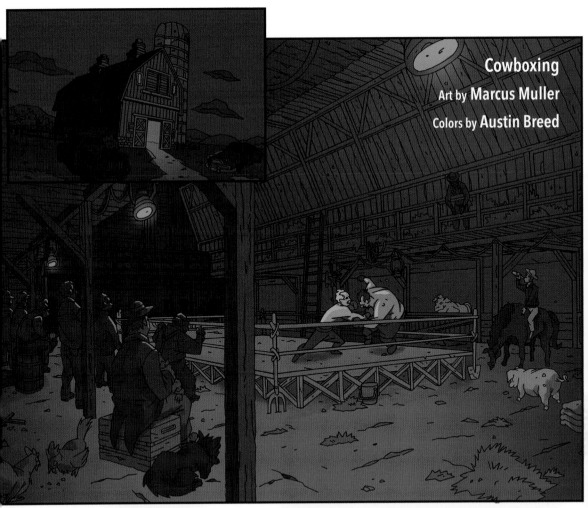

Cowboxing

Art by **Marcus Muller**

Colors by **Austin Breed**

THE MAN BUILDS A BOXING RING AND HE CAN'T EVEN BOX!

EVERY MONTH I GOTTA WATCH POOR HITCHENS GETS HIS FACE REARRANGED.

APPARENTLY, EDGAR, I LOST THIS ONE.

YOU LOSE EVERY FIGHT!

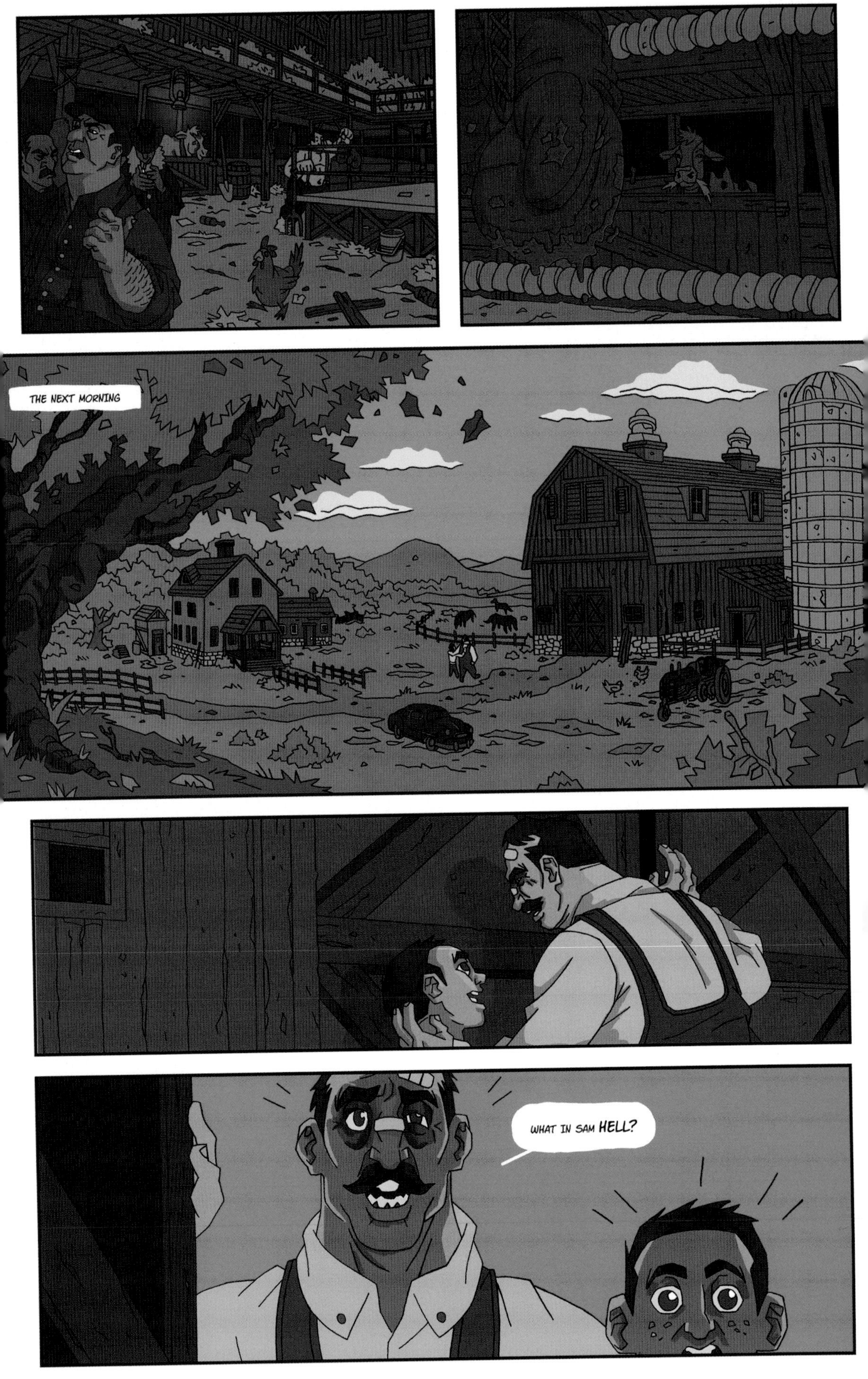
THE NEXT MORNING
WHAT IN SAM HELL?

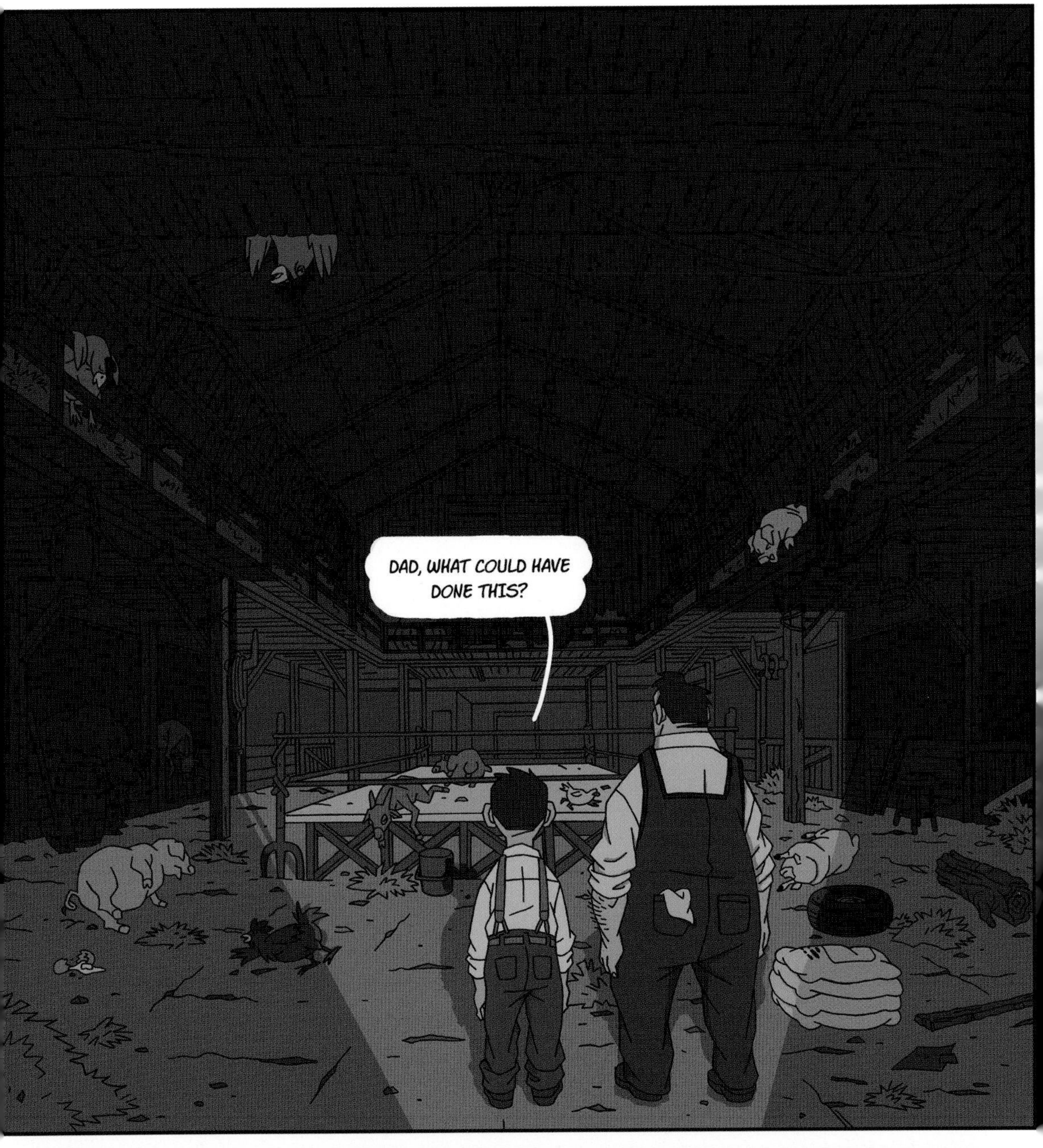
DAD, WHAT COULD HAVE DONE THIS?

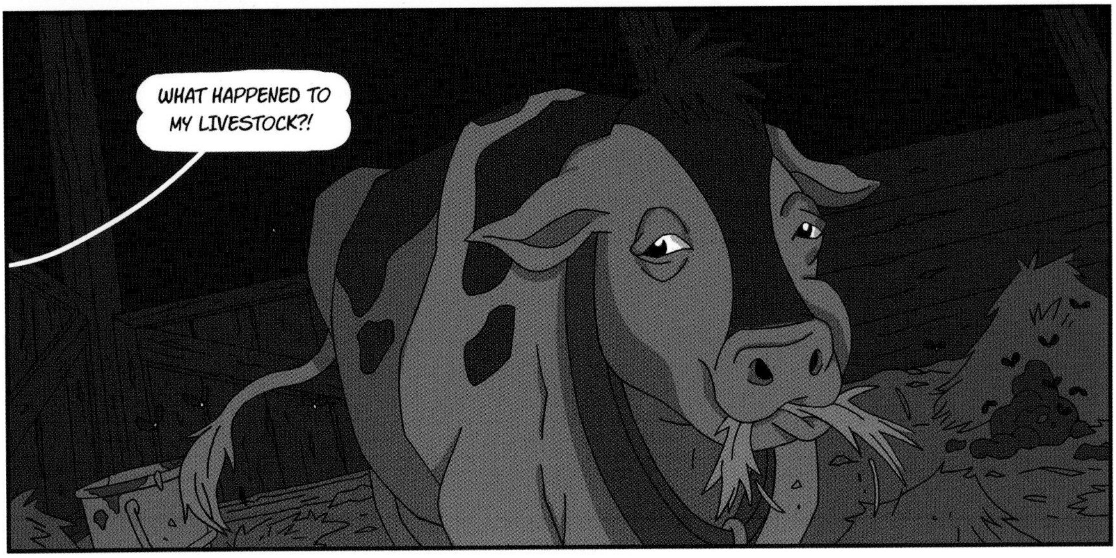
WHAT HAPPENED TO MY LIVESTOCK?!

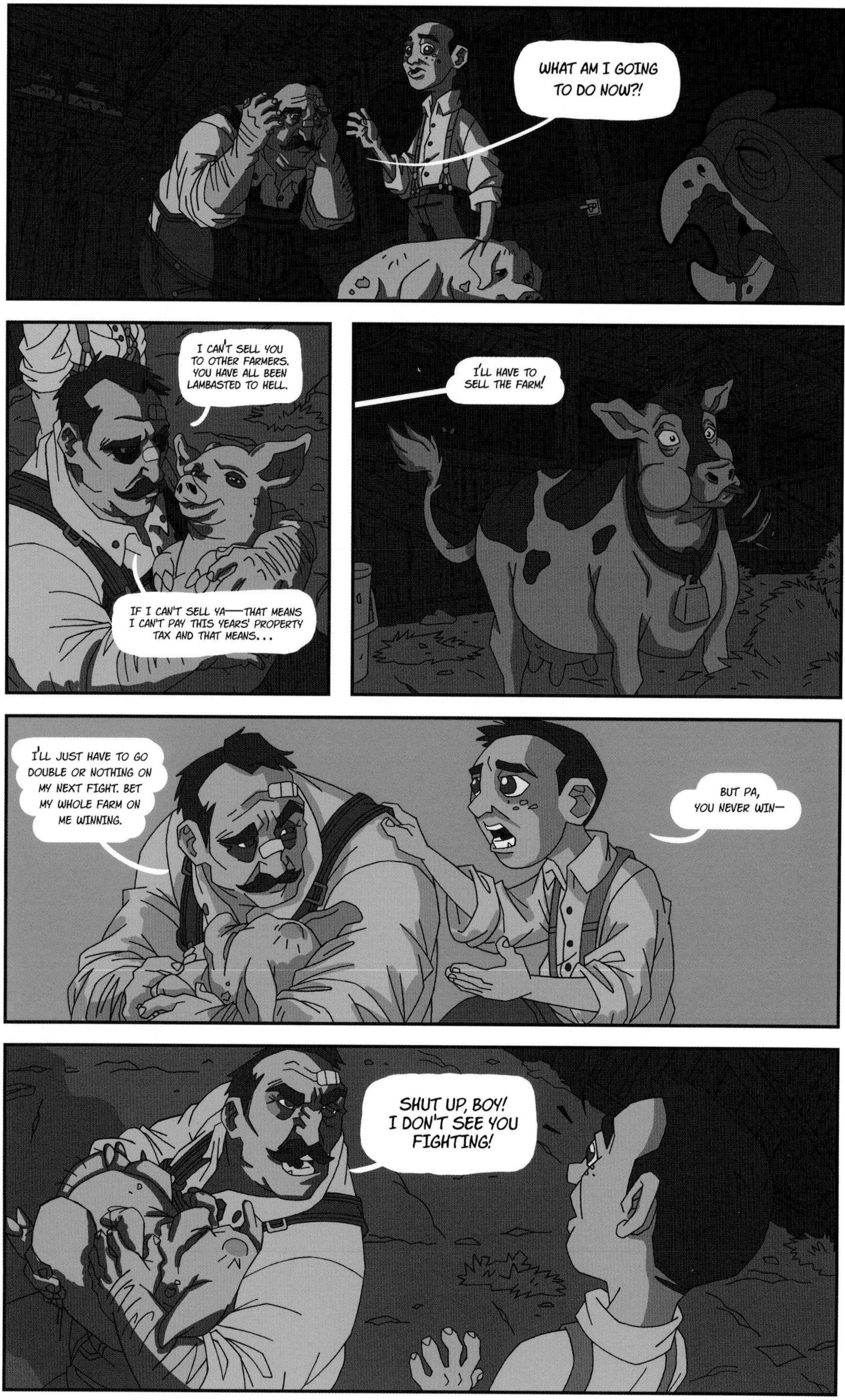

WHAT AM I GOING TO DO NOW?!
I CAN'T SELL YOU TO OTHER FARMERS. YOU HAVE ALL BEEN LAMBASTED TO HELL.
IF I CAN'T SELL YA—THAT MEANS I CAN'T PAY THIS YEARS' PROPERTY TAX AND THAT MEANS...
I'LL HAVE TO SELL THE FARM!
I'LL JUST HAVE TO GO DOUBLE OR NOTHING ON MY NEXT FIGHT. BET MY WHOLE FARM ON ME WINNING.
BUT PA, YOU NEVER WIN—
SHUT UP, BOY! I DON'T SEE YOU FIGHTING!

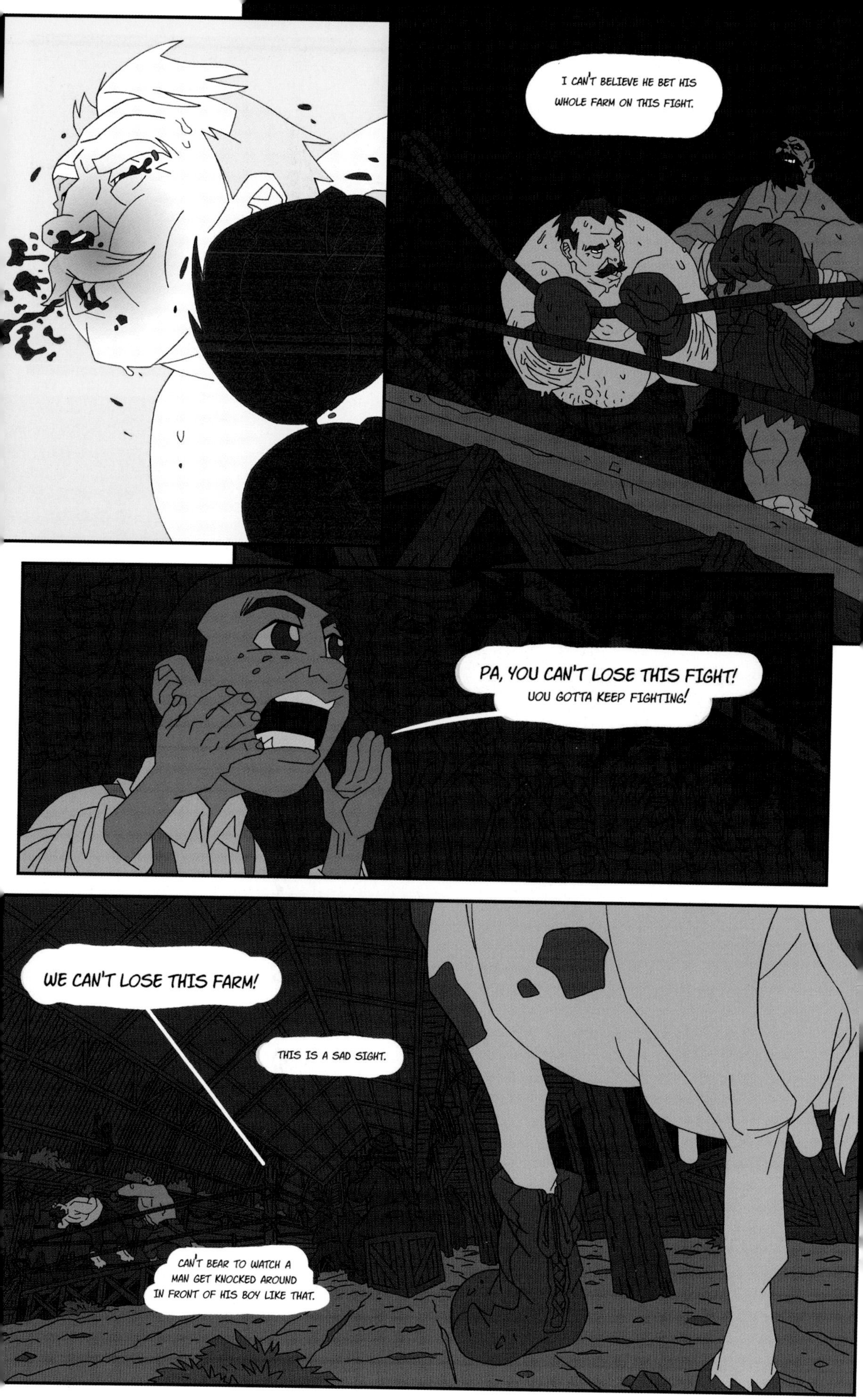
I CAN'T BELIEVE HE BET HIS WHOLE FARM ON THIS FIGHT.
PA, YOU CAN'T LOSE THIS FIGHT! UOU GOTTA KEEP FIGHTING!
WE CAN'T LOSE THIS FARM!
THIS IS A SAD SIGHT.
CAN'T BEAR TO WATCH A MAN GET KNOCKED AROUND IN FRONT OF HIS BOY LIKE THAT.

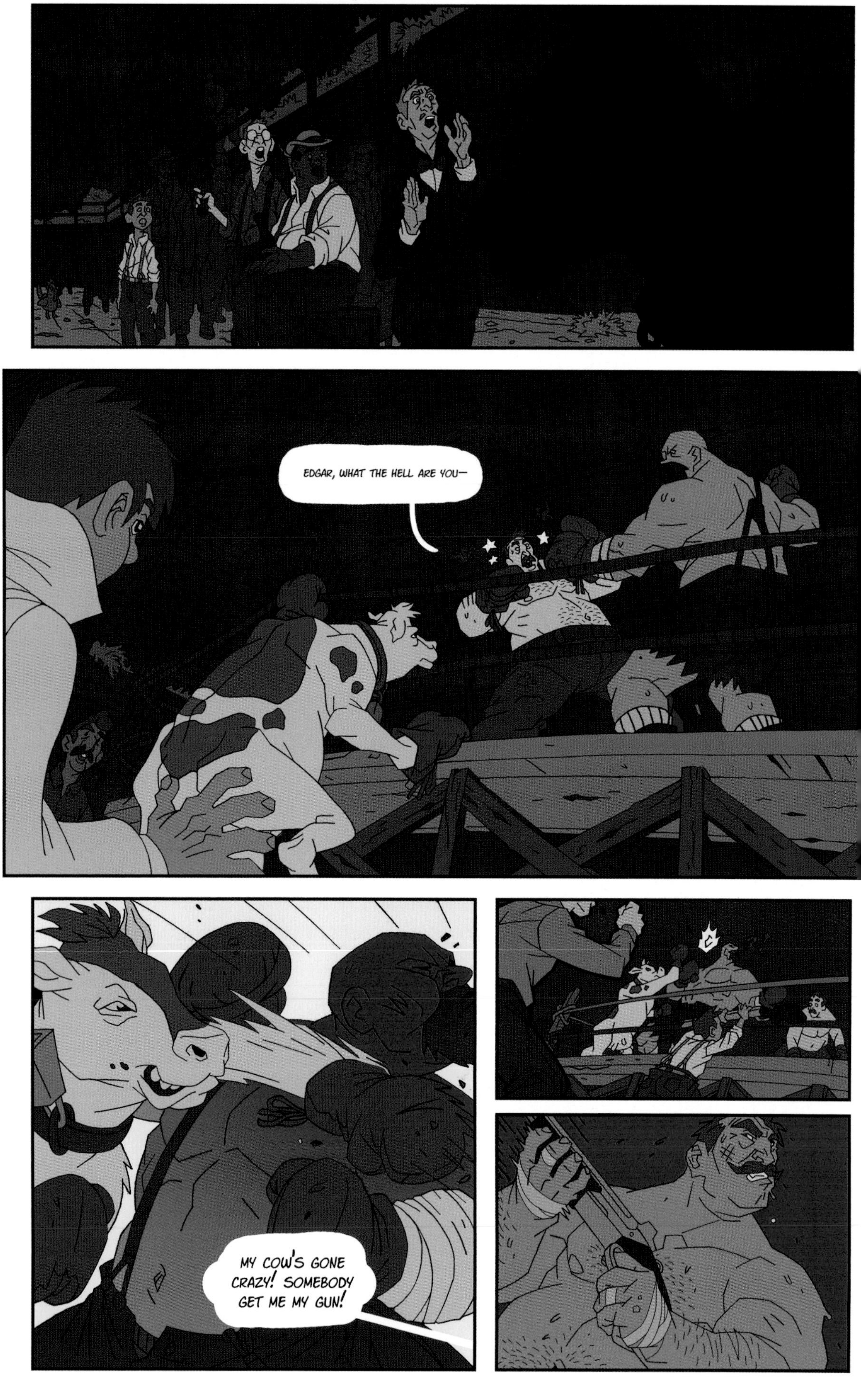
EDGAR, WHAT THE HELL ARE YOU—
MY COW'S GONE CRAZY! SOMEBODY GET ME MY GUN!

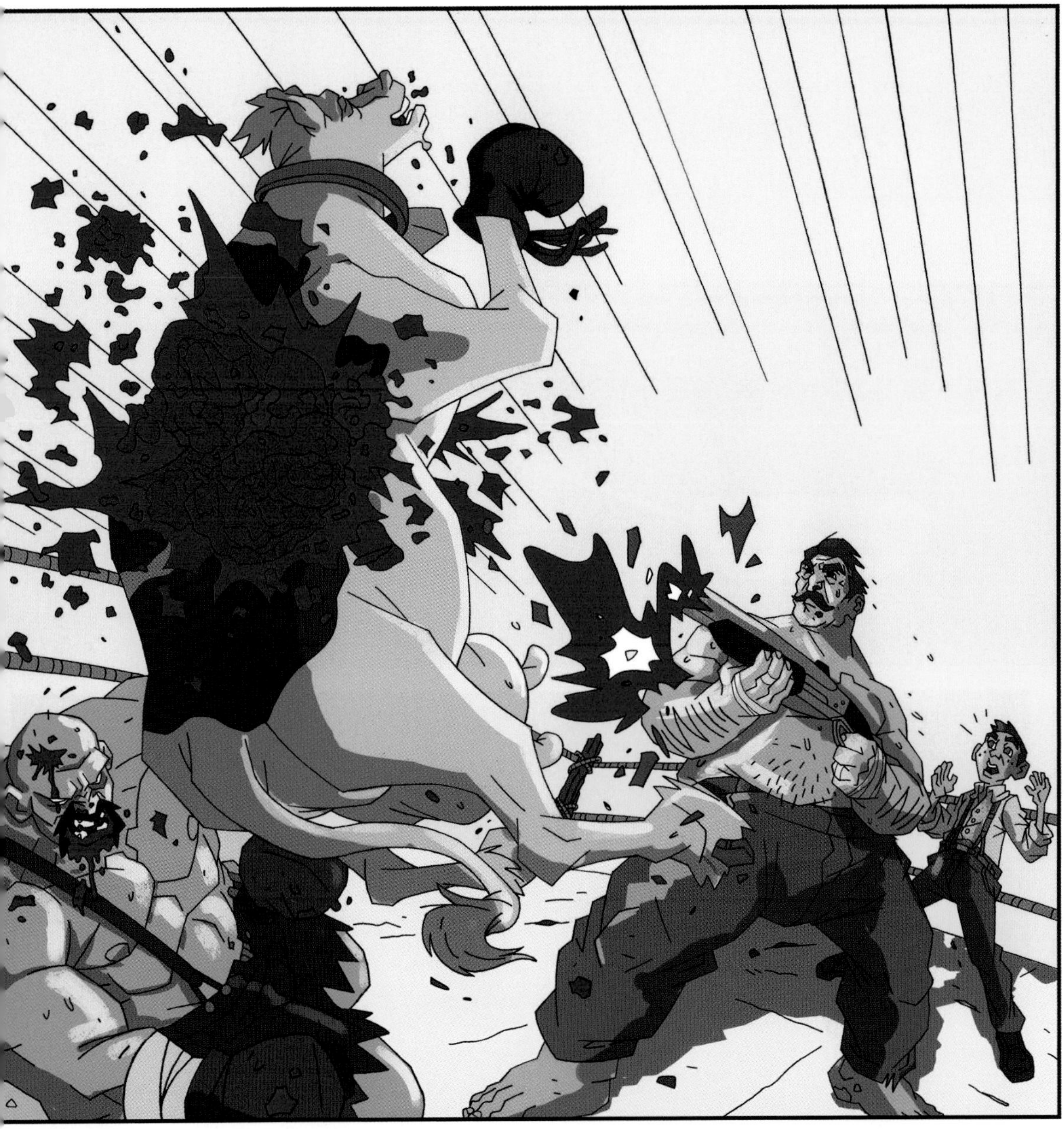

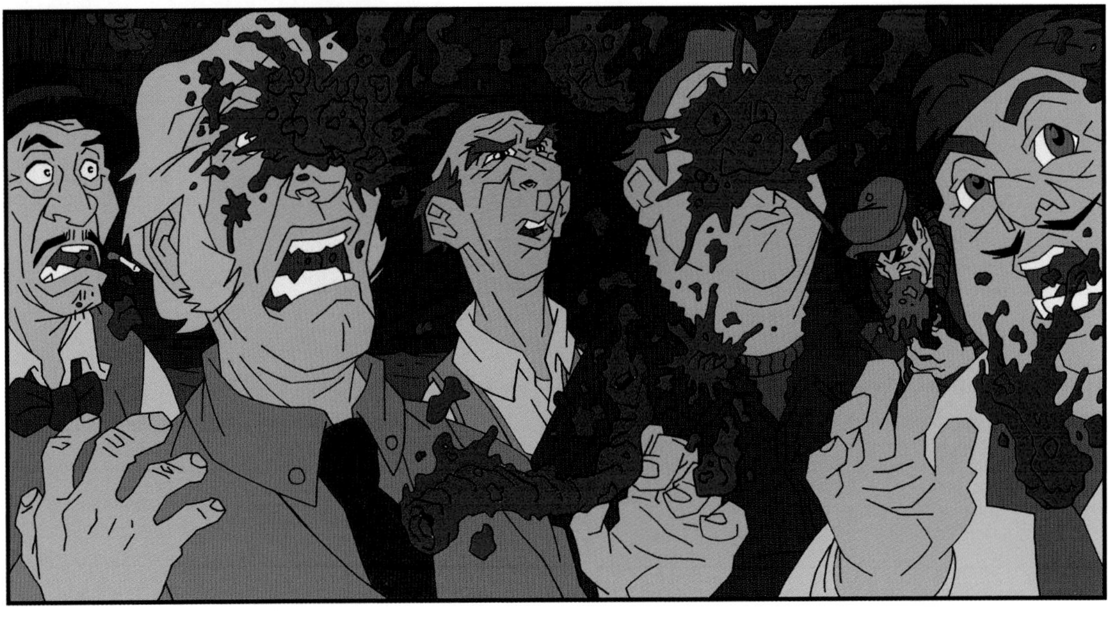

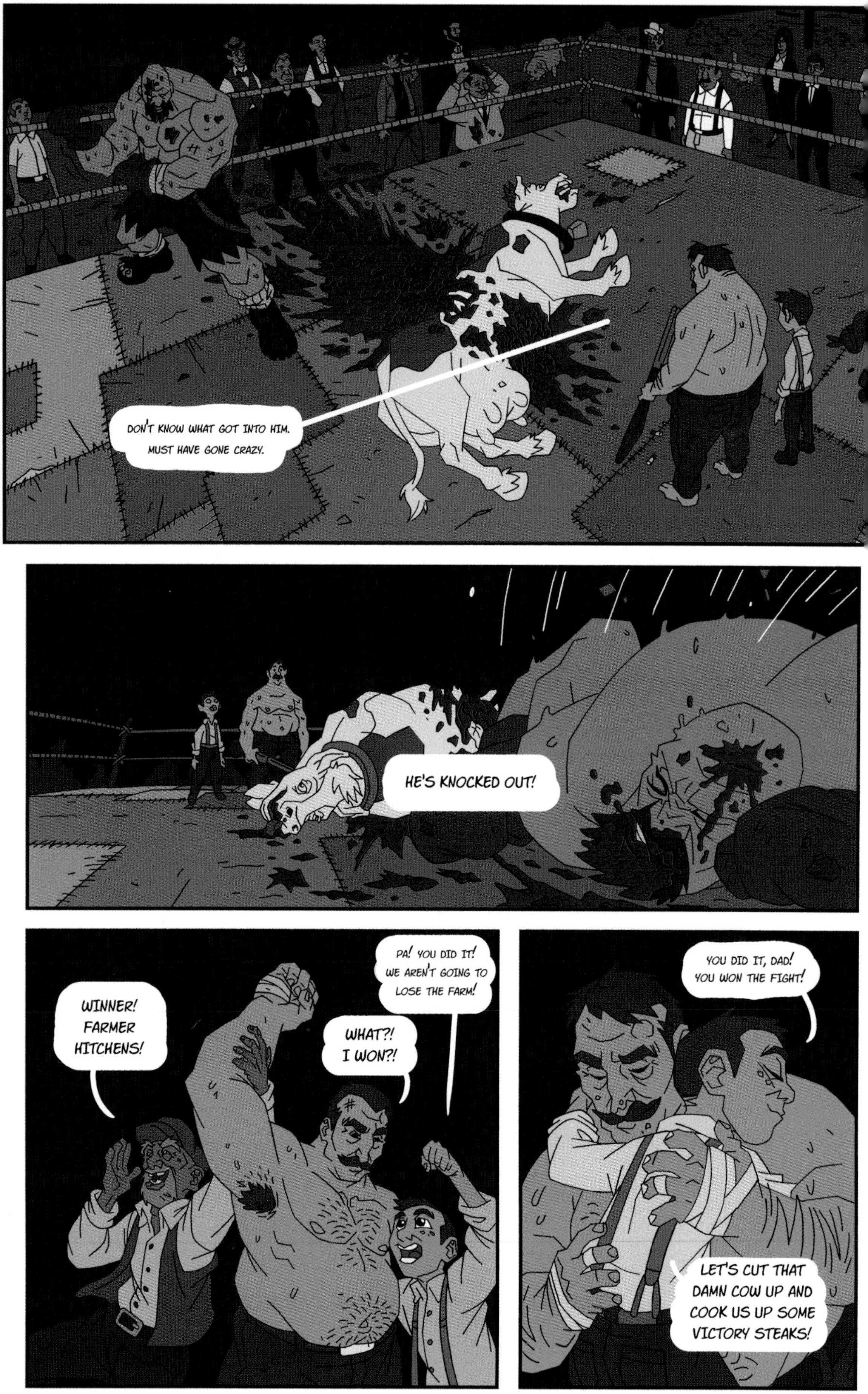

DON'T KNOW WHAT GOT INTO HIM. MUST HAVE GONE CRAZY.
HE'S KNOCKED OUT!
WINNER! FARMER HITCHENS!
WHAT?! I WON?!
PA! YOU DID IT! WE AREN'T GOING TO LOSE THE FARM!
YOU DID IT, DAD! YOU WON THE FIGHT!
LET'S CUT THAT DAMN COW UP AND COOK US UP SOME VICTORY STEAKS!

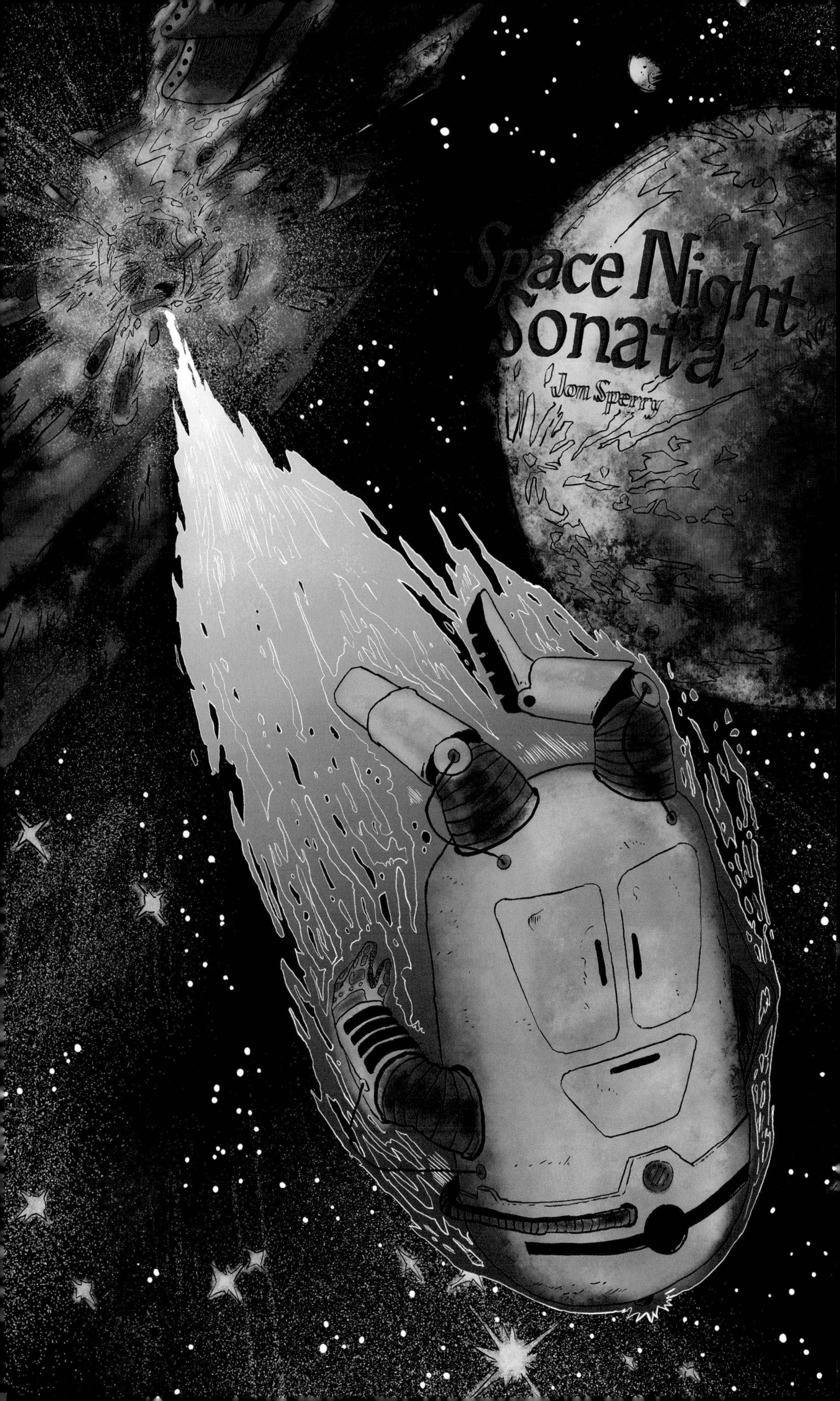
Space Night
Sonata
Jon Sperry

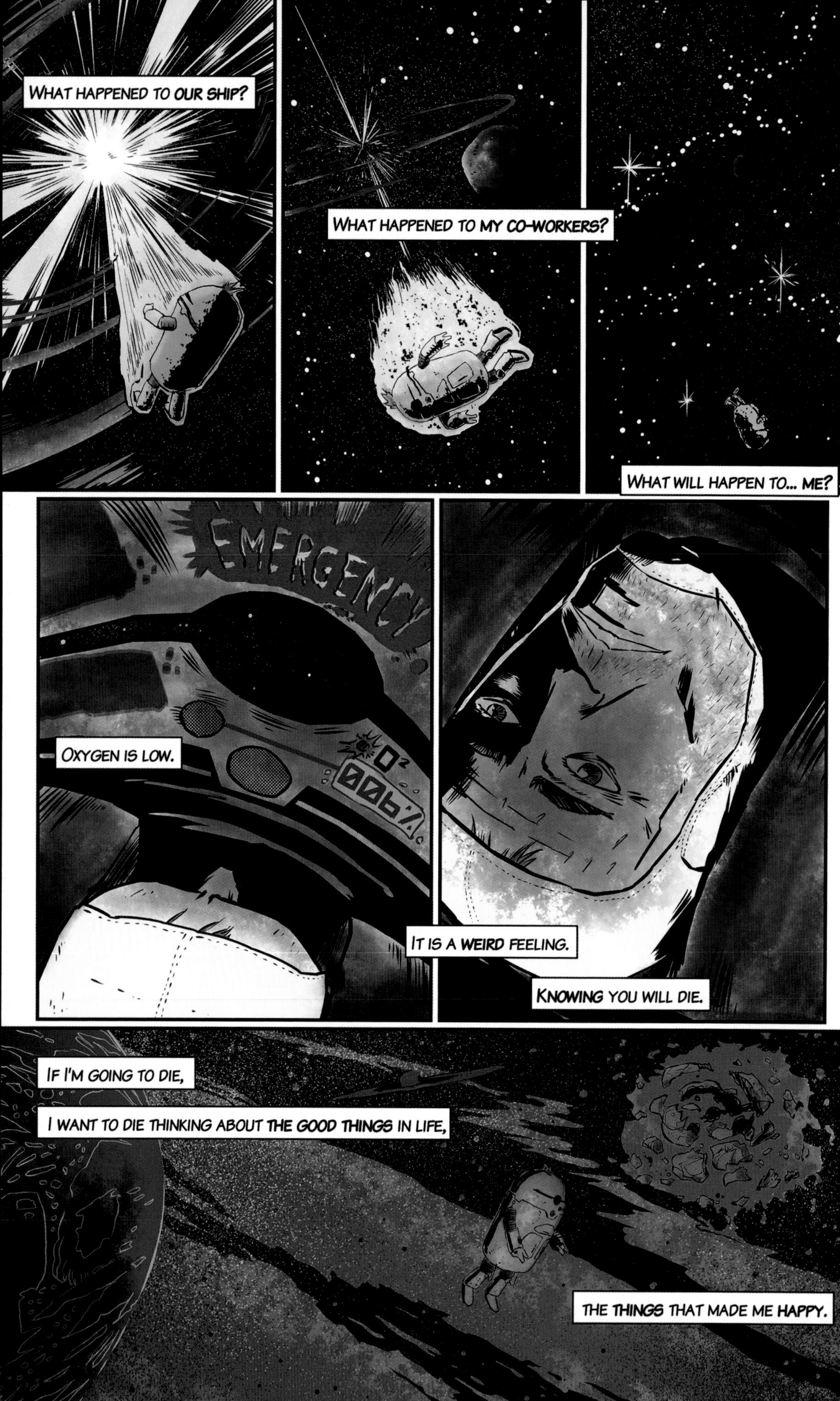
WHAT HAPPENED TO OUR SHIP?
WHAT HAPPENED TO MY CO-WORKERS?
WHAT WILL HAPPEN TO... ME?
EMERGENCY
OXYGEN IS LOW.
O2
006%
IT IS A WEIRD FEELING.
KNOWING YOU WILL DIE.
IF I'M GOING TO DIE,
I WANT TO DIE THINKING ABOUT THE GOOD THINGS IN LIFE,
THE THINGS THAT MADE ME HAPPY.

THE UNIVERSE IS A **PEACEFUL** PLACE.
A MAN CAN HAVE HIMSELF SOME **GOOD**
THOUGHTS OUT HERE. **NOT** LIKE ON **EARTH.**

I WAS TRYING TO KEEP TRACK OF TIME,
BUT I **LOST** MYSELF.

I HAVEN'T DIED YET...

IT FEELS LIKE **WEEKS**
OR EVEN **MONTHS** HAVE GONE BY...

OR MAYBE I HAVE.

TIME **DOESN'T MATTER** ANYMORE ANYWAY.
NOTHING **MATTERS** OUT HERE.
I CAN'T BELIEVE HOW **EASY** IT IS
TO **UNDERSTAND** THAT OUT HERE.

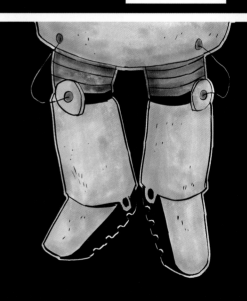

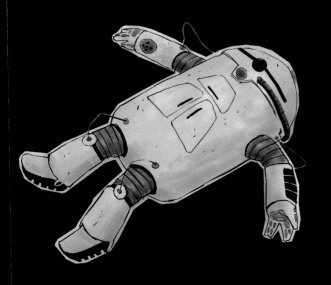

I AM STARTING TO LOVE THE ABYSS.

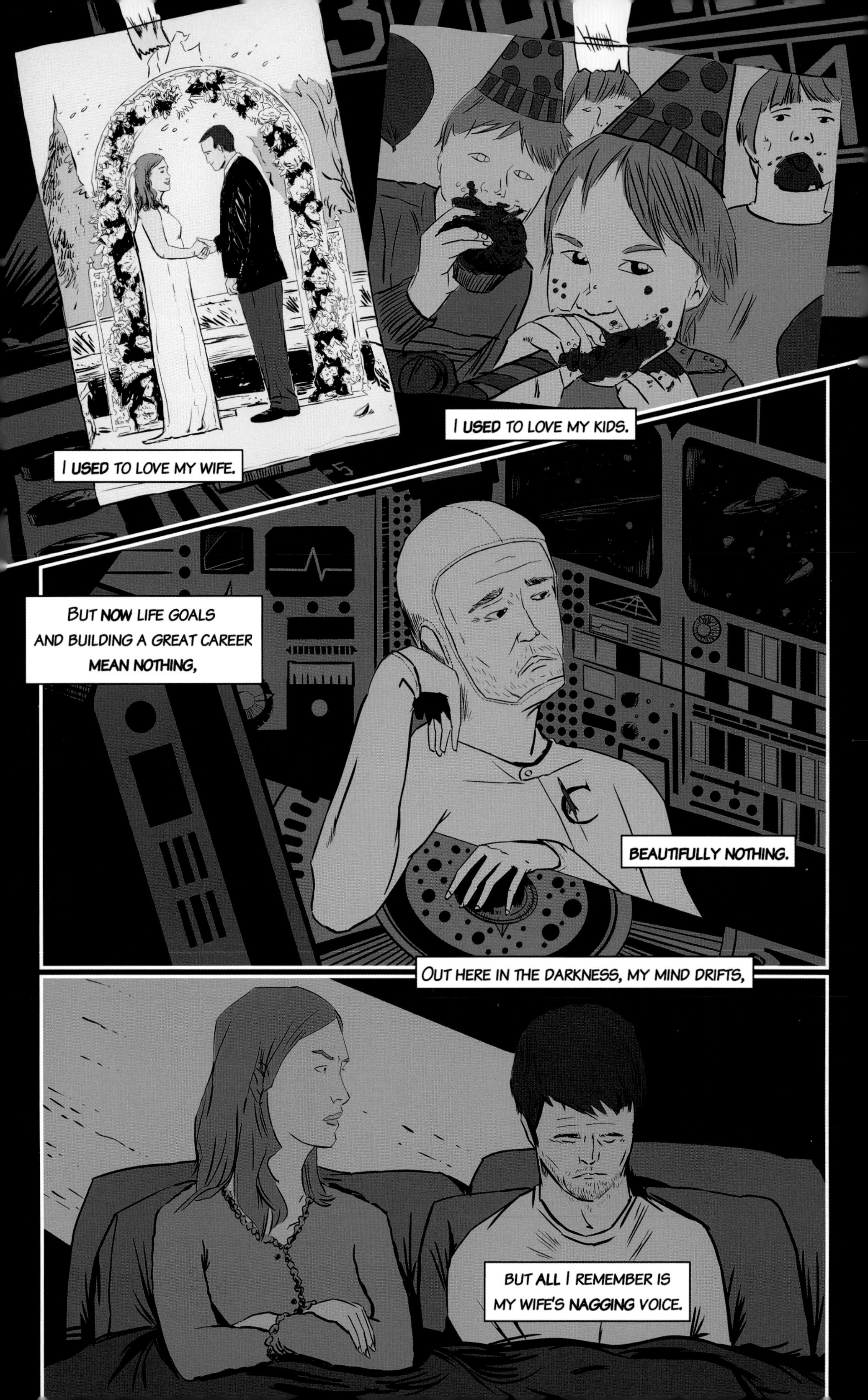
I USED TO LOVE MY WIFE.
I USED TO LOVE MY KIDS.
BUT NOW LIFE GOALS AND BUILDING A GREAT CAREER MEAN NOTHING,
BEAUTIFULLY NOTHING.
OUT HERE IN THE DARKNESS, MY MIND DRIFTS,
BUT ALL I REMEMBER IS MY WIFE'S NAGGING VOICE.

OUT HERE, IT IS QUIET.

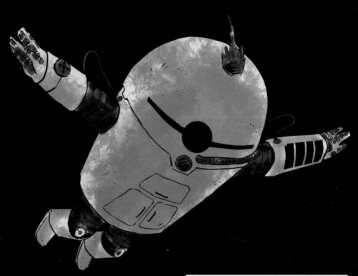

OUT HERE, EVERYTHING IS PURE.

I REALIZE THIS IS THE MOST PEACE I EVER HAD, MY WHOLE LIFE.

I HATE THEM.

I HATE THEM ALL.

THIS IS WHERE I BELONG.

BOOP BOOP BOOP BOOP

TOM?

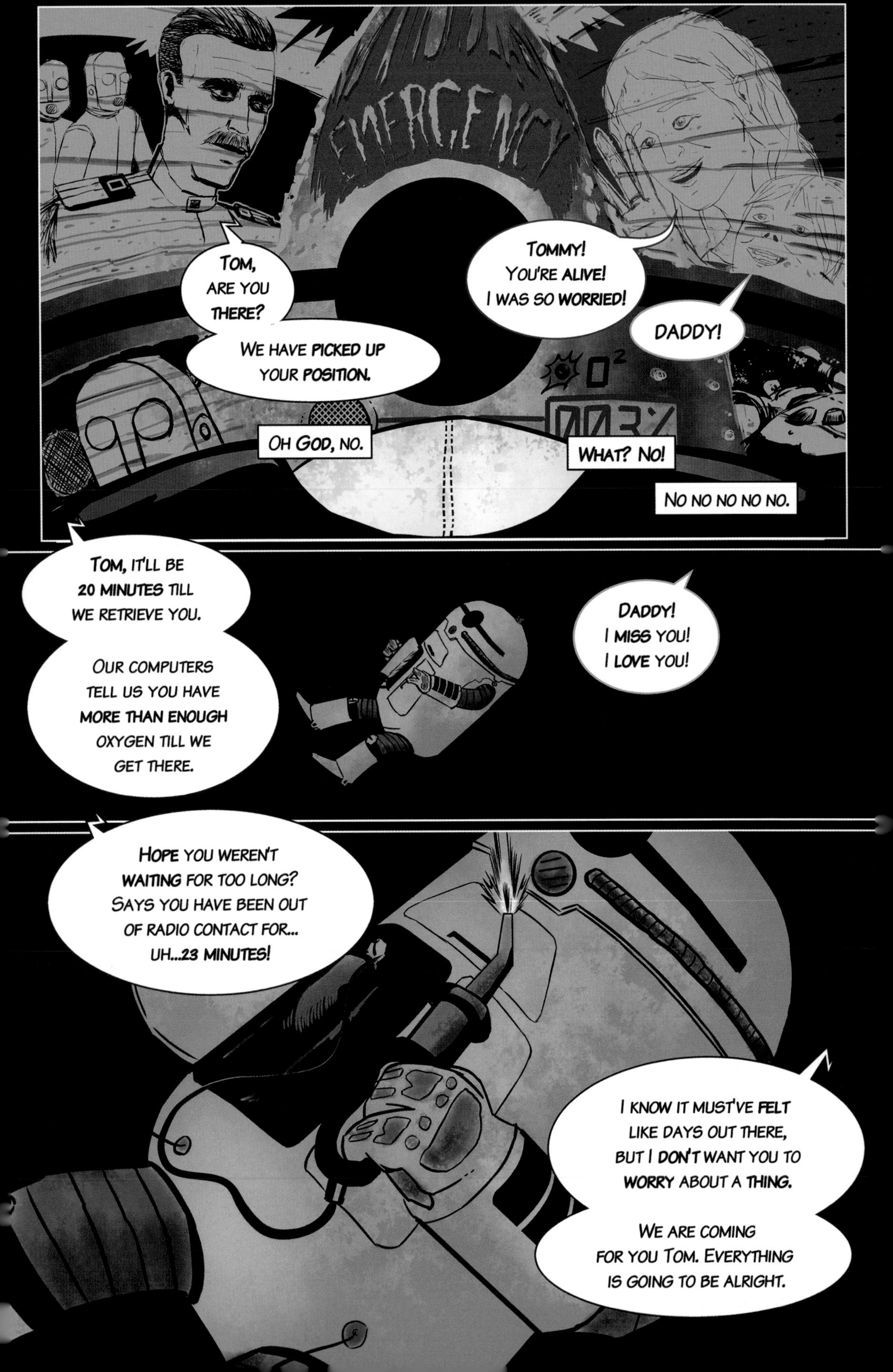
EMERGENCY
TOM, ARE YOU THERE?
WE HAVE PICKED UP YOUR POSITION.
TOMMY! YOU'RE ALIVE! I WAS SO WORRIED!
DADDY!
OH GOD, NO.
WHAT? NO!
NO NO NO NO NO.
TOM, IT'LL BE 20 MINUTES TILL WE RETRIEVE YOU.
OUR COMPUTERS TELL US YOU HAVE MORE THAN ENOUGH OXYGEN TILL WE GET THERE.
DADDY! I MISS YOU! I LOVE YOU!
HOPE YOU WEREN'T WAITING FOR TOO LONG? SAYS YOU HAVE BEEN OUT OF RADIO CONTACT FOR... UH...23 MINUTES!
I KNOW IT MUST'VE FELT LIKE DAYS OUT THERE, BUT I DON'T WANT YOU TO WORRY ABOUT A THING.
WE ARE COMING FOR YOU TOM. EVERYTHING IS GOING TO BE ALRIGHT.

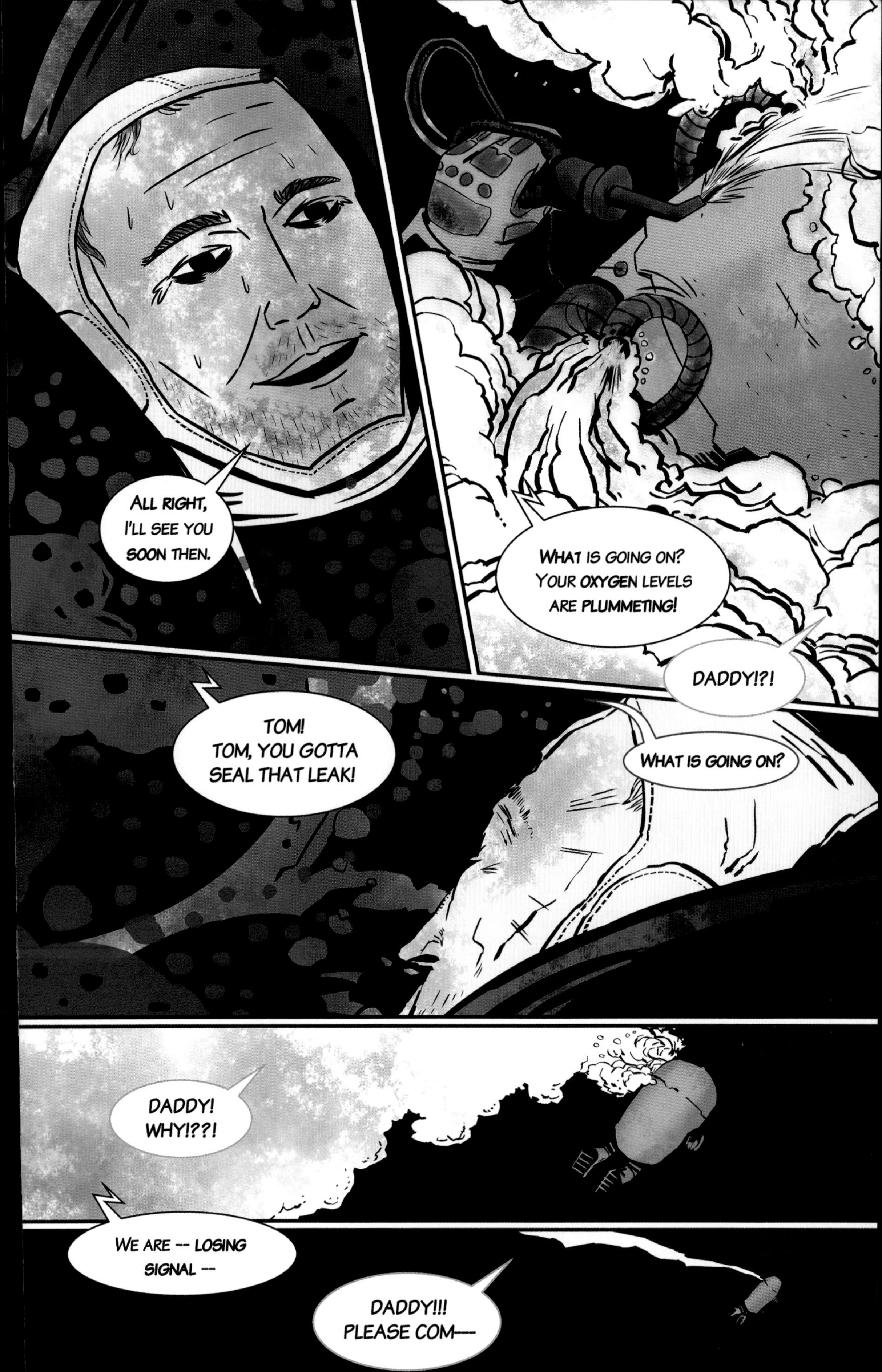
ALL RIGHT, I'LL SEE YOU SOON THEN.
WHAT IS GOING ON? YOUR OXYGEN LEVELS ARE PLUMMETING!
DADDY!?!
TOM! TOM, YOU GOTTA SEAL THAT LEAK!
WHAT IS GOING ON?
DADDY! WHY!??!
WE ARE -- LOSING SIGNAL --
DADDY!!! PLEASE COM---

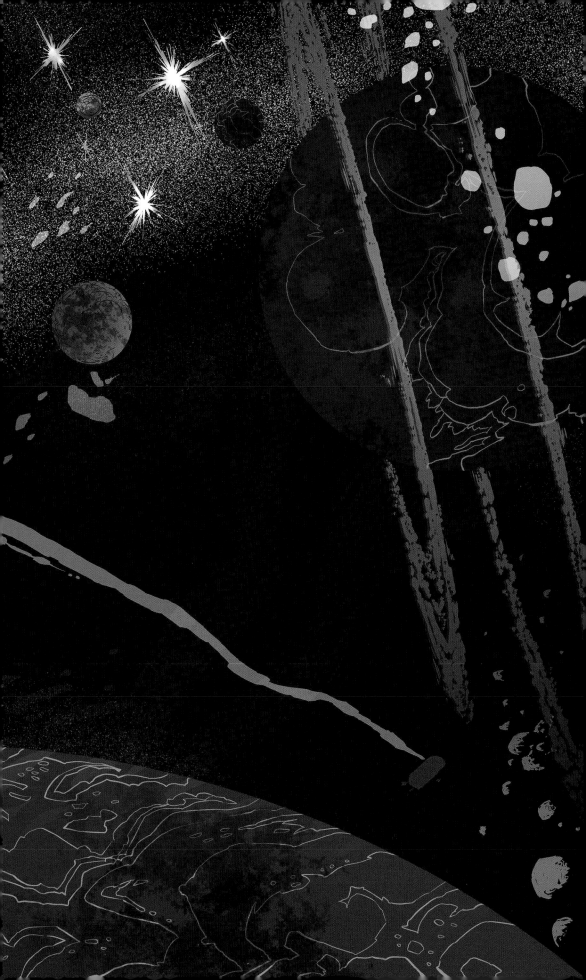

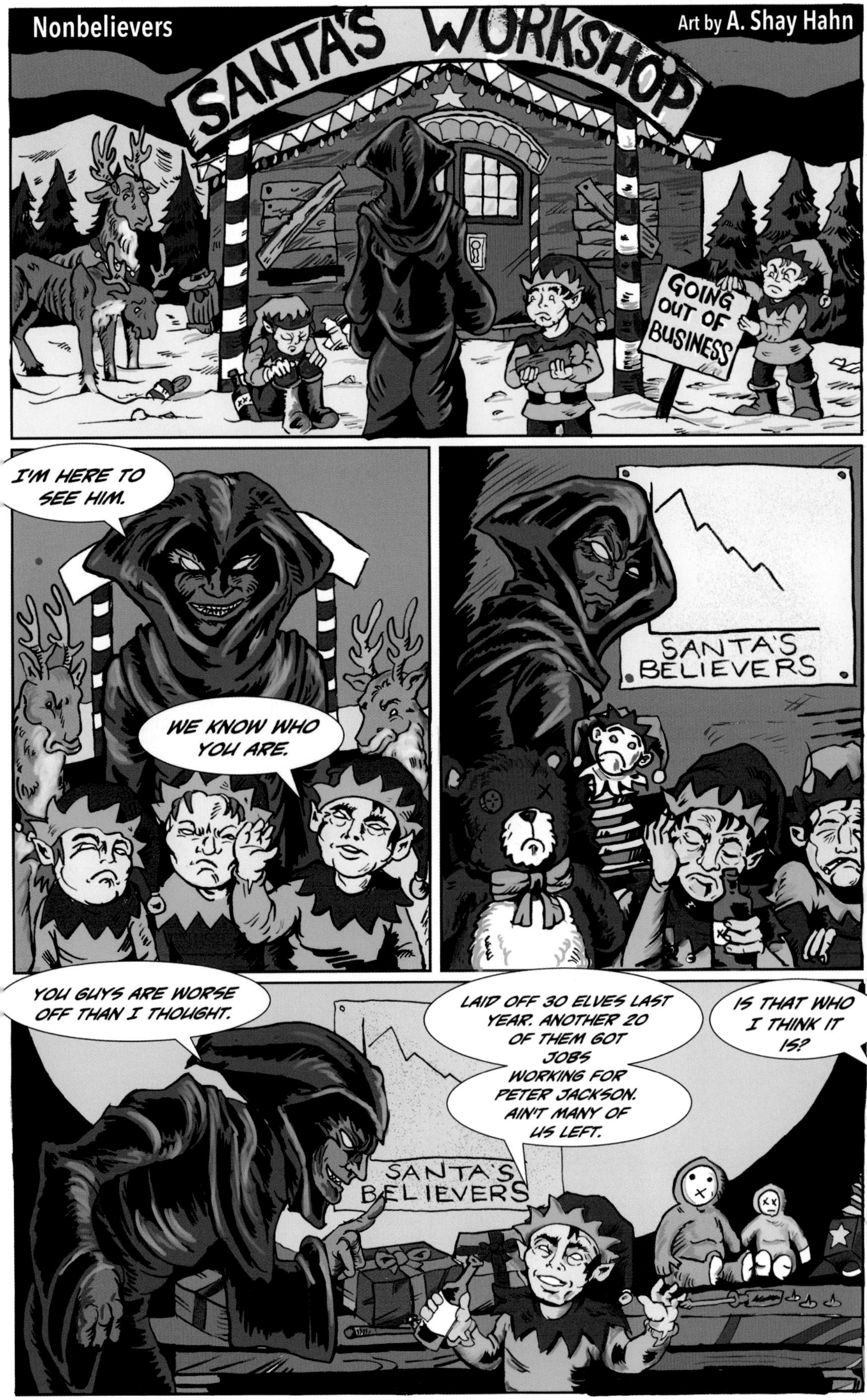
Nonbelievers
Art by A. Shay Hahn
SANTA'S WORKSHOP
GOING OUT OF BUSINESS
I'M HERE TO SEE HIM.
WE KNOW WHO YOU ARE.
SANTA'S BELIEVERS
YOU GUYS ARE WORSE OFF THAN I THOUGHT.
LAID OFF 30 ELVES LAST YEAR. ANOTHER 20 OF THEM GOT JOBS WORKING FOR PETER JACKSON. AIN'T MANY OF US LEFT.
IS THAT WHO I THINK IT IS?
SANTA'S BELIEVERS

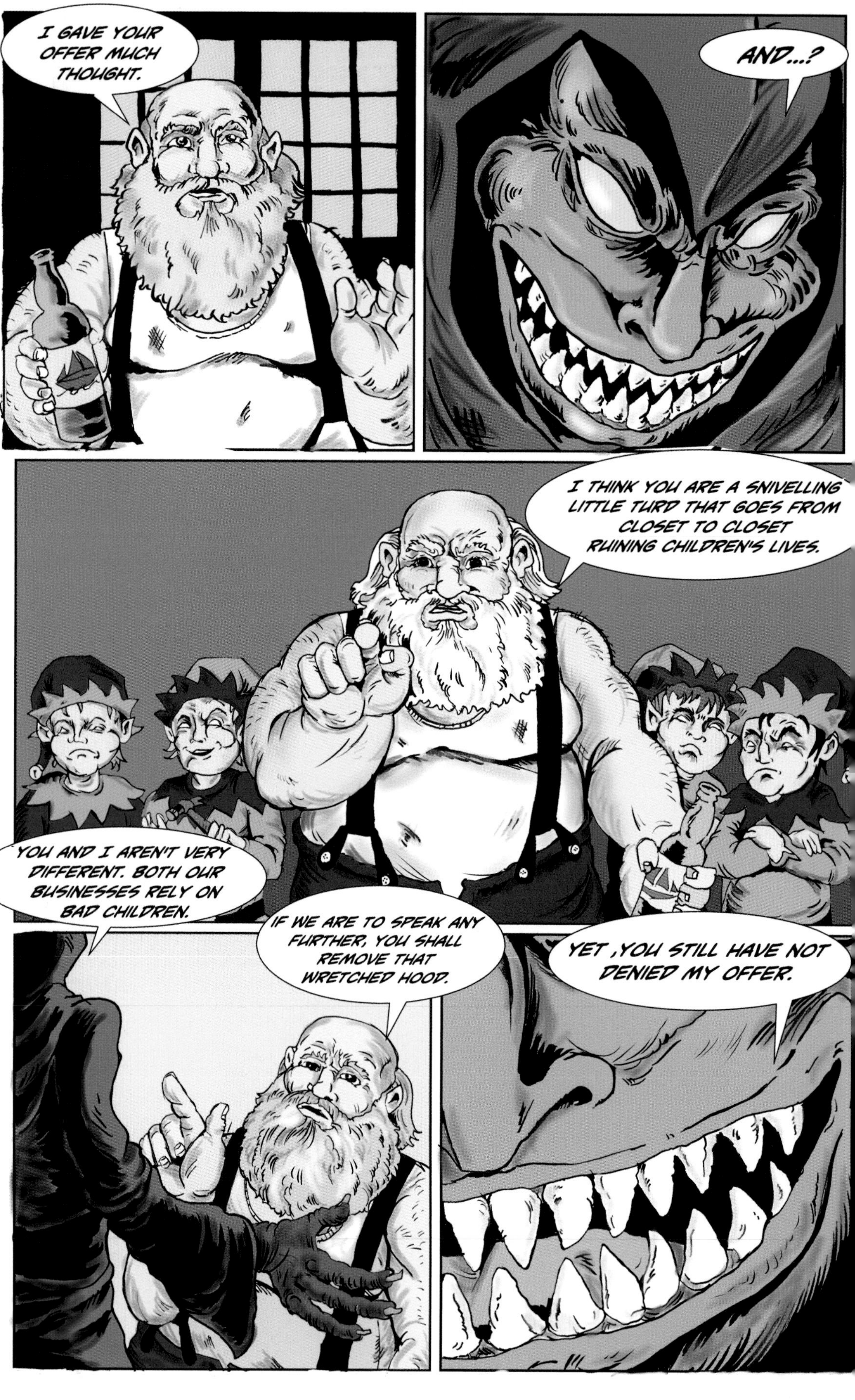
I GAVE YOUR OFFER MUCH THOUGHT.
AND...?
I THINK YOU ARE A SNIVELLING LITTLE TURD THAT GOES FROM CLOSET TO CLOSET RUINING CHILDREN'S LIVES.
YOU AND I AREN'T VERY DIFFERENT. BOTH OUR BUSINESSES RELY ON BAD CHILDREN.
IF WE ARE TO SPEAK ANY FURTHER, YOU SHALL REMOVE THAT WRETCHED HOOD.
YET ,YOU STILL HAVE NOT DENIED MY OFFER.

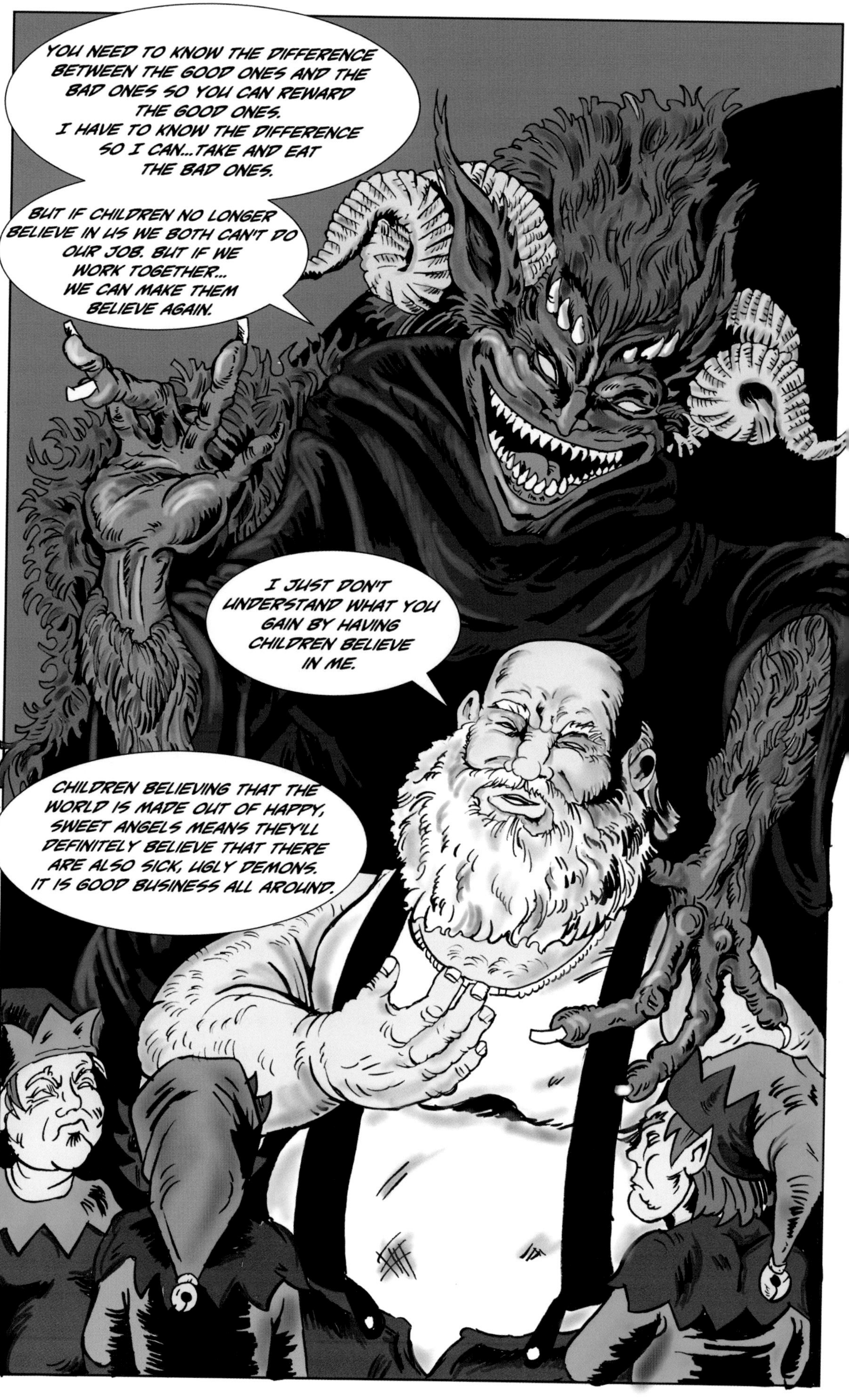
YOU NEED TO KNOW THE DIFFERENCE BETWEEN THE GOOD ONES AND THE BAD ONES SO YOU CAN REWARD THE GOOD ONES. I HAVE TO KNOW THE DIFFERENCE SO I CAN...TAKE AND EAT THE BAD ONES.
BUT IF CHILDREN NO LONGER BELIEVE IN US WE BOTH CAN'T DO OUR JOB. BUT IF WE WORK TOGETHER... WE CAN MAKE THEM BELIEVE AGAIN.
I JUST DON'T UNDERSTAND WHAT YOU GAIN BY HAVING CHILDREN BELIEVE IN ME.
CHILDREN BELIEVING THAT THE WORLD IS MADE OUT OF HAPPY, SWEET ANGELS MEANS THEY'LL DEFINITELY BELIEVE THAT THERE ARE ALSO SICK, UGLY DEMONS. IT IS GOOD BUSINESS ALL AROUND.

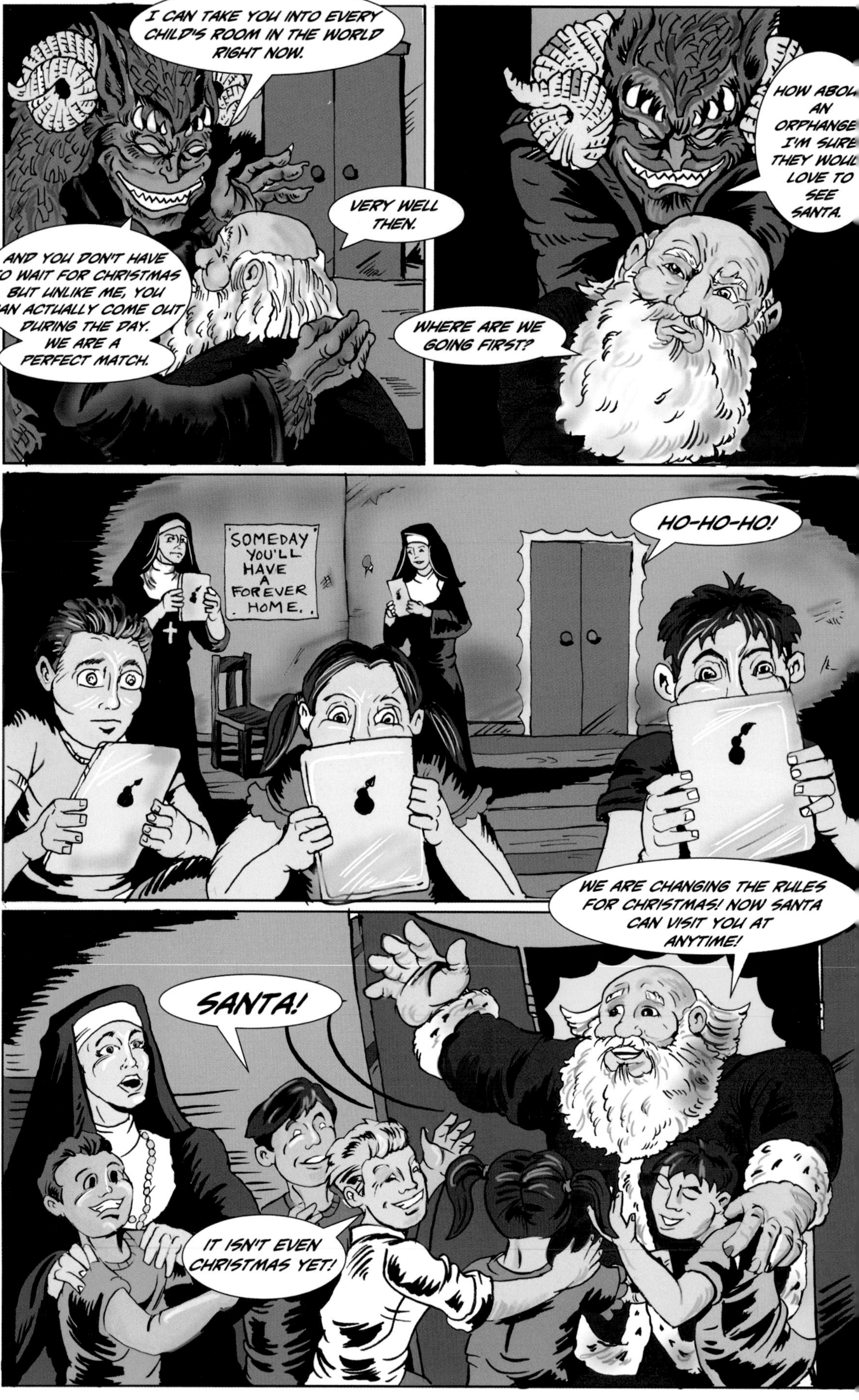
I CAN TAKE YOU INTO EVERY CHILD'S ROOM IN THE WORLD RIGHT NOW.
AND YOU DON'T HAVE TO WAIT FOR CHRISTMAS BUT UNLIKE ME, YOU CAN ACTUALLY COME OUT DURING THE DAY. WE ARE A PERFECT MATCH.
VERY WELL THEN.
WHERE ARE WE GOING FIRST?
SOMEDAY YOU'LL HAVE A FOREVER HOME.
HO-HO-HO!
WE ARE CHANGING THE RULES FOR CHRISTMAS! NOW SANTA CAN VISIT YOU AT ANYTIME!
SANTA!
IT ISN'T EVEN CHRISTMAS YET!

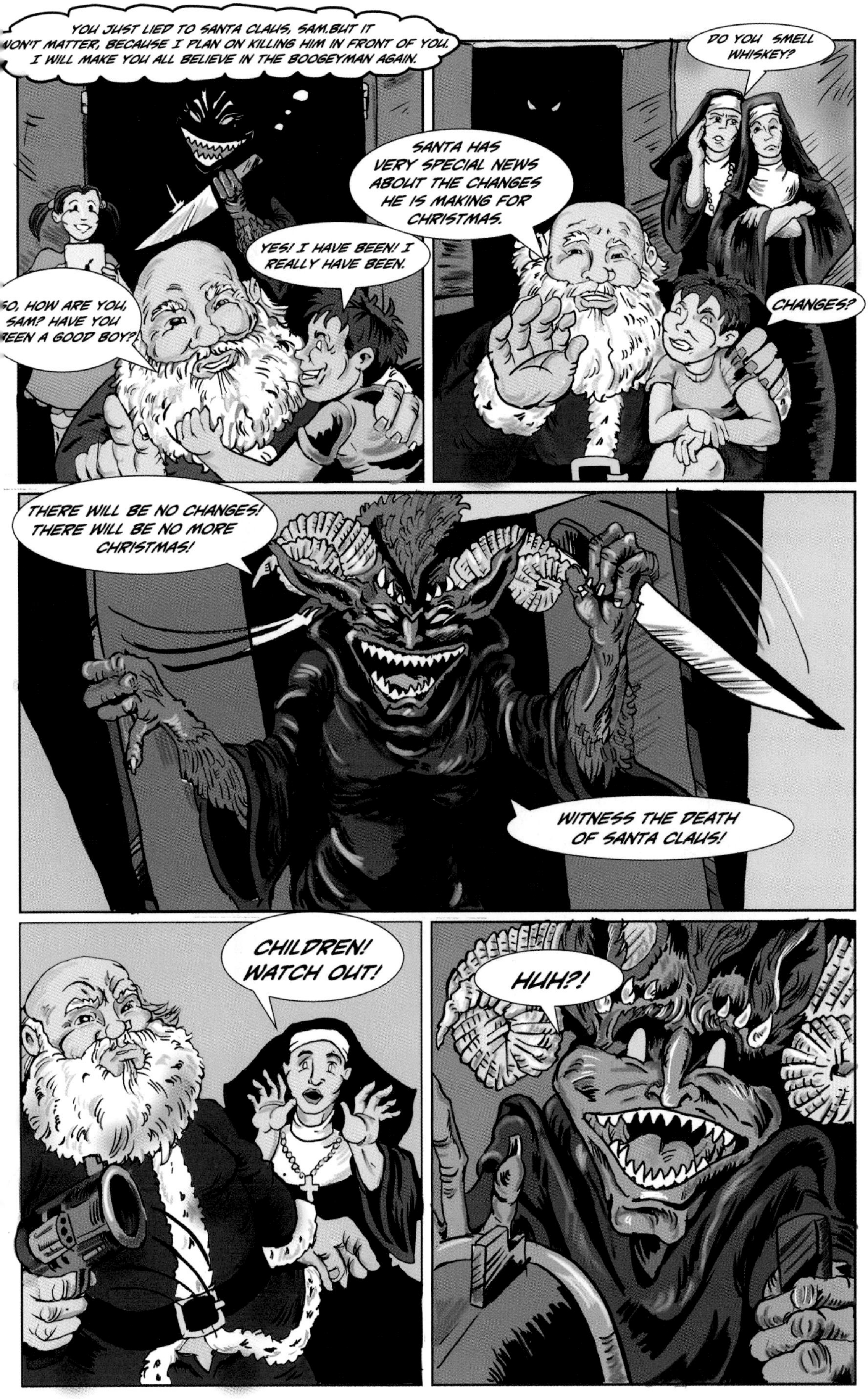
YOU JUST LIED TO SANTA CLAUS, SAM.BUT IT WON'T MATTER, BECAUSE I PLAN ON KILLING HIM IN FRONT OF YOU. I WILL MAKE YOU ALL BELIEVE IN THE BOOGEYMAN AGAIN.
SO, HOW ARE YOU, SAM? HAVE YOU BEEN A GOOD BOY?
YES! I HAVE BEEN! I REALLY HAVE BEEN.
DO YOU SMELL WHISKEY?
SANTA HAS VERY SPECIAL NEWS ABOUT THE CHANGES HE IS MAKING FOR CHRISTMAS.
CHANGES?
THERE WILL BE NO CHANGES! THERE WILL BE NO MORE CHRISTMAS!
WITNESS THE DEATH OF SANTA CLAUS!
CHILDREN! WATCH OUT!
HUH?!

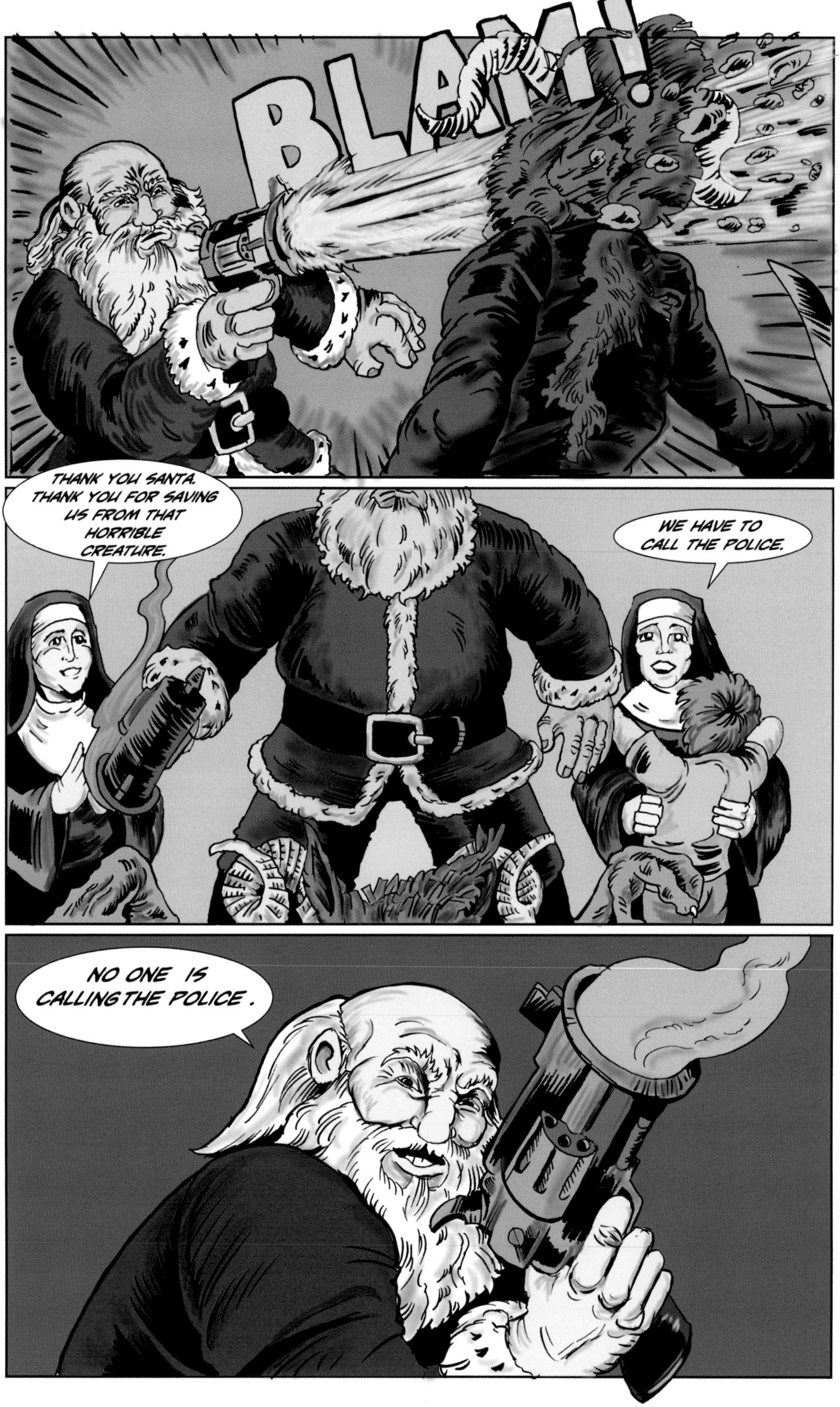
BLAM!
THANK YOU SANTA. THANK YOU FOR SAVING US FROM THAT HORRIBLE CREATURE.
WE HAVE TO CALL THE POLICE.
NO ONE IS CALLING THE POLICE .

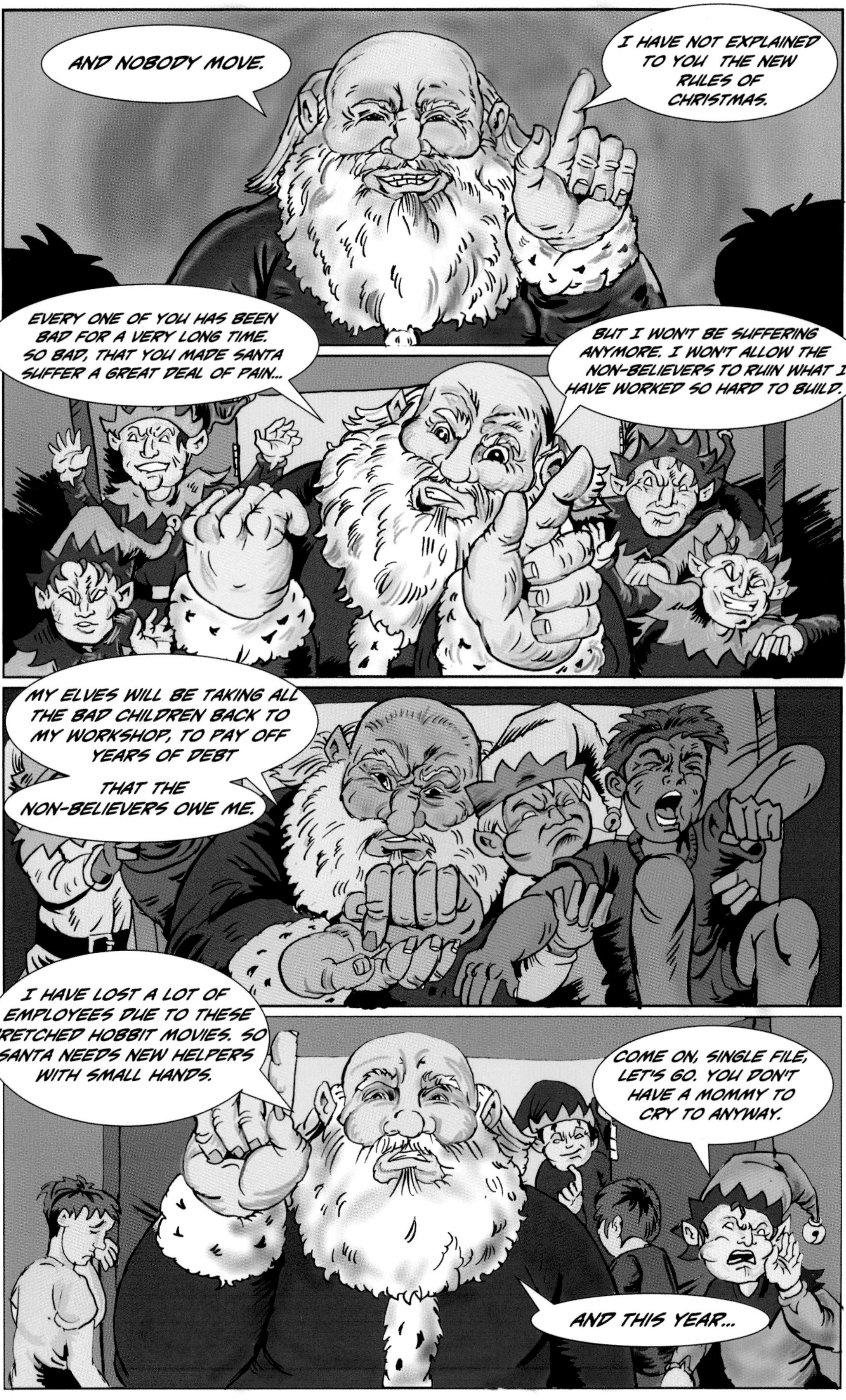
AND NOBODY MOVE.
I HAVE NOT EXPLAINED TO YOU THE NEW RULES OF CHRISTMAS.
EVERY ONE OF YOU HAS BEEN BAD FOR A VERY LONG TIME. SO BAD, THAT YOU MADE SANTA SUFFER A GREAT DEAL OF PAIN...
BUT I WON'T BE SUFFERING ANYMORE. I WON'T ALLOW THE NON-BELIEVERS TO RUIN WHAT I HAVE WORKED SO HARD TO BUILD.
MY ELVES WILL BE TAKING ALL THE BAD CHILDREN BACK TO MY WORKSHOP, TO PAY OFF YEARS OF DEBT
THAT THE NON-BELIEVERS OWE ME.
I HAVE LOST A LOT OF EMPLOYEES DUE TO THESE WRETCHED HOBBIT MOVIES. SO SANTA NEEDS NEW HELPERS WITH SMALL HANDS.
COME ON, SINGLE FILE, LET'S GO. YOU DON'T HAVE A MOMMY TO CRY TO ANYWAY.
AND THIS YEAR...

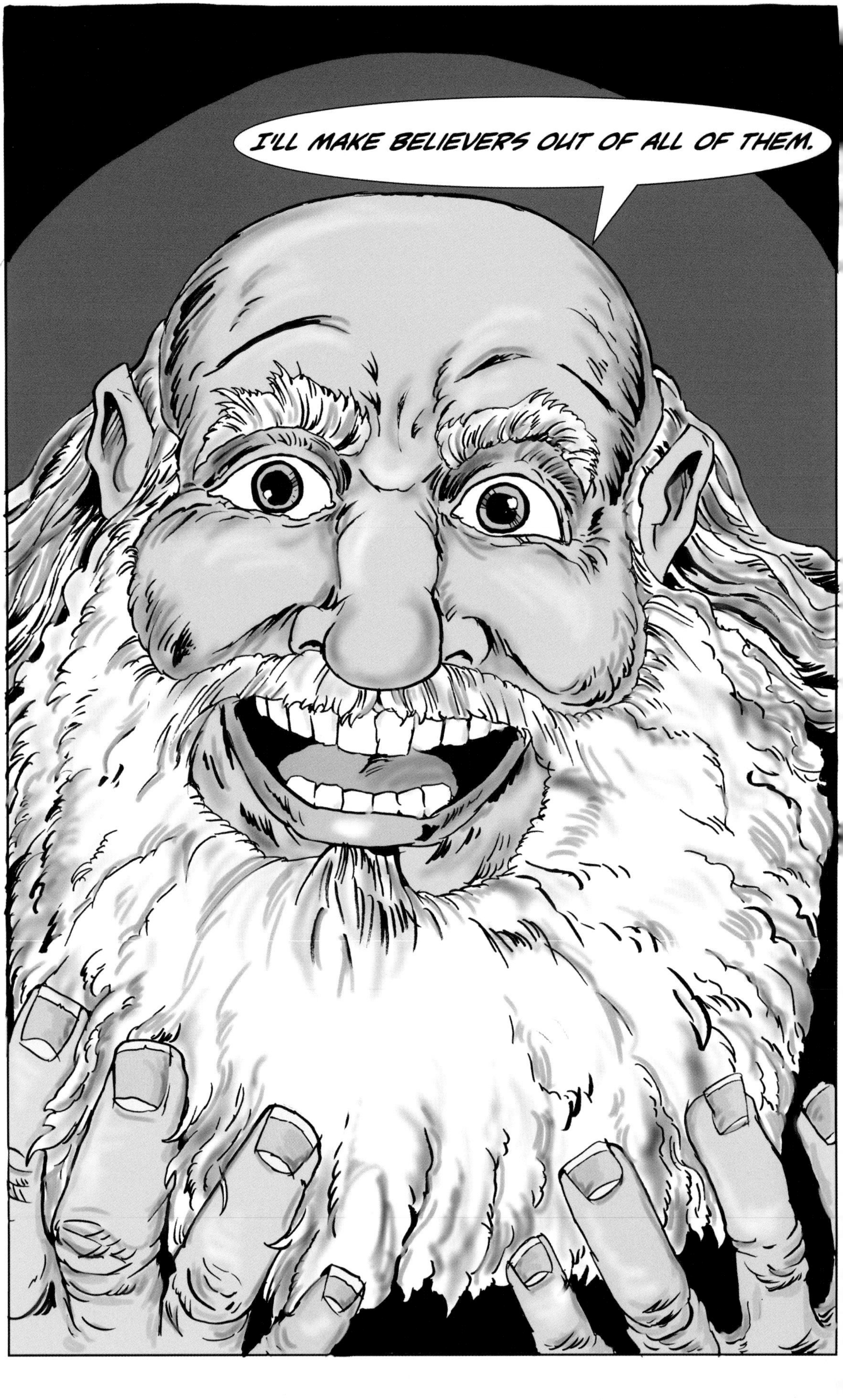
I'LL MAKE BELIEVERS OUT OF ALL OF THEM.

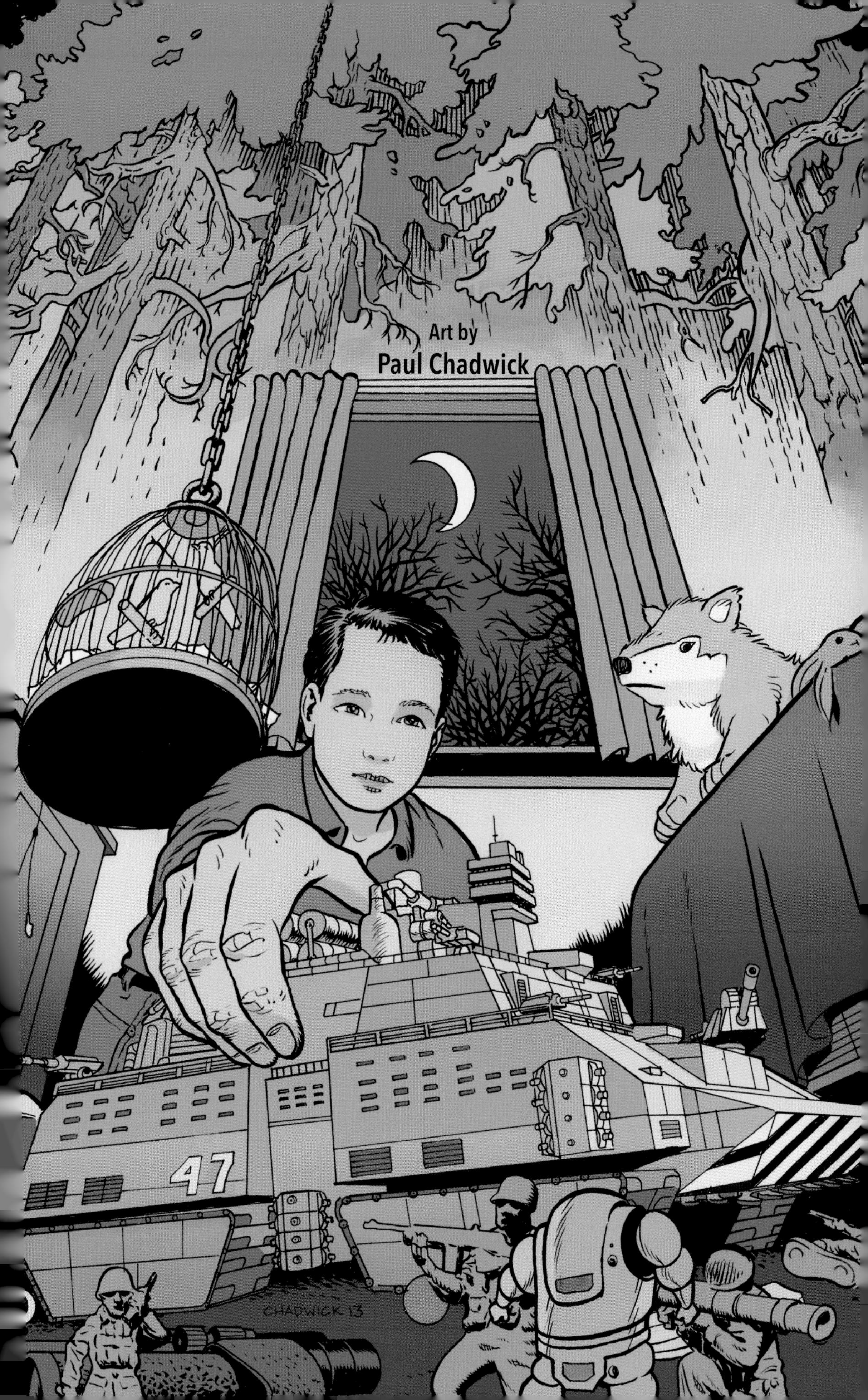
Art by
Paul Chadwick
CHADWICK 13

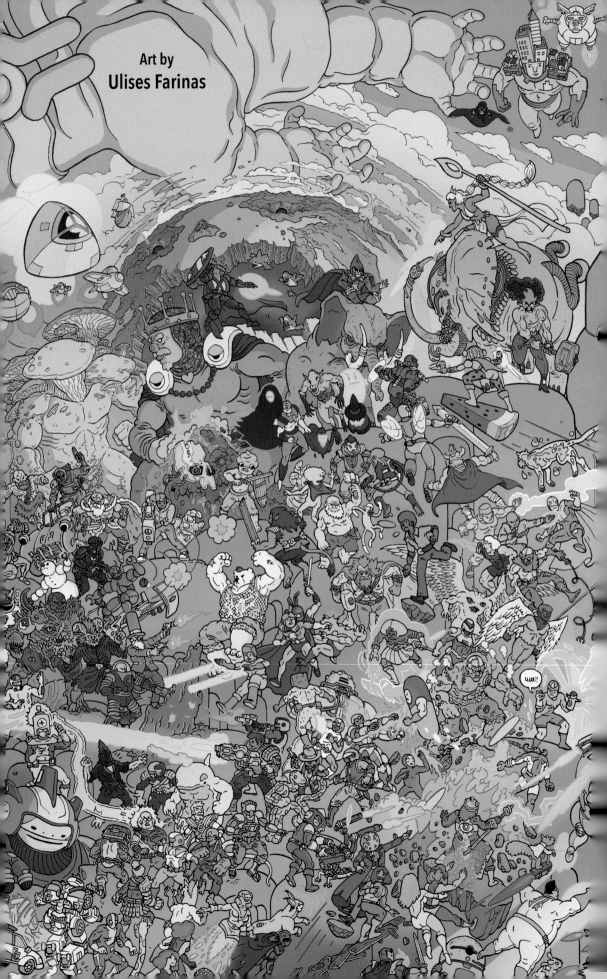

Art by
Ulises Farinas

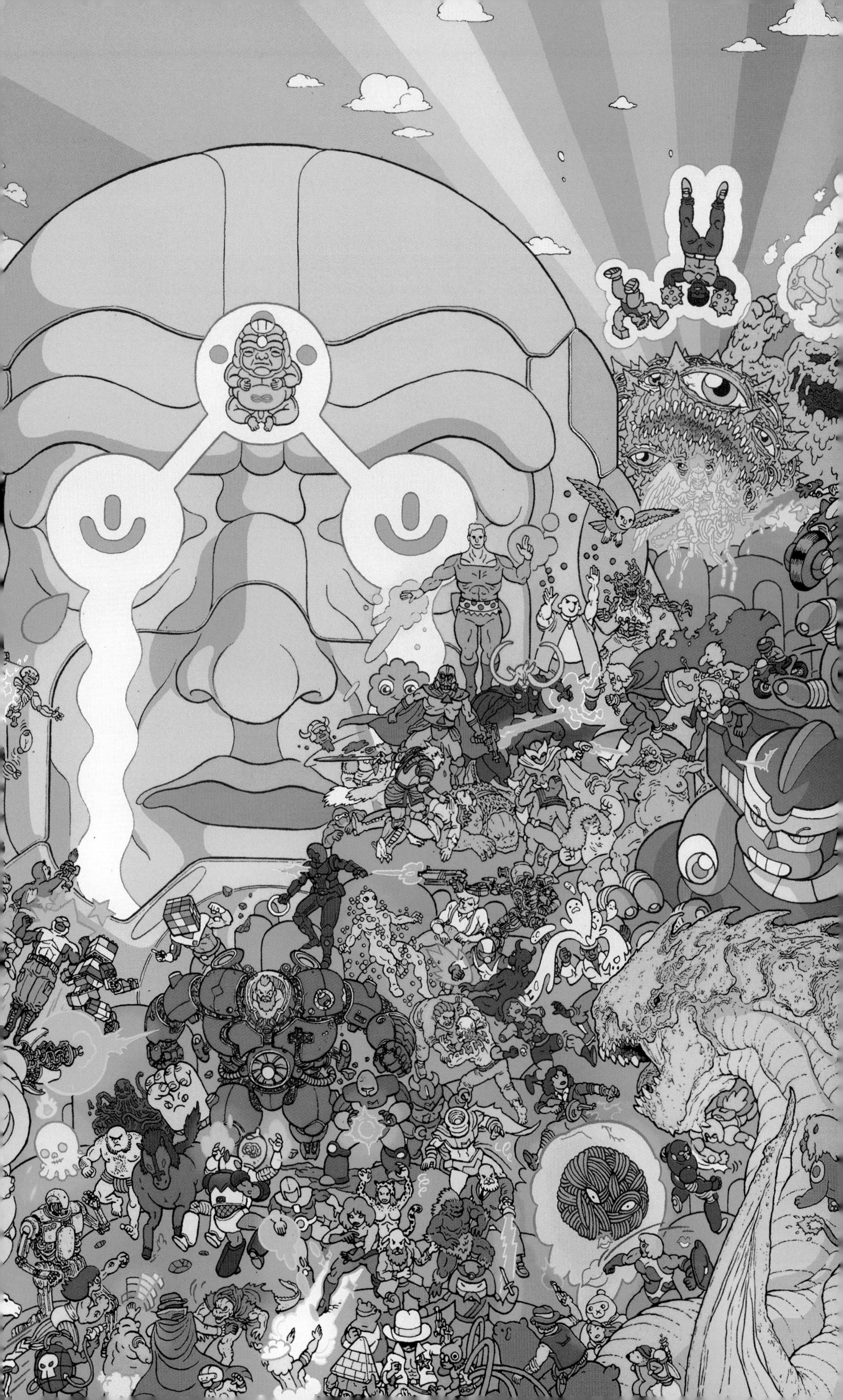

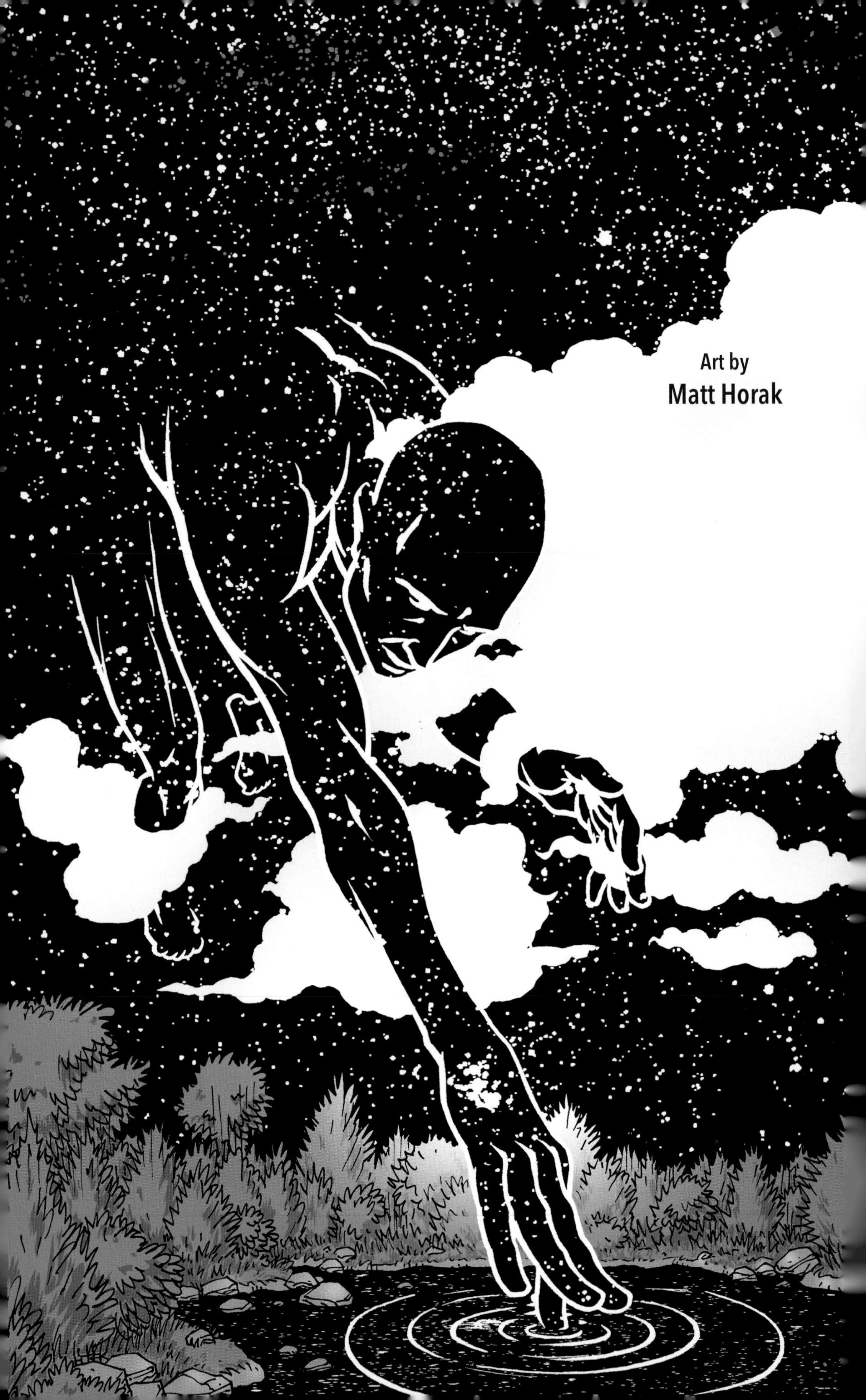
Art by
Matt Horak

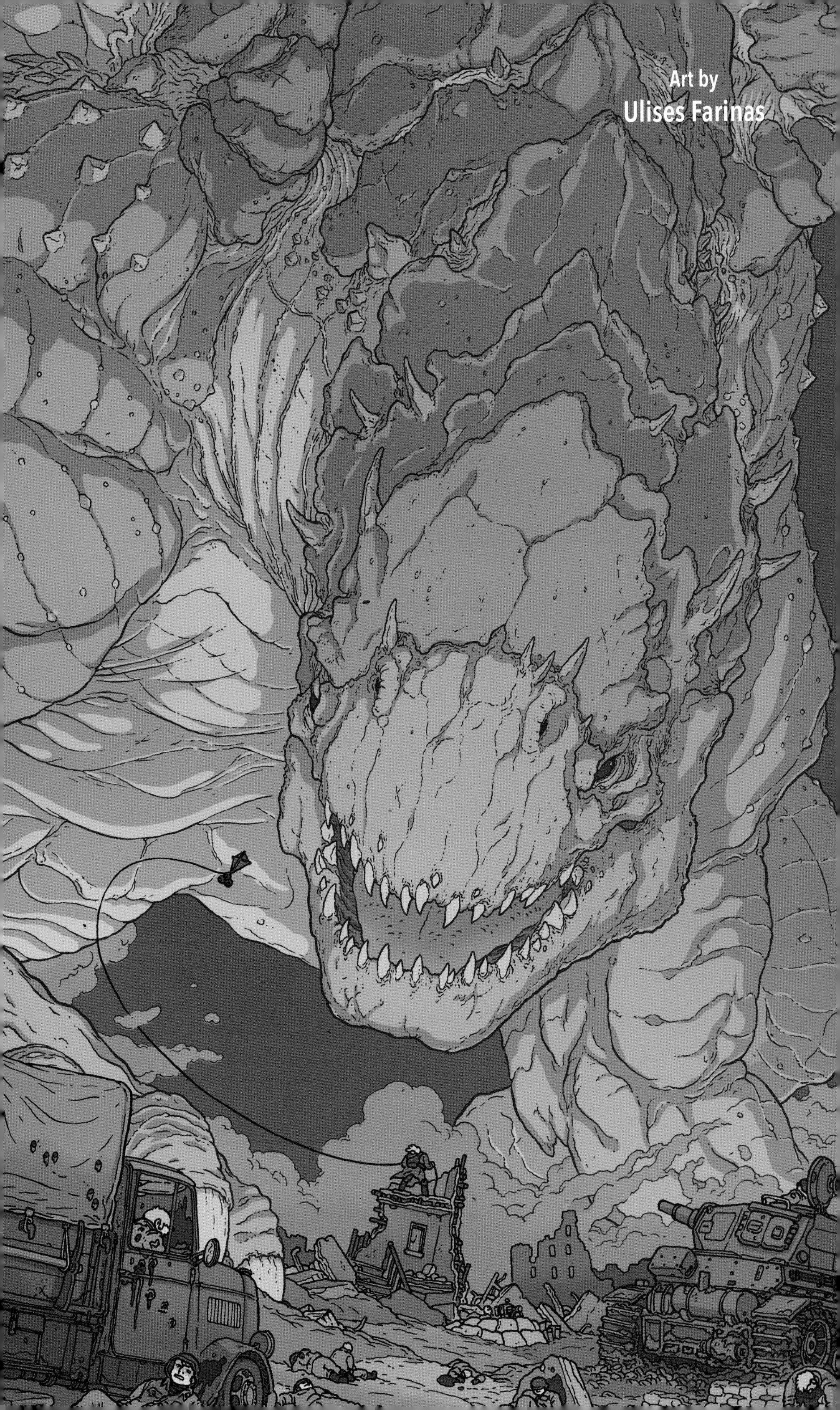
Art by
Ulises Farinas

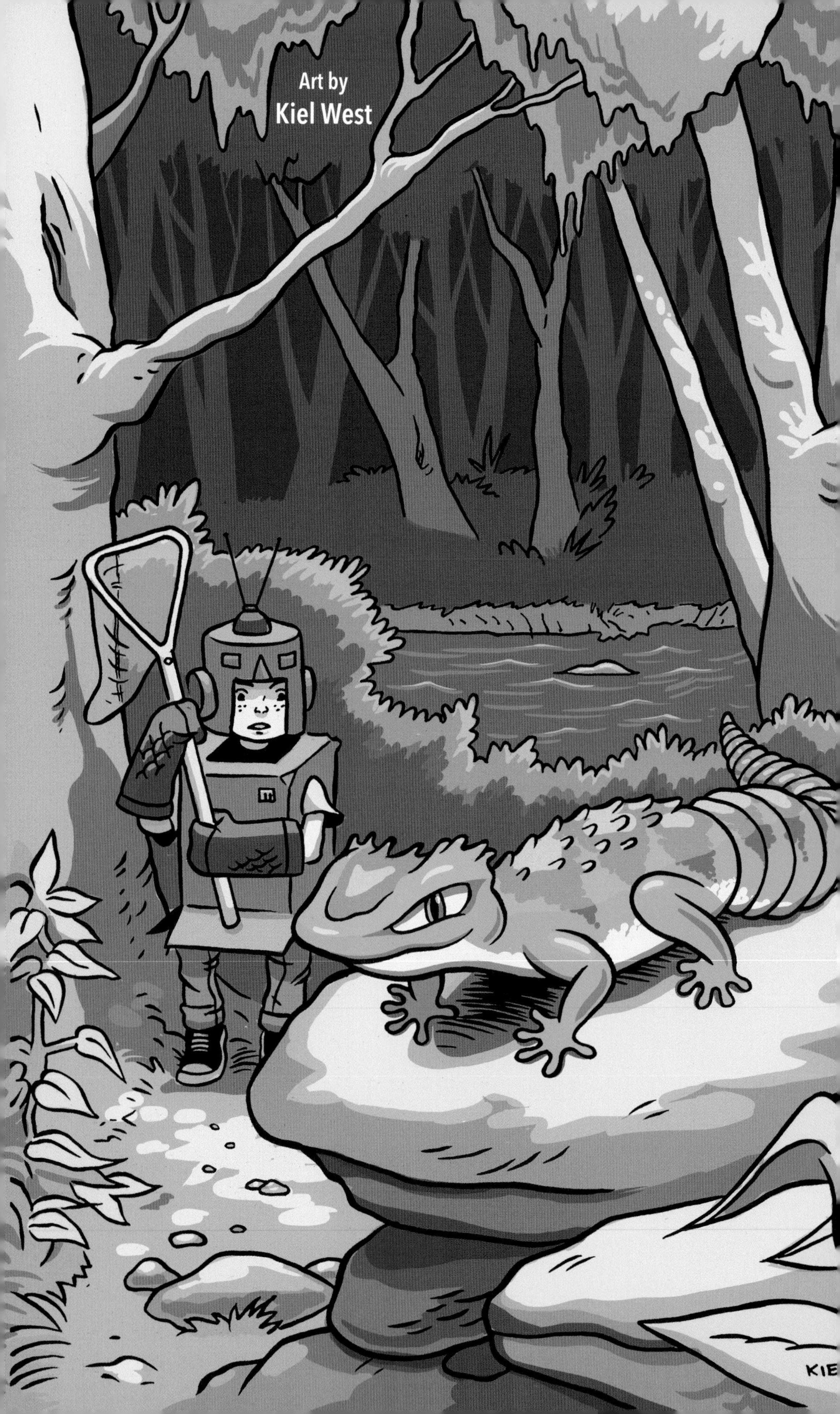
KIE

Art by
Kiel West

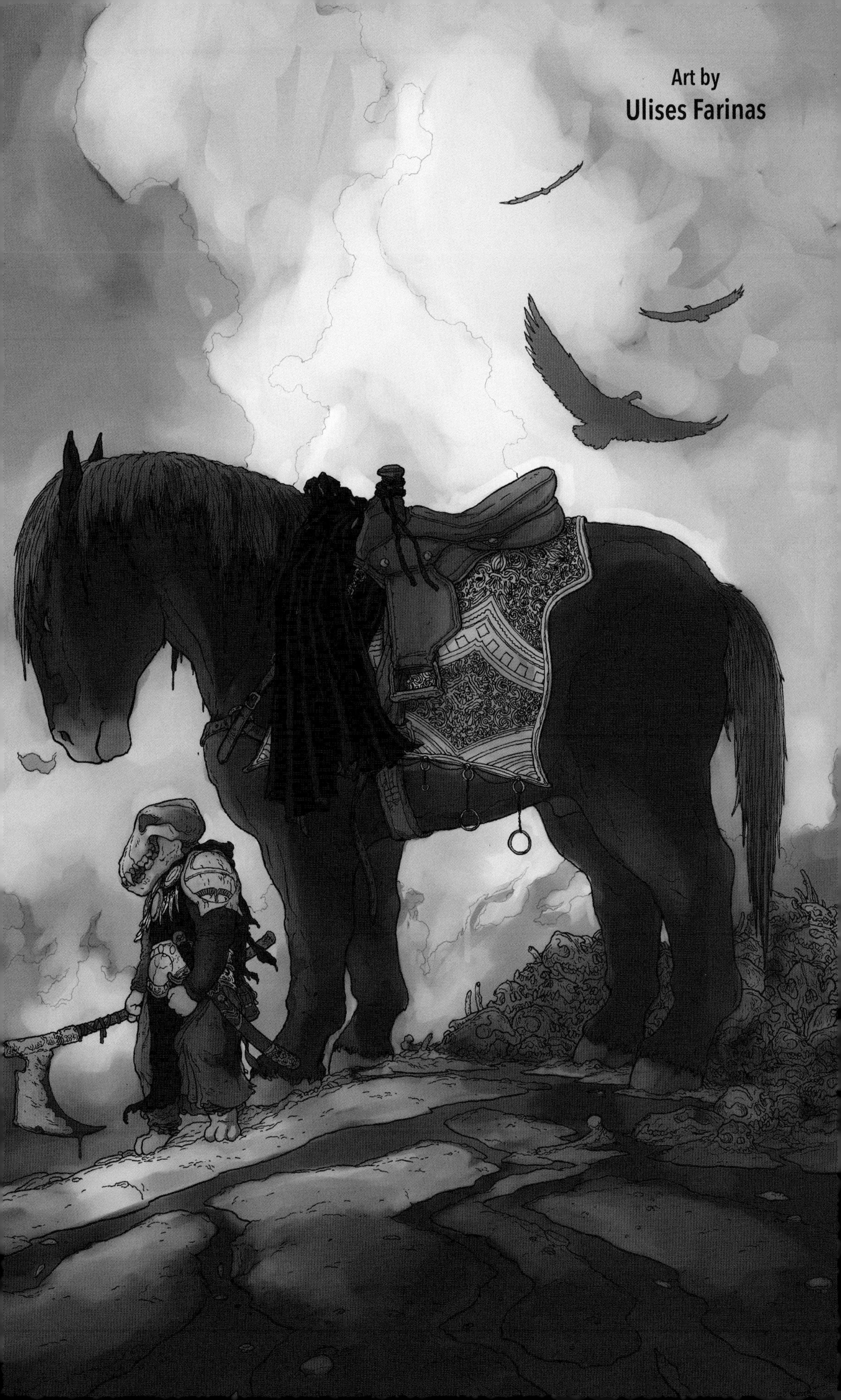

Art by
Ulises Farinas

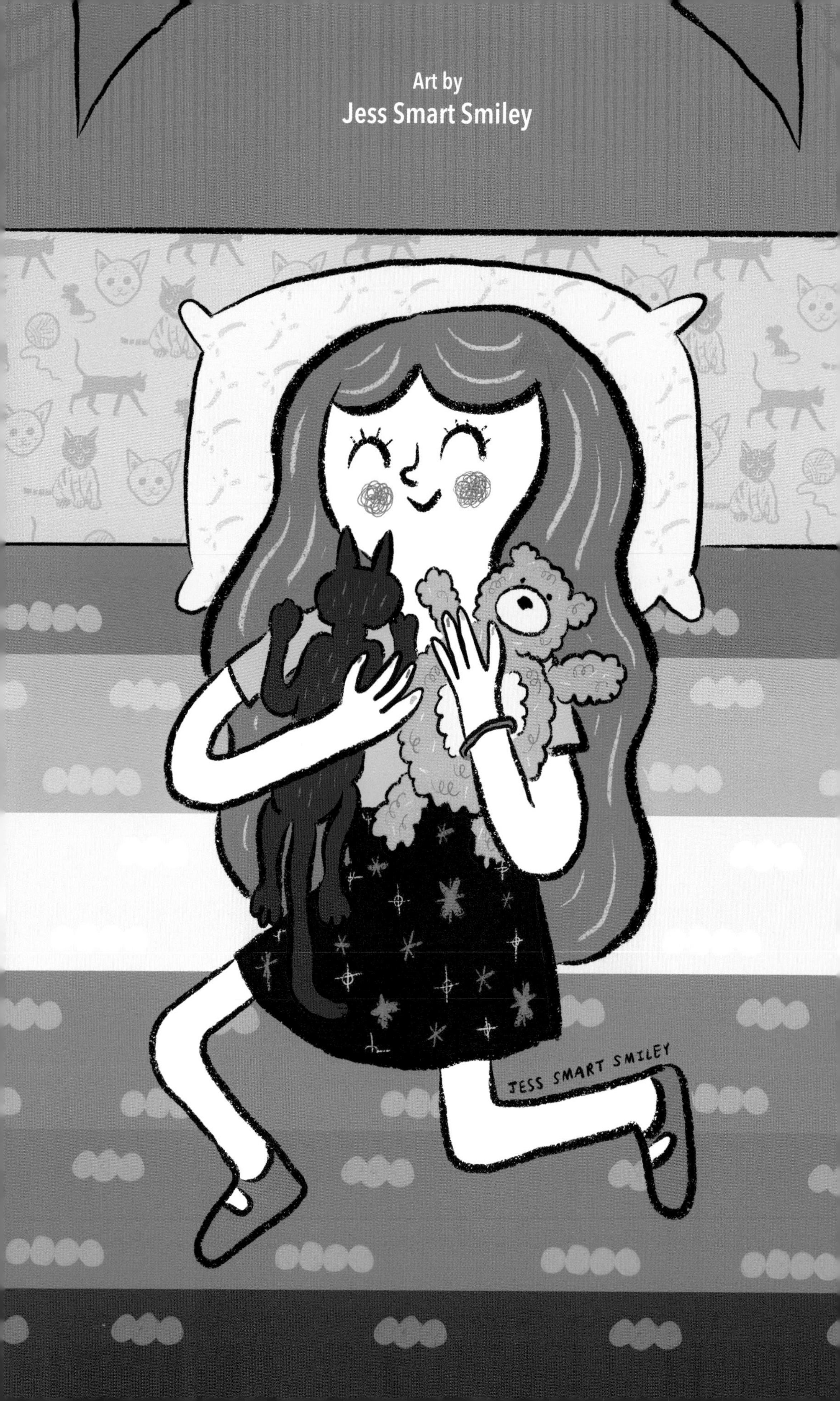
Art by
Jess Smart Smiley
JESS SMART SMILEY

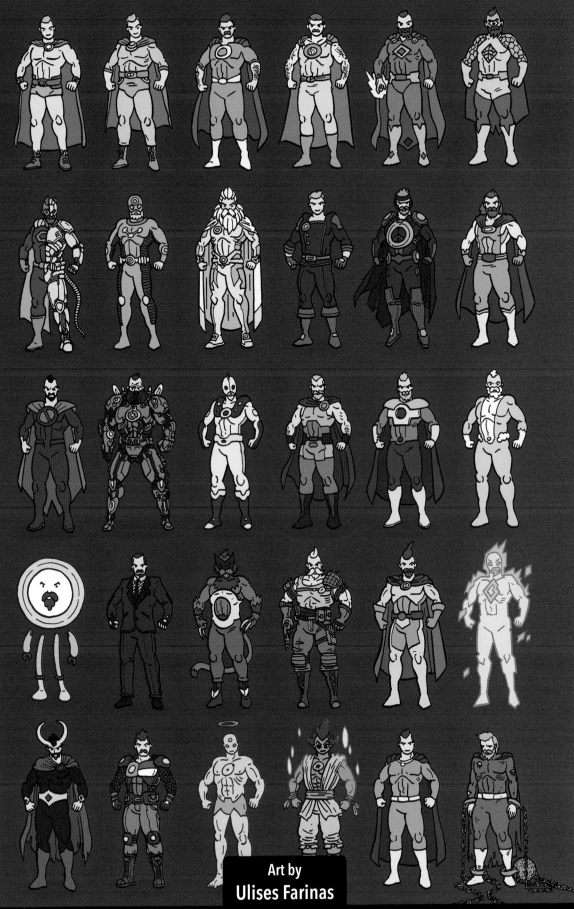

Art by
Ulises Farinas

75 Years of The Flying Captain - Every Significant Costume He's Ever Worn.

Art by
Steven Russell Black

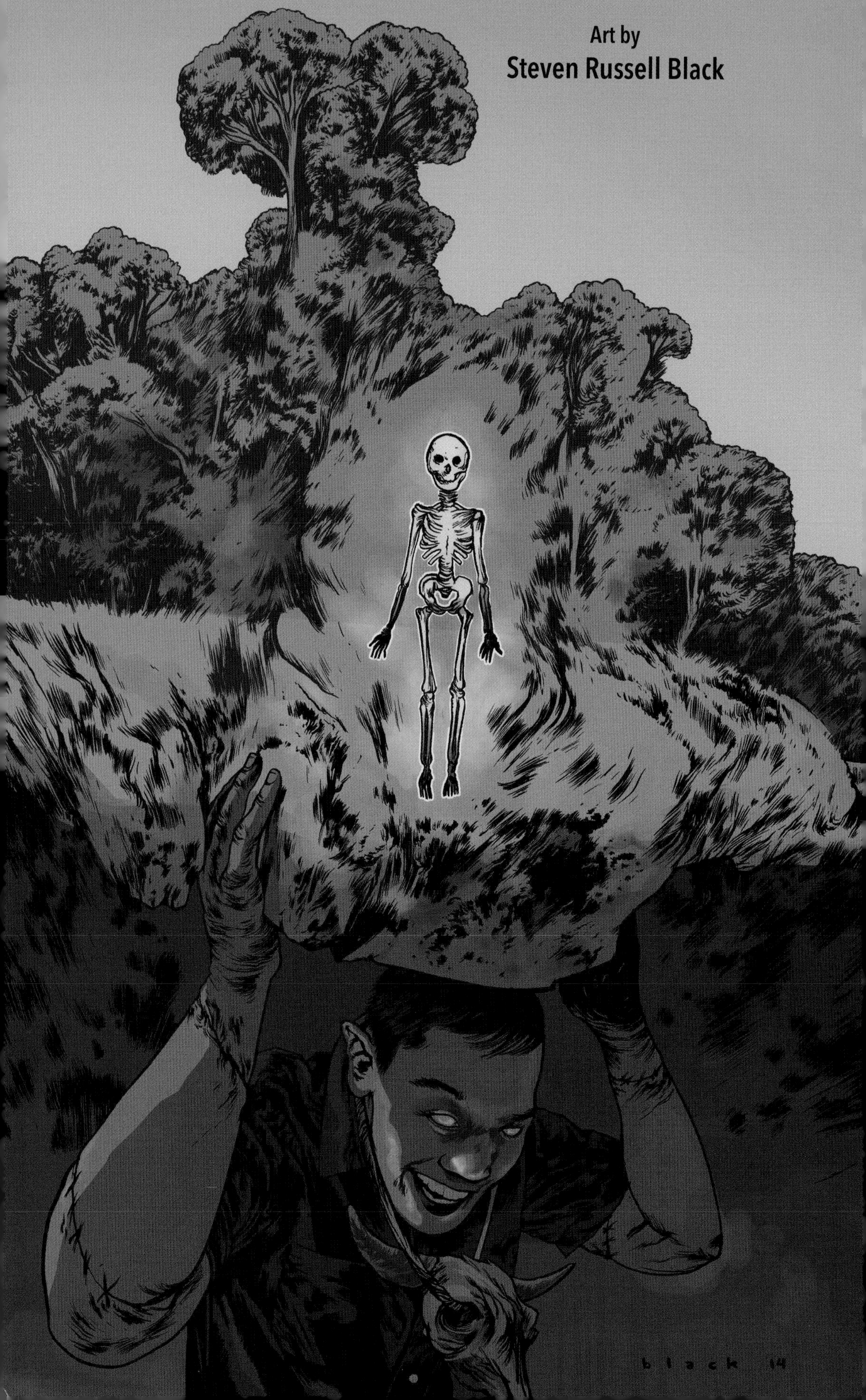
black 14

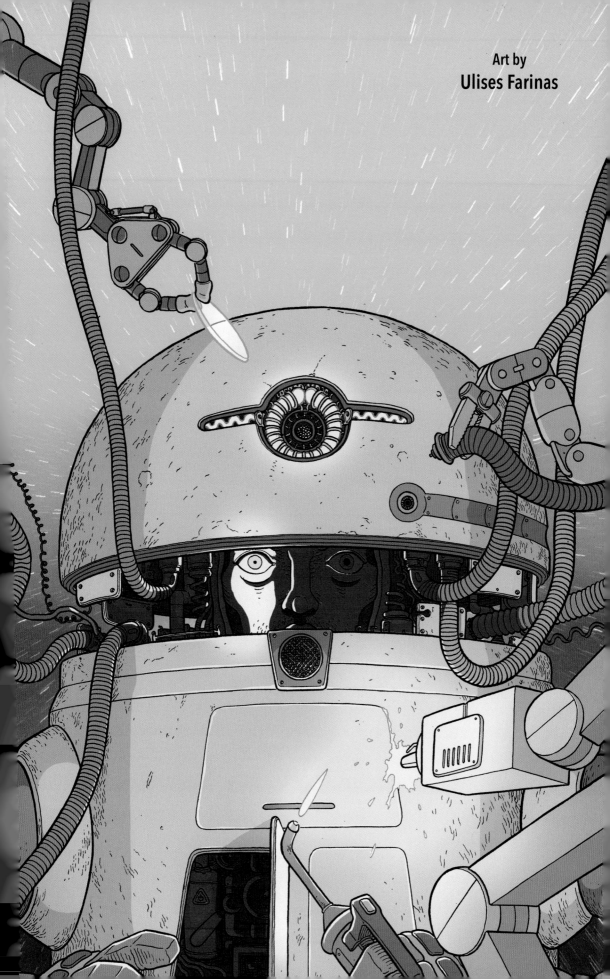

Art by
Ulises Farinas

Art by
Alexis Zirritt

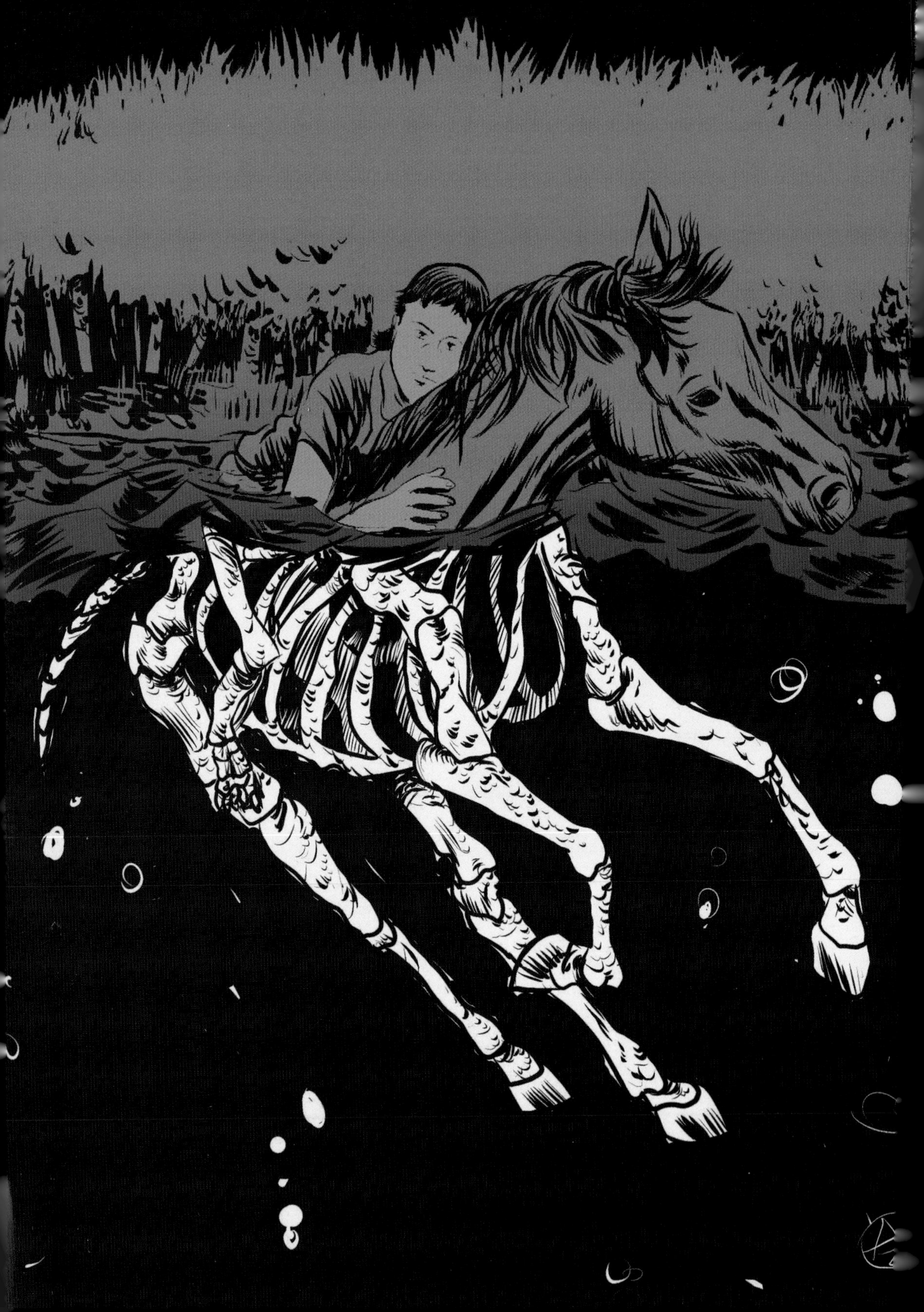